The Columbia Knight-Bagehot Guide to
Economics and Business Journalism

THE COLUMBIA KNIGHT-BAGEHOT GUIDE TO ECONOMICS AND BUSINESS JOURNALISM

Edited by Pamela Hollie Kluge

Written by the alumni of the Knight-Bagehot
Fellowship in Economics and Business Journalism

COLUMBIA UNIVERSITY PRESS
NEW YORK

Columbia University Press
New York   Chichester, West Sussex

Library of Congress Cataloging-in-Publication Data
The Columbia Knight-Bagehot guide to economics and business journalism
  / edited by Pamela Hollie Kluge ; written by the alumni of the
  Knight-Bagehot Fellowship in Economics and Business Journalism.
      p.   cm.
    Includes index.
    ISBN 0–231–07072–1
    ISBN 0–231–07073–x (pbk.)
    1. Journalism, Commercial—Handbooks, manuals, etc.   I. Kluge,
Pamela Hollie.   II. Knight-Bagehot Fellowship in Economics and
Business Journalism.
PN4784.C7C65   1991
070.4—dc20   90–20935
                       CIP
                        AC

Casebound editions of Columbia University Press books are
printed on permanent and durable acid-free paper

Printed in the United States of America
c 10 9 8 7 6 5 4 3 2 1
p 10 9 8 7 6 5 4 3 2 1

Book design by Ken Venezio

Contents

Preface and Acknowledgments

More than forty individuals contributed to this guide as writers, editors and reviewers. The essays were written by alumni of the Knight-Bagehot Fellowship in Economics and Business Journalism, a mid-career program at the Graduate School of Journalism, Columbia University. The initial editing was done by Bagehots, as the fellows call themselves. And several former fellows reviewed parts of the text. This guide is their gift to the Fellowship on its fifteenth anniversary.

The idea for the guide grew out of discussions with many former Bagehots and with the Fellowship's past directors. I wish to especially thank Chris Welles, a senior writer editor at *Business Week* and a former director, for his guidance and enthusiastic support of the Fellowship. His introductory essay puts business and economics journalism into an historical context.

The Fellowship owes a special thanks to Stephen Shepard, Editor-in-Chief of *Business Week,* who with Soma Golden, National Editor of the *New York Times,* developed the idea for the Fellowship in 1975. With the encouragement of Elie Abel, then dean of the Graduate School of Journalism, the Fellowship was born.

In recent years, the Fellowship has flourished under Joan Konner, who became dean of the Graduate School of Journalism in 1988. She has provided a lively, innovative environment for economics and business journalism education. The program also owes thanks to several of the members of the Graduate School of Journalism, in particular Assistant Professor Steve Ross, who provided computer and statistical assistance, and Steve Isaacs, associate dean for academic affairs, who supplied a code of ethics for this guide.

Many of the speakers and guests who take part in the nine-month Fellowship program also offered help with the guide. Gary Gigliotti, associate professor of economics at Rutgers University, kindly supplied a list of economists whose theories journalists should know. Others made helpful suggestions about the form and content of the guide.

The Fellowship is indebted to many corporations, foundations, and individuals for its annual financial support. Because of the commitment of these supporters, the Fellowship has been able to make a valuable contribution to journalism education, to the profession and to the public. The Fellowship is especially grateful to the Knight Foundation, which in 1987 committed $3 million to an endowment for the program.

In particular, I would like to thank the following people: Myron Kandel, deputy managing editor, Cable News Network, Inc.; Dr. Adelaide Katz, director, special programs, Graduate School of Journalism, Columbia University; Julia Martinez, a 1988 Bagehot and a business reporter at the *Philadelphia Inquirer,* and Stewart Taggart, a 1989 Bagehot and bureau chief for Knight-Ridder News Service in Rotterdam.

The Guide

by Pamela Hollie Kluge

Business and economics journalism is risky. Everyday there's a chance for mistakes, misunderstandings and misrepresentations. A misplaced decimal point can cause untold grief. And the difference between "no growth" and "zero growth" can spark intense debate in the letters to the editor column.

The information in this guide should help journalists, as well as students of business and public relations, reduce the risks and feel more confident. The essays assume little or no experience with economics or business terms and concepts. For that reason, the Guide may be especially useful to those who skipped economics in college and dodged courses in accounting, marketing or banking.

Some of the information will be familiar and useful right away. Other information may seem technical and obscure. But all the topics are important to understanding the scope and demands of economics and business journalism.

The Guide is divided into two parts. The first provides guidance on topics such as reading an earnings statement and understanding corporate finance. The second part tells journalists how to tackle everyday stories.

To get the most from this guide, it may be necessary to overcome some misconceptions about business and economics journalism. First, it isn't necessary to be an accountant to analyze a company. Financial reports simply tally a company's process beginning with an idea and ending, in some cases, with a profit. It's the *process,* regardless of the profit or loss, that's the heart of the story.

It's also a misconception that business stories aren't about people. The best business stories are about the individuals who create business, make it work, profit from it, support it and complain about it.

Finally, journalists often assume that making money is easy. But developing an idea, marketing it, advertising it, producing it and distributing it is not an easy task and the risks are great.

PART I

The Guide's first essay may be the most important. In it Jaye Scholl, the West Coast Editor of *Barron's,* helps journalists understand business performance. Her essay leads a Business section which includes essays on the role of corporations, on corporate strategies, marketing strategies and regulation. Step-by-Step sections will help journalists understand balance sheets and earnings statements.

A section on finance begins with an introduction to the language of Wall Street, where deals and dealmakers create wealth. Finance is a lucrative business for investment bankers, for corporations and venture capitalists, who are often the focus of business coverage. But it's the shareholders, the owners of public corporations to whom business journalism owes a thanks. It was to inform public shareholders—private individuals as well as corporate raiders, institutions and other companies —that most business sections were created. An essay on shareholders discusses their rights and powers.

Business journalists begin to call themselves financial journalists when they cover markets. Essays on the equity, commodities and credit markets explain the structure and function of each. Journalists who cover markets tend to be specialists, but understanding how markets work will help all journalists understand the principles of market economies.

The economy is perhaps journalism's most intimidating single subject. Economic stories never seem to be as clear or meaningful as journalists would like. One reason is that economists, the economic translators, are seldom certain about what's going on. And the federal government, despite tinkering with interest rates or budgets, doesn't actually "manage" the economy. Understanding the U.S. economy and the data produced to measure its performance, may be one of the most important stories of the 1990s. And as many countries around the world shift from centrally-planned economic systems to market economies, intelligent economic coverage will become increasingly important.

PART II

The second part of this guide is designed to provide practical information, such as how to find and develop sources. For those interested in broadcast, Jan Hopkins, a producer and anchor at Cable News Network, discusses the broadcast journalist's approach to business and economic stories. And Philip Moeller, the business editor at the Baltimore Sun, discusses the code of conduct for economic and business journalists.

This guide would be incomplete without a "how-to" section. The final section of the Guide helps journalists learn the structure of everyday economic and business stories. It also provides guidance for approaching stories about investment planning and tips for covering an annual meeting. The writers have provided advice on several important beats, such as insurance and taxes, as well as help in handling big stories like trade and policy.

While many journalists will not need all the information in this guide, an aspiring business editor certainly will. Still, the Guide does not attempt to answer every question about economics and business. The goal of the contributors is simple: to demystify business and economics and help journalists overcome the anxiety associated with facing a business subject for the first time.

The contributors believe, however, that even the most sophisticated journalist can make use of the Guide, since it acknowledges an unchanging truth of journalism: sooner or later, all journalists are confronted with stories they never foresaw, with issues they never considered, with information that baffles them. The Knight-Bagehot Fellows hope this guide will help journalists get started and that reading it will make them feel less alone, less overmatched and much closer to doing an important job well.

Pamela Hollie Kluge

Economics and Business Reporting

by Chris Welles

For years business and economics journalism was a bleak wasteland —"the most disgracefully neglected sector of American journalism," according to former NBC-TV correspondent and Columbia Graduate School of Journalism School Dean Elie Abel. If you did a lousy job covering city hall, couldn't hack it writing obits, weren't much good taking classified ads over the telephone, then they sent you to the business section. Maybe they even made you business editor.

That was the way it was at countless newspapers. And it wasn't much better at most business magazines. Business writing was tedious and boring, little more than jargon-ridden rewrites of corporate press releases about earnings results and executive promotions. And because business writing was tedious and boring, good journalists considering specializing in the field tended to conclude that business itself was tedious and boring. They regarded the business pages as a dead-end Siberia. Writer Dom Bonafede once described business reporters as "city room castoffs and journalistic drifters, bit players in a raw profession, fulfilling a melancholy task requiring little talent and less imagination in a cramped corner of a newsroom."

Today everything has changed. Business and economics are considered almost glamour beats, if not yet quite as prestigious as the White House or the Paris bureau. The ranks of business journalists include some of the best-known and most talented editors and writers in the profession. Business and economics is luring record numbers of aspiring journalists who have come to appreciate that the field is among the few journalistic specialties experiencing real growth. Despite the growth, the competition for jobs is intense. But while that poses problems for job-seekers, it has contributed to a dramatic elevation in the quality of business and economics coverage.

Readers of this book, who may have been attracted by the new glamour aura or the job opportunities, need to understand that the field of business and economics is quite different from other journalism specialities. It provides special satisfactions. But it also requires special skills and presents formidable demands and frustrations. Some of the difficulties associated with covering business and economics stem from the complexity of the subject matter. Others are more subtle, such as the reluctance of many story subjects to cooperate with reporters and the economic pressures that business interests can exert on the media.

Why has business and economics journalism risen from obscurity to prominence? Why is the field so essential to readers and viewers? Why does it offer journalists such unusual rewards and challenges?

The bleak wasteland era came to an end during the late 1960s and early 1970s. Several major business and economic events and trends made it to page one on a regular basis, and editors and reporters realized that the field was much more important and compelling than they had thought. The events and trends included:

- The excitement on Wall Street during the late 1960s: the superheated bull market, the rise of conglomerates and the takeover boom, the "money game" played by colorful mutual fund managers.
- The oil price shock of the early 1970s and its many aftershocks, including gasoline shortages and the disturbing new phenomenon of "stagflation."
- Discrediting of the well-entrenched belief, developed during the 1950s, that economic policy makers could "fine-tune" the economy to produce perpetual prosperity.
- Erosion of U.S. hegemony over world markets and the emergence of Japan, Germany and other nations devastated by World War II as potent business competitors.
- Escalating financial problems during the 1970s of America's major cities, especially New York City, which nearly went bankrupt.
- Growing awareness of health and environmental dangers stemming from products produced by corporations such as asbestos, tobacco, toxic wastes, and pesticides.

Newspapers reacted to these developments by rapidly expanding their business sections, which in turn stimulated an equally rapid growth in financial advertising. Big-city dailies such as the *New York Times, Washington Post, Los Angeles Times,* and the *Chicago Tribune,* as well as papers in smaller cities such as Atlanta, Louisville, Denver, Miami, and Philadelphia, doubled and tripled the size of their business staffs and sharply enlarged their news roles. Dozens of regional business magazines and newspapers sprang up. The roster of industry trade journals and newsletters all but exploded. New categories of magazines focusing on small business, minority business, and personal finance emerged. Business journalism as a career came to be regarded as a fast track and attracted some of the most able young reporters and editors.

The quality of business journalism improved. Reporters started digging behind the press releases to find out what really happened. Writing became livelier and more accessible to uninitiated readers. In order to capture the drama of events such as corporate takeovers or labor strikes, stories came to include more personalities, color, anecdotes, and narrative. Business editors overhauled the tombstone-like design of their pages and became adept at using arresting graphics to explain often abstruse subjects.

Editors staffing business sections came to realize that, to cover the field effectively, reporters needed specialized experience and training. Journalism generally had already become more and more specialized. The old notion had faded that any good general-assignment reporter could turn out a quick, authoritative story on any subject. The world had become too complex and readers were demanding more sophisticated coverage. Yet business and economics writing, it became abundantly clear, required more background knowledge than most other specialties. The Bagehot Fellowship was only one of several mid-career programs established to meet this need. Most journalism schools introduced business writing courses. More reporters sought MBA's and economics degrees. Former Council of Economic Advisers Gardner Ackley once remarked that he wished reporters who wrote about economic affairs had two qualifications: first, that they had taken a course in economics; and second, that they had passed the course. But as the field improved, Ackley's remark was no longer valid.

Business and economics journalism today still has plenty of room for improvement. The quantity of coverage is still more impressive than the quality. Too many older managing editors, who began their careers when the field was a wasteland, refuse to acknowledge changed perceptions, and expect their business sections to get by with only 3–4 staff members. Too many business editors shy away from sharply critical stories and refuse to allocate resources for investigative projects to take their coverage beyond the daily news flow. Too many reporters do not venture beyond handouts and lunches with public relations people. Too many business pages still have the visual appeal of the classified ad section. Too many trade magazines are little more than sycophants for the industries they cover.

Broadcast coverage of business remains particularly laggard. TV news directors still have not successfully overcome the relatively non-visual nature of business and economics and the difficulties in explaining complicated developments in less than a minute. Creditable business shows have recently been flourishing on cable channels, especially Cable News Network, and on public television. But business and economics coverage by the three major TV networks, especially on their widely-watched evening news shows, remains sparse and superficial.

But, undeniably, business and economics journalism has at last come of age. Most editors and reporters have come to appreciate the profound impact that business and economics has on our lives. Economics may seem very arcane and abstract. Yet such indicators as the inflation rate, money supply, unemployment, interest rates, and the gross national product directly affect our jobs, our salaries, the taxes we pay, the interest on our mortgages, the return we get on our investments. Large corporations may seem remote and somewhat mysterious. But the decisions they make about where to build plants, what technologies to use, what kinds of products to manufacture, and how to market them directly affect us as consumers: the choices we have and the prices we have to pay for what we buy.

Readers and viewers now depend on business and economics journalists for news and advice about a wide range of topics. Indeed, perhaps no other journalistic speciality provides people with information that is as essential to their daily lives. Other specialities offer intellectual stimulation, relaxation, diversion, titillation, and fantasy. But business and economics coverage offers information that people need and use. Consumers want easily understood guidance about practical matters such as how to buy a car or invest in the stock market. Dozens of magazines and the business sections of virtually every newspaper provide an abundance of personal finance information. But many people—including not only consumers but also business executives and millions of us who are simply lower-level employees of companies—want a much broader perspective, which the media by and large still do not do an adequate job of providing. They want to understand how business and economics really works. These people want to know who makes economic decisions for the country, how the Federal Reserve operates, what causes inflation, how serious the budget and trade deficits are, why the value of the dollar in world markets is important. They want to know what sorts of people run major corporations, what their goals and priorities are, what their attitude is toward ethics, how they decide on strategies to pursue and products to make, how they exercise power in Washington, what their policies are toward the environment and the health and safety of their employees.

For the business and economics journalist, tackling such questions is an enormously daunting task. In my view, covering business and economics is more demanding than any other speciality, much more difficult, for instance, than writing about a football game, a school board meeting, a robbery, a new music fad, or a political campaign. Business and economics journalists must be able to understand the intricacies of the field and write about them in clear, concise, intelligible prose. And the fact that business and economics touches people's lives so directly puts unusual demands on journalists for accuracy, reliability, and thoroughness. A careless mistake in an investment story can cost a reader thousands of dollars.

Covering business and economics poses other special obstacles. Economics at first glance may seem easy, for economists are typically eager to be interviewed by the press. Tons of economic data and studies are available for the asking. Unfortunately, economists are notorious for their propensity to disagree with one another and to change their own views from one moment to the next. It is often said, not without reason, that if you laid a thousand economists end to end, they would not reach a conclusion. Economic data is no more helpful: the same figures can often be used to substantiate two completely disparate interpretations. In reporting an economics story, one discovers that it is virtually impossible to come up with a definitive answer to numerous economic conundrums, such as whether the dollar should sell higher or lower in foreign markets, whether the negative effects of a tax hike on consumer spending would outweigh the positive impact on the budget, whether the federal deficit is an alarming crisis requiring immediate action or a minor problem that will fade away over time. Was Reaganomics a dramatic success or a terrible failure? You can find plenty of economists on both sides.

Despite appearances to the contrary, economics is as much an art as a science. It is much closer to sociology than physics. Reporters writing about a business event may, if they work hard enough, come up with a reasonable approximation of reality. But reporters covering an economic trend, who must contend with far larger masses of people and far more intricate patterns of behavior, typically find precision and tangibleness maddeningly elusive. The best economic writers, though, do not resort to on-the-one-hand/on-the-other-hand stories. They strive to report in which direction the preponderance of the evidence points.

Reporting on business presents quite different dilemmas. In their attitudes toward the press, corporations are quite different from hospitals, schools, police departments, and other government or nonprofit organizations. The latter, essentially public bodies, recognize an obligation to serve the public and thus tend to be responsive to reporters seeking information. Corporations often do not feel that obligation. Though many are "publicly owned," in the sense that their stock is owned by investors, corporations really serve private ends: making money for their employees and their shareholders. Many corporate executives do not feel that the public has any special right to know how they run their business. Politicians, movie and sports stars, and other public figures actively seek publicity. Popular story subjects such as doctors, district attorneys, ministers, and fire fighters are usually quite amenable to interviews. But corporations tend to be very secretive about their internal affairs. To be sure, they aggressively advertise their products and employ public-relations people to polish their image and spread the word about positive developments. Yet they are typically far less forthcoming to reporters about negative events. In many cases, they will refuse to cooperate with the press. It is not unusual for a corporation to forbid its employees to talk to a reporter seeking to write about the company.

Corporations may have good reasons to be reticent. They may not want to reveal plans to competitors. They may see no reason to air dirty linen in public or expose the mistakes of their senior executives.

But there are deeper attitudes at work. Business and the press have inherently conflicting goals. As Daniel Seligman, a columnist for *Fortune* magazine put it, a corporate executive "is not always looking for the unvarnished truth about his enterprise" and doesn't "necessarily want coverage that is comprehensive, thoughtful, and fair." Seligman observed that "there is that inevitable collision of interests between a corporation that is concerned with its own public image, and is eager to put its best foot forward, and the journalist who wants a story." Journalists will inevitably want to print things that business executives don't want to see printed. And business executives will often want journalists to print things that journalists don't want to write about.

It is no surprise, then, that the relationship between business and the press has often been acrimonious, with heated recriminations on both sides. Business' beef with the press is often well founded. As was noted earlier, the press's performance is often laggard. Virtually any corporate executive can display examples of inaccurate or distorted stories about that company. More than mere sloppiness or ineptness is often to blame. Too many business journalists allow biases and preconceptions to affect their stories. Business executives often claim that journalists are left-wing radicals out to undermine capitalism and free markets. Though far less radical than this stereotype, journalists do tend to be more liberal than business executives. But their liberalism usually does not significantly taint their coverage. Other basically nonideological biases are much more important. Like all journalists, business writers and editors seek out and often exaggerate stories containing elements of crisis, conflict, and controversy. Business journalists also tend to be skeptical of authority, large organizations, and repositories of power. And they are often suspicious of people who have made a lot of money. This sometimes leads business reporters to believe the worst about a corporation's or a wealthy executive's motives and actions and to write stories that are slanted and unfair. Louis Banks, a former *Fortune* managing editor, stated that "most ranking editors of mass media see business as suspect until proven innocent." Responsible journalists, of course, do not allow predispositions or biases to affect the fairness of a story. They always seek a response from a company on a negative story before publication. And they do not draw unfavorable conclusions if the company chooses not to respond. Unfortunately, too many journalists are not that responsible.

Much of the time, however, business complaints about the press are a matter of blaming the messenger for the bad news. "Business has always been yelling about coverage by the press," Timothy Hubbard, a professor at the Newhouse School of Public Communications at Syracuse University, said. "In all too many cases, they've been caught by the press with their hands in the cookie jar up to their elbows and they don't like it."

Most major corporations in recent years have learned to be more open to the press. A sophisticated public relations executive knows a company usually benefits from talking with reporters, even those planning negative stories. The company may be able to correct errors and convince the reporter to take a different tack. At the very least, it should be able to get the company's point of view reflected in the story.

Fortunately, there are many ways for journalists to get information about companies which refuse to talk to the press. All companies whose securities are publicly traded are required to file detailed financial reports with the Securities and Exchange Commission. These reports can provide an astute reporter with a great deal of information about a company's financial health and prospects. (You don't need to be a CPA to understand and interpret corporate financial statements, but many business reporters do find it helpful to take accounting courses.) There are many other document sources such as court records, congressional hearings, brokerage firm research reports. And there are many people sources outside the company who are knowledgeable: former employees, competitors, consultants, customers, suppliers, government regulators, labor union officials.

Many business reporters have become much more adept and aggressive in employing investigative techniques to pursue difficult stories. Yet too many others succumb to often powerful forces that have pushed business coverage toward stories that are insufficiently tough and probing. Too many journalists, when confronted by complex business issues, the arduousness of most investigative projects, or merely the uncooperativeness of a corporate subject, take the easy way out. They either do a superficial piece or drop the story altogether.

Business journalists are also frequently under pressure from their editors and publishers to take a softer line. Unlike story subjects in other fields, corporations have the power to exert considerable economic pressure. They will often retaliate against negative stories by canceling their advertising. Newspaper columnist Patrick J. Buchanan, who worked in the Nixon and Reagan White Houses, once advised, "These puppies of the press need to be given an occasional jerk on the leash of the advertising dollar." Journalists also have to reckon with the fact that their publishers often have close personal and even business relationships with corporate executives and don't like to embarrass their friends. Fear of angering advertisers or publishers often causes editors to spike negative stories. Some newspapers or TV stations have reassigned or even fired reporters and editors who offended business interests.

Large media organizations, which have broad advertising bases, can easily withstand these pressures. The *Wall Street Journal,* for instance, is seldom accused of caving in to business interests. But the situation is much different at smaller newspapers or broadcast stations, where the displeasure of only a few members of the local business community can have devastating financial consequences. Few small newspapers are willing to risk incurring the wrath of local bankers, realtors, insurance agents, or supermarket managers. In many communities, business doesn't have to flex its muscle; self-censorship by editors usually ensures that business has little to be upset about. John F. Lawrence, former assistant managing editor for economic affairs at the *Los Angeles Times,* observed that "the media are far more guilty of being too soft on business than being too hard."

Some observers go even further. They point out that as the media has coalesced into huge conglomerates and business journalists have become better paid and more socially respected, the press has abandoned its traditional function. It is the press's job, according to A. J. Liebling, to "afflict the comfortable and comfort the afflicted." Reporters are supposed to be gadflies, feisty, irreverent critics of the status quo. Now, observers argue with some justification, journalists—especially those covering business and economics—have joined the establishment. They have become defenders of the status quo and disseminators of the conventional wisdom. It is not easy for journalists to resist and subtle but powerful forces of co-optation.

But there is a flip side to all of these problematic demands, challenges, and pressures. Writing about business and economics is rewarding for the very reason that it can be so difficult and frustrating. Speaking as someone who wrote about a great diversity of subjects before concentrating on business, I can say that nothing matches the special satisfactions and pleasures of business reporting: when the former executive finally decides to disclose to you the behind-the-scenes details of how a billion-dollar deal was put together, when you stumble on a document that provides conclusive evidence of serious corporate wrongdoing, when you finally figure out why the once high-flying corporation suddenly plunged into bankruptcy. It is more than worth the effort. And I'm sure that readers of this book, after they've been in the field for a while, will feel the same way.

The Columbia Knight-Bagehot Guide to
Economics and Business Journalism

PART I

BASIC INFORMATION

Section 1

Business

Financial Documents

by Jaye Scholl

"Get the financials." This order is going out with increasing frequency at business publications. Depending on the publication's budget and deadline, a packet arrives either by messenger or by mail from either Bechtel or Disclosure, the two major suppliers of Securities and Exchange Commission documents to the public. Strictly speaking, the financials include the balance sheet and income statement. But a complete packet of information about a company also includes disclosure documents filed with the SEC: annual reports, and a more detailed, no-nonsense version of the annual report called the 10–K, quarterly financial updates called 10–Qs, proxy statements, and, if the company went public or sold additional common stock in the past couple of years, there will be a prospectus, too.

Can a reporter who majored in English literature uncover anything new in these documents, something Wall Street has missed? Absolutely. Just because XYZ Corp. and its auditors say the company has $153 million in assets, it doesn't mean you necessarily have to agree. Oh sure, one way or another, the company's various possessions add up to $153 million. But once you get familiar with a company and its industry, you can start to make judgments about the quality of assets for yourself. If XYZ Corp. is an urban business institute, you can ponder the likelihood that students who sign up for a $4,000 computer programming course may not complete the course. Their tuition has been paid up front. It's an asset. But if you're familiar with drop-out rates among vocational technology schools, you can raise questions about whether the company set aside enough money for refunds.

When an outside accounting firm gives an "opinion" about a company's financial statements, it's not judging whether the company is good or bad in the same way a financial analyst or a portfolio manager or a reporter might. Quite the opposite. A company's bookkeeping can be done in accordance with "generally accepted auditing principles," and the company can still be in serious financial trouble, even if it's not a case of fraud.

In reality, auditors aren't even bean counters. When they sign off on a company's books, they're saying, in effect, "Here's how the company says it counts its beans, and if they do what they say they do, then we agree that it is the right way to do it." And the auditors assure outsiders that the beans have been counted in a consistent fashion, from one quarter to the next. But they're not passing judgment on the color or the taste of the beans themselves, or even confirming that all the beans exist. They don't check, for example, to find out if for every $4,000 of tuition paid, a real person exists.

While financial documents can't be called advertising, they certainly can be promotional in nature. The information in them has to be factual, and the statements can't omit materially important information. Otherwise, the companies risk a Securities and Exchange Commission investigation and a shareholder suit. But the statements should be viewed as documents written on behalf of the company, with financial footnotes stated in as favorable a fashion as possible. In other words, financial documents can be biased, but are still a good place to start.

Here's a list of financial documents which can be especially useful to a reporter, and in any case, should be on file in the newsroom for each publicly traded company covered by the newspaper or magazine. Some of them can be obtained from the company itself. Try its public relations department first, and if the company doesn't have one, deal with its investor relations or shareholder services departments. Ask to be put on the mailing list for future filings. If that fails, order the documents from Disclosure, Inc., Bethesda, Maryland, or Bechtel. Other useful documents, alas, must be ordered from outside sources at some expense.

THE ANNUAL REPORT

Big, beautiful and boastful, the annual report must be filed 90 days after a company's reporting year ends. It usually begins with the chairman of the board's letter to shareholders, a revealing piece of prose as much for what it doesn't say as for what it does. In recent years, the SEC has permitted companies to issue shorter, simplified annual reports and, as a result, the amount of information in the reports varies from company to company. Therefore, always ask for the accompanying 10–K unless you're told specifically that it's included in the annual report.

Even in its shortened version, the annual report usually includes a balance sheet, an income statement, a statement of changes in financial position, and a "management's discussion and analysis of financial condition and results of operations," an answer, of sorts, to the question, "So, how's business?"

THE BALANCE SHEET

The balance sheet is a snapshot of the company taken on a specific date. (That day is December 31 if the company reports on a calendar year. Otherwise, the company operates on a fiscal year.) By comparing the most recent year's photo with a photo from a year earlier, you can see whether the company looks more haggard or more robust with the passage of time.

Conceptually, there are two sides to a balance sheet. The assets are on one side, and the liabilities and shareholders' equity on the other side. That's because assets equal liabilities plus shareholders' equity. When you actually read a balance sheet, though, the assets, liabilities and equity are presented in one long column.

Assets are current or fixed. Think of a current asset like cash in your pocket, very liquid and, in the case of a corporation, likely to be spent before the year is up. Inventory is a current asset. Presumably there is a ready market for the goods and the company expects to sell them this year. Current assets also include cash, accounts receivable, marketable securities such as a money market account holding the company's idle cash, and prepaid expenses such as an insurance policy.

Fixed assets, by contrast, are like your house or car—difficult to unload if you need cash quickly. Fixed assets are more interesting than current ones; they often serve as the hunting ground for "value investors," leveraged buyout artists and corporate raiders. That's because fixed assets are often unique to the company and hard to put a price tag on. Value is in the eye of the beholder. Who really knows how much an entertainment company's film library—a fixed asset—is worth? What value should be placed on 125 reruns of "Leave It To Beaver?" Similarly, real estate, franchises and patents and even reputation—part of an intangible asset called goodwill—are seldom carried on the books at their true value.

But by the same token, assets can be worth much less than their stated value. Among the more infamous examples of overvalued assets were real estate development loans held by many savings and loan institutions in the late 1980s. Not only did the borrowers default on their loans, but also the projects fetched far less than they were carried at on the books. (At lending institutions, loans are assets and deposits are liabilities. Repeat that ten times. Even people in the lending industry get confused.) Or suppose a product is discovered to be hopelessly defective. The company has to write down the value of the product—an asset— to reflect the fact that nobody wants to buy it.

Liabilities are a company's financial obligations, current and long-term. "Current liabilities" usually means any debt that has to be paid within a year. This includes accounts payable (what the company owes its suppliers), notes payable (the short-term loans which the company must pay back this year), accrued liabilities (what the company owes on this specific day to its employees, any outstanding interest on its bonds, contributions it will make to its pension fund and other indirect costs of doing business) and income taxes payable (what's owed this year to the feds and state.)

Long-term liabilities include repayment of bonds and other debt instruments and deferred taxes, deferred because the company got a tax break as an incentive to make an investment in say, a new plant, but is expected to pay the taxes eventually.

shareholders' equity

Subtract total liabilities from total assets, and you get shareholders' equity. That's the portion of the company owned by equity investors, otherwise known as book value. If a company is well run, shareholders' equity increases because the company takes whatever profits remain after paying dividends and reinvests them. As a result, the asset side grows in relation to the liability side.

THE INCOME STATEMENT

profit margin

It's just as important as the balance sheet. It shows how much money the company made or lost over the past year by adding up all the sources of revenue and then subtracting all the expenses. What's left is net income. What you're looking for in the income statement is an idea of how well the company's core business performed. The profit margin from core operations, (net income divided by net sales) is, after all, a key factor in determining a company's financial health. (Investment bankers' favorite rule of thumb for sizing up a company's ability to handle debt in case of a leveraged buyout, or LBO, is "net earnings before interest and taxes," or NEBIT. It's the net profit from the core business, and gives them an idea of resources available to cover interest expense should there be an LBO.)

Of course, it's nice when a book publishing company sells its old warehouse for a bundle of money. But the real estate sale says nothing about the management's ability to attract good authors and market books profitably. That's why the warehouse sale shows up as an extraordinary item on the income statement. It's a one-time gain. Watch out for this. Some companies herald record revenues and earnings even though the record profits result from an extraordinary gain. Of course, the opposite can apply; companies can have one-time, extraordinary losses which artificially depress earnings.

STATEMENT OF CHANGES IN FINANCIAL POSITION

In recent years, some companies have begun calling this statement "Reconciliation of Net Income to Net Cash." Here's where you'll find the tools to measure cash flow, the financial equivalent of blood pressure. It will let you determine how much cash the company has to work with. Cash flow is usually a higher figure than net profits because it includes depreciation and deferred taxes, money that the company has theoretically set aside for the future. But do you and I put $2,000 in the bank every year because our $10,000 cars are depreciating and will be worthless in five years? Of course not. Similarly, companies don't actually set aside cash as their assets depreciate. Nor do they put future tax payments in a box, waiting for the day they'll hand the money over to the IRS. That means the money is available for the company's use today.

The statement also gives sources of cash not spelled out anywhere else —a stock sale or a debt issue, for instance. And it also gives more detail as to what the company actually spent money on last year.

FORM 10–K

This document gives much more detail about companies than their annual reports and is indispensable if a reporter plans to write a company profile. Form 10–Ks are filed annually with the SEC, due March 31 of each year. Here's where a company talks about its origins, competition and the outlook of its industry in general. The 10–K lists property the company owns or leases, and sometimes how much it pays for space. It gives detailed backgrounds of directors and officers. If a company has changed outside auditors, it has to give the reason in the 10–K.

But remember to ask for a list of exhibits accompanying the 10–K. Exhibits contain equally valuable information which has been filed along with the 10–Ks or in 8–Ks. Exhibits can include such items as executive employment contracts, details about loans to the company and profit-sharing plans. It's a good idea to order all of them.

FORM 10–Q

In order not to confuse it with the 10–K, remember the "Q" stands for quarter. This quarterly statement is due 45 days after each calendar quarter ends or after the end of the three fiscal quarters. (The fourth 10–Q is 10–K.) The 10–Q gives an unaudited financial update on the company. 10–Qs are always worth reading on a timely basis because, in addition to presenting financial figures, they must mention significant, one-time events such as the beginning of a big lawsuit.

FORM 8–K

Sure to become a favorite with reporters, the 8–K must be filed 15–days after a "reportable event" occurs. When the SEC says "reportable," it's thinking of shareholders, not newspaper readers. But the two groups overlap, so assume any time a company files an 8–K that it will be of interest to your readers.

What's a reportable event? The same thing as a "materially important" event. Legally, something is materially important if its disclosure would affect a shareholder's decision to buy or sell a security. That's a pretty broad definition and so accountants and lawyers use the "5 percent rule." That is, a company should file a report if the event would affect earnings or revenues or the number of employees, for instance, by 5 percent or more.

Reportable events include a change in control of the company. Most likely, you would hear about a takeover days before the 8–K is due. But once it has been filed, you can get background information on change in ownership. If the company buys or sells a "significant amount of assets," it must file an 8–K, or if it files for bankruptcy or receivership. Here's the first place you'll read about a director resigning from the board because of disagreements about the company's policies. Here, too, is the first discussion about a change in accountants, one which must say whether the accountant issued an adverse opinion about the company in either of the past two years. Most 8–K information becomes part of the 10–K for that reporting year. But if you want to find out the reason for changing accountants four years ago, you will have to ask for the four-year-old 10–K and its exhibits.

How can you find out if a company has filed an 8–K? Often an 8–K event merits a press release. Ask the company if an 8–K has been filed. Or you can check periodically with Disclosure or Bechtel. Otherwise, you'll have to wait for the 10–K.

SCHEDULE 13–D

Anyone who buys 5 percent or more of a company's securities must file a 13–D within 10 days after the purchase. The 13–D tells how many shares have been purchased, the date of the purchase and the purpose of the acquisition. Is it for investment purposes or control of the company?

Amended 13–Ds have to be filed each time there is a material change. A 1 percent change in ownership, either by selling or buying additional shares, requires an amended 13–D. So does a decision by the 13–D filer that he'd rather take over the company than simply invest in it. Amendments must be filed promptly, but the SEC has left the definition of "promptly" purposely vague. If a company is already "in play," the amended 13–D would probably be filed within 24 hours.

FORM 4

This form deals with securities sales by company insiders. Insider trades can be a leading indicator about a company's fortunes. When a chief executive officer goes on a buying spree of his company's stock, it's safe to assume he thinks business is going to be good. By the same token, insider sales can be a tip off that bad news is on its way. Whenever a director, officer or someone who owns 10 percent or more of a company's decides to buy or sell stock, they must file a Form 4 with the SEC by the 10th of the following month.

There are a handful of reporting services which keep tabs on Form 4 filings. Subscribing to one of these services is the only easy way to get the information. The reporting services also pick up Form 144 filings which are stated intentions to sell restricted stock within the next 90 days. Restricted securities have to be held a minimum of two years; if the owner unloads them the first chance he or she gets, it could be worth investigating why.

THE PROXY STATEMENT

This arrives with the annual report and notifies shareholders when and where the annual meeting will be held for the purpose of electing directors. Proxy statements also give background information about changes in company policy which, under state law, require shareholder approval. They also show who owns 5 percent or more of the stock, how much stock each director owns and executive compensation. If you want to do a wrap-up of the highest paid executives in your area, you'll find the information in the proxy statement.

THE PROSPECTUS

When a company goes public, it files a registration statement called an S-1 with the SEC. Part of the statement includes the prospectus, one of the most interesting financial documents available to reporters. The prospectus tells a story about the company—its line of business, its top managers and their past experience and its competitors. It's the company's attempt to drum up interest in its stock. While the SEC doesn't guarantee that the information in the prospectus is true, there are all of kinds of penalties awaiting the company and its underwriters if the document turns out to be willfully false. So, while the company tries to put its best foot forward in the prospectus, it must also explain the risk factors associated with investing in the company.

The company's underwriters distribute a preliminary prospectus called a "red herring" to investors. It's preliminary because it doesn't show the per share price of the stock or the date of the offering. That information becomes available after the SEC declares the registration statement effective. The underwriters then offer the stock to the public a day or two later. Call the underwriters to obtain a preliminary prospectus.

Securities and Exchange Commission: Documents and Filings

The Securities and Exchange Commission is a good place to begin research if you are interested in any of the nearly 12,000 companies in this country selling stocks to the public—or the nearly 12,000 brokers and the estimated 5,000 management investment companies.

The SEC collects reams of financial and organizational papers from these companies, and the documents are available to the public. They can be obtained from the SEC through the mail, or you can rummage through them at public reference rooms in Chicago, New York City and Washington, D.C. Some business school libraries have some documents on file or available through a computer search.

The following list of SEC documents is supplied by Disclosure Inc., Bethesda, MD, a company specializing in SEC records.

FORM 10–K

This is the annual report filed by companies with over 500 stockholders and $1 million in assets. It includes the following information about organization and finance:

Part I

Business. Identifies principal products and services of the company, principal markets and methods of distribution and its "material," competitive factors, backlog and expectation of fulfillment, availability of raw materials, importance of patents, licenses and franchises, estimated cost of research, number of employees, and effects of compliance with environmental laws. If there is more than one line of business, for each of the last three fiscal years, a statement of total sales and net income for each line which, during either of the last two fiscal years, accounted for 10 percent or more of total sales or pre-tax income.

Properties. Location and character of principal plants, mines and other important properties and if held in fee or leased.

Legal Proceedings. Brief description of material legal proceedings pending; when civil rights or environmental statutes are involved, proceedings must be disclosed.

Principal Security Holders and Security Holdings of Management. Identification of owners of 10 percent or more of any class of securities and of securities held by directors and officers according to amount and percent of each class.

Part II

Market for the Registrants' Common Stock and Related Security Holder Matters. Includes principal market in which voting securities are traded with high and low sales prices (in the absence thereof, the range of bid and asked quotations for each quarterly period during the past two years) and the dividends paid during the past two years. In addition to the frequency and amount of dividends paid, this item contains a discussion concerning future dividends.

Selected Financial Data. These are five-year selected data including net sales and operating revenue; income or loss from continuing operations, both total and per common share, total assets, and long-term obligations including redeemable preferred stock; cash dividends declared per common share. Also, additional items that could enhance understanding and trends in financial condition and results of operations. Further, the effects of inflation and changing prices should be reflected in the five-year summary.

Management's Discussion and Analysis of Financial Condition and Results of Operations. Under broad guidelines, this includes liquidity, capital resources and results of operations; favorable or unfavorable trends as well as significant events or uncertainties; causes of any material changes in the financial statements as a whole; limited data concerning subsidiaries; discussion of effects of inflation and changing prices. Projections or other forward-looking information may or may not be included.

Financial Statements and Supplementary Data. Two-year audited balance sheets as well as three-year audited statements of income and changes in financial condition.

Part III

Directors and Executive Officers of the Registrant. Name, office, term of office and specific background data on each.

Remuneration of Directors and Officers. List of each director and three highest paid officers with aggregate annual remuneration exceeding $40,000 and total paid all officers and directors.

Part IV

Exhibits, Financial Statement Schedules and Reports on Form 8–K. Complete, audited annual financial information and a list of exhibits filed. Also, any unscheduled material events or corporate changes filed in an 8–K during the year. A list of schedules follows:

1. Marketable securities. Other security investments.
2. Amounts due from directors, officers, and principal holders of equity securities other than affiliates.
3. Investments in securities of affiliates.
4. Indebtedness of affiliates (not current).
5. Property, plant and equipment.
6. Reserves for depreciation, depletion, and amortization of property, plant and equipment.
7. Intangible assets.
8. Reserves for depreciation and amortization of intangible assets.
9. Bonds, mortgages and similar debt.
10. Indebtedness to affiliates (not current).
11. Guarantees of securities of other issuers.
12. Reserves.
13. Capital shares.
14. Warrants or rights.
15. Other securities.
16. Supplementary profit and loss information.
17. Income from dividends (equity in net profit and loss of affiliates).

FORM 18–K

Annual report for foreign governments and political subdivisions thereof.

FORM 19–K

For American certificates against foreign issues for the underlying securities of a foreign issuer.

1. Changes in ownership and control.
2. Changes in character of the business.
3. Changes in property.
4. Modification of securities of the registrant.
5. Limitations affecting security holders.
6. Securities of other issuers guaranteed by the registrant.
7. Increases and decreases in outstanding equity securities.
8. Exchange control.
9. Directors and officers of the registrant.
10. Remuneration of officers and directors.
11. Amount set aside for pensions and similar benefits.
12. Options to purchase securities from registrant or subsidiaries.
13. Financial statements and exhibits.

FORM 20–F

The annual report filed by certain foreign issuers of securities trading in the United States.

Item 1. Business
Item 2. Management discussion and analysis of the statements of income
Item 3. Property
Item 4. Control of registrant
Item 6. Remuneration of directors and officers
Item 7. Options to purchase securities from registrant or subsidiaries
Item 8. Pending legal proceedings
Item 9. Nature of trading market
Item 10. Capital stock to be registered
Item 11. Debt securities to be registered
Item 12. Other securities to be registered
Item 13. Exchange controls and other limitations affecting security holders
Item 14. Taxation
Item 15. Changes in securities and changes in security for registered securities
Item 16. Defaults upon senior securities
Item 17. Interest of management in certain transactions
Item 18. Financial statements and exhibits

FORM 10–Q

This is the quarterly report of companies trading stocks publicly, and their subsidiaries.

Financial data required include income statement, balance sheet and inventories; sources and application of funds; effects of any dispositions or purchases; earnings and dividends per share; any defaults or nonpayment of dividends; any increase or decrease in securities or indebtedness.

The report also must include a narrative analysis of operations covering changes in revenues and expenses between that quarter and the previous quarter, and corresponding periods during the previous year (this could contain sales volume, prices, productivity and labor costs); nonroutine legal proceedings; matters voted on by security holders.

FORM 8–K

This form calls for information about important current developments. It is filed by the public companies.

Documents filed describe any change in control of the company, including who obtained control, the nature of the transaction and any loans or contracts that could result in future changes of control; major acquisitions or dispositions of income, including sources of funds for acquisitions; bankruptcy or receivership proceedings; balance sheets for any business bought or sold.

FORM 10–C

Over-the-Counter companies use this form to report changes in name and amount of NASDAQ-listed securities. It is similar in purpose to the 8–K.

FORM 6–K

Foreign companies selling stock in this country, which do not have to file Form 8–K, must file Form 6–K. It requires that they submit information they have made public abroad.

Only information not previously furnished to the SEC, and information that is important to investors, is required. If the information is available only in a foreign language, it does not have to be translated into English.

The documents show the financial condition of the company and its subsidiaries; changes in business; major acquisitions or disposition of assets; changes in management or control; remuneration to directors and officers and any transactions with directors, officers or principal stockholders.

SCHEDULE 13–D

Schedule 13–D must be filed by a person or company that acquires more than 5 percent of the securities of a company that is listed on a stock exchange or is worth more than $1 million and has 500 or more shareholders.

It requires a description of the securities and issuer; background information about the issuer, including directors, partners, parent or subsidiary companies; sources of funds for the purchase; purpose of the transaction (for example, the purchase was made as an investment or to obtain control of management); plans for the issuer, if management control is acquired; amount of shares owned; contracts with others concerning those shares.

SCHEDULE 13–G

This must be filed when a person or company acquires more than 5 percent interest in a firm such as a brokerage company (which acts as an agent in a stock transactions), bank, investment adviser or insurance company.

It is a shortened version of Schedule 13–D. It requires less information if the interest was acquired in the normal course of business, and not in an effort to obtain control of management.

SCHEDULE 14–D1

This describes tender offers made to companies trading on a stock exchange or to those worth more than $1 million with 500 or more shareholders. It is filed by the target company.

It identifies the securities; past major dealings between the two companies or their directors; source and amount of funds required; purpose of the transactions; persons, such as brokers, retained to help with the transactions; material financial information; documents such as the tender offer itself, loan agreements and contracts.

SCHEDULE 14–D

This form must be filed by companies that are the subject of tender offers if they make recommendations for or against the offer.

It tells why the recommendation was made; describes the security and issuer; describes the background of the company; identifies persons retained as a result of the tender offer; gives information about any transactions with the other company during the previous 60 days.

FORM N-5

This form is used to register small business management investment companies.

Management investment companies, such as mutual funds, purchase a variety of securities. Investors then buy into the investment companies and earn profits from the securities owned by the companies.

Form N-5 includes type and amount of securities being registered; maximum offering price per unit and proposed maximum aggregate offering price; a prospectus.

Description of business being done, including type of businesses to which loans are made and kinds of loans; major lawsuits in progress; any special tax status; diagram illustrating controlling persons, giving names, addresses, affiliations and remuneration of the directors, executive officers and advisory board members; identification of investment advisers.

Explanation of policies on matters such as borrowing and lending; underwriting; concentrating investments in particular industries; sale of real estate and commodities; types and concentration of investments.

Financial data, including balance sheet, profit and loss; description of long-term debts; holders of portfolio securities; a summary of earnings for the past five years including net sales, cost of goods, gross profit, interest charges and net income; per share earnings and dividends or, for long-term debt preferred securities, annual interest requirements.

About capital stocks, it includes explanations of dividend rights, voting rights, liquidation rights, pre-emptive rights, conversion rights, redemption provisions, sinking fund provisions and liabilities.

For long-term issues, it includes interest rights, maturity, conversion rights, redemption provisions, amortization provisions, sinking fund or retirement provisions and liens and restrictions.

FORM N-5R

This is the annual report of small business management investment companies.

It gives the type of security and the exchange on which it is traded; information about companies that the registrant owns or controls; a diagram of the companies or persons controlling or controlled by the registrant, and their relationships; information about persons who own the equity securities, showing percentage of the class and number of holders.

Information about the directors, executive officers and the advisory board members, including remuneration; class and number of full-time and part-time employees of the registrant and its investment advisers; identification of who has custody of securities and similar investments; interests any affiliated persons have in transactions.

Financial statements, showing income and expenses, investments, receivables, payables, controlled companies and affiliated persons.

FORM N-8A

This is the notice of registration investment companies must file. It tells name of registrant, form of organization (corporation, partnership, trust, etc), state and date of organization.

If the business has directors, it tells the address of the principal office, names and addresses of directors, officers, advisory board members and investment advisers, and, if it is an open-end company, the underwriters.

If the business is unincorporated and has no board of directors, it shows the name and address of the trustee or custodian, sponsor, investment advisers, principal underwriters and officers and directors of the sponsoring company.

If the business is a management company, the form shows whether it is open-end or closed-end, diversified or nondiversified and whether it is an employee securities company.

The form must tell whether the registrant sells periodic payment plan certificates and whether it issues its own securities to the public. Companies in which the registrant holds 25 percent or more of the voting securities must be listed, and the last report to security holders is attached.

FORM N-8B-1

This form is used to register management investment companies. It requires a great deal of information, including date, form and state of organization; any new business entered into, name change, bankruptcy, receivership or similar proceedings; interest of affiliated persons in transactions; whether it is open-end or closed-end and diversified or nondiversified.

Descriptions of policies on matters such as issuance of senior securities, borrowing and lending, underwriting securities of other issuers, concentration of investments in particular industries, purchase and sale of real estate or commodities.

Security investment policies, such as types of securities in which the company may invest and proportion of assets that can be invested, percentage of assets that it may invest in the securities of any one issuer, percentage of voting securities any one issuer may acquire, interest in companies for the purpose of exercising control, investment in securities of other investment companies and portfolio turnover.

Information about diversification of assets, including class of assets, value of each and percentage of total assets; information about companies the registrant invests heavily in, or controls 5 percent or more of the voting securities; underwriting commitment, tax status, legal proceedings, capitalization; defaults and arrears on senior securities.

Financial information, including income and expenses, capital changes and comparative securities information for the past 10 years.

Information about affiliated persons including a diagram illustrating persons or companies controlling or controlled by the company, showing their relationships; holders of equity securities; names, addresses, remuneration, positions and outside occupations of directors, officers and advisory board members.

Pension or retirement benefits to be paid; indemnification of officers and directors; class and number of employees; holders of portfolio securities; connections and employees of investment advisers.

Information about capital stock, long-term debts and other securities, including the rights of security holders; distribution of securities; information about the underwriters.

Financial data, including balance sheets, income and expenses, assets and liabilities, gain or loss on investments; historical financial information, including increases in tangible or intangible assets.

FORM N-1R

Form N-1R is the annual report of registered management investment companies. Part II of the filing sometimes is confidential.

Part I includes class of securities and the exchanges they are traded on; information about companies in which the registrant invested more than 5 percent of its assets, or in which the registrant owns more than 5 percent of the voting securities; underwriting commitments; tax status.

Financial data, including balance sheet, assets and liabilities, income and expenses, dividends, capital changes and ratios (such as the ratio of operating expenses to total investment income).

Diagram of the companies or persons controlling or controlled by the registrant and their relationships; information about persons owning equity securities; information about directors, officers, advisory board members and legal counsel, including social security number, dates of service, occupation and remuneration of some officials.

Type and number of full- and part-time employees investment advisers; identification of who has custody of securities, including their business connections and personnel.

Portfolio turnover; information about restricted securities held; monthly sales of the registrant's shares; information about shareholders' meetings including proxies; policies; information about underwriters.

Part II gives formal meeting attendance by directors and advisory board members; purchase and sales transactions; vacancies in the board of directors and percentage of the board elected by securities holders; transactions with controlled or affiliated companies; remuneration of agents or brokers; deposits of funds in banks other than custodian banks; cross or circular ownership; brokerage commissions paid.

Familiar relationships of certain affiliated persons; exchange offers made to shareholders; the 10 largest dealers in the registrant's stocks; correspondence relating to shareholders' accounts.

FORM N-1Q

This form is the quarterly report filed by management investment companies.

It lists principal executive officers and investment advisers; total net assets; changes in portfolio securities; amount of government securities held; information about securities bought and sold, including symbol on the stock exchange, acquisitions or dispositions increased by stock dividends or splits and information about matters submitted to a vote of the securities holders.

Changes in investment policy regarding type of securities, proportion of assets invested in each type; percentage of assets which may be invested in the securities of any one issuer; percentage of voting securities any one issuer can acquire; investment in companies for the purpose of controlling management; investment in the securities of other management investment companies; portfolio turnover.

Any significant legal proceedings, including bankruptcy or receivership; changes in securities or debt; default or arrears on securities changes in control of registrant; terms of new or amended securities.

FORM BD

This form is for registration, licensing or membership as a broker or dealer (a person or company trading securities).

It shows the form of the organization; if it is a corporation, the date and state of incorporation, and class of equity security; if it is a sole proprietorship, the person's residence and Social Security number; if it is a successor to previous broker or dealer, the SEC file number of the predecessor.

Persons with controlling interests; how the business is financed.

The firm's or person's standing with the SEC and other regulatory agencies, including disclosure of having made false statement to the SEC in the past; been convicted in the past 10 years of a related felony; been enjoined in the past 10 years from financial activities; aided anyone in violating related laws or rules; been barred or suspended as a broker-dealer; been the subject of a cease and desist order; been associated with a similar firm that went bankrupt.

Information about the person or business that maintains the applicant's records and holds funds of the applicant or its customers; details about companies which control or are controlled by the applicant; whether the applicant is an investment adviser, types of business done (such as floor activity, underwriting or mutual fund retailing); descriptions of any nonsecurity business.

Information about principals including positions, securities held, Social Security numbers, education and background.

FORM X-17A-5

This is the financial and operating report of security brokers and dealers.

It includes a statement of financial condition, showing cash, securities, investments, obligations, assets, bank loans, liabilities and expenses, ownership equity, net capital, total indebtedness, ratios, statements of income or loss, credit and debit balances, changes in ownership equity and promotional costs.

REGISTRATION STATEMENTS

These are of two principal types: (1) "offering" registrations filed under the 1933 Securities Act, and (2) "trading" registrations filed under the 1934 Securities Exchange Act.

"Offering" registrations are used to register securities before they may be offered to investors. Part I of the registration, a preliminary prospectus or "red herring," carries all the sales features that will be contained in the final prospectus. Part II of the registration contains detailed information about marketing agreements, expenses of issuance and distribution, relationship of the company with experts named in the registration, sales to special parties, recent sales of unregistered securities, subsidiaries of registrant, franchises and concessions, indemnification of directors and officers, treatment of proceeds from stock being registered, and financial statements and exhibits.

"Offering" registration statements vary in purpose and content according to the type of organization issuing stock:

S-1 Companies reporting under the 1934 Act for less than 3 years. Permits no incorporation by reference and requires complete disclosure in the prospectus.

S-2 Companies reporting under the 1934 Act for 3 years or more but do not meet the minimum voting stock requirement.

S-3 Companies reporting under the 1934 Act for 3 years and having at least $150 million of voting stock held by non-affiliates, or as an alternative test, $100 million of voting stock coupled with an annual trading volume of 3 million shares. Requires minimal disclosure in the prospectus and allows maximum incorporation by reference of 1934 Act reports.

N-1 (Formerly S-5) Used by open-end investment companies.

N-2 (Formerly S-4) Used by closed-end investment companies.

S-6 Used by unit investment trusts registered under the Investment Act of 1940 on Form N-8B-2.

S-7 A short form which may be used by companies which have a relatively healthy operating history and have filed under both the Securities Acts of 1933 and 1934 in a timely manner.

S-8 Used to register securities to be offered to employees under stock option and various other benefit plans.

S-9 Rescinded in SEC Release No. 33–5791, December 20, 1976. Previously used as a short form similar to the S-7 for the registration of debt securities. The requirements are now incorporated in Form S-7.

S-10 Used for the registration of landowners' royalty interests, overriding royalty interests, participating interests, working interests, oil or gas payments, oil or gas fee interests, oil or gas leasehold interests and other producing and non-producing oil or gas interests or rights.

S-11 Used by real estate companies, primarily limited partnerships and investment trusts.

S-12 Used to register American Depository Receipts issued against securites of foreign issuers deposited with an American depository.

S-13 Used for the registration of certificates, agreements, etc. relating to voting and voting- trust agreements.

S-14 Used to register securities for the reorganization, merger, consolidation, transfer of assets or similar plan acquisition.

S-15 This new, experimental, optional, short registration form provides an abbreviated Prospectus to be sent to securities holders with the latest Annual Report in certain business combinations. It is anticipated that S-15 will be used primarily to register offerings made to small numbers of offerees so that inclusion of the Annual Report would not involve significant costs.

S-16 A short form which may be used for the registration of securities to be offered for sale by current or future security holders.

S-18 Short form registration up to $5 million.

"Trading" registrations are filed to permit trading among investors on a securities exchange or in the over-the-counter market. Registration statements which serve to register securities for trading fall into three categories:

1. Form 10 is used by companies during the first two years they are subject to the 1934 Act filing requirements. It is a combination registration statement and annual report with information content similar to that of SEC-required annual reports.

2. Form 8–A is used by 1934 Act registrants wishing to register additional securites for trading.

3. Form 8–B is used by "successor issuers" (usually companies that have changed their name or state of incorporation) as notification that previously registered securities are to be traded under a new corporate identification.

PROSPECTUS

When the sale of securites as proposed in an "offering" registration statement is approved by the SEC, any changes required by the SEC are incorporated into the prospectus. This document must be made available to investors before the sale of the security is initiated. It also contains the actual offering price, which may have been changed after the registration statement was approved.

ANNUAL REPORT TO SHAREHOLDERS

The Annual Report is the principal document used by most major companies to communicate directly with shareholders. Since it is not a required, official SEC filing, companies have considerable discretion in determining what types of information this report will contain and how it is to be presented.

Recent changes required by the SEC were made to standardize the presentation of disclosure items in annual reports to make them consistent with similar requirements in SEC filings. For example, selected financial data relating to a registrant's financial condition and results of continuing operations will be presented in the Annual Report in the same manner as in the 10–K.

In addition to financial information, the Annual Report to Shareholders often provides non-financial details of the business that are not reported elsewhere. These may include marketing plans and forecasts of future programs and plans.

HOW TO GET COPIES

Prices of documents differ depending upon their size and how you obtain them. The investor relations office of most corporations will provide the annual report, most recent proxy, quarterly statements and 10–K. Other documents should be obtained from the SEC.

The least expensive route is to visit one of four SEC public reference rooms and examine the papers.

The public reference rooms:

Chicago
230 South Dearborn Street
Chicago, IL 60604
312-353-7433 or 7434

New York
26 Federal Plaza, Room 1029
New York, NY 10007
212-264-1615

Washington, DC
450 5th St. NW, Room 1024
Washington, DC 20549
202-272-7450

You also can request copies from the SEC, to be mailed to you or picked up. The requests must be made in writing to:

Public Reference Section
Securities and Exchange Commission
Washington, DC 20549
202-272-7450

A company specializing in SEC records:

Disclosure, Inc.
5161 River Rd.
Bethesda, MD 20816
800-638-8241

NY 212-262-7070, 732-5955
Chicago 312-902-1550
LA 213-934-8313
SF 415-986-1775
DC 301-951-1350
London 01-278-7848

The Corporation

by John Holusha

For more than a century, the corporation has been America's dominant business structure. Like a person in the eyes of the law, the corporation is capable of owning property and making debts. It can sue and be sued.

The origins of the corporation can be traced to Roman law, which allowed religious societies to handle business transactions in guildlike groups. These guilds became state-regulated companies in the Middle Ages. By the seventeenth century, such companies as the East India Company and the Plymouth Company were operating around the world.

America's first corporation was the Bank of North America, chartered by the federal government in 1781. But it wasn't until 1811 that New York became the first state to establish a law making corporations legitimate enterprises.

In the United States, most corporations choose to incorporate in individual states where rules governing corporate behavior are most lenient. For this reason, Delaware is a popular state for incorporation.

Corporations vary in size from a one-person company to the massive General Motors Corporation, which has thousands of employees around the globe. Corporations may be publicly held or private. Most are organized to make a profit.

The corporations that journalists cover tend to be large businesses whose shares and bonds are traded in public markets such as the New York Stock Exchange or the American Stock Exchange.

Legally, a corporation is owned by the holders of its common stock and is responsible to them. But that doesn't mean that individual stockholders exercise real control. Management usually maintains its leadership because the top officers of the company represent enough shares to constitute a majority. In any vote of shareholders, these officers are practically guaranteed more than 50 percent of the vote. In recent years, however, a wave of takeovers has upset the comfort of the executive suite.

THE CHAIN OF COMMAND

Corporations are organized so shareholder interests are represented by the board of directors. There are two types of directors, inside and outside. Inside directors are executives who work for the corporation. Outside directors are not employees and are supposedly more independent in their judgment of management's performance. In practice, many outside directors are executives of other corporations who share management's attitudes and goals. In larger corporations, the board of directors is subdivided into committees, which may concentrate on finance or the nomination of new directors.

Corporations are hierarchies with the chief executive officer, or CEO, at the top. Many companies list the highest corporate officer as the chairman of the board, but it is the CEO who runs the company. The chairman presides over board meetings and sets the agenda.

Some corporations have one or more vice chairmen. These posts are usually honorary positions for executives who didn't quite make it to the top. Boards may also retain past chairmen with the title of emeritus.

The second highest ranking executive in most corporations is the president, who may also carry the title chief operating officer, or COO. In many corporate hierarchies, the COO is expected to be "Mr. Inside," focusing on the daily operations of the company. The CEO's responsibility, then, is to be "Mr. Outside," focusing on dealings with the financial community and general public. In some cases, a president is the CEO with an outside director functioning as chairman of the board. But many executives prefer control of the board and the company as well.

While corporations needn't become large bureaucracies, management often includes a long list of vice presidents, division heads and supervisors. After the top management, which includes the chairman, president, financial officer, corporate secretary and treasurer, comes the middle management, which includes division and department heads, plant managers, superintendents and operations officers. This management group is responsible for overseeing day-to-day operating decisions, evaluating personnel, handling minor problems and setting internal goals. This group implements decisions made by top management.

In recent years, American corporations have been accused of developing layer upon layer of middle management, which adds to the payroll but not much to the efficiency of the company. Many corporate restructurings are aimed at decreasing the number of management layers between the employees at shop level and corporate executives.

American corporations resemble the military—battalions of workers answering to superior officers who answer to more senior officers. Corporation divisions are part of this military model. And so are subsidiaries, which are independent legal entities with their own officers and boards of directors, even if the subsidiaries are wholly owned by the parent corporation.

Whatever an employee's title, there are basically two corporate functions: operations and staff. Operations is involved in production, the running of factories, the procurement of goods and services and the responsibility for deliveries. Staffs aren't directly concerned with the daily output. Staff activities include personnel, legal, labor relations, public relations, governmental affairs and financial analysis.

As in the military, rank is important. A senior vice-president usually outranks a vice-president and, in turn, is outranked by an executive vice-president. Some organizations, particularly advertising agencies, have a tendency to embellish titles. Senior executive vice-presidents have been known to exist.

The structure of a corporation is determined by the business it's in. Redrawing organizational charts is a favorite pastime of top executives. The structure of management will also reflect the company's strategy. In companies producing durable goods like appliances, cars or computers, there will be heavy emphasis on marketing. In others, such as drug companies, research may be the most important activity. If a company is anticipating expansion into a new market, it may begin searching for executives to run the new divisions. Some companies will be top heavy with lawyers, while others will have dozens of engineers. The test of a good corporate structure is profit.

Takeovers, some argue, is a natural way for business to correct mistakes in management and strategy. A takeover may actually make a business more efficient and profitable by changing the management, the product mix or the market strategy. To be sure, many corporations that had become too large, or unprofitable, were "reorganized" by corporate raiders in the 1980s. The raiders shed unwanted businesses and reduced overhead until the companies yielded profits for the raider.

CORPORATE BEHAVIOR

Corporations are immortal, yet they grow, shrink and often die. Sometimes one company merges into another as when the American

Motors Corporation was absorbed into Chrysler Corporation. At other times, a company fails to adjust to the market or to produce goods its customers want and goes out of business. Sometimes newcomers take over.

Journalists like to write about companies as if they were living things. We talk about companies "slimming down" or becoming "lean and mean" or being "fat and happy." But companies do not have personalities of their own. Corporations are neither good nor evil. They simply reflect the styles and temperaments of those who manage them. And yet, journalists and the public expect corporations to behave as people do— to feel pity, to feel shame, to feel embarrassed or to feel charitable.

The "corporate conscience" is an expression reflecting the desire to personalize corporations. Business schools teach courses about the role of business in society and, as journalists, we often find ourselves in the midst of debates over ethical and unethical business behavior.

There are areas where companies agree they have responsibility to the public for good behavior. For example, companies agree they should be efficient users of energy and natural resources; they should not pollute the environment; they should treat employees fairly; they should acquiesce to State Department requests to avoid establishing businesses in certain countries; they should encourage and promote minorities and women. Such voluntary behavior is becoming part of what we expect from corporations.

The theory behind the good corporate citizen concept is "enlightened self-interest," a doctrine that holds that by helping others, a business helps itself. Consequently, companies are expected to donate to education and to community and cultural activities. Many of these activities are tax-deductible.

While there are pressures on business to behave ethically in the United States, outside the United States the rules are different. For some companies, a more favorable corporate environment abroad encourages them to look to business outside the U.S.

MULTINATIONALS

The key event for America's corporations has been the internationalization of markets. After World War II, new markets opened up for American goods and the rebuilding of economies in the Far East and Europe provided opportunities for expansion. Now many American companies have global networks of subsidiaries tied into a single corporate strategy.

Despite the size of the American market, U.S. companies have built profit-generating empires in other countries. The advantages can be considerable. For example, it may be possible to sell older versions of goods Americans will no longer buy, thereby extending the useful life of equipment and technology. It may even be possible to sell a poorer-quality product for a higher profit in a country where the product is scarce. There can be production savings because labor is cheaper in other countries. Taxes may be less, and the host foreign country may give generous incentives.

But the multinational strategy is not one-sided. While American companies expanded overseas, so did foreign corporations, many of them to U.S. markets. Companies in the Far East targeted the U.S. consumer electronics business and parts of the semiconductor industry, effectively squeezing out American competitors. Some of the most successful overseas companies are establishing integrated operations in this country. Honda, for example, has design and engineering centers in the U.S. in addition to sales and manufacturing operations. In the 1990s, Honda executives say, the American arm of the company will be capable of operating independently of the Japanese parent.

While many American companies have done well overseas, journalists should recognize that the multinational corporations may carry the seeds of their own destruction. First, multinationals must operate in two or more business environments, under different laws and exchange rates. What's more, it is difficult for a company to transplant its "corporate culture"—the company's unique personality and business practices—to far-flung offices since companies routinely hire a high percentage of local workers, including executives, to meet local regulations of the countries that require foreign companies to hire locals.

And there is the problem of American policy. If the government decides the dollar is either too weak or too strong, earnings from overseas operations can vary wildly. If the U.S. Congress decides American factories must be protected against imports, some U.S. companies that manufacture abroad for import here may be hurt. The political and economic uncertainty of the late 1980s resulted in a reexamination of the value of multinational operations at some American companies.

BUSINESS STRUCTURES

American business takes many forms. Here is a list of common business arrangements:

Corporation: A legal entity chartered by the state or the federal government, in which each owner buys shares of ownership but does not necessarily participate in the management. The shareholder can expect some return on the investment in the form of dividends or appreciation in the value of the shares, but is not responsible for debts. Corporations may be public or private.

General Partners: Investors who have the right to enter into contracts in the name of the firm. They have unlimited liability, which means they can be called upon to provide additional money to pay the debts of the partnership.

Joint stock companies: A cross between a partnership and a corporation. Shares are sold in the company by its owners, who may be temporary. Professional management is required since the original owners do not wish to be managers.

Joint Ventures: A partnership in which two or more individuals combine resources for a single transaction or undertaking, such as the purchase of land for resale. When the business is complete, the partnership dissolves.

Limited partners: Individuals who invest in a partnership but do not participate in management.

Partnership: A business owned by one or more individuals who combine their resources, participate in the management and share the profits and losses.

Silent partners: Owners of a business who do not wish to have a voice in the operations of the company. They may also not want to be known to the public.

Sole proprietorship: A business owned by an individual who has exclusive control. The owner receives all the profits and must bear all the losses.

Syndicates: A partnership which is formed primarily to conduct a financial transaction. Participants might pool their money to buy controlling interest of a business.

Corporate Strategies

by Charles G. Blaine

Writing the corporate strategy story requires a bit of intellectual guerrilla warfare. The reporter must determine: What is the company doing? What does the company say it is doing? Does the company really know what it is doing? Do I?

There is a fair amount of risk associated with strategy stories, since analysis and an evaluation of risk are key components in a good article. The first problem is to understand just what a strategy is: A strategy is not to be confused with corporate goal, which, generally speaking, is to make money. The strategy is the process by which the goal is achieved.

Thus, the strategy spreads across all business disciplines: marketing, finance, accounting, etc. The writer's job, then, is to judge how well these disciplines work together. Sometimes they don't ; sometimes they work splendidly.

IDENTIFYING THE STRATEGY

General Motors became a hugely successful enterprise not because it decided to be big. Rather, in the early 1920s, it formulated one of the most successful corporate strategies ever devised.

Unlike Henry Ford who, legend has it, said a buyer of a Model-T automobile could have any color so long as it was black, GM understood the need to develop demand for its products by identifying what buyers wanted. Its strategy was to create, and then satisfy, consumer desires for automobiles of many colors and styles. To reach the maximum number of buyers GM developed a strategy built on a number of products that together would create high demand for GM products. Result: Different product lines that competed against each other as well as against other manufacturers' products. And lots of different colors. Ultimately, Ford had to add colors, too.

Corporate strategies are dynamic and must be measured in terms both of the ultimate results and of success over time. Time is a crucial part of the equation because investors, both large and small, tend to be impatient about getting income and appreciation from their investments. If a company embarks on a strategy that has middling results for several years, the shareholders may become frustrated and sell their holdings. Remember: A company is always under pressure to demonstrate that its strategies result in a more profitable enterprise.

At the same time, companies don't operate in a vacuum. Competition may increase dramatically or collapse, technology may change, or the economy might crash. A home building company has to change its strategy if mortgage rates rise to 18 percent. When personal computers became a fast-growing business in the late 1970s, smart companies, including IBM, shifted their business strategies to exploit the emerging market.

Some strategies are fairly simple. If a company is young, it will want to grow at a faster rate than a more mature company with established products in established markets. So, it's common for young companies to reinvest their earnings in new plants and equipment.

Many strategies are deliberate moves to challenge competitors. Consider Wal-Mart Stores, Inc. in Bentonville, Arkansas. It offers everyday low prices, a huge selection of goods, and brand names. The overhead is low because it operates in the suburbs in huge warehouse-like stores and advertises mostly by circulars.

This strategy has been devastatingly successful: Wal-Mart has expanded out of the South with all the subtlety of a tidal wave. Wherever it operates, its pricing strategy puts tremendous pressure on department stores, whether locally-based or not. No less than Sears, Roebuck & Co. was forced to change its own strategy.

Forbes magazine regularly dubs Sam Walton, the retail chain's folksy founder, as the richest man in the country. He is calculatedly colorful. He drives an old pickup truck. And, once, to fulfill a promise to his employees who beat his profit goals, he danced in a hula skirt in front of the New York Stock Exchange.

Often, in the acquisitive eighties, the fastest way to grow was to buy another company. Chevron bought Gulf Oil. Phillip Morris bought General Foods and Kraft Inc.. Bank of New York bought Irving Trust.

Texas Air took over Continental Airlines, then Eastern, then People Express and Frontier.

STRATEGIES CAN FAIL

Once the writer has identified the strategy, he or she has to determine whether it works. This means knowing enough about business to state the case with authority and examples.

People Express will go down as one of the classic cases of a failed strategy. The airline's initial success resulted from the choice of under-utilized Newark Airport as its network center. Helped by low costs and prices, the airline's business exploded across the highly populated Northeast, then on to Florida, to Texas, ultimately to Europe. But the strategy unraveled when People Express bought Denver-based Frontier Airlines, and moved into head-to-head competition with United Airlines and Continental Airlines, which had hubs in Denver.

It was one thing to expand. But People Express had some internal weaknesses that had never been addressed. It didn't have the management systems in place to handle the increasingly complex business. Luggage was lost. Flights were late. Also, it had paid too much for Frontier. Finally, People was buried by its competitors.

Not all writers recognized the risks involved when the deal was first announced. They soon did.

Even though companies, already sold on a strategy, will attempt to sell the public on their plans, reporters should be skeptical. What may seem like a logical strategy may not be in the long run.

Oil companies decided in the late 1970s that buying minerals companies made sense. There indeed was a certain logic, since both extracted natural resources. Their professional disciplines—geology, engineering, seismology, geophysics—were similar. But the energy and minerals businesses aren't alike, as Atlantic Richfield (ARCO) found out when it bought Anaconda Copper in the late 1970s. Less than a decade later conditions changed. Copper prices had tumbled, losses mounted at Anaconda. Raiders started to nibble at ARCO. So, ARCO unloaded Anaconda.

There was no way to predict whether the strategy would be successful. But a business writer does his audience a disservice by not raising questions about the short-term or long-term risks of a strategy. It helps to know a bit of history.

Most strategies are deliberate efforts to enhance a company's competitiveness or profitability. But, at times, the strategy reflects situations when the management has no choice about the company's direction.

For example, top management may also decide (or a corporate raider will decide for them) shrinking the company is more prudent. So its strategy will be to sell pieces of the company and distribute the cash to shareholders. To prevent situations like this, many companies have adopted anti-takeover strategies, which are aimed at discouraging corporate raiders.

Some strategies may make sense to management but not to the public. This is what happened to a company called UAL Inc. Once its major assets were United Airlines and Westin Hotels. Then, UAL bought Hertz Rent-A-Car. Then, it decided to change its name. So it became Allegis and began promoting itself as an all-inclusive travel business. Unfortunately, few people liked the name or the strategy. The company was too big, and raiders like Coniston Partners of New York moved in, because they reasoned that selling off the assets would be lucrative. That is exactly what happened.

Management may find that a company can't avoid a takeover by another company. In such a case, its strategy may be to find a partner other than the initial bidder. Management cannot simply ignore an offer to buy a company. Shareholders can sue managements for violating their fiduciary responsibility to shareholders. But management can head off an unfriendly takeover. When word of a possible offer for Gulf leaked out in the winter of 1984, chairman James Lee had little choice but to put the company up for auction (see "Analyzing the Acquisition" in this volume). Ultimately, three companies bid, and Gulf sold out for $13.2 billion, or $80 a share. Not bad for a stock that was selling in the 30s nine months earlier.

ANALYZING THE STRATEGY

Like any business story, the strategy piece needs to be firmly backgrounded in the company's history, past financial and market performance and the condition of the industry in which it competes.

It is not enough to say Boise Cascade's stock is selling at $42, down 16 percent from its 52–week high. The writer has to keep in mind that Boise Cascade is in forest products and paper. If the housing industry is in a slump, Boise's stock will be in one, too. When interest rates drop and housing starts to show signs of life, Boise's stock will move up quickly.

Moreover, the stock price and the current earnings don't necessarily reflect whether the strategy is working. Remember, the strategy takes time to implement, and it takes time to see if the strategy is working. And it can always be changed.

Reporters cannot rely solely on a company to determine if the strategy is a good one. Having a Value Line Survey or the Standard & Poor's Industry Survey handy is extremely useful. So are the S&P stock reports, usually available in good libraries, brokerage firms and business schools —if not at your office.

The research that pours out of investment houses and trade associations as well as a working relationship with the analysts who cover your company are useful.

And it is wise to cultivate academic sources and corporate refugees with experience in the industry you're interested in. Often, these turn up in university business schools, banks or consulting firms. Also, most industries usually have a band of consultants hovering about doing market research and the like. This group often can explain a strategy better than stock analysts can.

Corporate strategy often involves a change in how the management approaches the company's business. The change may involve spending more advertising dollars for a product, the renaming of the company or the development of a new business. Sometimes, the strategy means the complete restructuring of the company, a reduction in the labor force or the acquisition of a competitor. Here are some typical strategies:

Acquisition

An acquisition is a polite way of saying a purchase of one company by another. Usually a larger company buys a smaller one. The terms of the purchase may involve cash, stock or debt such as bonds. Acquisitions come about for many reasons. A home delivery pizza company may find it easier to expand in a new market by buying an existing participant in that market.

But let's say you run Popeye's Famous Fried Chicken and Biscuits, the number 3 player in the fried chicken business, which has an eye on becoming number 2. (No one is close to challenging number 1 Kentucky Fried Chicken.) The only way to get there was to mount a hostile bid for the number 2 player, Church's Fried Chicken.

Diversification

Diversification means getting into a number of different, and not necessarily related, businesses. A company usually pursues this strategy to offset the swings in its industry's business cycle. A hugely profitable diversification move was made by Quaker Oats in the late 1960s when it bought Fisher-Price, now the powerhouse of children's toys. What forces a diversification move is the realization by management that the company can't grow quickly enough with its current product mix to justify additional investment.

A number of companies have taken the concept to extremes. Gulf + Western grew into a massive conglomerate under Charles Bluhdorn in the 1960s. Beginning with an automobile bumper maker, the G+W empire included more than 100 businesses including cigar making, racetracks, and sugar plantations. After his death in 1983, the company began focusing on two businesses: publishing and entertainment. G+W owned Paramount Pictures, Madison Square Garden and Simon & Schuster publishing. Likewise, ITT Corp. has expanded, once owning everything from hotels to insurance companies to bakeries, and contracted.

Divestiture

The shedding of an unwanted asset or business. Mobil Corp.'s spinoff of Montgomery Ward was a divestiture.

Downsizing

Downsizing shrinks a company. Operations are shut down or sold off. Employees are laid off, though many may continue to work at companies that are sold. The goal is to reduce the size of the operation so that it is easier for the company to achieve its profit goals.

ARCO's restructuring, after it admitted that its copper venture was a bust, is a classic downsizing. It lopped off the copper operation plus its refining and marketing operations east of the Mississippi River—a full third of the business.

Going Private

This means that a publicly held company buys back all of its shares traded publicly. Afterward, the company doesn't have to report results to anyone except its new owners, its bankers, and the Internal Revenue Service. Some companies much prefer to operate privately because they really don't like to talk about results. As a corporate strategy, it has another clear advantage: It keeps the company out of the hands of the raiders.

Going Public

This involves the registration of stock and securities with the Securities and Exchange Commission and the sale of the securities to the public. The strategy is usually employed because a company needs to raise some capital, either for expansion or acquisitions, and the capital markets are an efficient way to get at the money.

Leveraged Buyout

The LBO is a form of restructuring. A small group of investors, typically an investment company and a company's management, propose to buy out all the other shareholders and take the company private. They accomplish this with huge amounts of debt that's paid off either from the cash flow of the company or by selling assets.

The goal of the strategy may be, ultimately, to fix up the company and take it public in the future at a higher share price than is currently available. Or the strategy may be to allow management to operate without the pressure of large numbers of public shareholders. The LBO can be used to fend off corporate raiders or solve other problems. One of the biggest buyouts ever was the $25.2 billion buyout of RJR Nabisco Inc. by Kohlberg, Kravis, Roberts & Company, one of the best known practitioners of the art.

Merger

A merger occurs when two companies merge their operations and, sometimes, even their philosophies after one company has acquired the other.

The term has become very broad, however. When one hears that Engulf & Devour (with apologies to its originator, Mel Brooks) merged with Disgorged Inc., the odds are that E&D actually bought Disgorged.

Redeploying Assets

This is a cute way of saying that a company is getting out of one business and sticking its money into something new. Gould Inc., once a maker of batteries and other products, decided in the late 1970s to get into high technology. Singer Inc., likewise, got out of the sewing machine business and into aerospace.

Repositioning

When a company repositions itself, it is saying, in effect, that its products aren't producing the kinds of profits that keep stockholders happy, raiders at bay and management in their jobs. As a result, the company's managers reconfigure the products, push them at different customers, and hope that the new strategy works.

When Philip Morris Companies took over Miller Brewing Company, it bought a dowdy beer-maker that called its product "the champagne of beers." The marketing whizzes dumped that quickly and aimed the beer at the young macho types. Miller vaulted into the number 2 spot in the U.S. beer market.

Restructuring

Restructuring means rebuilding a company's financial structure. That usually also means refocusing the company's strategy. With takeover mania a reality, a company that's restructuring usually substitutes a lot of debt for its equity, thus enriching current shareholders. Often, this maneuver is forced onto a company. A prime example: The T. Boone Pickens-Carl Icahn raids on Phillips Petroleum Co. Phillips had to substitute about $4.5 billion worth of debt for equity and shed a lot of businesses, including a hotel in Florida.

Spinoff

A company may decide to turn a certain operation out on its own. For example, Allied Corporation unloaded all the businesses it didn't want into a new corporation called Henley Group. Sometimes, the company that's spun off must buy its freedom.

But companies have been known to create spinoffs and give the shares in the new firms to its existing shareholders. The strategy here is to help boost the overall value of the shareholders' original investment.

Pennzoil Company. and Freeport-McMoran Inc., both oil and gas and natural resources companies, have done this frequently. The strategy for both companies has been to let the stock market value the assorted assets independently of the main corporate structures. Shareholders can come out way ahead.

BANKRUPTCY PROCEEDINGS

Business journalists deal most often with two types of bankruptcy: Chapter 7, when the company throws in the towel, and the assets are sold off to pay off its creditors and Chapter 11, when the company works with creditors in order to survive.

Chapter 11 is the more interesting story. A company is placed under the protection of the court. It doesn't pay interest on debt or taxes. It submits a plan of reorganization, which lays out how and when the company will pay off all its creditors. After some argument, a deal is settled, and the plan, however modified by the company and its creditors, is put into effect.

For existing shareholders, a Chapter 11 is rarely a happy experience because they lose most or all of their investment. Their place is taken by debt holders or by new owners.

Bankruptcy as a corporate strategy is used to buy time to solve a problem. Sometimes, the problem can't be solved and the company is sold off or liquidated.

In the summer of 1982, Manville Corporation showed how creative a strategy bankruptcy can be. Manville, though financially healthy, faced millions of dollars in liabilities from asbestos claims and saw no end to the suits against the company.

Filing for protection under the 1978 federal bankruptcy code gave the company time to work out a solution that it and everyone else found equitable. Six years later, Manville emerged from Chapter 11, still healthy and the claims settled.

Texaco Inc. used Chapter 11 to prevent Pennzoil from seizing all its assets in the war that broke out over whether Texaco stole Getty Oil from Pennzoil. Texaco bought a lot of time in the move, and it paid $3 billion to settle the case. It could have been far worse: a jury had awarded Pennzoil $10.5 billion.

Wall Street has no trouble understanding Texaco's use of a bankruptcy strategy. When Texaco went into Chapter 11 in April of 1987, its stock crashed, landing in the high 20s. By the end of July, it was at $46 a share.

Marketing Strategies

by Joshua Levine

Many business journalists regard marketing with a mix of mistrust and outright hostility. If you write business news for a living, you're probably best acquainted with marketing through the advertising that appears in your own news organization and the department down the hall that solicits it. These are the folks who coddle the same companies you try to write about objectively, the church to your state. Any journalist who has seen an advertiser pull its ads from a publication after an unfavorable story—and who hasn't?—gets the queasy feeling that advertising and journalism make uneasy bedfellows at best.

But there's much more to marketing than advertising, both as a business discipline and as a source of rich and exciting stories. Marketing includes a diverse array of business activities: the strategy behind a product, the design of a product, its packaging, pricing and distribution, as well as its advertising and promotion. Marketing is the process that begins with learning what consumers want and ends with satisfying those needs. Through advertising, marketers cajole and persuade. Through marketing, they try to develop a loyalty and long-term relationship between product and customer. Marketing is only successful if the customer comes back for more.

Marketing is therefore much more than appending "new and improved" to yesterday's product. It is the business of creating a market, either by attracting customers who have never purchased the marketer's products before or by taking customers away from a competitor. And it's the marketer who disciplines the company's romance with innovation and forces the R&D (research and development) department to answer several key questions: Does anybody want this thing, and if so who? Are there enough buyers to justify making it? And will they pay enough for it to cover costs and generate a reasonable profit?

THE MARKETING PROCESS

The process begins with market research to get preliminary answers to those questions. More market research will guide the formulation of the product itself—what color should the soda be? Should it taste more lemony or more limey?

That makes the marketing department central to corporate strategy. Marketing assumes an even greater role in nontechnology companies, where form is often more decisive than function in making a sale. There isn't much you can do to catsup or coffee. With the exception of products based on revolutionary technology—a new drug or an advanced computer chip—most consumer products differ very little from each other. Succeeding or failing in such businesses often depends more on how they are packaged, distributed and advertised.

With every product, the marketer must explain why potential buyers should want it. Very few products sell themselves. In some cases, the message is obvious. It doesn't take much explaining to convince people that a car is a better mode of transportation than a horse. But once everyone owns a car, the marketer must convince car buyers that a new model is either better or cheaper than existing models.

This isn't easy to do in an age when only superficial details distinguish most products. To compensate, marketers often substitute hype for persuasiveness—something the marketing reporter should keep in mind. New products are often treated as news, particularly when the accompanying press release includes profit or sales projections. Tread warily here. Marketers will often attempt to use news stories as unpaid ads. There's no reason why the marketing reporter should oblige them.

Companies differ in how they approach marketing. Standard practice for years at consumer companies was something called the "brand management system." Brand management, pretty much invented by Procter & Gamble, assigns each of the company's brands to an individual or team, which is responsible for all of the brand's marketing activities. Brand management survives today, but even its most ardent supporters are tinkering with it. The system encourages brand managers within the same company to compete with one another—the brand manager for P&G's Tide, for instance, regards the brand manager for P&G's Cheer as a competitor. As a result, P&G recently created a higher level of "category managers" to oversee marketing for all of P&G's detergents.

Regardless of the marketing setup at a company, the mission remains the same—to make a product profitable. That may dictate creating a unique image and market for a single product. Or it may dictate adopting a new product into an existing family of goods sold under a single brand. Over time, successful brands develop trust and loyalty among steady consumers—if you're happy with your Frigidaire refrigerator, you'll probably buy a Frigidaire to replace it, even if other products offer the same quality, price and selection. You may even buy a Frigidaire air conditioner on the assumption that folks who can make such fine refrigerators ought to be able to make good air conditioners. If a brand is properly managed, a company can introduce numerous products under the brand umbrella and be assured a certain degree of consumer acceptance.

Creating brand loyalty takes time, often decades. But in recent years, brand loyalty is much less of a factor in marketing. Brand loyalty was probably strongest just after World War II, when American goods were considered the best in the world. In the 1950s, for example, it was not uncommon for a family to have a history of purchasing only Fords or Cadillacs year after year. Most Americans were fiercely brand loyal to American automakers. But the energy crisis of the 1970s changed those purchasing habits. Young consumers startled their parents—the World War II generation—by buying German and Japanese cars which were smaller and more fuel efficient.

Corporate image is now part of the marketers' job. How the public feels about a company will not only affect consumers' confidence in the company's products, but also their willingness to buy the company's shares.

THE MARKETING STORY

Much business coverage overlooks the yawning abyss between the creation of a product and its appearance on the shelf. Just because a product can be made doesn't mean it can be sold.

It is important not to forget an important component of marketing: getting the product to the customer. This has become an increasingly thorny problem in an age of plenty. From the retailer's point of view, a new product creates problems. Where do you put it? Every product wants to be displayed at eye level. Marketers spend millions deciding the right color for a package based on how it will look on the shelf. As a result, marketers get involved in coaxing and encouraging retailers. Sometimes there's a good story in how one product muscled its way onto the shelf. Keep in mind that retailers sometimes extort payoffs in the form of promotional allowances to carry products.

Only after a company's marketing department has shepherded a product to the store, does marketing's handmaiden—advertising—show up. Advertising in America pervades the culture so profoundly that it tends to overwhelm the discipline that spawned it. As a cultural phenomenon and national art form, advertising has a life apart from commerce. "You can tell the ideals of a nation by its advertisements," wrote pundit Norman Douglas. Unfortunately, he was right.

But advertising also has a life apart from culture. It is a role that should concern a journalist covering marketing, since it exists to articulate a preconceived strategy forcefully and persuasively—Calvin Klein's Obsession perfume was a good example of a product whose advertising, strong with images and emotion, was its sole raison d'être. Many business journalists confuse artful advertising with successful advertising. The two often don't go hand in hand (although it's nice when they do). Mr. Whipple spent years making viewers cringe while selling boatloads of Charmin bathroom tissue for Procter & Gamble. Reebok's "Let U.B.U." commercials fiddled stylishly while its sneaker sales burned.

Marketing as it evolved in the 1950s and 1960s rested on the tripod of national media, national advertisers and large advertising agencies. At the time when America was still learning to brush regularly, Procter & Gamble could indeed whip up a better toothpaste (its research powers are legendary). Its straightforward advertising explained its benefits ("Look ma, no cavities") and easily conveyed its message to the nation through the nascent television networks. It could garner sizable economies of scale through national distribution—no problem at all in those days— and fend off any competitors by out-advertising them.

Market strategy is not so easy today. And covering marketing in this decade means realizing that it is a process that is reinventing itself. The tripod is collapsing. Network television is wrestling with videotape recorders and cable TV for viewers, and it's losing. The din of advertising messages often comes through as white noise, obscuring individual commercials in a general buzz from the tube. What's more, most basic needs have been met. Few teeth are left unbrushed. Most consumer product markets aren't growing faster than the population.

All of which makes marketing far more interesting to cover today. To grow, most companies must wrest customers from their competitors—a struggle that gives reporters the chance to see business at its most violent and dramatic. The eternal verities have been upended. Instead of gearing their marketing toward the largest possible group of buyers to keep the assembly line churning, marketers are carving the market into small segments with specific needs. For many companies, the only way to lift a product above the level of a commodity is to customize it to the tastes and requirements of a select group. Mass marketing is giving way to regional marketing, which tailors products and services to one area of the country. And even now, regional marketing is giving way to something called "micromarketing," which treats the clientele of a particular supermarket or department store as the basic marketing unit.

At the most basic level, covering these and other marketing issues means making the consumer—horrible word, but there it is—the arbiter of business success or failure. The preponderance of business coverage views a company's stockholders and the financial community as its bedrock constituencies. Much of the time, this is fitting. At the end of the day, a company must answer to its owners. It's also handy. Financial measurements abound, and most of them are public.

Marketers don't ignore their income statements, of course, but they answer to their customers first. Often, this puts their agenda out of sync with demands to meet quarterly earnings projections. It may be advisable for a company to cut prices temporarily to outflank competitors, bruising profits in the process. Any gains may show up only later on, after a competitor has been driven from a market, or when gains in unit volume compensate for the discount.

In covering marketing, a business reporter must learn first to leave behind the financial guideposts that mark the road in other stories. The guideposts do appear, but at odd and unexpected turns in the route.

The reporter setting out in this territory should keep the consumer— that word again—uppermost in mind. Who exactly does the company intend to buy a product or service? Why should they buy it? How big is this group? Several years ago, Pepsi Cola tested a new diet cola called Jake's, which had 70 calories a can—on the surface, a quixotic exercise. A reporter covering the story could only make sense of the venture by pointing out Diet Coke's advantage over Diet Pepsi among men and the reasonable assumption that men are generally less obsessive about watching their weight and would sacrifice calories for better taste. If it caught on, Jake's could conceivably have cut into Coca Cola's lead among men without undermining Diet Pepsi's standing with women. (As it happened, Pepsi's reasonable assumption turned out to be wrong; Coca Cola bludgeoned Jake's on the calorie issue, and the new product died a quick death.)

GETTING THE STORY

A company will rarely divulge its strategy to a reporter, so covering marketing means finding back doors. Fortunately, the marketing department is full of them. First off, there's the company's public advertising. It may not deliver a blueprint of the strategy, but it will usually telegraph the basic thrust—after all, that is exactly what it's designed to do. Take the commercials for Jake's. Most of the actors were men.

A good reporter can occasionally develop good sources at an advertising agency willing to disclose an upcoming ad campaign before it breaks, but such scoops are rare. An advertising agency depends on the client for its livelihood and usually won't jeopardize the arrangement. Ad agencies have been fired for far less.

There are several other avenues. Many magazines require ads for a forthcoming issue long before the publication date. Ad salesmen at magazines generally work with particular industries. They usually have an excellent sense of what their advertisers are up to, and often know the details of an ad campaign months before it appears. (The same does not hold true for television, since broadcast commercials need not be delivered to TV stations until shortly before they are due to air.)

Companies also cue their distributors and retailers to the fine points of marketing strategy ahead of time. Distributors and retailers function as selling agents of a company, but they owe no debt of loyalty and often regard their suppliers more as adversaries than allies. They can be excellent sources.

Ironically, Wall Street financial analysts make perhaps the least useful sources for either hard facts or informed speculation in marketing stories. There are exceptions, of course. The best ones know about buying and selling as intimately as they know balance sheets and income statements—particularly, analysts covering companies like beverage or household-product manufacturers that depend on marketing savvy to survive. On the whole, though, the obligation to render a judgment on the advisability of buying or selling a stock makes the financial analyst a myopic observer of marketing. RJR Nabisco under the stewardship of F. Ross Johnson delighted Wall Street with the predictable march of its earnings. At the same time, Nabisco impoverished many of its brands by cutting advertising expenditures to meet those goals, and stinted on new product introductions.

Since standard financial criteria give only a fuzzy picture of the realities marketers confront daily, how does a reporter tell what's working and what isn't? Mostly by viewing marketing against the backdrop of competition. For a marketer, it is no sin to grow slowly in a flat market where the competition is stagnating. To some extent, marketing stories invariably concern competition, and the legendary practitioners are distinguished by an aggressiveness that verges on the homicidal—McDonald's founder Ray Kroc reportedly averred that if his competitor were drowning, he would stick a garden hose in his mouth and turn on the water.

The best measure of competitive success is market share—the proportion of sales in a market a company controls. Companies with large shares and high market rank consistently show far better return on investment than weaker rivals. There are several sources for such measures. A. C. Nielsen, the same folks who measure television ratings, and SAMI/Burke both measure market shares for products sold through supermarkets and drug stores. These figures are confidential, but can usually be obtained through third parties. Most other industries also have at least one market research firm that measures market share on an ongoing basis.

Market shares yield only a snapshot of success, however. As in the definition mentioned earlier, a marketer only accomplishes his or her mission if a buyer feels good enough about a purchase to repeat it. Many business stories award laurels prematurely to companies whose products score early triumphs, only to succumb to the buyer's subsequent disappointment. In reporting on marketing, it is always advisable to ascertain whether it has raised unreasonable expectations it can't sustain.

Finally, a stylistic caveat. Given marketing's warlike nature, most reporters find it impossible to resist splattering their stories with military metaphors. The coverage of marketing abounds with companies launching headlong assaults at rivals or outflanking them. Thrusts are met with parries. Second fronts are opened, often leading to full-scale retreats. In the stirring first phase of a marketing reporter's tour of duty, this is probably unavoidable. The hardened vet should know better. It tends to give the reader battle fatigue.

THINGS YOU SHOULD KNOW

Simmons Market Research Bureau and Mediamark Inc., both in New York, have voluminous data on which demographic groups use which products and how heavily. When writing about a product, new or old, it is often enlightening to see who's using it, who's using the competition, and whether a product's marketing strategy fits into those usage patterns. Both SMRB and Mediamark are happy to disclose this data.

Advertising spending in all media except newspapers is measured and recorded by the Bureau of Advertising Research in New York. If a company will not disclose its ad budget (or it will, but you don't trust them), ad spending for companies and products can be checked directly.

Test markets are good places to get an advance peek at forthcoming products. Often, a company will experiment with different marketing approaches for a product by testing alternatives in several different markets. Test marketing is highly secretive, and companies will rarely divulge details. But local media and local retailers are often less reticent.

When reporting on a company or an industry, read trade magazines not just for their editorial coverage, but for their advertising as well. Before American Express unveils a new strategy for its travelers cheques, say, it will inform the bankers who sell them through trade magazine ads. If Kraft General Foods is preparing to launch a new coffee brand, it will attempt to pique the interest of supermarkets through trade magazine ads.

Beware succumbing to the marketer's hype, which comes with the territory. Common wisdom has it that between 80 percent and 90 percent of all new products fail, a sobering statistic that should mute the fanfare accompanying new product introductions. The true test of a new product is not the immediate response to its appearance; many people will try anything once. It's the response to the product six months to a year later.

Marketing success, like most business success, is measured in profits, not sales. It is comparatively easy to obtain sales figures for most consumer goods, but very difficult to get profit figures in such detail. Short-term sales success can often be bought by discounting, by giveaways or by comparative advertising. At the end of a year, product managers will often resort to sales promotion of one sort or another to make sure they hit their sales targets. A reporter should guard against counting a sudden leap in sales as a marketing victory. As was the case with automobile rebates, today's sales are often borrowed from tomorrow's.

Reading the Balance Sheet

The balance sheet lists what the business owns—the assets—and what the firm owes to others—liabilities—and what the owners have invested—capital—at a certain moment, usually the end of the business year. The basic balance sheet (see table 1) expresses the relationship between these accounts:

$$ASSETS = LIABILITIES + CAPITAL$$

The capital account (or owners' net worth) is calculated by subtracting liabilities owned to creditors from total assets owned by the enterprise. The right side of the equation can be viewed as the sources of funds supplied by either creditors (liabilities) or the owners (capital). The left side of the equation shows the uses of the funds (assets).

A balance sheet forecasts the financial needs of a business and is usually divided into three sections: current assets, fixed assets and intangibles. Balance sheets will vary. Public utilities, for example, will have most all of their investments in fixed assets—property and equipment. Service or financial companies will have most of their investments in current assets.

Table 1   A Typical Balance Sheet

International Digi-Widget, Inc.

Balance Sheet	December 31, 1991	December 31, 1990
Assets		
Current Assets:		
Cash	$2,031,400	$1,398,000
Marketable securities	2,187,230	2,008,900
Accounts receivable	2,089,520	1,850,020
Inventories	2,869,990	1,900,340
Prepaid income taxes	587,770	603,000
Other prepaid charges	201,650	90,820
Other current assets	53,120	48,340
Total current assets	10,020,680	7,899,420
Fixed assets:		
Net property, plant, equip-ment	6,082,330	5,590,050
Other fixed assets	1,397,200	1,465,000
Total fixed assets	7,479,530	7,055,050
Total Assets	17,500,210	14,954,470
Liabilities and shareholders' equity		
Current liabilities:		
Accounts payable	$4,523,000	$4,288,030
Notes payable	549,000	480,000
Accrued expenses payable	987,000	1,005,600
Income taxes	78,980	32,000
Total current liabilities	6,137,980	5,805,630
Long-term liabilities:		
Deferred income taxes	1,005,600	1,200,700
Debentured	3,890,000	3,084,030
Total long-term liabilities	4,895,600	4,284,730
Total liabilities	11,033,580	10,090,360
Shareholders' equity	6,466,630	4,864,110
Total liabilities and equity	$17,500,210	$14,954,470

CURRENT ASSETS

Cash

Because current assets are those assets which can be turned into cash quickly, usually within 12 months of the date of the balance sheet, petty cash—bills and coins—and the deposits in the bank are the most current of a company's current assets. Cash means liquidity.

Marketable Securities

These investments including commercial paper and short-term government securities can also be converted quickly. Usually marketable securities appear on the balance sheet at the "cost" of purchase or at "current market value," whichever is lower.

Accounts Receivable

This is the money owed the company, usually the result of the sale of goods or services. Customers normally pay on a 30–day, 60–day or 90–day billing cycle. The balance sheet shows what the company expects to receive minus bad debts.

Inventories

A manufacturer's balance sheet will show three kinds of inventories: supplies and raw materials, product in the process of manufacture and the finished goods. Like accounts receivable, companies prefer to value inventory at the lower figure reflecting either cost or the market value. But, inventory accounting is subject to change. The more popular method LIFO (last in, first out) assumes the goods last purchased are the first to be sold. This method shows a lower profit and reduces taxes. FIFO (first in, first out) assumes the inventory contains the most recently purchased products, since the goods that have been in the inventory longest are sold first. During inflationary periods, this method inflates profits.

Prepayments and Deferred Charges

These are bills paid in advance for services or goods the company has not yet benefitted from such as insurance premiums or computer rentals; and bills not yet paid for goods or services already benefitting the company such as research and development.

FIXED ASSETS

Property

Land, buildings, machinery and office equipment. These are assets the company doesn't intend to sell, since they are important to the production of the company's goods and services. The value of these assets is generally set at "cost," minus depreciation. Depreciation can be calculated by several methods. Assuming a machine is expected to last three years and cost $9,000, it can be depreciated by the "straight-line" method at $3,000 a year. Some companies can also claim economic depreciation due to technological obsolescence.

Depletion

Used by resources companies, it assumes that the assets of the company will be used up over time.

Intangibles

These are valuable assets that don't exist physically such as patents, trademarks, copyrights and franchises. "Goodwill" is an intangible since it represents the difference between the price of an acquired company and the value of its assets.

Total Assets

This figure represents the size of the company and the total property owned by the enterprise.

CURRENT LIABILITIES

Accounts Payable

This item on the balance sheet represents what the company owes its suppliers and other providers of services within the next 12 months on "open account"—unpaid balance. In analyzing a company, the relationship between accounts payable to purchases is an indication of the health of the company's financial management.

Notes Payable

This is the money owned a bank or other short-term lender, usually holders of "promissory notes"—a promise to pay a sum of money on demand on a fixed date, with or without interest.

Accrued Expenses Payable

This item includes attorney and accounting fees, insurance premiums as well as unpaid salaries, bonuses, pensions.

Federal Income taxes

Income taxes will vary.

LONG-TERM LIABILITIES

Deferred Income Taxes

The government provides some corporations with tax incentives to do business. This includes, in some cases, the postponement of tax payments.

Debentures

This item represents loans made to the company by bondholders and the interest expense of these bonds, usually paid twice a year. A debenture is a general debt obligation backed by the reputation of the borrower and its promise to honor the terms

Total Liabilities

This figure represents the total amount of financing obtained by borrowing.

SHAREHOLDER'S EQUITY

Capital Stock

This is the proprietary interest shareholders have in the company represented by stock certificates of authorized and issued company stock that is either preferred stock or common stock. Preferred stockholders have preference over other shareholders and get dividends at a promised rate. Some preferred shareholders have cumulative rights, which means that if dividends aren't paid in any year, they accumulate in favor of the preferred shareholders. Common shareholders' dividends can be cancelled or lowered if the company cannot afford to share its profits with shareholders.

Capital Surplus

This is the money shareholders have paid to the company in excess of the par value of the company's stock. Par value is the nominal or face value of the stock. It has no relationship to market value and represents the amount assigned by the company to its stock when it was issued.

Accumulated Retained Earnings

This is money that the company earned that will not be paid out to shareholders in dividends, but will be kept by the company for reinvestment.

BALANCE SHEET RATIOS

In analyzing a company, the balance sheet provides several clues to the health of a business (see table 2). The ratios of an individual company should be compared to industry figures, which are available from firms such as Dun & Bradstreet and Robert Morris Associates.

Current Liquidity Ratio

Divide current assets by total current liabilities. This ratio, also called the current ratio, shows whether a company has enough current assets to pay current liabilities. It's the most widely used ratio because it indicates whether a company can meet its obligations and has a sound working capital position. As a rule of thumb, the ratio should be 2 to 1, so that the amount of assets in excess of liabilities could shrink 100 percent in case of a forced liquidation.

Acid Test

Divide total current assets minus inventories by total current liabilities. This ratio, officially known as the quick asset ratio, shows whether a firm can meet its current obligations if sales stopped. It is called the quick asset test because it's a measure of assets available to cover an emergency—assets quickly converted to cash, excluding inventories. A ratio of 1 to 1 or better is satisfactory, since this means a company can theoretically pay for all current liabilities immediately.

Cash Plus Marketable Securities Ratio

Divide cash plus marketable securities by total current liabilities. The result of this equation shows the company's ability to pay current liabilities without relying on inventories or accounts receivable.

Net Working Capital to Total Assets

Current assets minus current liabilities. This ratio indicates the importance of net working capital in the balance sheet.

Net Worth to Total Debt

Divide net worth by current debt. Net worth includes capital stock, reserves and retained earnings. The ratio is useful in the evaluation of the current ratio (current assets divided by current liabilities) since a company might try to improve its current ratio by increasing the total

Table 2 Balance-Sheet Ratios

Current liquidity (current assets/current liabilities	1.63
Acid test (current assets-invent/current liabilities)	1.16
Cash plus marketable securities/current liabilities	0.69
Net working capital/total assets	0.22
Net worth to total debt	4.21

for current assets through an increase in its long-term debt. Keep in mind that the ratio of net worth to total debt should be kept high, especially for companies subject to fluctuating earnings and high risks.

Total Shareholders' Equity to Total Debt

Total equity divided by total short-term indebtedness. This ratio indicates the extent of leveraged financing. Divide total stockholders' equity by the total of short-term loans, current installments on long-term debt and long-term debt due in more than one year.

Net Book Value per Share of Common Stock

If a company were liquidated, how much would each common shareholder get? (Preferred shareholders and bondholders would come first in line.) To find the value, take total assets (minus intangibles) and subtract from it current and long-term liabilities and preferred stock. Divide that number by the number of common shares outstanding to arrive at net book value per share of common stock. The calculations of balance-sheet ratios are shown in table 2.

Reading the Earnings Statement

While the balance sheet is a snapshot of the company's financial situation, the earnings statement is a motion picture of its quarterly performance, a simple list of the company's income-making activities and its expenses. A successful profit-making enterprise will take in many more dollars than it spends. The excess, called profit, is usually expressed in dollars and also by an earnings per share (EPS) figure. A portion of the EPS will be paid out to shareholders if the company pays dividends.

Every earnings statement (see table 3) will begin with a revenue, or sales, number which represents all the money that the company has collected. The costs of the company's activities are subtracted from sales until you reach the "bottom line," which is the profit, or earnings. The following terms are listed in the order they usually appear on an earnings statement. The key items are sales, operating profit, net profit and earnings per share. Revenues and expenses represent actual cost with no adjustments for inflation.

NET SALES (REVENUE)

This number includes the total funds collected by the company during the reporting period, usually divided into 90-day periods, or quarters, of the year. After the first quarter, a company will report both the second

Table 3 An Earnings Statement

International Digi-Widget
Earnings Statement

	Three Months Ended:	
	Sept. 30, 1992	*Sept. 30, 1991*
Net sales	$6,872,640	$5,530,800
Costs and expenses:		
Cost of goods sold	3,286,460	2,602,220
Marketing and distribution	1,443,320	1,143,920
Depreciation & amortization	532,840	562,440
General and administrative	1,024,950	963,000
Other	103,840	—
Total expense:	6,391,410	5,271,580
Operating income:	481,230	259,220
Other income:		
Interest and dividends	154,880	168,000
Foreign currency transactions	(102,000)	63,000
Total operating income:	534,110	490,220
Extraordinary items		
Sale of X-Glop division	(380,000)	—
Net income before taxes	154,110	490,220
Provision for income taxes	73,800	180,700
Net income:	80,310	309,520

quarter and the first half; the third quarter and the 9–months results; the fourth quarter and the full year. Some companies have a "fiscal year," which ends on a date other than December 31.

Cost of Sales and Operating Expenses

Cost of goods sold. Because a company must produce a product or service to sale, there is a cost associated with getting the product. This expense is subtracted from net sales. For a manufacturing company, the cost of goods is determined by taking the company's beginning merchandise inventory; adding the purchases, then subtracting the cost of the merchandise in inventory at the end of the reporting period. The result is the "gross profit on sales."

Depreciation and amortization. Since assets wear out, companies are allowed to deduct the loss in the productivity of machinery or resources over time.

Administrative expenses. This item includes salaries, advertising, office expenses and any other cost of doing business. Often depreciation is included in this item.

OPERATING INCOME

This item is important because it is the difference between the total sales of a company and what it costs to earn those sales. The operating profit or loss may be a truer reflection of a company's performance than net income, since net income includes extraordinary items and other usual business activities.

Other Income

Dividends and interest income. Companies make investments and may receive interest, dividends or other income. The income may also come from ownership of subsidiaries or other companies or joint ventures. This money isn't the result of doing business, even though it adds to the bottom line.

Foreign currency transactions. For companies doing business overseas, the fluctuations in exchange rates can be large. This item may be a gain or a loss.

Extraordinary Items

Sometimes a company buys or sells stocks, writes off a division, settles a lawsuit, or engages in an activity outside its usual pattern of business. It's assumed that an extraordinary item is a nonrecurring event. An extraordinary item can be a gain or a loss.

Total Income

Before a company can determine how much money it actually earned, it must account for the cost of borrowing money to banks or bondholders. The company's interest expense is subtracted from total income (the sum of all the previous items). The result is "income before provision for federal income tax." This number is less important than operating income.

Net Income (Profit)

This is the money left after the federal income tax is paid. It represents all the funds that have come into the company minus all the funds that were paid out. The remaining money is profit.

Earnings Per Share

The dollar amount of earnings per share represents the total of after-tax earnings available for distribution to common shareholders (minus the amount owed the preferred shareholders who get theirs first). The figure is the result of dividing the net income by the number of common shares outstanding. The amount of the earnings per share that will be paid to shareholders is determined by the company's dividend policy. Dividend policies change; some companies don't pay any dividends.

ANALYZING THE INCOME STATEMENT

A company's performance isn't measured only in profit. A journalist may want to know how profitable the company actually is or whether the company has enough "coverage," a measure of financial risk, to handle the financial charges it must pay. The following calculations will aid your analysis:

- Operating profit from operations: *Divide the operating profit by revenue.* The resulting percentage, say 9.5 percent, means that for each dollar of sales, 9.5 cents remained as a gross profit from operations. Compare the results with previous years and the industry average.
- Net profit ratio: *Divide the net profit by the sales.* This result, say 6.5 percent, means that for each dollar of product sold, 6.5 cents went to the company.
- Price/earnings (P/E) ratio: *Take the market price for the company's stock and divide by the earnings per share.* If a stock sells for $66 a share on the Big Time Exchange and the company's annual earnings per share are $6 a share, the ratio would be 11, which means the stock is selling for 11 times earnings. Low P/E stocks generally have higher yields than high P/E stocks, even though low P/E stocks tend to be mature companies with slow growth.
- Cash flow coverage ratio: This ratio indicates a company's ability to service its debt. Divide the annual cash flow before interest and taxes by the interest on bonds plus the company's principal repayments.
- Net profit ratio: *Divide the net profit for the year by the net sales.*

THE ACCUMULATED RETAINED EARNINGS STATEMENT

It can be difficult to determine how profitable a company really is. Clues can be found in the accumulated retained earnings statement (see table 4), found in the annual report. The company's value rises when the retained earnings rise.

Retained earnings are an important source of finance for corporate assets, although high retained earnings may attract corporate raiders. The statement should show what happened at the company from the first day of its annual year to the end. The statement begins with the

Table 4   A Retained Earnings Statement

International Digi-Widget, Inc.
Retained Earnings Statement

	December 31, 1991
Retained earnings, 1990	$2,386,420
Profit after tax, 1991	1,090,840
	3,477,260
Less dividends	920,830
Retained earnings, 1991	$2,556,430

accumulated earnings the company reported at the end of the previous year. The arithmetic looks like this:

The total at the end of the previous year.

Add: this year's net profit.

Subtract: dividends paid to stockholders, both preferred and common.

Result: the balance for the current year.

Retained Earnings Ratios

• Dividend payout ratio: *Divide the dividends paid to common share-holders by the income available for common shareholders.* The ratio for most American companies will be over 30 percent. In general, the higher the payout the more mature the company, because they tend to invest less in growth. The ratio tends to fall in good times, when a company has had a spurt in earnings —directors usually decide to keep the actual dollar payout stable and save the excess earnings for poorer times.

• The earnings retention ratio: *Divide the earnings retained by the earn-ings available for payout.* This percentage tells you how much of the available funds for payout were retained. It usually rises in profitable times.

OTHER FINANCIAL RATIOS

Return on assets: *Divide the total income by total assets.*

• Return on equity (ROE): *Divide net income for distribution to com-mon shareholders by the total equity of common shareholders (net worth).* ROE tells common shareholders how effectively their money is being used. Compare with industry figures.

• Net profit to net worth: *Divide net profit by net worth.* Net worth is the amount that assets exceed liabilities. The ratio of net profit to net worth indicates the rate of return on the ownership investment. For a company to continue to operate, it should meet minimum industry standards. Check the ratios for the industry.

Private Companies

by Pamela Luecke

Chances are your first job in business writing will be at a newspaper in a small to medium-size community. Many of the companies in that community will be privately—rather than publicly—owned. And that fact will make your job different than the job of a business writer at *The Wall Street Journal,* where the coverage is of listed, public traded companies.

Technically, a private company is one with fewer than 500 shareholders, and thus does not fall under the purview of the Securities and Exchange Act of 1934. Private companies are usually smaller in sales than public ones. There are notable exceptions, such as Estée Lauder, which is one of the cosmetics industry's largest firms, or Cargill, the nation's largest commodities firm.

The distinction between public and private companies is more than semantics. From a reporter's point of view, a private company is required to disclose little information to you, the public or the government. What's more, there are few executives of private companies who want to disclose information; sometimes, that's why companies are private in the first place. Being a private company is a lot less grief for executives—no public annual meetings, no pressure from the stock exchanges. In addition, many owners of small—or even large—private companies are private people. They do not want their management styles made public, their hiring practices discussed or their acquisitions questioned.

GETTING INFORMATION

Your job as a business journalist is nonetheless to write about these companies. And there are ways to accomplish the writing.

While some private companies are flattered by a call from the press and will cooperate from the start, others may require some gentle persuasion. One approach is to convince the president (or the public relations manager, if the company is large enough to have one) that the company is of interest to the community because it provides jobs. Almost every company feels some responsibility to its community and tries to be a good citizen. You might also take the approach that it is always wise for a company to establish a rapport with the local newspaper at a noncrisis time, rather than wait for a chemical spill, strike, or layoff.

The next step is to get some background on the company. If you're writing about a public company, you can prepare for the interview by studying its annual reports, tracking down past articles in the business press or talking to stock analysts. For a private company—particularly a small one that hasn't received national attention—preparation is more difficult. Your newspaper library might be a good starting place. Clips—even ancient ones—can give you a sense of history about a company.

Standard & Poor's *Register* is also worth a check—either in your newspaper library or the public library. It lists 45,000 companies, both public and private, and includes basic information such as directors, top officers, number of employees, and estimated revenue.

The office of the secretary of state may also be helpful. In most states, corporations are required to be chartered and to file annual reports, but not necessarily financial statements. Information required varies from state to state (just ask what reports are available), and sometimes an interesting tidbit will turn up. The secretary of state's office is generally in the state capital, and you can probably find the correct department by asking for "corporate reports." There is typically a small charge for the records and a slight time lag in getting them.

Lawsuits can also be a useful source of information. If you don't have time, ask your paper's court reporter to check the local (and federal, if possible) court dockets for the past few years for any suits in which the company was a plaintiff or defendant. The charge itself may or may not be material to your story, but depositions by company officers may reveal useful details about a company.

It doesn't hurt to check bankruptcy court, while you're at it, particularly if you have reason to suspect the company has financial troubles. The U.S. Tax Court in Washington, D.C. is also a potentially rich source. And if any of the company's owners has recently been divorced, those suits might reveal financial information about the company as well.

If a company has used government financing, that's another possible source of background information. Applications for some types of bonds and grants are public record. And some leases with public agencies are based on a percentage of sales, which should enable you to extrapolate a company's business volume.

Real estate transfers on record in county courthouses can yield important information, too—especially if a company or businessman is property-rich. And don't overlook "uniform commercial code" filings, which govern commercial transactions and are designed to bring uniformity to the laws of various states. The UCC, generally in the county courthouse, shows what property a company or individual has used as collateral for loans. While the filings might not list the amounts of the loans, they will list the lenders and give you a sense of the company's general level of secured indebtedness. (Filing systems differ from courthouse to courthouse and finding a helpful clerk can be essential.)

Don't forget to check more general references such as *Who's Who* or the historical society or the alumni offices of the schools the chief executive officer attended. Is the CEO a chemist, an engineer or an accountant? Is the company interested in helping the local orphanage because the CEO was an adopted child? Nothing is more flattering to an executive than to think you have taken the time to know something about what interests him. It may also help you find an angle that will get you in the door.

The greatest frustration in doing a story about a private company is that you can't easily check what you are told against unbiased documentation. And it may seem impossible to get past the company's need to project well-being in order to find the heart of the story. To get another perspective takes some creative thinking. Here are some possibilities to help you balance your story:

Employees. It's relatively easy to get an employee perspective if the company's workers are represented by a trade union. Your business staff or labor writer should have a state directory of unions and their locals. (If not, get one from the state AFL-CIO or the state Labor Department; it's a handy resource.) If the company's workers are not organized, the job is tougher. Word of mouth might be a good way to find names of a few people who work there.

Another option is to drive past the company's parking lot and jot down license plate numbers. Then determine the owners' names through the motor vehicle registration office (procedures vary from state to state) and give them a call. Otherwise, ask the company for the names of some seasoned workers you could interview. Admittedly, you are unlikely to get names of people who are unhappy with their work, but even satisfied employees can sometimes be surprisingly candid.

Former employees can also provide a useful perspective. Whistleblowers and people who have been discriminated against have led to many good business stories. Be cautious, though, of those with an obvious axe to grind. Some people are fired for legitimate reasons.

Industry trade associations. Even the most obscure industry seems to have a trade association these days. Just look at the *Encyclopedia of Associations,* which should be available in your newspaper library or your public library. The usefulness of these associations varies from group to group, but it's worth a try. After finding the association that applies to your company's industry, call the executive director. The director may be reluctant to give much specific information about sales or earnings, but he may be able to say whether it is one of the larger or smaller players in the industry, or give you a sense of the industry's current climate. That can lead to some intelligent questions in your interview. Also ask if there are any trade magazines for your company's industry and where they are published. Tracking down some recent issues or interviewing the editor will help bring you up to speed on the industry's current problems and trends.

Industry analysts. While most Wall Street analysts follow companies with stock that can be purchased by the public, some analysts might be familiar with a private firm. Does it have a competitor whose stock is publicly traded? Chances are an analyst who follows the public company knows something about the private one, if it is a significant force in the industry. Is your company a heavy user of a raw material? An analyst for that raw material might be worth a call.

Community groups. Don't rule out contacting such groups as the Better Business Bureau, Chamber of Commerce, neighborhood associations, etc. If the president of the company is a pillar of the community, that's good to know. If the neighborhood has long complained about the company's factory smells, that's good to know, too.

Regulatory agencies. Does the company emit any wastes that are monitored by the Environmental Protection Agency? Is it a public utility? A financial institution? An insurer? State and federal agencies can be helpful in learning about private companies because much of the information filed with them is for the public record.

Competitors and suppliers. It is the rare company that will publicly throw bricks at a company with whom it is competing or on whom it depends for business. But conversations with such firms, even if only "on background," can help tip you off if the company is about to go belly-up, have an internal shake-up, etc. Ask competitors and suppliers what questions they would like to ask the company president.

THE INTERVIEW

Interviewing an executive of a private company requires a great deal of skill. Remember, most private company CEOs are not practiced at interviewing. They can't anticipate what you want. They might not have answers to your questions. An executive who runs a company with a firm hand may try to manage the interview. You may be forced to interrupt and possibly offend the executive to get to the point

Many executives are nervous about interviews with the press because they assume that you wouldn't want an interview unless you plan to say something bad about the company. It sometimes helps to start an interview by explaining the nature of the story, where it is likely to appear, etc. Sometimes, it is also necessary to explain certain basics of journalism, such as: No, you cannot let the executive see the story before publication. Yes, you do intend to quote what the executive says unless you both agree that a portion of the interview is off the record.

Since some executives like to have help during interviews, don't be surprised if the financial officer, the public relations person or the corporation counsel is present. Don't let that bother you; just make sure the ground rules are clear. And if you can, at the time you are setting up the interview, limit the people who will be present. The quality of the interview generally decreases with each additional person present.

Two areas that private companies are typically squeamish about are sales and earnings. Ask, but don't be surprised if they don't give you figures. They don't have to. Still, it's important for your story to give some idea of how large an operation the company is. When you don't get figures, give the executive some options that will give an indication of the size and financial health of the company.

One option is the range. Mr. Executive Officer declined to give precise sales, but said annual sales last year were between $40 million and $75 million.

An alternative is the trend. Ms. Executive Officer said the firm's sales increased 15 percent per year for the last five years and should exceed $100 million next year.

And there is the confirmation. Mr. Executive Officer declined to discuss sales, but said the Standard & Poor's estimate of $25 million was "in the ballpark."

Profits are a little trickier. If you can determine from a competitor or trade association the typical industry profit margin—the relationship of gross profits to net sales—you can run those figures past your executive for a reaction. That could lead to a statement such as: Ms. Executive Official declined to discuss the company's profits, but said the firm's profit margin was consistent with the industry average of 18 percent.

Private company executives may also be guarded about who actually owns the company. If so, be alert to possible minority shareholders, who may not be pleased with the way the company is being run.

FUTURE PLANS

If a private company is fairly large, it is always a good idea to ask if it might consider going public in the future. There are a number of situations that might be clues to the company's intentions:

Does the CEO hold most of the shares in the company and does it represent nearly all of his wealth? If so, he might want to diversify his investment, by selling some of those shares to others.

How old is the executive? If he is older than 60, are there members of his family who will take over the company? If there aren't, might the heirs consider taking the company public and hiring professional management.

On a less selfish level, the CEO may have ambitious plans for the company. In that case, you might ask how he intends to pay for acquisitions and mergers. From earnings? From borrowing? From selling stock in the market, which would mean going public?

TIPS AND TRAPS

Avoid the one-interview story. Even if you're profiling a Mom and Pop grocery, Mom might see things differently than Pop.

Beware of the company that harangues you for a story. Some troubled firms look for "free publicity" as a last resort.

If the company refuses to talk to you, don't give up. In some cases, a company is so newsworthy that it is worth doing a story even if the subject won't cooperate. Simply base your story on the people and organizations you would call anyway for perspective and note in your story that the company declined repeated requests for interviews. Make sure you give the company several chances to comment, however. Sometimes, once a company is convinced you are going to do a story, it will cooperate.

If a company is structured as a partnership rather than a corporation, try to interview several of the partners.

If a public company has "gone private," remember that documents from its public days are still obtainable.

For general information on private companies:

The Small Business Administration
1441 L. St. NW,
Washington DC 20416

National Federation of Independent Business
150 W. 20th Ave.
San Mateo, CA 94403

Center for Family Business,
PO Box 24268
Cleveland, OH 44124

The Center for Entrepreneurial Management
180 Varick St.
New York, NY

Regulation

by Cynthia A. Kasabian

If you're a business reporter, you can't ignore the enormous impact of regulation. In fact, you probably wouldn't have much to say about business if regulators didn't force companies to make certain information public; if breaking the rules didn't make companies newsworthy; or if your own activities weren't guided by Securities and Exchange Commission rules. Since this country is always increasing regulations or decreasing them, it's important for journalists to understand the effects these trends have on corporate America and business journalism.

Regulation is intended to protect the public and bring order to the business environment. Many of the regulations we now live under are the result of increased government involvement in the private sector following the Great Depression. Such agencies as the National Labor Relations Board formed in 1935 owe their existence to this period in American economic history.

It's a mistake to assume that regulations are anything more than rules of conduct. They don't prevent criminal activity. And while there's a penalty for breaking some regulations, that doesn't prevent individuals from trying to get around them. In the 1980s, for example, we seemed to go through an unprecedented period of lawlessness. It was a time when infamous deal-maker Ivan Boesky lectured to Harvard business school students that "greed is good." (Ivan Boesky was arrested for securities violations in 1986 and sentenced in December 1987 to three years in prison and a $100 million fine.) It also was a time when major brokerage houses fired scores of executives for brazenly breaking insider trading rules; when brokers were handcuffed and arrested in their Manhattan offices; and when securities fraud seemed commonplace.

In such a climate—a takeover frenzy followed by huge gains on the New York Stock Exchange and multimillion dollar commissions for takeovers and leveraged buyouts—a reporter can assume a simple fact of life: When there are millions of dollars changing hands, some rules are going to be broken.

The regulations are designed to protect against such behavior. But I cite this period in American business history to make a larger point about regulation: The regulatory climate was probably one of the underlying causes for the greed on Wall Street.

Take a look at what was happening with regulation in the ten years preceding the stock market crash in 1987. Since the late 1970s, there had been a move toward deregulation—the relaxation of government involvement in American industry. By the end of the 1980s nearly every major industry, including airlines and financial services, had undergone a regulatory transformation that reverberated not just at corporate headquarters but in the homes and pocketbooks of American consumers. The rumble was felt on Wall Street, too. In an environment of decreasing regulations, companies had less fear of the Federal Trade Commission power over mergers. Even the most daring deals—some of which were financed in unconventionally creative ways—were allowed to be completed. The ways that new and bigger deals could be constructed and financed fueled a frenzy of takeovers and deals. Stock prices rose higher and higher. And even after the crash, the deals continued.

DEREGULATION

As these events illustrate, deregulation is as important as regulation. Behind deregulation is the belief that companies operate more efficiently in an environment of less regulation. The freer the market the fairer the trade. The first wave of deregulation began in the 1970s and continued in the 1980s. Banking, broadcasting, airlines, transportation and telecommunications were deregulated.

It is assumed that too much regulation prevents healthy competition and makes "creative" management virtually impossible. Profits are reduced by the paperwork required by regulators or, from another point of view, customers pay higher prices for goods because of regulations. Regulations, such as the ones enforced by the Food and Drug Administration, may lengthen the time it takes to bring drugs to market and increase the cost of research, resulting in fewer new drugs and the development of only those drugs with the greatest commercial potential.

In covering any beat, it's critical to anticipate the regulatory climate, since it drives business strategy and will help you understand management's motives. One aid in doing this is to focus on the regulatory trends in key industries—often harbingers of the bigger picture.

The banking industry is a good example. In the late 1970s interest rates were on the rise and people were pulling their savings out of banks and savings and loans (S&Ls) and plunking them into higher-paying money market funds. No longer was "cheap" money rolling into banks and savings and loans, which could use those funds for making higher-priced loans.

The bankers wanted to pay savers more in interest for the money they put in savings accounts so that they could compete on a "level playing field" with the brokerage houses and mutual funds which offered higher interest rates. The bankers won. The Depository Institutions Deregulation and Monetary Control Act (a long name, but one you should remember, since it changed the American financial system more dramatically than anything since the 1930s), over a period of years, abolished interest rate caps imposed on banks and S&Ls. The result was that these financial institutions began to win back deposits. But since the bankers had to pay savers more, their costs rose.

It soon became clear that if the bankers were going to pay more, they had to start charging more for their services to maintain the traditional profit on their activities. And so, a change in regulations began to affect consumers, who soon learned that savings accounts offered a variety of interest rates. And if a consumer chose certain kinds of accounts, certain fees would be charged. It soon became clear that customers who could maintain higher balances paid less in fees.

Banks were forced to manage their balance sheets as never before because they could no longer count on depositors putting money into savings accounts that paid a low interest. Consequently, they could no longer count on a safe spread—the difference between the cost of funds and the lending rate—that had yielded bankers high profits in the past.

What complicated the management of financial institutions further was that deregulation coincided with a severely weakened dollar and sharp economic swings in various geographic areas—recession in the oil-producing states, the decline of the heavy industry in the north central states and agricultural failures in the West and Midwest. The result was a record number of bank and S&L failures. In 1991, it was estimated that as much as $200 billion would be needed over the next ten years to rehabilitate the industry.

REPORTING ON REGULATION

Where does reportage on an S&L story begin? At the Federal Home Loan Bank Board, which regulates the industry. It will provide you with basic facts about failures and its approach to reviving an S&L. But that is just the beginning.

The S&L industry, as with any industry, is made up of individual companies. And it's those companies, their managements and their financial statements that will be of greatest value to you. Information about them is required by the Securities and Exchange Commission. In fact, probably one of the most important regulatory bodies to a business reporter is the SEC because it regulates all publicly traded companies.

It's the job of the SEC to protect investors, in part by requiring various types of disclosure documents (see the section on SEC documents herein). There is a wealth of information in even the most basic documents required by the SEC. Remember, this is the watchdog agency responsible for public companies. Its required company disclosure statements will provide the fodder for some of the hottest stories you'll ever cover.

As basic as it sounds, you need to keep up a good filing system on the SEC reports. When something breaks, you'll be ahead of your peers if you can refer to previous documents that are full of details about companies and their managers. Also, keep up with the changes in the reports required by the SEC.

A key step to covering any business beat is to introduce yourself to the head of your local SEC office. Keep in touch with him or her and if possible get to know the staff. While the SEC officers are restricted in the types of information they can provide about a company, a personal relationship with SEC officials can prove helpful in guiding you when you're on to a story. One way of maintaining the relationship is to ask them to keep you up-to-date on SEC guidelines. Remember, whether you're a business writer or on the police beat, the better you get to know your potential sources, the better the potential for exclusive stories.

Another industry that's worth taking a close look at when attempting to understand the forces of regulatory change is the airline industry. In 1978, the Airline Deregulation Act decontrolled air routes and prices, thereby deregulating the entire industry. This deregulation opened the door to a flood of entrepreneurs who began their own airlines and competed with the major airlines. Many of the new, smaller carriers attempted to make their way into the market by offering cut-rate fares. But costs soon caught up with them and their independence didn't last long. Within a few years, many decided to let themselves be gobbled up by the majors rather than continue to struggle for survival, or more likely, face failure. The result: ten years later, the airline industry is dominated by only eight major carriers, which account for more than 90 percent of the industry's operating income.

Who won? Passengers of the most heavily traveled air routes saw a significant decline in prices. However, fares for less popular routes rose dramatically and the availability of flights declined. In addition, since deregulation, consumer complaints about time delays rose so dramatically that in 1987 the Department of Transportation began publishing "on-time" records of the airlines. These lists receive a lot of press, and therefore put pressure on the airlines to better serve their customers.

It's regulatory upheavals, such as those in the airline industry, that generate a variety of stories: the rise and fall of corporations, the winning and losing of fortunes, as well as a host of consumer issues.

The most successful companies and business people are those who anticipate change and act accordingly, and those who create the change to serve their interests and those of their industry.

ETHICS

Many of these stories are related to ethics—or the lack thereof. The high visibility mega-takeovers, junk bond-financed leveraged buyouts, and the huge fees paid to the investment bankers who made these deals happen all raised issues about the "go for greed" attitude of Wall Street in the 1980s. But even in the more routine stories that involve regulatory changes, ethical questions arise: Is it ethical to charge exorbitant fares on less traveled routes and cut-rate fares on routes routinely traveled by business commuters?

Increasingly, corporations today have codes of ethics—standards by which their corporate decisions are made. Taking a close look at these codes can often lead to interesting stories that give you perspective on corporate values. One organization that follows codes of ethics published by companies is the Washington D.C.- based Ethics Resource Center.

Another place to look for the values of a company is their social policy committee. Do they have one? Who sits on the committee, senior officers or functionaries? How involved are the officers in the community? What's the agenda of the committee? Digging at the answers to these questions often leads to enlightening and provocative stories.

THE REGULATORS

In nearly any business or financial "trend" story you'll find that regulations, and therefore regulatory agencies, will play a role. Depending on your beat, some of these agencies will be more important than others, but there are a couple that will be essential no matter what your speciality. They are the Securities and Exchange Commission, mentioned earlier, and the Federal Trade Commission, which challenges monopolistic mergers (although, in the 1980s, critics claimed it focused on small mergers instead of the multibillion dollar mergers allowed by the Reagan administration). The FTC is also a good source of information on consumer protection issues.

While the hub of regulatory activity is in Washington, D.C., where all major regulatory agencies are based, many of the regulators have regional offices and it's worthwhile to get in touch with your local office. Among the regulators you should be familiar with are the following:

Comptroller of the Currency. This office of the Department of the Treasury grants charters for national banks and examines banks. It also keeps track of "troubled" institutions—information which is supposed to be confidential but often leaks when a bank is obviously in bad shape. The agency was created by the 1864 National Banking Act.

Consumer Product Safety Commission. This independent agency, created in 1972 by the Consumer Product Safety Act, conducts consumer product research and collects information about injuries. The National Injury Information Clearinghouse sets mandatory product standards.

Environmental Protection Agency. The EPA is responsible for water and air pollution regulation and sets standards for all pollutants including radiation and pesticides. The agency, established in 1970, enforces environmental laws.

Equal Employment Opportunity Commission. The EEOC, created as part of the Civil Rights Act of 1964, enforces laws prohibiting discrimination on the basis of race, sex, creed, age or national origin.

Federal Aviation Administration. The FAA regulates airlines and airport traffic. It is concerned with the safety of aviation.

Federal Communications Commission. The FCC oversees all communications vehicles including television, radio and satellites. It was created by the Communications Act of 1934.

Federal Deposit Insurance Corporation. The FDIC insures all nationally chartered bank deposits up to $100,000 per customer. Most state chartered banks also have FDIC insurance. The FDIC was created by section 12B of the Federal Reserve Act of 1933.

Federal Home Loan Bank Board. The FHLB regulates and supervises savings and loan institutions. It was formed in 1932 by the Federal Home Loan Bank Act. It operates the Federal Savings and Loan Insurance Corporation.

Federal Reserve System. The central bank of the United States and responsible for administering monetary policy. It approves state banks. The Federal Reserve was created by the Federal Reserve Act of 1913.

Federal Savings and Loan Insurance Corporation. FSLIC insures deposits at savings institutions up to $100,000 per customer. It establishes reserve requirements for savings and loans institutions.

Federal Trade Commission. The FTC was established by the Clayton Act to prevent unfair competition and deceptive practices. It oversees consumer advertising as well as mergers. It has a tradition of opposition to monopolies.

Food and Drug Administration. The FDA sets standards for drugs, foods, labeling and other health-related practices.

Interstate Commerce Commission. The ICC regulates interstate ground transportation. It was formed in 1887.

National Labor Relations Board. This agency oversees the rights of workers to organize and has the power to remedy unfair labor practices.

Occupational Safety and Health Administration. OSHA sets rules for safety and health and conducts inspections of workplaces. It is a part of the Department of Labor.

For a complete listing of regulatory agencies and other federal offices, see the Congressional Quarterly's Washington Information Directory.

Section 2

Finance

Street Talk

by Jack Willoughby

"Hey Bob, those zeros really have a big dollar pop," says one young man to another. "They've taken off since Treasuries dropped 50 ticks these last four months," the other confirms. Translation: Two bond traders are congratulating themselves on the smart purchase of some zero coupon bonds. When interest rates fell one half of one percentage point, these two made a nice profit.

One of the first things business journalists realize when they walk into the business section is that they have entered a foreign country with a language of its own. There are dialects too. Bond traders and commodities dealers use a slightly different language than investment bankers and merger lawyers. The computer industry requires a different vocabulary than the aerospace industry. Work your way through an acquisition and there will be dozens of new words and concepts, all in need of careful translation for your readers and listeners.

Much of the jargon comes from Wall Street. The actual Wall Street is a rather short, narrow street running east from soot-darkened Trinity Church on Broadway past a dozen financial sites including Irving Trust Company, the New York Stock Exchange and Morgan Guaranty Trust of New York. George Washington was inaugurated at Federal Hall, located on Wall and Broad Streets. Wall Street gets its name from the mud and brush barrier built around a dirt path which marked the edge of a seventeenth-century Dutch settlement.

Today, Wall Street is synonymous with New York's financial district. Everyone knows what Wall Street represents. Journalists freely refer to it and conjure images of pinstriped gladiators vying for control of America's biggest companies. Some of this business activity happens in commonly known venues, such as the "Big Board," or New York Stock Exchange; the AMEX, the American Stock Exchange; and the Over-the-Counter, or Nasdaq market, which is an electronic exchange where stocks are nationally traded over computer terminals.

Wall Street is also the home of banks, investment houses, brokerages and law firms. Consequently, using the term Wall Street may bring a variety of meanings to your story. To many it means power. To others it means greed. Regardless of what it may mean to you, it represents much of what financial reporters write about and struggle to interpret. Journalists can't ignore Wall Street. As Will Rogers put it: "Let Wall Street have a nightmare and the whole country has to help get them back in bed again."

THE LANGUAGE

Wall Street has a colorful language rich with historical references that extend far beyond its geographical borders. Take "watered stock"—a term credited to Daniel Drew who ran the Erie Railroad during the era of the robber barons in the mid-1800s. It refers to the practice of watering cattle just before they are weighed. A bloated animal meant a higher price per pound at the stockyard. Today, watered stock is a stock issue in which the issuers, often the founder and principal investors of the company, inflate the price of the stock and then offer it to investors. The actual price, the book value of the shares, is lower than the price at which the shares are offered.

Some of the language of Wall Street has become part of contemporary speech. Take "bull." Everyone knows that a bull is an optimist. One of the great bulls of the nineteenth century was J. Pierpont Morgan, father of the swank J.P. Morgan bank and Morgan Stanley Investment banking house. He coined the phrase: "The man who goes short on America will go broke," which means that anyone who does not believe in the future prosperity of America can't succeed.

Morgan would have scoffed at businessmen who were "bears"— pessimists, who believe things will get worse, rather than better. Bears might be expected to sell short; the technique of borrowing stock to sell on the expectation that the market for the stock will then fall, making it possible to buy the replacement shares at a bargain price and make a profit. Daniel Drew, called the "Great Bear," is famous for an ominous maxim on short selling: "He that sells what ain't his'n must buy it back or go to prison."

Because Wall Street and business were largely the domain of men until the 1960s, much of the language is aggressive, competitive and warlike. Take the business of mergers and acquisitions. If the individual or company proposing an acquisition of a company is buying stock to gain control and the company doesn't like it, it's called a "hostile takeover attempt." A "raid" is an attempt to buy a company despite the company's "defenses." A raid generally assumes that the buyer wants control of a company to "loot" it of its assets.

When there are raiders around, there will also be "speculators," buying stocks of companies "in play." Speculators aren't interested in longterm investments. They seek a quick profit.

Both can be foiled by a "white knight," a friendly buyer who seeks control of a company with the approval of the company's management. The knight promises to work with management.

When a besieged company wants to end a battle with a raider, it might try to "buy him out." Raiders, however, are unlikely to sell at the price they purchased a stock. In fact, a raider will want compensation for all efforts at amassing the company's stock. A greedy raider may want a lot more. If the raider holds out for an exorbitant amount of money to release the shares and the company is forced to pay it to get rid of the takeover threat, the raider is said to have gotten away with "greenmail." (See "Analyzing the Acquisition.")

If a white knight cannot be found, the company may be sold to the raider when the public shareholders "tender," or sell, their shares to the raider. To pay for the purchase of the company, the raider will "obtain financing," which means going through investment bankers to get loans to pay off the cost of the takeover. To pay back the debt, raiders often sell some of the acquired company's assets for cash. Therefore, a raider may "strip" the company to "pay down" debt. Because the shareholders have tendered their shares to the raider, the company may have become a "private company," which means it no longer is required to meet certain disclosure requirements of federal regulatory agencies, like the Securities and Exchange Commission. Often the intent of the raider is to return the company to the public's hands. "Taking the company public" means selling stock to the public to raise even more cash.

TAKEOVER TALK

The takeover business makes lots of money, attracts lots of attention and generates lots of colorful expressions. Takeover artists are notorious for giving "bear hugs," takeover discussions involving prices well above what the company's stock is selling for in order to force management to publicly disclose that the company is in play. Sometimes the haste with which managements must deal with these offers results in announcements called "Saturday Night Specials" because they often are announced over the weekend. (In 1968, restrictions on tender offers made Saturday Night Specials more difficult.)

It is the unfriendly takeovers, where the "target" attempts to free itself using "poison pills" or "shark repellent" that make the best stories. Managements spend millions on corporate lawyers to protect themselves against hostile takeovers. And companies have devised numerous defenses. For instance, there's the so-called Pac-Man defense made famous in the Marietta-Bendix takeover war in 1982. Why Pac-Man? Because that was the video game that was the rage at the time. In the game, if a character does not consume its opponent, it gets consumed.

If a company gets consumed, its managers are out of a job. Some managers prepare by obtaining "golden parachutes"—hefty severance packages which ensure a soft landing when they bail out following an acqustion. Some parachutes are so expensive they discourage raiders from nibbling at the company. But some severance packages are not part of an "anti-takeover" strategy, leading to chargers that these expensive severance packages are just one more sign of managements' irresponsible rule by divine right (see "Publicly Held Companies," herein). The industrialist W. Edwards Demming, an American partially responsible for Japan's postwar manufacturing success, claimed industrial progress suffers from management self-interest. "Management is 80 percent of the problem," he said. Business philosopher Peter Drucker, who also considered the high cost of management a business encumbrance, noted: " 'Absorption of overhead' is one of the most obscene terms I have ever heard."

The jargon of the late 1980s owed a great deal to the "leveraged buyout." That's when managers buy a company the same way people buy houses—by putting a little money down and borrowing the rest. So-called LBOs frequently make managers rich, thanks largely to a tax act that allowed them to deduct the interest payments on their takeover loans. Most LBOs succeed by severely chopping overhead: that means jobs.

IT'S A JUNGLE OUT THERE

If corporate raiders weren't enough to worry about there are a group of performance junkies known as "arbitrageurs." These stock market players buy and sell companies, and other securities and indexes as well, in multiple markets to make a profit. A successful "arbitrage" results in the purchase of securities in one market and the simultaneous sale in a second market at a profit. Sometimes arbitrageurs work for a big house, say First Boston Corporation. But more often they work alone. The word arbitrageur was little known by the public before the "insider trading" scandals put a spotlight on these wheeler-dealers. Inside information is any information about a company that affects its operations but is known only to officers of the firm, such as an upcoming public announcement about the company's earnings. Under SEC rules, a person who knows this information can't trade the stock on the basis of this information. Sometimes information leaks or is ferreted out of a company, but since it is still nonpublic information, people who use it are breaking the law. It was arbitrageur Ivan Boesky, whose securities laws violations resulted in a three year prison sentence and a $100 million fine, who gave the word a sinister meaning.

Corporate managers hate the "arbs" because they always ask the question: What have you done for me lately? The arbs simply take advantage of the short-term volatility of markets. In cases of takeover talk, big institutional shareholders, pension fund managers and insurance companies often sell to arbs when it appears that a profit can be made without the risk inherent in holding stocks until the conclusion of a bidding war. Pension funds, in particular, are compelled to sell stocks when a higher price is offered for them. Besides, there is no guarantee the bidding war will end satisfactorily for investors.

Of all the animals on Wall Street, the meanest of all are the "shorts." Their specialty is scavenging off bad news. They spot a company with problems and make money by selling stock in expectation of a price decline. An investor will borrow stock certificates to sell, expecting the price to fall so he or she can buy replacement shares at a cheaper price. One of the greatest short sellers was financier Bernard Baruch. Another was Joseph Kennedy, who made a fortune in the Great Depression speculating in film stocks. "I wish I hadn't acquired respectability," lamented Kennedy. "I'd be out selling the market short."

Shorts need gossips—reporters will do—to make their game work, because the public must learn how bad things are before they can line up to sell stock. The shorts are under intense pressure because the minute they take a position in a company, the interest clock starts ticking on the borrowed stock. They won't want to buy, however, until the price of the stock drops low enough to produce a profit.

THE THEORIES

On any given day, it is difficult to determine what makes the markets move. But when logic fails there are theories that reflect some interesting thinking. The "Aspirin Count Theory" says the production of aspirin leads market downturns. The "Hemline Theory" equates market prices with women's hemline; if they go up, so does the market. Sports fans watch the "Superbowl Omen," which claims the stock market will rise if a team from the old National Football League wins the Super Bowl.

There are more serious theories. Burton Malkiel's famous "Random Walk Theory" says stock pickers can pick stocks just as easily with darts as with computers. On the other side is Benjamin Graham, author of *The Intelligent Investor*. He got rich by looking behind the stock price for the real value backing the stock of a company. Hence the term "value" investing. The "Nifty Fifty" was a term used to designate 50 institutional favorites. These are "blue chip" stocks and industry leaders with proven records and long dividend histories. Blue chips—such companies as International Business Machines and General Electric—provide the most value in a high stakes poker game.

PUBLIC JARGON

A brief word about new products dreamed up by Wall Street's rocket scientists, known as "quants," or quantitative analysts. These are PhDs who sit around in front of computer screens figuring out new ways of buying and selling the same old stocks and bonds. They come up with things like CATS. Not the Broadway play. It is an acronym, invented by Salomon Brothers, for Certificate of Accrual on Treasury Securities. These represent ownership in future payments of selected U.S. government securities. These securities trade in the secondary market. Merrill Lynch has similar securities called TIGRs and COUGARS.

Besides the world of the white shoe firms—those big ones like Goldman Sachs and Solomon Brothers—there are boiler rooms run by cigar chomping salesmen who don't care one whit about economics. They sell penny shares on lesser exchanges to investors with dreams much too big for their pocketbooks. The great havens for these promoters are Denver and Vancouver, B.C. Canada's Dodge City of stock investment.

This is the world of the "shill" or "customer's man." They have more in common with the carnival barker. Using customer lists from investment newsletters, they make "cold calls" to prospective investors, sight unseen. Once investors send money to these folks, they can forget about it. As O. Henry, who spent a few years cooling his heels in an Ohio penitentiary for bank fraud, observed: "Everbody's moving so fast. Even the hayseeds are baled hayseeds. The only problem is there's too big a protective tariff on bunco."

What about flim flam? The Ponzi scheme is one of the most famous. A Ponzi scheme promises high returns but survives on using funds from new investors to pay off old investors. Charles Ponzi cost investors millions before being exposed in the *Boston Globe* in 1920.

Another classic confidence scam is the advance fee con. This is one of the meanest frauds around because it turns desperation into despair. An agent who claims to represent some big spenders, say in the Middle East, puts an ad in the paper calling himself a venture capitalist or financial planner or something. What this guy is looking for is people who are having difficulty getting money from the usual sources, banks, to finance their dreams. Our Mystery Guy will listen to the proposal earnestly, then jump up and exclaim that is exactly what his people in Bahrain want. He will take the proposal to them. But he needs $5,000 in advance for his services in arranging the $130,000 venture capital loan. Sounds reasonable. After all, it is only a downpayment on the first half of his fee. The eager businessman pays, fully expecting to have an answer within weeks. The cruel truth becomes evident much later. No sugar daddy. No money. Nothing.

Jargon is sometimes a barrier to finding out what is really happening. If you are ignorant of the meaning of words, you run the risk of misunderstanding or missing valuable information. Of course, the task for journalists is to translate jargon and analyze the processes it represents. Don't be afraid to look silly in an interview. Remember two great things about journalism. First, it is the only job where you are paid to ask the kind of silly questions everyone else is too arrogant or stupid to ask. Second, if your source can't explain it chances are he or she doesn't understand it either.

Scandals Galore: A Guide to the Biggest Business Scandals of the Twentieth Century

by Stephen J. Govoni

"Each generation repeats its leaders. Each sees men endowed with superior inventiveness, energy and genius for business, inspired by love of power and possession, launch selfish schemes—Carnegies, Rockefellers, Goulds. If each of these strong men left something sinister behind, each also contributed to higher living standards and hurried on the nationalization of the country. The public without whom they could not have lived a day saw in their greedy grandiose undertakings whatever was for its benefit, and took it while ordering its government to control whatever was sinister."—From "Nothing New Under the Sun," a chapter in the 1939 autobiography of Ida M. Tarbell.

Nearly a century ago, Ida Tarbell was considered one of America's leading muckrakers. What cemented that reputation was a two-volume *History of the Standard Oil Company,* one of the best accounts of corporate monopoly of the day. Indeed, Tarbell's reporting eventually led to federal antitrust laws and the break-up of that oil empire. But it would have taken scores of people like Tarbell to cover the greed and arrogance that followed. Among the more infamous examples in chronological order:

The Meltdown of 1902: In a single day the stock price of International Paper Co. dropped 78 points, to $121 a share, on news that the company had cooked the books. Three investment houses closed, and 20 banks that had lent money to the company took huge losses.

The Panic of 1907: This is the year when speculation suddenly became joke material. "The safest way to double your money is to fold it over twice and put it in your pocket," advised humorist Frank Mc-Kinney Hubbard.

The patriotic con artists: To pay for World War I, thousands of Americans invested in liberty bonds. Unfortunately, over $400 million of the bonds were fraudulent.

Coster's last stand: His real name was Philip Musica, but after serving time for cheating Uncle Sam of import duties on cheese and borrowing money on trumped-up securities, he changed his name to F. Donald Coster. In 1923 Coster founded Girard & Co., a Mount Vernon, New York-based hair tonic manufacturer that also peddled denatured alcohol to bootleggers. So profitable were the two enterprises that in 1926 Coster merged Girard with McKesson & Robbins, an ailing drug manufacturer and gained control of the new company. Coster ran the crude drug division, in which the parent company invested $21 million. But when the company's treasurer a (former investment banker who had helped arrange the merger) tried to find out why some of the crude drug division's assets weren't making a contribution to the parent, he discovered that its Canadian "warehouses" were in fact one-room offices set up to perpetrate an elaborate fraud. In 1938, as authorities closed in, the swindler shot himself in the bathroom of his palatial Fairfield, Conn. home.

Ivar the Terrible: At his peak Ivar Kreuger, a Swedish-born international financier, who controlled three-quarters of the world's match production, boasted the friendship of Herbert Hoover and a long list of female companions. But a 13—year investigation of his business by authorities showed that Kreuger had bilked shareholders and moneylenders out of some $500 million.

Big Board Bunco: Imagine how embarrassed the New York Stock Exchange was when its president, Richard Whitney, pleaded guilty to illegally pledging customers' securities and the exchange's gratuity fund as collateral for loans. In 1938, the Securities and Exchange Commission issued a report condemning an "unwritten code of silence" that had covered the misdeeds of exchange members. That code, the report contended, allowed Whitney to conceal his activities.

War Scams—Part II: While new laws continued to be written to protect the public, they hardly stopped wily con men from dipping into the $179 billion of savings accumulated by the American public during World War II. The president of the National Association of Better Business Bureaus labeled the investment scams an epidemic. Among the victims were thousands of investors who trusted Canadian swindlers who sold mining stocks then manipulated their prices.

Brazil Nuts: One of the most famous swindler/fugitives of the 1950s was Lowell Birrell, a flamboyant, sharp-witted attorney who fled to Brazil after looting various companies of some $14 million. Brazil's popularity with shady businessmen increased thereafter.

The Goldfine Standard: Bernard Goldfine, a 70–year-old Russian immigrant, became wealthy in textile and real estate businesses. Unfortunately, his penchant for bribing influential politicians contributed to his downfall. Accused in a shareholder suit of embezzling nearly $6.7 million, Goldfine was said to have bragged that he had Sherman Adams, chief White House assistant to President Dwight D. Eisenhower, "in his pocket." Adams resigned on Sept. 22, 1958, after it was disclosed that he had accepted favors from Goldfine. Goldfine was later jailed for criminal contempt and tax evasion.

Mob Security: By the early 1960s, when securities theft, fraud and counterfeiting were rampant, authorities sounded the alarm about an underworld invasion of the financial community. In fact, Robert Morgenthau, then U.S. Attorney for the Southern District of New York, classified securities fraud as "organized crime." And as mobster involvement in legitimate business increased, some federal and local investigators started calling Carmine Lombardozzi, a "capo regime" in the Carlo Gambino crime family, "the Wall Street representative of the Mafia."

Mr. Ed: One of the most sensational cases during the John F. Kennedy Administration involved Edward Gilbert. This former financial wonder of Wall Street fled to Rio de Janeiro to avoid prosecution for the theft of $1,117,000 from E. L. Bruce Company, the hardwood flooring company he once headed. Most of the money Gilbert stole was believed to have gone toward his personal debts, stemming from stock market losses suffered when stock prices tumbled in May 1962.

Texas Crude: Sometimes scandals come very close to people in power. The notorious Texan Billy Sol Estes, for example, eventually became an embarrassment to former President Lyndon B. Johnson. Estes was convicted of mail fraud and conspiracy for having sold financial companies $24 million of mortgages on nonexistent fertilizer tanks.

Salad Daze: In 1963, the country was mourning the assassination of President Kennedy and Wall Street was quaking over the $150 million salad oil swindle masterminded by Anthony (Tino) DeAngelis, a Bronx New York-born former butcher who eventually ran a dozen businesses around the country, with combined annual sales of $250 million. But DeAngelis was highly leveraged. When the house of cards folded, Allied Crude Vegetable Oil Corporation, the country's largest supplier of edible oils for export, was bankrupt. That bankruptcy led to the failure of more than 20 lenders, banks and commodities and securities firms because many of the Wall Street firms had unwittingly used warehouse receipts for the salad oil as collateral for millions of dollars in bank loans. Allied alone used such receipts to secure bank loans of $150 million. But creditors discovered that a large portion of the edible oils purportedly stored in Allied's tanks, or by other companies, was missing. Actually, a lot of the oil never existed.

Network Crime: As the business of banking and finance expanded internationally, criminal cooperation became disturbingly widespread and sophisticated. Jonathan Kwitny, a former reporter for the *Wall Street Journal,* described these operators in 1971 as a "new white-collar Mafia." Some of the notable con men were Clifford Noe, Peter Crosby, Leslie Zacharias, Philip Wilson and Michael Strauss. In Kwitny's book, "The Fountain Pen Conspiracy," he describes the infamous Bank of Sark, an empty shell corporation from which phony documents were used to defraud banks of more than $40 million. Merely a rented third-floor office on the Isle of Guernsey in the English Channel, the "bank" played a role in the securities fraud cases of such spurious companies as Picture Island Computer and Trans-Continental Casualty Insurance Company.

Vesco: Fugitive financier Robert Vesco "made monkeys out of the United States," a federal prosecutor once said. That's putting it mildly. Vesco and IOS Ltd., the firm he headed, were accused in 1972 of looting more than $224 million from four IOS-managed mutual funds. While the SEC was investigating Vesco, Harry Sears, a director of one of Vesco's companies arranged a $200,000 cash donation (which was later returned) to Richard M. Nixon's 1972 presidential reelection campaign while the SEC was investigating Vesco's activities.

The Goldblum Standard: As Nixon approached a landslide victory, the Equity Funding Corporation of America, a leader in insurance and mutual funds, was earning praise as an outstanding investment because of its rapid and aggressive expansion. But in the months that followed, the story of a colossal fraud unfolded; it involved thousands of false insurance policies, forged bonds and millions of dollars in nonexistent assets. Stanley Goldblum, co-founder and former chairman and president of Equity Funding, was sentenced to eight years in federal prison and fined $20,000 for his part in the insurance and securities fraud. He was also a defendant in two state criminal cases and in more than 60 civil lawsuits.

Nixon's Phony Crony: Here is an early example of the type of fraud that has mushroomed among the nation's thrift institutions. Less than two months after the Equity Funding scandal, C. Arnholt Smith, the prominent California financier and friend of Nixon's, was accused of defrauding the U.S. National Bank of San Diego and a conglomerate controlled by Smith. According to the SEC, he was part of a group that systematically appropriated conglomerate assets for its own use while issuing false and misleading financial statements. The bank was declared insolvent by the Federal Deposit Insurance Corporation and taken over by Crocker National Bank. The FDIC assumed liabilities that included $389.9 million in questionable loans—more than half of the bank's total loan portfolio—made on Smith's authorization. Smith was eventually convicted of grand theft and state income tax evasion.

Sinner Sindona: Far eclipsing Smith's troubles was the 1974 collapse of the Franklin National Bank. Michele Sindona, who had controlled the bank, was convicted of transferring $15 million to Italy through improper foreign currency speculation in an attempt to salvage two banks he owned there. Italian authorities accused Sindona of illegally siphoning $225 million from banks he controlled in that country.

The Drysdale Crisis: Wall Street was stunned in 1982 when a new brokerage firm called Drysdale Government Securities defaulted on $180 million in interest payments to Chase Manhattan, Manufacturers Hanover Trust Company, and other primary dealers. To help avert a disaster, the Federal Reserve Bank twice injected funds into the banking system. Investigations resulted in a number of convictions. The biggest involved two of Drysdale's top officials, Joseph Ossorio and David Heuwetter, who pleaded guilty to cheating major banks of more than $270 million.

When E. F. Hutton Launders . . . : In the famous "Pizza Connection" case federal investigators discovered that one of the defendants, Franco Della Torre deposited several million dollars in cash with a friendly broker at an E.F Hutton office in downtown Manhattan. The money was later wired to a Swiss account. Subpoenaed by a grand jury regarding the incident, Hutton employees were instructed not to discuss the proceedings with anyone. But a wiretap showed that one Hutton employee wasted no time notifying a person known only as "Rossini" in Switzerland. An E.F. Hutton attorney later described this leak as a "misunderstanding."

The list goes on: Marc Rich, the commodities trader indicted in the nation's largest tax-evasion ever; J. David Dominelli and the multimillion-dollar bankruptcy of his San Diego investment firm; Jake Butcher and his banking scams; rogue journalists Foster Winans and Rudy Ruderman; E. F. Hutton's check-kiting; the insider-trading adventures of the Dennis Levine/Ivan Boesky network; John (the gun-toting Springsteen fan) Mulheren; the Yuppie Five, Drexel Burnham Lambert, Mike Milken, et al.; the great S&L crisis of the 1980s, and futures shock in the commodities pits—etc., etc., ad nauseum.

APPENDIX

Among the more notable books that touch on individual Wall Street scandals are:

Bloom, Murray Teigh. *Rogues to Riches*. Putnam, 1971.
Blumgarten, James. *Up Against the Wall (Street)*. Hawthrone Books, 1974.
Confessions of a Wall Street Insider. Playboy Press, 1972.
Cormier, F. *Wall Street's Shady Side*. Public Affairs Press, 1962.
The Equity Funding Papers. Wiley, 1977.
Floyd, William. *People vs. Wall Street*. Vanguard, 1930.
Goldberg, Stuart C. *Capital Games*. American Institute for Securities Registration, 1978.

McClintick, David. *Stealing from the Rich*. 1977.

Plummer, A.N. *The Great American Swindle*. 1930.

Shapiro, Susan. *Wayward Capitalists*. Yale University Press, 1983.

Sobel, Robert. *Inside Wall Street*. W.W. Norton, 1977.

Steele, John Gordon. *The Scarlet Woman of Wall Street: Jay Gould, Jim Fisk, Cornelius Vanderbilt, the Erie Railway Cars, and the birth of Wall Street*. Weidenfeld & Nicholson, 1988.,

Unmasking Wall Street, The Stratford Co., 1932.

Where Are All the Customers' Yachts? Simon & Schuster, 1955.

Deals and Dealmakers

by Leslie Wayne

When people say Wall Street, they don't mean the narrow street extending from Trinity Church nearly to the East River in lower Manhattan. They mean the marketplace where stocks and bonds are bought and sold, deals are made—and billionaires, too.

It's the heart of a multibillion dollar industry that's fundamental to the raising of capital for American business. Even if the deals and the dealmakers aren't physically on the street, Wall Street is still the site where those who have money and those who need it come together. In crude terms, Wall Street is where people make money—some by selling something for more than they paid; others by assisting in the buys and sells; and still others, who through creative finance, seem to create money from thin air.

For more than two hundred years Wall Street—named for the brush and mud wall built by Dutch traders in 1609 to keep the cows in and the Indians out—has been the home of high finance. In Wall Street's Federal Hall, the first order of business for the first Congress of the United States in 1789 was to authorize the issue of $80 million in government bonds. Two years later, on March 21, 1792, several Wall Street businessmen met at Corre's Hotel to discuss the establishment of an auction market. Shortly thereafter, the financial market which was to become the New York Stock Exchange was formed.

THE INVESTMENT HOUSES

The financial markets, which are so important to Wall Street, couldn't operate without the middlemen who bring together the two sides of American finance—the investors and the investments. Investment bankers, therefore, play a major role as intermediaries in the process of getting product—stocks, bonds, options—to the financial market. In turn, these securities are the fuel of investment banks; the selling, trading and holding of them is what creates jobs and brings profits to an investment house.

To begin, investment houses usher securities from issuing corporations or municipalities to the financial markets in their capacity as an "underwriter." Underwriters assume the risk of buying new issues from the corporation or government issuing the securities and then resell the securities to the public. A profit is made on the difference between what the security was bought for and what it's sold for to the public.

Once the securities are in the market, investment houses act as brokers for others and as "agents" for themselves. They maintain a portfolio of securities for their own account. Investment houses also participate in the market, using options and futures, to protect themselves and their customers against financial loss.

Investment houses fall into several categories. Some, like Goldman Sachs, are best known for their corporate finance prowess and specialize in underwriting securities and financial advisory work. Others, like Bear Stearns and Salomon Brothers, are "trading powerhouses" and are known for making money for themselves and others through the trading of securities. And still others are known as "wire houses" because of their big retail brokerage operation.

Trading powerhouses generally have billions of dollars in securities of all types in inventory. Some are traded for the firm's own account. Some are traded for others. Firms "make a market" in hundreds of different securities, which means they will always have enough securities of a certain type on hand to satisfy customer demand. Firms need such vast inventories because the appetites of their institutional clients—insurance companies and pension funds—run into the multimillion dollar range. In addition, to attract these institutional clients, and the large commission revenues they generate, an investment bank needs a full staff of institutional salesmen, a research staff to provide investment information, ample securities in its portfolio and savvy traders to execute the client's orders.

The state of the financial markets directly affects earnings at an investment house. In a rising market, where there's a lot of buying and selling, firms make money as the value of their own holdings rises and as their customers trade more, giving the house more in commission revenues. But, when the markets fall, so does the value of these securities. Sudden market reverses can lead to multimillion losses for an investment firm. And any lessening of demand for securities by customers reduces commission revenues.

THE RETAIL BUSINESS

Another aspect of the business is called "retail," because it caters to small investors. Big retail houses like Merrill Lynch or Paine Webber hire thousands of brokers across the country to handle the accounts of individual investors, some with as little as $5,000 in investments.

The retail business, is sometimes referred to as the "secondary market," so called because the business involves Securities and Exchange Commission "registered representatives" who act as agents. These "stockbrokers" or "account executives" are employed by a brokerage firm and are paid a "brokerage commission" unless they're executing orders in the over-the-counter market, where "mark-up" or "mark-down" fees are paid. Commissions vary. (The major institutions such as pension funds, insurance companies and banks have the greatest bargaining power when buying and selling in the secondary market and so tend to pay lower fees than individuals.)

Brokerage firms in the 1980s moved quickly to expand their investment offerings to individual clients. There's intense competition between firms, based on service and fees. Discount brokers, however, should be used primarily by investors who don't need investment advice.

Because it's important for firms to have direct access to the financial markets, every large brokerage firm owns a "seat" on the major exchanges. Since there are a limited number of seats, there is a market in exchange seats.

THE PROCESS OF FINANCING

Most reporters get their first look at the Wall Street community through coverage of a deal. Wall Street is where the savviest of the dealmakers work their magic. Because the beauty of the deal is measured in the amount of money it generates, it's important to keep a careful tally of the fees and profits, not just the final cost or the amount of available financing. The numbers can be tricky.

First of all, there are many types of deals. There are initial public offerings, the first stock offering by companies switching from private ownership to public hands. When there's a lot of interest in a company's products or future, like the public offerings for Apple Computer, MCI or Genetech, going public is a major business event. The proceeds of these deals are the first big payoff to the company's founders and are a signal of how enthusiastic investors are about the company's prospects.

Then there are leveraged buyouts. Leveraged buyouts are, in effect, the reverse of going public. It's when a publicly held company is purchased by a small investor group which borrows heavily to buy the company's stock from public shareholders. When the company is as large as Beatrice or RJR Nabisco the numbers are in the multibillion range. The leading practitioners of this type of deal are firms such as Kohlberg Kravis Roberts and Wesray Capital. These firms line up a small group of equity investors, get management of the target company to go along with the plans and then borrow the billions of dollar to make the acquisition. The theory behind this is that the earnings of the target company will pay down the enormous debt burden and, in effect, pay for the deal.

LBO dealmakers argue that this debt is not a burden, but a discipline that forces the company's management to operate with greater efficiency than ever before. Many of the target company's assets are also sold off to help reduce the debt burden.

If all goes well, the company, over time, is returned to public ownership through a stock offering that provides enormous profits for the small investor group and the management equity holder. LBOs, however, are highly risky ventures. Many argue that these debt-laden companies could easily slip into bankruptcy should the economy sour or if the dealmakers' beliefs about the target company's potential earnings turn out to be too rosy.

Finally, there is the merger—hostile or friendly. This is when one company buys out the stock of another. Hostile deals make headlines because of the complicated tactics and the high stakes. Unfriendly takeovers pit some of the shrewdest brains on Wall Street against each other, either as defenders or attackers. Investment bankers and securities lawyers weigh in as the "hired guns" for the opposing sides. Millions in fees, and a lot in the way of prestige, is riding on the outcome of the takeover for them.

Often the merger can erupt into three- or four-way battles until a "winner" walks away with the corporation under siege. In the course of the battle, different constituencies have different agendas. Managers of the target company are fearful of losing control and their jobs. Shareholders want to get top dollar for their holdings and are waiting for the highest bidder. Arbitrageurs, professional investors, bet millions on the outcome of takeover battles by quickly buying up shares once a merger is announced. They want the merger to go through. Directors are worried about getting sued by disgruntled shareholders. And employees are uncertain what the battle—and the potential new corporate owners— will mean for them.

There's a grab-bag of other deals that often make news. Recapitalizations of different types are popular. This is when a company changes the structure of its balance sheet by repurchasing large blocks of its own shares or issues large amounts of debt. Stock repurchases are designed to make companies less vulnerable to corporate raiders and provide a one-time boost to earnings per share. What businesses a company buys —or sells—can also be newsworthy. If a company buys a new division, is this to strengthen a business it's already in, or to diversify into a new business? How will it finance that purchase? If it sells a division—why and what will the proceeds be used for?

TAKING APART THE DEAL

Deals are exceedingly complex and perhaps the safest way to cover one is to simply trace the flow of dollars and get to know the players.

Take a leveraged buyout. Who's proposing the LBO and where are they getting the money? Is it management, an outside leverage buyout company or a raider? What's their track record and their chances of success? Success here will be based on their ability to raise money to get the deal done. Remember, anyone can propose a deal; completing it is another matter.

It's interesting to see who the takeover group has lined up on their "team." This means the investment bankers and lawyers plotting the strategy and clearing away any legal hurdles. (These people become a reporter's primary sources.) Other team members are the banks, insurance companies or providers of funds. These players are usually looking for a rate of return on their investment—if the deal goes through. The quality of the providers of the money and their track record as investors will give a reporter a clue as to the strength of the deal.

Other team members are the management of the target company, who put in their own money as well. What are their motives? Do they inspire confidence among the money lenders? In a leveraged buyout, there are generally two types of money lenders: Management and the leveraged buyout company, which puts in a small amount of equity capital but stands to reap big potential gains at some time in the future. And there are the providers of debt—banks, insurance companies, pension funds—which are looking for a steady rate of return.

Once you have an understanding of how the deal is structured and who's behind it, then it's time to look at possible roadblocks. Are their legal barriers to the LBO? Will other bidders step into the fray? What about public opinion? Is there any chance negative publicity will derail the deal? Once the initial announcement of the deal is made, it often becomes open season for competitors to descend on the target company with competing bids. That's when the fun really begins.

If there are competing bids, the analysis is the same: Who's proposing it? How credible are the bidders? How solid is the money they have lined up? What are potential obstacles to their success? Again, it's important to have sources in all camps to beat your own competition on breaking developments.

Finally, a reporter must ask the question which investors are asking: Does this deal make sense? If the company plans to sell assets to pay its debts, a reporter should know what these assets may fetch. Will it be enough? Are the estimates of value off? Look at analyst's estimates of the actual cash generated from the company's business activities. Will future cash flow be sufficient to cover the debt payments? If not, the company's in real trouble. Don't forget the "what ifs." What if the economy sours? What if foreign competition or new technology kills demand for the target company's products?

In essence, the key rule to analyzing a deal is to question everything, to follow the flow of dollars and to understand the character, including the personal quirks, of the players. Remain skeptical all through the reporting process.

HOW TO COVER THE STREET

Covering Wall Street is a lot like covering the court house. There's intrigue. There's drama. And there are people who are in the know, and therefore, important to know. One of the differences is that Wall Street is a vast place, with hundreds of firms and thousands of employees. There's no easy way to develop sources and since many of the transactions are secret before official announcement, it's difficult to anticipate what's likely to happen. Besides, everyone is especially careful about information that might in any way be considered "inside information." Unlike the government, where politicians and officials feel some responsibility to respond to reporter's questions, Wallstreeters don't.

Generally, the best way to develop sources is to know something about financing and how it works. Generally, our sources will be people who talk fast and in code. They're usually not happy to decode and explain. And since the magic of Wall Street is the deal—the more complicated and innovative (and low tax), the better—getting the details right is crucial. Make sure your sources understand that it's in both your and their best interest to make sure you understand the finer points of a deal. It may be necessary, therefore, to ask the "dumb" question and request your Wall Street source to walk you through the deal.

There are no hard and fast rules for making contacts at investment houses. Some firms are closed and refer all phone calls to public relations personnel. These people, however, can be helpful in setting up interviews. The best approach is the direct one. If you can find out who's involved in the deal—the principals—call them.

Occasionally dealmakers need reporters in the same way that politicians do: to float trial balloons and get their side explained. If the door opens, make sure you're prepared to make the most of it.

Where do you find sources on Wall Street? I've found it's on a story-by-story basis. On any given deal, I'll find the names of the bankers working on that deal, often from the public relations people, and then call directly. One source will lead to another. It's good to stay in touch with these people, via phone, lunches, etc., since they may have the information you'll need on a competitive story on deadline. In many of these areas, especially in mergers, there are a small number of players, who all know each other. So after a couple of stories, you will have a handle on them.

The sources are different for each story. In the area of mergers and takeovers, there are two groups. One is the group of dealmakers who work in the corporate finance departments of the investment banks handling the deals. The other are arbitrageurs who invest in the stocks of takeover candidates. As with politicians, "arbs" are often as interested in getting information from reporters as they are in giving it. The relationship can be one of mutual benefit, but be cautious.

As with all sources, keep your guard up. With so many deals changing so quickly and with so much of what Wall Street does couched in technical language, it's easy to get taken. Sources have their own motives and it isn't always truth, justice and the American way. Misunderstandings are easy enough, given the complexity of Wall Street. Being misled is another matter—and it happens often enough.

Corporate Finance

by Kevin J. Lahart

Recently, corporate finance has been seen as a means for investment bankers to get rich. After all, Michael Milken, former head of the now defunct Drexel Burnham Lambert Inc.'s high-risk, high-yield "junk bond" department, was paid more than a half-billion dollars a year before his indictment on charges of violating securities law. Even the spear-carriers of corporate finance—the young investment bankers with three to five years of experience—earn a half million dollars annually.

But there is an older, more accurate vision of corporate finance: a system rationalizing and smoothing the allocation of financial capital— the money that businesses need. This older, quainter notion says the driving force of the system is financing businesses, not creating income for financiers.

In the old days, companies began with an idea: a horseless carriage, a dry breakfast cereal, a desktop computer. They still start that way.

But since bankers shy away from unproven ideas, private backers put up the seed money for these ideas. In all of the cases just mentioned, the business got started and, against all odds, prospered. (Years ago, the investors were typically individuals. Today the investors might be venture capitalists.) After some success, the next stop was the bank, the same one that had said "no" at first. But now there were assets and a flow of cash. There were profits. So the bank now said "yes."

The businesses continued to succeed. Revenues poured in, but the businesses needed to hire more workers, add more new equipment, open more offices or factories or stores in order to meet increasing demand. Along came the investment bankers. "Go public," they said. "Sell stock in your companies. We'll help you. For a fee." So the companies went public. Stock prices rose as the companies' fortunes increased. They sold more stock. They were noticed.

They needed still more money to finance further expansion. This time, the investment bankers said, "You've issued enough stock. You're successful. You have a track record. Issue bonds. We'll help you. For a fee."

So the companies issued bonds. As new issuers, they had to pay a bit more interest on their bonds than did well-established corporations, but as they continued to prosper and to pay the interest in a timely manner, the rating agencies raised their ratings, making it cheaper for the companies to issue their bonds. They called in the older bonds, paid them off, issued new bonds carrying lower coupon interest rates.

With their great track record in the stock market, with their credit quality at the bank, with their high ratings from the agencies like Standard & Poor's, the companies could pick and choose among the ways to raise money. They could borrow at banks. They could issue stock. They could borrow in the bond markets.

Life was sweet.

Corporate finance used to be a piece of cake, a fancy piece of cake perhaps, but a piece of cake. There were recipes. The recipes were straightforward. All you had to do was come up with the ingredients, follow instructions, and, bingo, you had what you wanted.

No more. The decade of the 1980s changed all that, and corporate finance is now salmon en croute, oeufs a la niege, medallions of venison served with a sauce whose stock base took days to simmer to perfection. The instructions may exist, but they are far more complicated, less widely available (often well-guarded secrets) and incomprehensible to boot.

Investment banks have whole departments whose sole purpose is to research and invent financing schemes—they call them "products"— tailored to a client's needs and the market's appetite. The products are driven by considerations of tax law, accounting principles and risk. In many cases, only a small proportion of the very bright professionals in the investment banks have more than a perfunctory understanding of the complex mathematics behind these schemes.

Further confusion arises from the flood of mergers and acquisitions, recapitalization plans and management buyouts, many of them relying on leveraging plans that load the companies with huge amounts of debt.

Nevertheless, to get a handle on what's going on in the netherworld where the adepts of contemporary corporate finance are cooking up their stratagems and in the world of the leveraged buyout (LBO), it's still necessary to go back to a smaller world.

All businesses need financing—from kids with a lemonade stand to the most widely diversified multinational corporation. It's easy enough for the lemonade entrepreneurs. They finance their enterprise by using their own cash to buy lemons, sugar, paper cups, or they borrow from their parents either cash or raw materials. If the children are successful after a day, they can take some portion of their profit and plow it back into the business to finance the next day's enterprise.

EQUITY AND DEBT FINANCING

For elaborate businesses it's more complicated. But even with the added confusion brought on by a bewildering array of financial instruments and the blurring of lines between institutions called on to provide the financing, it's not all that difficult to see through to the essentials of the financing.

The first cut is the one between debt and equity. With debt you borrow money. With equity you sell off a portion of the business, a share, representing a piece of the ownership. Equity can be sold via a private placement or in the public markets as common stock or preferred stock. Common stock is far more prevalent. With its purchase, generally come voting rights and a stake in the good, or bad, fortunes of the company. The not-so-common preferred stock usually comes with a more-or-less guaranteed dividend, but without voting rights.

The advantage to the company of issuing common shares is the cost. There is little in the way of direct financial obligation to the holders of such equity. Many companies declare dividends, but they needn't do so. And if a business is showing little or no profit, or if it's growing by leaps and bounds and wants to plow the profit it generates back into the business, it's not likely to pay a dividend.

The upside for the shareholders is that the company may grow and prosper by using the money it might have paid in dividends to finance its needs. Thus the value of the company increases and its stock is more attractive. The upside for the company is that issuing common stock provides cash that has no direct financial obligation attached.

The downside for the shareholder is the uncertainty of the company's long-term performance. It may turn into a dog and its stock may lose value. The worst case, of course, is that the company will go belly up. When that happens, shareholders have no recourse. They lose their investment.

The disadvantage of common share issuance for the company is that the ultimate control of the company, at least in theory, is diluted. It becomes harder to control the management of a company, since companies are supposed to have a responsibility to all their shareholders. Often shareholders demand that the management please them and enrich them by running the company with certain goals in mind, such as stock appreciation. In addition the structure of the tax laws is such that dividends come out of post-tax earnings. Debt service, on the other hand, is accounted for as a pre-tax expense. At a 35 percent tax rate, the savings can be huge.

Other forms of equity are common stock with no voting rights, or common stock with a diluted voting value, and preferred stock. They are alike in that neither makes much difference in determining the life of the company. Nonvoting or diluted-voting common is generally issued as part of a broader ploy by owners of large blocs of stock and/or company managements to protect the company (and their own autonomy and jobs) from hostile takeover. It has been particularly popular with dynastic media companies such as the New York Times Company. and the Times Mirror Corporation.

Preferred stock generally carries no voting power. Its attraction is that it carries a guaranteed dividend and a claim, albeit the weakest, on the assets of the corporation. Its attraction is the guarantee plus the potential for appreciation as the fortunes of the company rise.

The other main cut in financing is debt. Oversimply, it's divided between straight financing that is either secured or unsecured, such as bank debt, and publicly offered debt instruments, such as bonds, subordinated debentures and commercial paper.

Straight financing, or straight lending, has many sources. The most obvious and largest sources of such funding are commercial banks. They lend money, usually for no more than seven years. They charge interest, usually at a spread over some fluctuating benchmark rate such as the prime rate or the London Interbank Offered Rate (LIBOR) and pay very close attention to the fortunes of the business. In addition to the commercial banks, insurance companies and very well-capitalized financing companies that had their start as the consumer financing arms of large industrial companies (General Electric, General Motors, Ford) play an important role in this kind of financing. Such lending usually has a primary claim in the case of default and is often tied to company assets.

Lining up behind that kind of straight lending is the array of publicly offered debt. First, there are long-term bonds, with maturities that go out 10, 15, 25 years or more. They have a first claim on stated amounts of company revenues and assets. The claim on assets is stated as the bonds' face value. The claim on revenue is the coupon that states the interest rate. Generally, companies pay interest semi-annually. The face amount is due at the end of the period for which the bond was issued.

Second are long-term subordinated debentures. They generally have a term that's considerably shorter than the long-term bonds, and, like the bonds, have stated amounts of claim. But the claim is not as strong. In case of default, holders of such junior debt must line up behind the holders of senior debt. For this reason, the interest rate paid on junior debt is greater than on the bonds. The claim is less. The risk is higher. And the holder demands compensation for assuming greater risk.

Third on the list of plain vanilla debt is intermediate term debt. These are issues that have a maturity of one to five years.

Finally, there is short-term debt, debt with a maturity of up to one year. For large corporations with good credit ratings, this usually means commercial paper. The market and idea of commercial paper was invented in the 1970s. Prior to that time, even large corporations relied on commercial banks for their short-term financing needs. But when corporate treasurers, with significant visionary help from Goldman Sachs, the idea's inventor, saw that they could borrow more cheaply in the public debt markets, the new instrument was born.

Since then a vast array of new financing instruments has come to the market place, most of them variations in one way or another on the basic structures. Standing on the other side of such transactions is an army of investors. They range from the individual with a small portfolio of stocks or a money market fund share or shares in a mutual fund to the corporation with spare cash to put to work, to institutional investors with large pools of funds to invest in equities and in fixed-income instruments of varying terms and time horizons.

With all of them, the banking and investment banking and securities industries serve as intermediaries, always looking for their cut.

HOW FINANCING HAPPENS

What do those intermediaries do to earn their daily cake? They act in two areas in particular where they are said to add value. They structure deals, engineer them, advise on them. And they execute the deals, taking on the risk of holding for a short time the paper that they have agreed to peddle in the market and distributing that paper. Clients pay them large fees for their advice and financial engineering skills. On the distribution side, the investment banks take on the risk of holding the paper that they are to distribute. They're paid for the risk and the distribution in the margin between what they guarantee to the selling corporation and the purchasers of the paper. It's a gamble that almost always pays off in favor of the investment bank. But if they miscalculate public appetite for a particular issue, or if the market takes a turn, they often must eat the loss as well.

No corporation, save the investment banks themselves, has the expertise and means to distribute its own securities. But increasingly corporations, through their own financial staffs, have developed the competence to engineer their own deals. The Tisch's Loews Corporation has developed dozens of deals on its own and a reputation for a high level of financial sophistication. Banc One Corporation, the Columbus, Ohio based bank holding company had, by the end of 1988 acquired 83 banks in less than ten years, engineering the deals itself. Further afield, when Phelps Dodge, the giant copper mining company, wanted to diversify in the late 1980s, its chairman, G. Robert Durham, led his own in-house team in structuring the deals in which Phelps Dodge acquired a large carbon black producer and a wheel manufacturing company. Mr. Durham said he thought that relying on investment bankers would have been a waste of money. And besides, he said, investment bankers have a vested interest in making a deal work whether or not it's absolutely right for the company.

Such in-house deal-making remains the exception not the rule, and the potential profitability of such endeavors makes the fee-generating area of investment banking, as well as the profitability of distribution very attractive. The commercial banks, buffeted by losses of business to the investment banks, find it particularly attractive and have moved aggressively to get into what has been the domain of the investment bankers for the past five decades.

Since the late 1970s the lines between commercial banking and investment banking have grown increasingly blurred as the securities industry has moved into areas previously the domain of the commercial banks, and the commercial banks have broken through the wall separating commercial banking from investment banking established by the Glass-Steagall Act in reaction to the 1929 crash.

These days an investment bank is likely to put its own capital on the line. Doing the five month to six month bridge financing to make a LBO deal work, to own a bank that processes consumer credit cards or to engage in significant foreign exchange trading.

Even without the repeal of Glass-Steagall, the large commercial banking companies are likely to have well-capitalized investment banking subsidiaries through which they have entered, or plan to enter, the field of underwriting and domestic corporate debt and equity.

FINANCING TRENDS

Several factors drove the changes: the shift from relationship to transaction, deregulation, the tax laws and technology.

While the corporate finance business is still not a total meritocracy, overall it has changed from a business where your father's club memberships, where you grew up, where you went to school, who you grew up with and where your family summered made all the difference. Far more important today is competence in getting deals done most efficiently and at the best price.

Second is deregulation. Before 1975, brokerage commissions were set by the industry; legalized price-fixing. The change in competitive pricing created short-run chaos in the industry and drove from the business scores of inefficient firms. Then in 1982, with the advent of so-called self-registration, issues could be registered with the Securities and Exchange Commission but held off the market until banker and company felt the time was right for sale. On the commercial banking side, the steady weakening of the Glass-Steagall Act permitted the money center banks particularly to move more and more into areas previously closed to them.

Third is tax law. Beginning in the late 1970s a few shrewd investment bankers saw that the relationship between tax policy and the fundamental economics of the stock market created an arbitrage between the asset value represented by corporate shares and the market value of the shares. Quite simply, in many cases the real value was greater than the market value, particularly if you calculated the value as depreciated by the "due bill," a statement of money owed, the government whenever the corporation made money. Why not gain control of the stock, borrow the money to do it, and then load the debt onto the newly acquired, now privately held company? Presto, a leveraged buyout wherein equity is converted into debt and what would have been the taxable profits of the company are now used to pay off debt. The change transfers the due bill from the government to the investors, and the tax bill is eliminated.

Into that conceptual mix came Mr. Milken and Drexel Burnham Lambert, inventing the new-issue, high-yield (junk) bond and developing the market for it. At that point, the game changed considerably. (By 1988 more than a third of new bonds were junk bonds.) In the pre-junk days, less-than-investment-grade bonds were fallen angels, previously issued bonds issued of corporations that had fallen on hard times. With Milken and DBL advising them, hundreds of companies simply issued such bonds.

The junk market made it relatively easy to finance LBOs and takeovers friendly or hostile. Smaller corporations, moreover, who because of their size had previously been limited to bank financing, suddenly found themselves able to sell their paper in the public markets. And the commercial banks, which had seen short-term lending to large corporations taken away from them via commercial paper, now found many of their middle-market, long-term lending customers issuing bonds.

The final engine of change has been the technological revolution. Calculations that would have taken days or weeks can be done in a matter of seconds. That has made possible activities that would have been all but impossible only a few years ago. Risk can be calculated, and therefore managed more efficiently. Financial products can be invented and used.

For example, one of the revolutionary shifts taking place is the rush to securitization of debt, allowing bonds to be backed by anything from mortgages to student loans to credit card receivables to the corporate debt on the books of commercial banks. An early manifestation of that is the securitization of consumer automobile loans. Normally such loans are held by the lender for two or three or four years until they are paid off. The lender then recycles the funds into the next generation of loans. In one deal typical of large securitization schemes, General Motors Acceptance Corporation, instead of holding a block of loans it had made, combined billions of dollars in such loans in a huge pool, and sold bonds and notes backed by those pooled loans in the marketplace. The result was that GMAC executed a quick turnaround on the paper, got rid of the risk and increased its liquidity. Without the aid of computers to track historical default rates (very low) and payoff history (extraordinarily various), the debt instruments could not even have been considered. As an added wrinkle, because of the variety of the appetite among the potential buyers of such paper, three separate kinds of notes and bonds were created, each with a different term. The transaction simply could not have been accomplished without the use of sophisticated computers.

Over the coming years, these four factors—emphasis on transactions, the structure of the tax law, regulatory changes and technological change will continue to affect the way corporate finance is carried out. Commercial banking will change. The investment banking business will change. Greedy men and women will work very hard to distort the system to their own self-enriching ends. New instruments will be invented. It will take greater and greater sophistication and study to understand what is going on. But the basic instruments of financing—debt and equity—will remain despite the bells and whistles that are attached and despite the hybrids that will continue to be invented. And beneath the changes the real purpose of the system will remain the same: to rationalize and smooth the allocation and distribution of financial capital.

Venture Capital

by Udayan Gupta

Venture capital—American style—isn't an easy business to understand.

Not long ago I watched a veteran New York venture capitalist trying to explain the subtleties of the industry to a group of senior Japanese executives. After almost three hours of detailed and elaborate explanations, the Japanese didn't know any more about venture capital than before the meeting started.

The Japanese were bewildered by a system that provides money for new businesses but also encourages the defection of senior executives. Even though the system provides an opportunity for these executives to develop new ideas, the Japanese were baffled at the sometimes staggering financial rewards that accompany investment in a venture capital project. "Why can't these executives work within the corporation like we do? Why go through the suffering of being on your own?" asked one Japanese accountant.

But it isn't just the Japanese who are perplexed by the workings of venture capital in America. Some Asian and European countries have attempted to develop a brand of venture capital with the hope of replicating the phenomenon that gave the United States the financial and technological success of Silicon Valley and Boston's Route 128. What many countries have created instead is a system of collateralized lending to small, untested concerns—with few rewards for success.

Strangers to U.S.-style venture capital are awed by a system that routinely manages to give rise to dynamic new ventures without any perceptible drawbacks. Other economic systems also generate new ideas and concepts but often at great social and economic cost. Only Americans seem to have succeeded in regularly creating a generation of new and exciting companies and reaping financial rewards when they go public.

Take the example of Kleiner, Perkins, Caufield & Byers of San Francisco, which since the early 1970s has invested in some of the fastest growing U.S. high-technology companies, including Sun Microsystems, Compaq Computer, Cypress Semiconductor and Lotus Development Company. Between 1972 and 1988, the firm has invested an aggregate of $395 million and averaged a compound annual rate of return of 27 percent—higher than most investments in the stock market or real estate during the same period.

What makes venture capital so uniquely American? A combination of factors. First, there is abundant capital available for investment in risky startups. Second, the tax system, until recently, has favored equity investments with lower rates on long-term capital gains. Third, there is a stock market that, in cycles, has allowed young companies to sell stock to public investors. Finally, there is a social system that encourages and supports individual enterprise—more so in countries like Japan or France.

"You can mimic the financial conditions and tax incentives but you can't change the social system overnight," says a Boston venture capitalist, a strong advocate of the U.S. system.

HOW VENTURE CAPITAL WORKS

Venture capital funds (pools of investment money given to firms in the business of searching out and funding risky, startup companies) usually are structured as partnerships with a life of seven to ten years. Venture capitalists—the managers of the funds—are the general partners. And a passel of investors, including pension funds, foreign investors, corporations, endowments and foundations—the ones who provide the money—are the limited partners.

As managers, venture capitalists select investment strategies as well as the companies that will eventually receive capital. They decide not only who but also how much, as well as the terms and conditions of the investment. After the deal is done, some venture capitalists will sit on the board of directors of the companies to keep close watch on progress and to help companies make contacts with a network of suppliers, customers, and others. If things go wrong, venture capitalists may take charge: firing founders, replacing them with more seasoned managers, refocusing the goals and strategies of the business, or simply shutting down operations.

The aim of all this is to prepare a company to go public or to be acquired by another company. When that happens, the profits from the sale or the shares from the public offering are distributed to the limited partners.

But success isn't always guaranteed. And even though most venture capitalists are reluctant to talk about their blunders, more investments fail than succeed. A venture firm's rule of thumb on investments: About half its portfolio will go belly-up within the first four to five years. Of the survivors, 20 percent will amble along aimlessly (the living dead), another 20 percent will be moderate successes (the singles and doubles). And about 10 percent will prove to be staggering successes (home runs), making up for losses in the rest of the portfolio.

For all their efforts, venture capitalists receive an annual management fee of between 2 percent and 3 percent of the capital being managed, and either interest on their investment or a 20 percent to 30 percent share of the profits in the partnership. That is, of course, a much higher fee than managers of mutual funds receive but it pales in comparison to what LBO fund managers like Kohlberg Kravis & Roberts and Forstmann Little receive for their efforts.

HOW VENTURE CAPITAL BEGAN

In simple terms, venture capital is risk capital—money that is invested in a young company in exchange for a stake in that company. Then when the company matures, and either is acquired by another company or sells stock to public investors, the venture capitalists sell their own stake as well.

The idea itself isn't new. In the nineteenth and early twentieth century, Andrew Carnegie and J.P. Morgan, among others, practiced their own brand of finance capitalism by investing in new ideas or projects, which then became part of their giant empire. But it wasn't until after World War II that such wealthy families as the Rockefellers and the Whitneys institutionalized the process by creating private venture capital pools.

In 1958, President Eisenhower signed into law the act creating the Small Business Investment Program, creating the nation's first organized program for investing in small businesses. The resulting investment companies or SBICs would be private investment companies that would receive tax breaks and the right to leverage their capital by borrowing from the Small Business Adminstration.

For a while SBICs flourished. By 1964, for example, there were as many as 649 operating all across the country. But the rapid multiplication of SBICs meant that the SBA couldn't provide all the capital they wanted to borrow. Then came the market crash of the mid-1960s and the ardor of many SBIC managers cooled.

By the early 1970s venture capital pools had begun forming in various parts of the country as private partnerships. The investors mostly were corporations like General Electric Company and Xerox Corp. looking for new product ideas and new acquisitions, or university endowment funds such as those at Harvard University and the University of Rochester. Later, as the rules surrounding pension fund investments were relaxed, more pension funds aggressively began investing in the industry. Venture capital investments would not only provide higher, albeit risky, returns, but also shield them from the short-term fluctuations of the unpredictable stock market.

In 1990, the venture capital industry had over $30 billion in assets. New money continues pouring in at the rate of $4 billion a year.

There also are over 600 venture capital firms that manage more money than ever before and are being asked to bet larger sums of money on each deal. If the average deal size in the 1970s was less than $500,000, today it is four times as much, some venture capitalists say.

The industry is now a global one. Some venture capitalists from the United States are going abroad trying to replicate the successes they've had stateside. And a plethora of investors from abroad—Japanese and Australian, Taiwanese and German—are testing the waters here.

Federal, state and local governments have also established units to finance small, new companies. Universities are creating investment arms to commercialize research developed within their walls. And universities and state and local governments are banding together in order to create incubators and technology parks—to fund ideas too small for institutional venture capitalists.

GETTING INFORMATION

Still, amidst all this growth and diversity, venture capital continues to be one of the hardest businesses to obtain reliable data about—and one of the hardest businesses to report.

Most venture capitalists talk to the press reluctantly, and mostly to promote themselves or their companies. Only a handful, such as Benjamin Rosen, the major investor in Lotus Development Corporation and Compaq Computer Company are experienced at dealing with the press regularly and with sophistication.

Entrepreneurs are even worse when it comes to dealing with the press. Most of them are uncertain about how much information they should provide and often unwilling to provide key data on sales and revenues.

Others say that they are private corporations and don't have any obligation to talk to the press.

Corporations involved in venture capital also are poor sources of information. Many of them are restrained from talking by their internal bureaucracies. Others argue that their deals are private and aren't significant.

The handful of scorekeepers that the industry now possesses provide little help. Their information is usually historical and of little use to daily reporters and journalists. And since many of them also act as consultants and advisers to the industry, they provide little specific information.

Most of the useful information about venture capital, the riskiest part of their investments, comes from institutional investors—the people whose money venture capitalists invest. Institutional investors such as state pension funds feel that their activities in venture capital—the riskiest part of their investments—should be fully disclosed from day one "to avoid surprises." As a result, a great deal of information about venture firms, their track records, investment strategies and portfolio companies can be obtained from helpful and cooperative institutional investors.

WHAT'S THE STORY?

A major problem for venture capitalists and for the media is the absence of agreement on what constitutes real stories. And in many of the larger newspapers and magazines, important and meaningful stories often can be eclipsed by relatively uninteresting stories about large corporations.

Many small entrepreneurial companies have interesting stories to tell, not just about the problems and perils of starting an independent company but about successful management strategies, the application of technology to the workplace or socially responsible business behavior. But these aren't simple stories. And too often they are damn difficult to sell to editors with dual standards; one for large companies, quite another for the smaller ones.

The difficulty of reporting on venture capital isn't likely to go away in the years ahead. The industry now is strikingly different from what it was in the 1970s.

Venture capitalists aren't a clubby lot, sharing deals and information. More often than not, they are competing for deals and entrepreneurs and, sometimes inadvertently, bidding up prices in the process.

The industry's early fixation on technology has shifted to new and unfamiliar areas such as specialty retailing and aquaculture. And venture capitalists are investing in seemingly less risky buyouts or stock of public companies—instead of gambling on risky, untested technologies and young companies.

Some complain that success has spoiled the venture capital industry. Instead of using its vast spoils to invest even more aggressively in the dreams of corporate executives and restless kids, it has turned conservative.

And amidst a sea of players, venture capitalists now have to scramble to distinguish themselves from the rest of the pack. Some, like Boston's Advent International, have focused on the international arena. Others like Crosspoint Ventures in Menlo Park, California are focusing entirely on seed investments and very early stage ventures. Still others are aggressively hiring public relations firms to promote their activities.

Success in such an environment clearly isn't guaranteed. And recent predictions of the industry's performance is a cause of great concern to investors. Several studies of the performance of venture funds suggest that most partnerships formed in the 1980s will not have annual yields higher than 20 percent—a sharp drop from the 30 percent to 40 percent in the boom of the 1970s. In fact, most funds are expected to have yields of 12 percent to 15 percent or lower—higher than stocks and bonds but far short of the yields that attracted many investors to this industry.

Venture capitalists also are beginning to recognize their own limitations. They have a checkbook but many lack the knowledge and know-how to deal with companies in distress. That management void has encouraged a plethora of new players—market researchers, consultants and corporate executives—to enter an overcrowded arena.

What does this mean for the media?

Even before the media have had an opportunity to understand what traditional venture capital is, they're being asked to spot changes and describe the new battleground. That's not an easy task for those journalists who haven't been familiar with the business in the first place.

For others, the venture capitalist, stripped of the romantic veil of nurturing new ideas and new companies, just won't be as exciting as the strident figures of Tom Perkins working with Tandem Computers and Ben Rosen helping promote Lotus and Compaq.

But the contemporary image of the venture capitalist might prove to be the lasting image—the one that will stay with us for the rest of the millennium.

TIPS AND TRAPS

Trying to discover how well—or how badly—venture capitalists have done is a nightmarish task. One source of information is the offering memorandum used by venture partnerships to raise new capital.

These aren't public documents and only the venture capitalists themselves, or those they are calling on for money, have them.

Measuring the performance of any given venture capital fund isn't easy. You need to put a value—somewhat arbitrary—on the companies that are still private and come up with a price for the companies that have been sold or gone public. The final yield figures are then computed from the total amount that has been invested and the present value of the capital invested.

Documents filed by venture-backed companies at the time of their initial public offering are also useful in gauging what the returns of a venture firm are from a single deal. The filings not only reveal the number of shares held by venture investors but also the price at which the shares were bought and their transaction dates.

Sometimes, venture capitalists themselves will tell you how well their funds are performing. But you have to remember to ask how the valuations have been made. Some venture capitalists value the portfolio based on the last price at which each deal was done. That is fine, if the market doesn't change dramatically. But if the market is topsy turvy, the prices can be too high or too low.

Another problem is the way some venture firms value their portfolio companies that have gone public. Some firms will value the stock at the price at which they gave the stock to their limited partners. Others will continue to peg the stock at its current price—even though they may not hold the shares.

For overall industry statistics the two most popular sources are: National Venture Capital Association, the industry's trade group in Arlington, Virginia. Venture Economics, Wellesley Hills, Massachusetts, which publishes the Venture Capital Journal, an industry newsletter.

If you want a quick history of the industry read *The New Venturers* by John Wilson (Addison-Wesley). Written in 1985 and updated in 1988, it's still the most comprehensive book on the industry.

Publicly Held Companies

by Victoria Gits

Ownership in American companies is highly dispersed. The New York Stock Exchange estimates that more than 50 million individuals own stock in publicly held companies. Some is held as individual shares. Other stock is held in pension funds, mutual funds and other stockholding agents that make investments on behalf of individuals. And brokerage firms, companies, and institutions own stock.

Some companies are widely held. Take, for example, American Telephone & Telegraph. It's the most widely held corporation in America, with 1.07 billion shares outstanding and 2.6 million shareholders in 1989. Institutions, such as Wells Fargo Bank, Bankers Trust New York Corporation and California State Teachers Retirement Fund, held 261 million, or 24 percent, of the outstanding shares. AT&T officers and boardmembers held 642,976 shares, or .06 percent. The remaining 812 million shares, or 76 percent, belonged to individuals.

Among the various owners, reporters should pay close attention to institutions, members of the board of directors, officers, employees and those with 5 percent or more of the shares. Information on ownership can be found in the company's proxy statement, issued prior to the annual meeting, and in the 10–K, filed with the Securities and Exchange Commission. When an investor increases his ownership to 5 percent, he must file a 13–D with the SEC, and state the reasons for the purchase (see "SEC Documents").

Sometimes a careful look at who owns a company can lead to an interesting insight into its health and operations. Is the company increasing the opportunity for executives to own stock? Are executives jumping at the opportunity or shying away? Not buying stock may mean they are not as optimistic about the company's future as they say they are. Company executives are routinely conferred stock through bonuses and benefit plans.

Employees, through an Employee Stock Ownership Plan (ESOP) or other employee ownership program, may also own shares. ESOPs often vote their shares as a block. What has been the trend in voting? Other company stock plans, some of which allow employees to buy stock at a discount, disburse stock to employees as individuals. Consequently, employees vote their stock as if they were individual investors. Is this strengthening the voting for management proposals?

COMMON SHAREHOLDERS

What do common shareholders own? They hold a certificate of corporate ownership which doesn't carry any liability for debts. In the event of bankruptcy, those who have paid for stock can lose only what they have invested. Common shareholders can't be forced to pay debts incurred by the firm. The shareholder buys actual ownership or equity in the company and is entitled to dividends, if the company pays them, and capital appreciation on the stock.

The rights of shareholders vary according to the laws of the state where the firm is incorporated, but in general the shareholder has the following rights:

- To share in the surplus upon dissolution of the company.
- To vote at stockholders meetings, to elect the board of directors and approve certain structural changes in the firm, which may include amending the bylaws, authorizing the sale of property or approving a merger.
- To transfer stock.
- To examine the records and books.
- To go to court to prevent damage to the corporation due to negligent or fraudulent acts of directors, corporate officers or other shareholders.

VOTING PRIVILEGES

When a corporation comes into existence, its organizers decide how many shares of stock will be offered for sale. In most cases, a shareholder is entitled to one vote per share of stock owned.

The election of the board takes place once a year at a scheduled time and place. A "special meeting," prompted by some unexpected event, may be held at any time. By law, the corporation must give shareholders at least ten days advance notice of meetings.

Shareholders who don't attend in person may send a "proxy," which authorizes someone who will be present to vote in their behalf. The meeting may conduct official business only if a quorum is present. In this context, a quorum is the number of shares present, not the number of persons present. Without a quorum, the only action shareholders can take is to adjourn the meeting until a quorum can be obtained.

In general, a quorum consists of a majority of the voting shares of a corporation and action may be taken upon a vote of more than 50 percent of the shares.

COMPANY CONTROL

Since most shareholders don't invest with the idea of taking over a company—they want dividends and higher share prices—they tend to trust management to run the company. Often managements are in power because they control a majority of the company's voting shares. Control, considered to be 51 percent of the voting shares, isn't necessary, however, if management can convince other shareholders to support its decisions. Sometimes control can be achieved with stock holdings of as little as 25 percent, if a company is widely held by many investors and no other investor has more than a 25 percent stake.

Some corporations, in order to obtain greater control over the election process, create different classes of stock. For instance, the company may create a Class A stock which entitles its owners to elect seven out of 10 directors. This stock may be available only to company employees and may be a way to keep the board favorable to management, since the company officers may buy most of the Class A stock. Often a class of stock is available only to members of the founding family. Then a second class of stock, Class B stock, will be available to the general public. Obviously, Class B isn't as valuable as A, with full voting privileges.

Multi-class stock is a corporate strategy opposed by some shareholders because, they argue, it decreases the value of the stock and is prohibited by the one-man, one-vote principle, guaranteed by the Securities and Exchange Act of 1934 and other amendments. On July 7, 1988, the SEC passed Rule 19c-4, preventing firms from creating a second class of voting rights. (The exceptions are firms issuing stock for the first time or those with plans in effect before May 15, 1988.)

According to the Investor Responsibility Research Center in Washington, D.C., in 1985, only 119 companies on the three major national securities markets had disparate voting common stock. By 1988, the total had increased to 306.

SHAREHOLDERS AND TAKEOVERS

In recent years, a wave of takeover activity in the 1980s forced the issue of shareholders' voting rights into the limelight. When a corporation is faced with the prospect of a lucrative takeover offer, many shareholders want the option to vote on it. For that reason, the multi-class stock strategy, which makes takeovers more difficult, is an issue with shareholders who want the right to participate in the decision to sell.

The courts, however, have generally not been sympathetic to shareholders. For example, when Time decided to buy Warner Communications Inc., rather than to sell out to Paramount Communications, the Delaware Court ruled on July 14, 1989 that the Time officers weren't obligated to put the action to a vote of the shareholders. Regardless of how many shareholders wanted to sell, Time Inc. acted within the scope of its authority to conduct business affairs as it saw best, the court said.

In a previous landmark case involving Revlon in 1985, the Delaware Supreme Court ruled that directors must sell to the highest bidder, but only after they have decided to sell or drastically restructure the company. Time, the judge said, had not decided to sell itself and was justified in pursuing its chosen long-term strategy.

A takeover involves a purchaser's making a bid to the board of directors. The next step is the tender offer in which the buyer attempts to buy up the public shares, enough, that is, to elect a new board of directors and take control of the company. In a tender offer, shareholders have the option of bypassing management. They may simply "tender" or sell their shares to the acquiring party without the consent of the company. Shareholders in this instance usually get a premium for their shares. That is, the price is almost always above what the stock market is offering.

Shareholders usually oppose the tactics companies take to prevent takeovers. Such strategies as poison pills, supermajority voting, golden parachutes and restructuring are methods commonly used to prevent a deal from closing (see "Analyzing the Acquisition"). Shareholder groups have challenged such methods, because they can penalize shareholders by denying them an immediate high return on the sale of their stock.

In reality, shareholders of most large companies are rarely willing, nor will they be asked, to do much more than ratify the wishes of the board of directors. While they have the right to make proposals to the board or to offer recommendations on changes in the bylaws, most shareholders are happy to hold stock and collect dividends. There are provisions in the system which, at least theoretically, provide for democratic voting and a degree of shareholder influence over management, but they are seldom exercised.

SHAREHOLDER ADVOCACY

Individual shareholders are generally not powerful enough to reverse a corporate decision. But these days, individual shareholders are represented by large and powerful trustees such as retirement funds. Pension funds today own 20 percent of the publicity traded stock in America. In the 1960s and 1970s, they were relatively passive investors. But in the late 1980s, they began to organize against practices that in their view entrenched management at the expense of shareholders.

A number of shareholder organizations have become important to shareholder rights issues. They include The Council of Institutional Investors (mainly public funds), The United Shareholders Association (formed by T. Boone Pickens, Jr., chairman of Mesa Petroleum and a well-known corporate raider) and the Institutional Shareholder Services, an advocacy group for public and private funds and money managers.

Among the proponents of shareholder rights are prominent pension funds, such as the California State Teachers' Retirement System, the College Retirement Equities Fund, the New York City Employees' Retirement System and the California Public Employees' Retirement System.

Reporters will find information on shareholders issues at the Investor Responsibility Research Center, based in Washington, D.C., a not-for-profit corporation founded in 1972, which publishes a bimonthly newsletter.

The SEC provides some basic shareholder protection. The Securities Act of 1933 requires companies to supply investors with information about their activities. The act provides that a firm offering public securities for sale must file a registration statement and a prospectus with the Securities and Exchange Commission. While the SEC does not inspect the truthfulness of a prospectus, it may impose severe penalties for false or misleading information.

The Securities Exchange Act of 1934, which created the Securities and Exchange Commission, regulates securities trading after the initial offering. The law says that publicly traded companies must file periodic reports (see "SEC Documents," herein).

The 10–K is useful to reporters because it requires companies to state the amount of stock held by both managers and outsiders with more than 5 percent stock ownership.

The 8–K contains information about companies in bankruptcy. The 10–Q, issued quarterly, is often the source of good stories about lawsuits or new developments.

Under SEC rules, a registered company is required to furnish each stockholder a proxy statement and ballots for voting at the annual meeting. Proxy statements make good reading because they contain a listing of top officers and their annual compensation packages.

Investors are especially interested in the information statement required under section 13–D, which mandates disclosure whenever an investor acquires more than 5 percent of a registered security. Such a move may indicate the launch of a tender offer, an invitation to shareholders to sell their stock.

DELAWARE INCORPORATION

Most companies willingly comply with the requirements of the regulating agencies. But many are not as happy to comply with the demands of hostile shareholders or states with strict corporate laws. Consequently, many of the nation's corporations have sought a more favorable environment in Delaware. Shareholders rights are governed by the state in which the firm is incorporated. A company can be incorporated in the state of its choice, regardless of where it does business or is headquartered.

More than half of all Fortune 500 companies are incorporated in Delaware, as well as more than 40 percent of the companies on the New York Stock Exchange. Delaware in the late 1980s derived $170 million, or 17 percent of its revenues, from incorporation fees. The main attractions are an efficient judicial system and a pro-management climate.

Delaware offers the business firm certain options helpful in avoiding hostile takeover bids, primarily, the allowance of poison pills, or antitakeover strategies, without the vote of shareholders. But in recent years, even the Delaware courts have said that poison pills, in certain situations, are illegal. Consequently, some companies have considered moving to states more hospitable to poison pills such as New York, Hawaii, Ohio, Wisconsin, Idaho, Kentucky and Pennsylvania, which have bypassed the courts and enacted new laws to protect the validity of poison pills. Some 28 states in 1988 offered various anti-takeover laws that, like Delaware's, may go into effect without shareholder approval.

The legal roadblocks to takeovers may be formidable, but plenty of proposals succeed in spite of them.

TERMS YOU SHOULD KNOW

Beneficial owners. Actual owners of securities held in the name of a brokerage firm ("street name").

Closely held. A firm in which a substantial portion of the stock is owned by insiders, including officers and members of the board of directors.

Common stock. Stock that represents ownership of a portion of a company and has ordinary rights of participation in a corporation.

Cumulative preferred stock. An investment in stock that entitles the holder to dividend distributions that accumulate in years when dividends aren't paid. When a dividend is declared, all back accumulations are paid first.

Cumulative voting. In an election of directors, shareholders have a number of votes equal to the quantity of shares owned multiplied by the number of directors to be elected.

Derivative suit. A shareholder action on behalf of the corporation against its officers for mismanagement.

Dividend. A part of the corporate earnings given to shareholders on authority of the board of directors.

Ex-dividend. A stock marked with an "X" in stock tables means the dividend was declared and goes to the current owner, rather than the new buyer.

Full disclosure. SEC Rule 10b-5 which prohibits an inside director from profiting from information that can influence the price of the stock.

Limited liability. A shareholder cannot be held responsible for debts incurred by the corporation.

Market Sweep. When a bidder halts a tender offer to buy a large holding of stock from arbitrageurs.

Partial tender. A firm offers a premium price to the shareholders who first agree to tender their shares.

Pre-emptive right. Holders of the right to purchase newly issued stock in proportion to the amount already owned in order to maintain their relative proportion of ownership.

Preferred stock. Dividends are paid first to preferred holders of stock.

Proration. In a tender offer, the buyer agrees to accept an equal percentage of each lot tendered by a certain date, up to the total amount sought.

Registration statement. Issuers of new public stock are required to provide detailed information providing full and fair disclosure on the firm.

Street name. Securities held by a brokerage firm on behalf of their clients.

Tender offer. A means of obtaining control of a corporation by offering to buy enough shares to elect a majority of the board of directors. (see "Analyzing the Acquisition," herein).

Wall Street Rule. Investors who don't approve of management actions express their view by selling the stock.

Williams Act. Amendments to the Securities Exchange Act of 1934 that established disclosure requirements and procedures associated with tender offers.

The Exchanges

by Floyd Norris

In May 1792 a group of brokers met under an aging buttonwood tree in lower Manhattan. The purpose of that meeting was to set up the auction market that would eventually become the New York Stock Exchange.

The idea was to form a closed clearinghouse to bring order to the then-chaotic sales of securities. The group made this pledge:

We, the Subscribers, Brokers for the Purchase and Sale of Public Stock, do hereby solemnly promise and pledge ourselves to each other that we will not buy or sell from this day, for any person whatsoever, any kind of Public Stock, at a less rate than one quarter percent Commission on the specie value, and that we will give a preference to each other in our negotiations. In testimony whereof, we have set our hands, this 17th day of May, at New York, 1792.

In those days, there was not a lot to trade. Most of the action was in government bonds, which were known as stocks. The only common shares available were from two banks.

THE NEW YORK STOCK EXCHANGE

For the two centuries since the brokers gathered under that buttonwood tree, the New York Stock Exchange (NYSE) has reigned preeminent on the U.S. financial scene. Various efforts to start competing exchanges in the nineteenth century were generally failures, and the Big Board, as the NYSE is often called, showed an ability to change with the times and attract the biggest transactions.

For much of the nineteenth century, stocks were traded in ways that would seem very strange to someone accustomed to the action now. Rather than continuous trading, stocks were traded by an auction system, in which each stock was called in turn, and the members completed all the trading in that stock before moving on to another. In the 1817 rules of the New York Stock Exchange Board, there was a 25 cent fine levied on any member who asked that trading be resumed in a stock after the auction had moved on to other securities. There were also fines for brokers who failed to show up for the auction.

That system faded after the Civil War, when the auction system became too slow to handle the increasing trading volume and the "specialist" system gradually evolved. The specialist system allowed trading in individual stocks to be conducted at designated positions on the trading floor. While any stock could theoretically be traded anywhere on the floor, it was inconvenient to wander about looking for another broker willing to trade a certain stock. Some brokers began to specialize in certain stocks, and to stay in a certain place throughout the trading day. Other brokers with an order in that stock would know that the quickest way to get a market quote was to go to where that specialist was standing.

Specialists eventually came to dominate the NYSE, and while their power has been diminished, the specialist system lives on. Each of the more than 2,000 stocks that are traded at the Big Board is assigned to a specialist, who is charged with trying to maintain an orderly market. To do that, the specialist will post a bid (the price he or someone else is willing to pay) and an asked price (the price at which he or someone else is willing to sell). If no one else wants to take the opposite side of a customer order, it's up to the specialist to do it.

The "spread" between the bid and asked prices is normally an eighth of a dollar—12.5 cents—or a multiple of it. In general, the less active a market in a stock is, the wider the spread. Noting the size of the spread can be very important in writing about some stocks, notably stocks with low prices per share.

Orders get to the floor of the NYSE in several ways. Most individual orders now arrive electronically, and are executed by the specialist almost automatically. Her duty is to pair off such public orders if possible, and to execute them herself, if necessary. The simplest orders are ones that call for buying or selling at the current price, and are known in stock exchange lingo as "market orders." Those orders will generally be executed immediately when they come in, at the "bid price" if the customer wants to sell, and at the "asked price" if the customer wants to buy.

Another kind of order is a "limit order," in which the order is to be executed only if the price rises, or falls, to a specific level. Those orders go into the specialist's "book," which is generally available to other traders on the floor who ask to see it.

One type of order that gets special treatment is the "short sale," *short sale* which is the sale of stock that is not already owned by the seller. To make such a sale, the stock must be borrowed from a holder and then delivered like any other stock. The normal reason for such a sale is the expectation that the security will decline in price, although such sales can also be part of other trading strategies involving taking offsetting positions in differing markets, perhaps selling a stock and buying a "call option" on the shares. A call option is the right to buy 100 shares of a stock or stock index at a predetermined price before an agreed upon deadline, in exchange for a premium.

The reason short sales are handled differently is that after the 1929 crash, short-sellers were blamed for driving prices down. The evidence was dubious at best, but the "uptick" rule was nonetheless put into place. It requires that a short sale be made only if the price of the trade is higher—an uptick—than the last different price for the stock.

Customer orders of up to 2,099 shares can be handled through the electronic delivery system known as "Super-DOT." Larger orders must be hand carried to the specialist booth by a broker, who may be an employee of the brokerage firm receiving the order, or what is known as a "$2 broker," an independent broker who makes a living executing orders that the customer's broker, for whatever reason, chooses not to handle himself. The name stems from the fact that such brokers used to get paid $2 for each hundred shares traded. They now get far less, but the name stuck.

While the NYSE trading floor is a colorful and fast paced area, much of the real trading action takes place blocks or miles away, in the trading rooms of "upstairs" firms that specialize in institutional trades. An institution wishing to sell a million shares of General Motors would never have a broker take the order to the Big Board floor for execution, in the way an order for 1,000 shares would be handled. Instead, that order would go to one of the "upstairs firms," such as Salomon Brothers or Goldman Sachs. Depending on the institution's wishes, the broker may agree to take some or all of the shares himself, or may try to line up institutions that want to buy the stock. When the trade is ready, it will be taken to the floor of the Big Board, or perhaps another exchange, and "crossed" on the ticker tape so that everyone knows of the trade. In a cross, orders on the floor may be automatically included. Say that the General Motors trade was at $45 a share, 75 cents below the last trade.

An individual who had placed an order to buy 1,000 shares, if the price fell to $45.25 a share, might find he had bought them at $45, since he was simply included in the trade.

All brokers live on commissions, with trading profits sometimes playing a major role as well. From the days of the buttonwood tree until 1975, commissions were fixed. But on May 1, 1975, "Mayday" in Wall Street lore, the era of fixed commissions came to an end. The result has been sharply higher commissions on small trades, and much lower ones on institutional trades, where the commission may be five cents a share or even less. While individual investors can generally get lower commissions at a discount brokerage firm than at a full-service firm, the discounters' rates are still likely to be more than the individual would have paid in the era of fixed commissions.

Until the reforms of the 1970s, if a stock was traded on the New York Stock Exchange, that was just about the only place it could be bought by any individual. Trading the shares elsewhere was perfectly legal, but any brokerage house that did so would be booted out of membership in the Big Board. So while a handful of firms traded stocks away from the NYSE, there was little effective competition. That Big Board rule was eventually repealed, and now most NYSE stocks are traded at regional exchanges, as well as over-the-counter.

REGIONAL EXCHANGES

The largest of the regional exchanges are the Midwest Stock Exchange in Chicago and the Pacific Stock Exchange in San Francisco and Los Angeles. Of less importance for stocks are the Philadelphia and Boston exchanges. The Cincinnati Exchange, actually an electronic network, never caught on, isn't located in Cincinnati, and has little influence.

The regional exchanges function much like the NYSE, with specialists making a market in the same stocks as those listed on the Big Board. There are electronic hookups between the exchanges, making it possible for brokers to see where the best price is and execute a trade on the Midwest Exchange, for example, even if the broker is on the floor of the Pacific Exchange at the time. In practice, the Big Board still controls the overwhelming majority of trading in securities with NYSE listing.

Some stocks of regional interest are listed only on the regional exchanges, but this is true of fewer stocks now than in earlier years. The primary advantage of watching the NYSE and the Pacific Exchanges is that the Pacific exchange stays open for 30 minutes longer than the other exchanges, until 4:30 P.M. EST. It's for that reason that the consolidated tape operates until 4:30.

AMERICAN STOCK EXCHANGE

The American Stock Exchange, known as the Amex and, sometimes, as the Curb, has a shorter but perhaps more colorful history than its Wall Street neighbor, the NYSE. Until 1921 the exchange had no home. Trades were conducted at the curb. Even after it moved indoors, it was called the New York Curb Exchange until it became the American Stock Exchange in 1953.

When trading was conducted outside, brokers actually gathered in the street. Brokerage firms would have offices in buildings with a view of the proceedings, and men standing in windows would relay orders by hand signal to runners, who would give orders to brokers executing the trades.

The Amex long suffered from an inferior image in the shadow of the Big Board; many of the stocks it listed couldn't meet listing requirements for the NYSE, and its volume was lower. But it survived predictions of its demise and prospered.

In part, its success is based on the implementation of stock option trading in 1975, more than a decade before the NYSE began to do so. Its principal competitors in stock options are the Chicago Board Options Exchange, the Philadelphia Stock Exchange and the Pacific Stock Exchange. Until recently, the Securities and Exchange Commission allowed monopolies in listed options, so that if one exchange traded options in a given stock, no other exchange could do so. The SEC now allows dual trading of options.

THE NASD

The National Association of Securities Dealers is the other principal way stocks are traded in the United States. Its automated quotation system, known as Nasdaq, has gained considerable market share from the exchanges, trading in a fundamentally different way.

The Nasdaq system does not have specialists as do the NYSE and the Amex. Instead, it has competitive market makers, and electronic screens to let brokers pick the best bid. Nasdaq proponents say several market makers are better than one.

When a customer places an order in Nasdaq, it's always executed with a market maker on the other side of the trade. While many exchange trades are executed between two real customers, with the brokers collecting commissions from both sides but not otherwise taking part, at Nasdaq that's virtually impossible.

Calls for a change in the system have been rejected by brokers seeking to preserve a profit center. For that reason, it's entirely possible to have two customers who want to take the opposite side of the same trade, and never have them get together. Consider a stock with a bid price of

19 3/4 and an asked price of 20 1/4. Both the bid and the asked prices are posted by market makers, unlike the system at the stock exchange where the posted bid and asked prices may represent a specialist bid, or one by a customer.

Assume that a customer of one brokerage firm wants to buy the stock, but only if he can pay $20 a share, or less. A customer of another firm wants to sell it, but only if he can get at least $20. On an exchange, those two orders would be paired off, but not at Nasdaq. With the best bid at $19.75, the sell order at $20 cannot be executed, and won't be posted as an asked price. By the same token, the buy order at $20 is for less than the asked price of $20.25, and will not be executed. It is possible that a market maker would choose to execute one or both of the trades.

In some cases, Nasdaq trades can now be executed electronically, but for many trades, including all larger ones, it remains a telephone market, with brokers using the phone to make deals.

At one time, Nasdaq reported only the bid and asked prices of stocks, not the prices at which trades were actually made. Now for the most important stocks on the system, known as the National Market System stocks, trades are reported throughout the day, just as they are for exchange-listed stocks, and stock tables listed in newspapers show those actual trades.

There are two other lists, of Nasdaq stocks that aren't traded in the National Market System. The National list, and the Supplemental list show only the final bid and asked prices, and the total volume for the day, with no indication of the price at which trades were executed.

When it's said that a stock trades "over-the-counter," it usually means it is traded on Nasdaq, but there is also another, much smaller market that also trades over-the-counter.

PINK SHEETS

The final place where stocks are traded is the "pink sheets," published each day by the National Quotation Bureau in New York. Those prices are almost never published in newspapers, and are so called because of the color of the paper on which the quotes are printed.

These sheets show brokers offering to buy or sell stocks, some of which may be extremely illiquid. They may have wide spreads between the bid and asked prices, or there may be no asked price, just a bid price, for some closely held companies. The prices, unlike those shown on the Nasdaq machines or posted by specialists at exchanges, are not guaranteed. A broker reached by phone may have moved the price away from the quote listed on the sheets that morning.

While many reputable companies are listed on the pink sheets, so too are many "penny stocks" with much more hype than substance. Penny stocks, generally those trading for less than $2 per share, are low priced by definition, but they are seldom inexpensive. Penny stocks are issued by companies with short, sometimes erratic, histories of earnings and revenue performance. They are risky investments since such stocks are usually volatile and can be easily manipulated by brokers, who can benefit by making a market in a little-known company.

FOREIGN TRADING

While stocks are now traded in many countries, in general, the home market almost always remains the most liquid one. IBM, to cite one example, can be bought in London or Tokyo, as well as in New York or Los Angeles. That keeps the market for IBM open longer hours, but in practice, any institution with a really large order in IBM probably would choose to execute it in the United States. If the institution tried to place a large sell order in Europe, before the New York market opened, other traders would wonder what the hurry was. Did that institution know something they don't, perhaps about a negative news announcement that was imminent? Fearing that, the other traders would be likely to reduce the price they'd pay for the shares. Knowing that would happen, the institution is likely to wait until the New York market is open.

An exception is in cases where either taxes or high fixed commissions make it substantially cheaper to trade in another market.

While the most liquid market is in the home country, there are still some substantial foreign stocks traded in this country. Most often, those stocks are traded as American Depository Receipts—each ADR representing a specified number of shares in a foreign company. For many individuals, buying ADRs is the easiest way to buy foreign stocks.

OTHER PRODUCTS

A generation ago, describing the products traded on major securities exchanges was easy. There were stocks, and there were bonds. But a bewildering variety of other products have arisen. Options came first, in the mid-1970s. Options traded over the counter had been around for decades, but exchange-listed options created a booming business. As with many financial innovations, it was pioneered in Chicago. The haughty NYSE did its best to ignore options until it was too late, but the Amex moved in quickly enough to secure a major part of the business.

"Call" options provide the right, but not the obligation, to buy shares of a stock at a specified price until a fixed date, when the options expire. "Put" options are similar, providing the right to sell shares. The buyer of an option has a limited risk; the worst that can happen is that the option will expire worthless and she will lose all the money she has invested. But the seller of the option, known as the "option writer," has virtually unlimited risk if the price of the underlying stock moves rapidly.

When they were introduced, call options rapidly became the cheapest way to speculate in stocks. While an investor must put up 50 percent of the price to buy a share, he can buy options, and control the same number of shares, for much less money. But stock options lost some popularity in the late 1980s, as other financial instruments took some of their luster.

In the mid-1980s stock index futures were introduced at the futures exchanges, with the contract on the Standard & Poor's 500 index, traded on the Chicago Mercantile Exchange, becoming the most popular. A futures contract on the S&P 500 is a way to bet, on low margin, on the direction of stock prices. A buyer of such a futures contract will profit if share prices rise, while a seller will gain if prices fall. Options on futures were quick to follow (see essay on "Futures and Options Trading," herein).

The existence of futures contracts led to index arbitrage, a form of program trading. When stock index futures get too expensive relative to the underlying stocks, a way to profit is to sell the futures contract and buy, in a program trade, the underlying stocks. Since the futures contract is guaranteed to be worth the same as the stocks when the contract expires, on the third Friday of a month, the profit can be locked in then. The gyrations on the third Fridays of March, June, September and December, when the most important contracts expire, came to be known as "triple-witching hours," because index futures, options on index futures and options on individual stocks were all expiring at the same time. Some contracts now expire at the opening price on that Friday, and others at the closing price.

Why Markets Move

by Stephen Dunphy

On a mild Monday afternoon in 1987, former Secretary of the Treasury James Baker got off a plane in Texas. "How'd the market do?" he asked casually as he and his colleagues walked across the tarmac to a waiting car.

"Down five oh eight," came the answer.

"Not bad," said the treasury secretary.

"No, sir, that's down five hundred eight," came the somewhat shellshocked reply.

That day, October 19, 1987, will go down in stock market history. It was Black Monday. It was the crash. It was the largest single decline in the market's history as measured by the Dow Jones industrial average. Larger than the Crash of 1929. But while the "crash" set new standards for magnitude, it further complicated another, deeper question about markets.

Why and how do markets move?

In the wake of Black Monday, the economy held its breath. After all, this was the way the Great Depression began. This was a signal that the long awaited recession would begin soon. The financial press was filled with the stories of how closely the decline mirrored the experience of 1929.

But the dire forecast signaled by the market never happened. The economy slowed somewhat in that last quarter of the year and then resumed a slow growth. The stock market, changed and chastened, soon joined in and started to climb again.

So what does move markets? And how can you cover something that at times defies reason and seems to operate on its own internal logic? If you had an answer to that eternal market question, it would be worth much more than the cost of this book. A number of experts, analysts, seers, charlatans, investors, brokers, journalists, observers and stargazers have been wrestling with that idea for years. None is any closer to an answer.

There are important questions raised about how and why markets are regulated in the wake of Black Monday. The *Wall Street Journal* won a Pulitzer Prize for a series of stories that described how close the stock market came to collapse on that fateful day and the hectic days that followed it.

As a result of the sharp drop in the market and its impact on investors, particularly small investors, there are now some controls on the market. For example, some kinds of computer-generated trading are halted when the stock market advances or declines more than 50 points a day on the Dow Jones average.

Congress continues to study imposing further controls on the market, but faces some opposition from those who feel that too many rules would constrict the market, ending its freedom to respond.

PATTERNS OF THE MARKET

The daily movement up and down is largely a mystery. But there are some general patterns that a journalist should understand before tackling a story about the financial markets and the stock markets in particular.

One point to keep in mind is that the market is made up of people. That means the psychology of the market is important. How people feel about things can, and does, have an impact on the movement of the market. Stand in the gallery of the New York Stock Exchange just before the opening bell and you can almost feel what it's all about. Below you the specialists, who are the assigned market makers in stocks, and traders and clerks are moving about in a dizzying dance. On the walls the clocks begin to flash on and off as the final minute ticks by. The bell sounds and the noise level rises.

The noise level reflects the importance of the psychology of the market—is the noise the roar of enthusiasm for the expected gains of the day or the sound of fear for what might be ahead? Are the bulls running or are the bears growling?

The market, of course, is made up of individual stocks and how those individual stocks perform on a daily basis makes up the collective direction of the market. Some stocks are more important than others. A large company such as IBM can make the market itself move as investors look to IBM as a barometer of the market or the economy as a whole.

The market even has a macabre streak. There is a group of stocks called Death Watch stocks. The chairman of a company may be old and not expected to control the company for long, so the market begins to anticipate that, moving up or down depending on how the market observers view the impending change.

Takeovers also are a key element. When there's takeover talk about a specific company, its share prices may jump. The acquiring company's shares may fall, as investors consider the cost of the takeover. If it appears that airline companies are suddenly good targets for takeover, stock prices in an entire industry may rise. Companies "in play"—to use the market's jargon—at any given time push the entire market up. Northwest Airlines, for example, was selling for about $80 a share in 1989. A takeover battle for it developed, and it finally sold for more than $120 a share. But in the wake of that takeover, investors started looking around at other airlines. That helped to push the Dow Jones transportation average, a group of rail and airline stocks, to record highs. The rest of the market looked at all of this, reasoned that if things looked good in airlines maybe things were fine elsewhere in the economy and the entire market rose.

The result is that tracking the stock market can be a fairly complicated and humbling experience. Just when you think you've got it, the market psychology changes and a new set of circumstances is at work.

MARKET MOVERS

Here are a few of the more common factors that make the stock market move:

Economic indicators.

The market is often fueled by speculation, especially about economic indicators that come out on a regular schedule each week. The market focuses on indicators as conditions change. For a time it was money supply, because that gave a hint as to Federal Reserve policy. Another time the indicator was the trade deficit. Anticipation of a sharp turn in an indicator can be almost as important as the indicator itself. Remember that the market does not like surprises. An indicator higher or lower than expectations can make the stock market move dramatically.

Events.

A crackdown in China, the fall of the Speaker of the House, shifts in the sands of Middle East policy affecting the flow of oil. A shift in Federal Reserve policy. Inaction on key bills in Congress. All these things can affect the stock market.

Rumors

Don't discount them; a rumor can have as much an impact on the market as the most solid report about earnings from IBM. But rumors usually cause only short-term changes in the market as they are discounted or prove true. In the latter case, other factors then come into play.

Program trading

A new factor in the movement of the market is computer-generated program trading, so named for the computer programs that help keep large portfolios in balance. They are usually done by arbitrageurs—stock market traders interested in making money off small discrepancies in market prices.

The Triple Witching days

This is one of the harder concepts for new financial writers to grasp, but it's an important factor in moving the market on the day every three months when time runs out for investors to cash in on three different, stock market-linked investment instruments—futures contracts on stock indexes, options on stock indexes and options on stocks. The impact of triple witching was reduced by controls imposed by the Securities and Exchange Commission after the 1987 crash.

Stock indexes are based on one of several leading stock-market indicators, such as the Standard & Poor's 500. Traders can buy futures and options on the indices—for instance, on a block of one of each of the Standard & Poor's 500 shares. Futures are an obligation to buy or sell that block at a fixed price on a set date. Options give the right, but no obligation, to buy or sell at a set price on the given date. It's a way of protecting yourself against swings in stock prices—and a device for speculating, too. Both index futures and options, as well as options on individual stocks, expire on the same day four times a year. Since many investors own index options and futures, on expiration day many will try to liquidate their positions at the same time. The action gets hectic, especially if there is an excess of either buyers or sellers in the market.

Moves of 30 to 50 points in the market have been common on those days.

Profit Taking

This is usually the reason given for small declines in the market after a few days of increases. The thinking here is that investors sell some of the stock that has gone up, taking their profits out of the market. The opposite of profit taking is often called simply bargain hunting, trolling around the bottom of a market looking for stocks that may be rising. Enough bargain hunting can push stocks higher.

Window Dressing

Much of the stock market—especially the New York Stock Exchange—is in the hands of institutional investors, big pension funds, mutual funds and the like. Each quarter, the professional investors like to put the best face possible on the portfolio of stocks they hold. Some buying and selling of stocks is done in order to accomplish this. Stock movements usually are relatively small.

TIPS AND HINTS

Keep an eye on the differences in the movements of stocks within various markets. Blue chip stocks—that's the Dow Jones industrial average and a few other large-company stocks—can be down, but over-the-counter stocks could be gaining. Over-the-counter stocks are usually smaller companies and more interesting, and more accessible, to individual investors. As a result, good local stories can be developed using smaller stocks and how well they performed against the Big Board stocks.

Another area of stock market analysis is the difference between fundamental analysis and technical analysis. Each has its own devotees who think they are most nearly correct in describing how and why the market moves.

Fundamental analysis looks at the individual stocks that make up the market, imposes a scenario for the economy over that viewpoint and comes up with a view—the fundamentals—of how or why the stock market might move.

A fundamental analyst might look at the profits expected from corporations, consider inflation rates and the Gross National Product of the country and conclude that stocks are a good investment. Those kinds of reports, frequently published by the investment house that the financial analysts work for, can have an impact on the market when they turn bullish or bearish.

Technical analysis looks at the numbers. When dealing with the huge numbers involved in the market—millions of shares traded each day, thousands of investors—the numbers can have their own internal logic. The temptation is to dismiss the technical analysts because of the complexities of their calculations. Momentum, projections, moving six-month averages, oversold markets and the like can sound like a foreign language. But the serious practitioners of technical analysis can provide insight into why markets move, when and how they do.

Tip. Watch out for the charlatans here. Any number of people have said that they hold the key to the market and can predict its movements. While some of them have enjoyed some short-lived success with their methods, all of them eventually have been caught by the market forces. The stock market is simply too complex, too human, an entity to predict with any long-term consistency.

There are other markets to consider beyond the stock market. Two key ones these days are foreign currencies and commodities.

Many of the same factors that move the stock market—speculation, news events, fear and greed—exist in these markets as well. But there are some differences.

Take currencies, especially the dollar. More than $150 billion a day changes hands in the world's money markets, much of that in dollars. Before 1973, there was not much of a market in currencies because the U.S. and other countries maintained a fixed exchange rate for money. The dollar's volatility increased in 1973, when the United States stopped trying to maintain a fixed value for the dollar and allowed its value to "float" against other currencies. Since then, a series of economic crises has increased its gyrations, including the oil-price rises of the 1970's, rapid inflation and the growing imbalance in world trade.

Trading in currencies around the world has three sides to it: governmental, commercial and speculation. On the government side, countries try to maintain a value of their currency that reflects national policies.

For example, the U.S. joined with other nations in 1985 to push the value of the dollar lower. The trade deficit in the U.S. was getting out of hand and it was the only way the governments could see to get it under control. A lower value for currency makes U.S. products more competitive in world markets. When the Boeing Co. sells a new 747 to Japan Air Lines, the airline pays in yen. In 1985, the airline had to get 200 yen for each dollar to pay the bill. In 1989 it only had to get 125 yen for each dollar. In effect, the price is cheaper.

The Boeing deal shows how currency exchanges work in the commercial world. With billions of dollars in trade going on around the world, the deals have to be converted from one currency to another. As a result, banks frequently are in the market to buy and sell dollars for their business accounts.

SPECULATION

Just as in any market, a chance to guess which way the value of the dollar will move brings traders to the market, if only to make money on that movement. These speculators at times are accused of frustrating the designs of central governments that are trying to control the price of their currency.

It all can get very frustrating for the governments and confusing to all but the most intense watchers of the market. Here for example, is one way life has become more complex for the Federal Reserve and other central banks. Other nations are worried about inflationary pressures in their economies. If they tighten money and raise interest rates, that will strengthen their currencies and weaken the dollar. But Japan, West Germany and Britain, just like the U.S., are trying to work out the currency problem without a recession.

If "the Fed" eases money enough to bring the dollar down to its supposedly proper level, it could very well increase domestic inflation pressures. So there's likely to be more intervention in the foreign-exchange market. But that can cause problems for domestic money management, too. When the Fed intervenes in the foreign exchange market, it puts dollars into the economy. Since this is obviously inflationary, the Federal Reserve is likely to "sterilize" the transaction by selling an equivalent amount of Treasury bonds in the market and mopping up dollars.

But there's no easy way out. Selling government bonds puts downward pressure on interest rates. But lower interest rates could make foreign investors move funds to Japanese yen or West German marks where rates might be a bit higher. They sell dollars to do that, which in turn forces the dollar lower.

Confusing? You bet. New financial journalists may think it odd to be trading something like money. But if you think of money as simply a commodity like wheat or corn, it makes it easier. And that is what it is in many situations—simply a commodity to be used to either make some money or close a deal across international boundaries.

And that brings us to one final market to discuss. Commodities. What makes markets in commodities move up or down?

This is at one and the same time simple and complex. Again, you have to look at the two sides of a market in a commodity like wheat or pork bellies or gold. Most trading in commodities is done on a futures contract (an agreement to buy a set amount of a commodity at set price at a set time in the future). For farmers growing wheat, it helps them lock in what they'll get for their crops. They can hedge by selling a contract on part of the crop and let the market determine the price for the rest.

But as with the dollar, there are speculators in this market as well who have no intention of taking a load of wheat. The futures contract has a value that changes with such factors as weather and government actions. A drought in Australia, a country which grows wheat for export, can push the price of American wheat higher because of the laws of supply and demand. If the demand for wheat is high and the supply low, the price rises. It rises for the futures contract as well.

Government action also plays a key part in commodity trading since most commodities are international these days. A crackdown in China, reflecting instability in the government, can affect wheat prices, since China is a major buyer of wheat on international markets.

There are hundreds of commodities traded in the U.S. and around the world. And the reasons why the markets in each of those commodities move can vary, making it difficult to make any general statements about markets. But commodities may be one of the last places where the law of supply and demand really works. It's a starting place for a financial journalist who wants to know more about commodity markets—anything that affects either the supply (weather, strikes, coups) or the demand (a glut, a slowing economy, political unrest) can and will affect prices.

Even commodity trading has become complicated in recent years with the introduction of futures contracts based not on any tangible commodity like wheat but on how various indexes of the stock market will move.

It's a complicated and tricky business (see Futures and Options Trading, herein). Suffice it to say, the new futures contracts have the power to move markets since sophisticated investors will sell stocks to buy futures contracts and vice versa.

How does it all come together? Take a look at this technical account of a typical day in the market near the end of a quarter.

NEW YORK- The Dow industrials closed lower Friday—off 18 points at 2440 although the market was able to pull back from a sharp 30 point drop early in the day.

While both index-arbitrage and outright selling—some of the latter apparently computer-executed—were largely responsible for the initial free fall in prices, bargain-hunting and some end-of-quarter institutional "markups" were cited as contributing to the afternoon rebound.

"Markups" represent end-of-quarter buying by money managers done to enhance portfolio valuations on quarterly reports to clients and mutual-fund shareholders.

At the close, the Dow stood at 2440.06, down 18.21, while declines outpaced advances on the Big Board by a moderate, 881 to 647 margin, in stark contrast to an early, lopsided ratio of 5 losers for every gainer.

The market hesitated for a few moments after the opening, then succumbed to what traders termed an unsettling replay of Thursday's malicious market, which swept the Dow to a 46–point loss—the second greatest of the year.

Thursday's debacle was built upon growing concerns about a weakening economy, upward pressures on interest rates overseas, sagging corporate earnings projections coupled with actual announced shortfalls, and perceptions of deteriorating technical underpinnings in the market itself.

Index-arbitrage executions were obvious, traders said. With S&P 500 and other key futures selling considerably below "fair value" against cash stocks in early trading, the opportunity to buy deflated futures, sell cash stock, and pocket the spread was undeniable, they said.

But some observers also detected asset-reallocation sell-programs, which represent computerized executions designed to significantly, and almost instantaneously, alter the mix of big institutional portfolios.

Evidence suggested there was a move from stocks to bonds. Indeed, as stocks bottomed after the first bout of selling, the U.S. long bond—which is hardly immune from a global environment of higher interest rates—was up almost half a point. Bonds also rose on Thursday despite severe losses in stocks.

Analysts said that, as anticipation increases that the Federal Reserve will have to ease monetary policy in order to sidestep a potential recession late this year or in 1990, a move from stocks to bonds makes sense. As interest rates ease, bond prices must rise—perhaps sharply—while the stock market must still wade through a spate of corporate earnings that look to be more sluggish than anticipated earlier in the second quarter.

Some traders noted, however, that the price free fall of the first half hour terminated precisely as the Commerce Department released its report on May factory orders, which showed a 2.5 percent decline under April's level—dead on Street expectations. Observers said that, had orders been much weaker than anticipated, the market's losses Friday could have been far worse.

But as selling finally relented in late morning, so did volume, and bargain-hunters were left the luxury of bidding up, at their leisure, the depressed targets of morning liquidation and futures-related selling.

Traders said they did not have a clear idea of how much "marking up" was actually conducted by domestic pension funds, mutual funds, and the like, but it was probably a factor in the afternoon rally.

Got that? Good luck.

Futures and Options Trading

by Ovid Abrams

The electronic clock on the wall shows 9:24 A.M. The microseconds are whizzing by. Men and women wearing colored jackets with name tags pinned to their lapels take up their positions on the steps of this octagon-shaped trading pit. Note pad and pencil in hand, they're gazing at television screens and monitors suspended from the ceiling and walls. There's scarcely any motion, except for people passing notes. Anxious as expectant fathers, they wait for the opening bell to ring. It's the signal that chaos is imminent.

The clock flashes 9:25 A.M. The bell rings again and pandemonium breaks out. Everyone goes into action. The noise rises to a near deafening level. Traders begin screaming buy and sell orders, each person trying to shout louder than the next to attract the attention of a buyer or seller. Hands flailing, fingers flashing, heads bobbing up and down, they rise to their toes to gain a little more height and a little more attention. Young men with slips of paper dart between phone banks and the people who are screaming in the trading pit.

Welcome to the arcane world of commodity trading, where people routinely sell what they don't own and buy things they never expect to receive. This scene is the copper pit, or ring, at New York's Commodity Exchange (Comex) one of the nation's largest commodity futures exchanges. Before this day is over, more than 8,000 copper futures contracts representing 100,000 tons of the red metal valued at over $300 million are traded here.

Trading is by "open outcry," which means that brokers shout the price at which they would either buy (bid) or sell (offer) the commodity. Open outcry operates on the principle of a public auction. Under this system, the price of a commodity is known to all those present at any given time. With business being done in the open within earshot of everyone present, current prices should reflect all known factors of supply, demand and other information pertinent to that product. Prices change every time a trade is made. Sell orders push prices down. Buy orders cause them to increase.

Open outcry trading is used on virtually all futures exchanges in the U.S. but exchanges in Europe and the Far East often employ other trading systems. On some exchanges, typically in London and Tokyo, bid and ask prices of commodities are fixed by brokers sitting at a table and matching their "buy" and "sell" orders. A broker who is willing to pay the highest price gets the trade, while low bidders are priced out of the market. Exchange rules stipulate that a broker can't bid below another broker's high bid or offer a price that is above someone's low offer.

Futures trading is also taking place at more than a dozen locations on this trading floor, which is shared by five exchanges trading in futures and options on metals, crude oil, currencies, stock index and other products. Commodity futures and options trading also takes place at other exchanges in New York, Chicago, Winnipeg, Montreal, London, Hong Kong, Tokyo, Singapore, Sydney and other major cities throughout the world. Gold is traded virtually 24 hours a day, with markets in different time zones complementing each other—New York, Sydney, Hong Kong and London.

In the U.S., there are 11 futures exchanges. The Chicago Board of Trade (CBOT) is the nation's oldest futures exchange, founded in 1848, and now the largest, accounting for 47.5 percent of all futures contracts and 53.5 percent of the total futures options traded in the U.S. in 1988. More than 140 different types of futures contracts have been approved by the Commodity Futures Trading Commission (CFTC) for trading.

It's not unusual for exchanges to trade similar contracts. For example, both the Comex and the CBOT trade contracts for gold (100 oz) and silver (5,000 oz).

HOW FUTURES TRADING WORKS

What appears to be chaos to an outsider is actually one of the most efficient market systems, some economists say. Futures trading involves buying or selling commodities at current prices, for delivery on some future date. The contractual price can't change, regardless of how much the actual price of the physical commodity may rise or fall when the delivery date arrives. For this reason, about 75 percent of all futures transactions are liquidated before the delivery date comes around, particularly if the price turns unfavorable. Actually, most people who trade commodity futures and options are speculators seeking to profit from market volatility.

Suppose you are a speculator and you believe corn prices will rise because of a drought in the corn belt. You buy 10 corn futures contracts with a small deposit now for delivery in six months. (This means you are now "long" on corn). You sit tight and watch corn prices go up. But you must remember to sell back those 10 corn futures before the last trading day, or you will be forced to cough up the balance of cash and take delivery of 10 corn contracts (50,000 bushels). If the price falls lower than the purchase price, you must meet "margin calls" (pay an additional deposit) or liquidate (sell) those 10 corn contracts at a loss. If corn prices rise, you liquidate the 10 contracts at a profit.

If, on the other hand, you forecast a decline in corn prices you would sell 10 corn futures at today's high price (selling short), for delivery in six months. If corn prices increase rather than decline as you had expected, you have a problem. You are losing money and you have two options: either meet the margin call and wait in the hope that prices will decline again or liquidate (sell) the position at a loss. However, if the price should fall lower than your contract price, you're in the money. Since you sold 10 corn contracts which you didn't own in the first place, you must offset the position by purchasing 10 corn futures contracts.

THE GROWTH OF FUTURES TRADING

Although the concept of commodity trading is several centuries old, futures trading began in earnest in the U.S. just over 100 years ago. Commodity futures trading is now an integral part of the world's financial network. It involves not only commodities such as pork bellies and wheat, but also currencies, stock indices, precious metals, base metals, livestock, interest rates, crude oil and a vast array of other products. In other words, futures trading doesn't only apply to commodities which can be physically delivered, but also to nontangibles such as the inflation index.

Until the early 1960s commodity futures trading was chiefly confined to farmers, grain elevator operators and a handful of commodity brokers and speculators. Farmers and grain merchants bought futures contracts (a hedge) to safeguard the value of their inventory, or lock in the price of their product. Now trading in futures and options occupies a prominent position in the portfolios of aggressive investors and portfolio managers.

In 1960, the total number of futures contracts traded (trading volume) on all exchanges in the United States was a mere 3.9 million contracts. Since then futures trading has grown in geometric proportions. In 1970, the total annual trading volume reached 13.6 million contracts. The trading volume then rose to 92.1 million contracts in 1980 and rose to more than 250 million contracts in 1990.

The explosive increase in trading volume can be attributed both to increased futures trading activity and to the increase in futures and options contracts traded. Previously, futures trading was confined mainly to agricultural commodities traded principally at exchanges in Chicago and New York. Now, there are eight groups of commodities futures: agricultural commodities, precious metals, nonprecious metals, interest rates, equity indices, energy products, foreign currency/index, and a miscellaneous category.

Banks, for instance, need to maintain a foreign currency trading department to hedge their foreign currency transactions. Oil companies trade on the futures exchanges to hedge their inventory; portfolio managers buy stock and bond indices futures contracts to hedge their portfolios of stocks and bonds; and jewelers buy precious metals futures to hedge their inventory.

OPTIONS ON FUTURES

For risk-averse investors, or those who lack the financial means to trade futures contracts, there are options to most futures contracts which can be traded at virtually no risk for a fraction of what it cost to trade futures contracts. Options on futures offer a lot more flexibility to the buyer or seller, providing the same leverage as futures contracts but at a much lower cost and with less risk of financial loss.

With an option on futures, the investor actually buys the right to purchase a specific futures contract at a specified price. (This, in effect, is an option on an option, since a futures contract is an option to buy the physical commodity.) The worst that can happen is that the option expires worthless. There are no margin calls involved. If the price moves in your favor, then you would exercise the option at the "strike price" agreed to when the option was purchased.

For example, if gold is now trading at $400 an ounce and you believe the metal's price will rise to $450 by December, you could buy a $410 December call option for $670. The option gives you the right to buy a gold futures contract (100 troy ounces) at $410 an ounce for a total of $41,000, at any time before December. If the price of gold goes to $480 in October, you can exercise your option to buy the gold futures contract at $410 an ounce, or you can sell the option at a profit since your option is now "in the money." Your profit before deducting brokers' fees is ($480 − $410) × 100 − $670 = $6,330. If the price of gold had declined instead below $400 and remained there until the end of December, the option would expire worthless. Your risk or loss is limited to $670, the option's cost.

Options on futures have gained considerable popularity because of the relatively low risk involved and the small investment required. Options trading on commodity futures began in earnest in the U.S. in 1982. (Trading in stock options has been going on for more than a decade prior to that.) In 1987, total volume of futures options was 2.8 million contracts. It swelled to nearly 50 million contracts by 1989. Options are now being traded on most types of commodity futures, including metals, grains, currencies and stock index futures.

REGULATION OF FUTURES AND OPTIONS TRADING

Futures and options trading can be manipulated by unscrupulous individuals—both by brokers and persons who are wealthy enough to acquire large positions. The most notorious example involved the billionaire Hunt brothers, who made their fortune in Texas oil. They were convicted for manipulating the silver market in the late 1970s and early 1980s. Silver prices soared from $6 an ounce in early 1979 to $50 in January 1980 as the Hunt brothers bought silver futures in hopes of making huge profits. But before the spring of 1980, silver plunged to $10 an ounce. The Hunts faced billion dollar losses.

The primary watchdog of commodities trading is the exchange where trading occurs. The exchange is a membership organization which provides the facilities for its members to conduct business. An exchange doesn't own or sell any commodity, but it's the venue for trading. To trade, a broker or trader must purchase a seat, which often costs in the six-figure range. Each futures exchange makes its own rules governing its internal operations. However, the exchanges must also meet government guidelines enforced by the Commodity Futures Trading Commission (CFTC), which is the ultimate regulatory authority for commodities and options futures trading.

Regulation takes place at several levels. Brokers organizations censure their members caught in irregularities; exchanges make sure that their members adhere to their rules, and monitor the solvency of brokers and firms whose members trade futures and options; and the CFTC maintains a constant surveillance of the activities of exchanges and their members. The Federal Bureau of Investigation has been active in investigations in cases where brokers have allegedly manipulated the execution of clients' orders and made huge profits for themselves.

IMPORTANT INFLUENCES

The computer age is beginning to catch up with the futures industry, threatening to permanently change the way commodity futures are traded.

Actually, computers have been in use for years in commodity board rooms where traders and analysts employ sophisticated programs to develop trading strategies. The last areas where computers have penetrated is the exchange floor and the transmission and execution of trades. Old timers view any form of computer trading with suspicion, maintaining that open outcry and the phone order system provide the fairest method of doing business. Not so, say the computer-trading advocates. They argue that computer trading can't be easily manipulated by unscrupulous traders, as often occurs under the present system.

Computers, of course, will be used in any global system of commodity trading linking exchanges in a 24–hour commodity futures and options market. Two independent systems have been developed by the world's two largest commodity exchanges, the CBOT and the Merc. The Merc's system called Globex, developed jointly with Reuters Holdings P.L.C., is an electronic trading system that can do all of the steps between receiving an order and executing a trade to informing the client. The rival CBOT system, called Aurora, can replicate the open outcry system on a computer screen. It, too, can link world markets.

HOW TO COVER FUTURES TRADING

This beat requires a certain amount of specialization and it's wise to familiarize yourself with the markets before you write your first story. It's especially important to learn the basic fundamentals of various commodities—the basics of supply and demand and the economic and political factors that normally influence these markets.

For example, the weather report says there's a major drought in the grain belt of the USSR which can lead to a poor crop. This means the Russians will probably need to import a larger quantity of grain from the West. That assumption could trigger a rally in the grain market, which would mean higher exports for western producers and higher grain prices. In turn, this probably means the Russians will sell more gold or platinum to pay their bills. Consequently, precious metals prices could decline. Can you see the chain reaction from just one simple report on the weather? This is a likely scenario, but it won't always happen this way because there are always other factors influencing the market. In other words, there are no set rules and "A" doesn't always lead to "B."

The first fundamental fact you'll realize is that markets tend to react in sympathy to one another. Also, markets sometimes react differently to the same news. For example, the U.S. Treasury Secretary talks about an increase in government spending. The stock market may react to the news by assuming it will lead to higher inflation. So, the stock market might decline. And investors may sell their dollar holdings, since a dollar buys less in an inflationary economy, leading to a decline of the dollar in the foreign currency markets. High inflation and a weak dollar are good news for gold, so precious metals prices will rally because gold, silver, platinum and palladium prices often move in the same direction. Fears of inflation can send stock and bond prices tumbling. All, or none, of these things may happen in reaction to the Secretary's speech.

While supporters of the futures industry regard it as the most efficient market, the system is subject to abuse. Commodity prices generally fluctuate during the trading session, due to brokers placing large buy or sell orders and news affecting the market. Thus, the price at any given moment is supposed to reflect all known facts about that commodity. However, it's not unusual for brokers and traders to start their own rumors in order to influence the market in their favor. Rumors of a strike in South Africa, for example, could trigger a rally in precious metals.

You should always try to find out what's behind any unusual price move in any commodity. The system of open outcry is not immune to fraud. Brokers sometimes work in collusion to manipulate the market. For example, a broker has a large order from Big Oil Co. to buy crude oil on the New York Mercantile Exchange. The broker tells other traders about the order. They know that when the order hits the trading pit crude oil will rally. Before placing the order, these brokers buy crude oil futures for their own accounts. The Big Oil Co. order hits and crude oil prices rise. The brokers sell their own futures contracts at a profit. That is why you should try to get to the root of any unusual commodity price movement. You may wind up with a juicy story.

Also, you should be on the lookout for scams. This industry is awash with them. Beware of the commodity broker based in Miami or Denver making cold calls to farmers in Illinois offering to sell them titanium sponge stored in Rotterdam. The company that advertises on late night cable TV offering to sell precious metals at a discount, or with only an initial down payment, providing that the metal be held in storage for investors, can also turn out to be phony. When any of these happen, bells should go off to let you know that something isn't quite right.

There's a reason behind any unusual price move, either up or down. You should be vigilant and try to find out what's going on. Some price moves are caused by a market squeeze. Every commodity has what is called "visible stocks," or inventory in the exchange warehouses. Suppose Comex had only 100,000 ounces of silver in its warehouse and there are outstanding silver futures totaling 150,000 ounces. This means that if all of those persons who are "long" on silver try to take delivery, the exchange wouldn't be able to deliver. This is a potential squeeze situation and silver prices can react upward.

How do you find out if someone is trying to squeeze the market? Well, you should have news sources or contacts in the industry. Try to establish contact with floor traders and brokers at the different exchanges, analysts, futures and options marketing personnel at brokerage houses and on the exchanges, commodity fund managers, research organizations, trade publications, trade organizations, the Futures Industry Association (FIA) and the CFTX. Besides, you should try to cultivate a healthy working relationship with commodities specialists at the various government departments: Agriculture, Commerce, Bureau of Mines, Treasury, etc. Some of these departments publish authoritative reports that have an impact on the markets. Get on the mailing list. Most of these publications are free.

Here is a partial list of likely sources:

1. A speculator who has lost money.
2. A broker who went bust. (This happens frequently. Some people rent or lease seats on the exchange and trade for their own account.)
3. Programmers who design trading strategies. Find out their track record.
4. Regulatory agencies. Talk with attorneys and enforcement agents about pending cases.
5. The Washington-based FIA publishes a wealth of statistics about futures and options trading volume and other information about exchanges. The PR person there can be of much help as a quick reference.
6. Attend dinners, seminars, trade shows, conventions, meetings and other events staged throughout the year by various groups representing different aspects of the industry. Become part of the crowd and know the members on a first name basis. This is your passport to great story leads.
7. Research analysts are a good source of information. Their job is to constantly study the factors influencing the market and to make oral and written commentaries. They also make trading recommendations for the markets in which they specialize. For market forecast, analysts are a better source than traders, who have a vested interest and can be biased, or technical analysts, who interpret price charts and give short-term forecasts and commentaries.

You shouldn't be without story ideas. There's always something going on in futures and options trading. You will find that many marketing and public relations executives are willing to help you, because they need you to provide a conduit for information they wish to get to the public. Sometimes after sifting out the pulp, you get some good story leads.

Exchange personnel aren't allowed to make trade recommendations or price forecasts. Still, they can be good sources of historical information or rumors. Exchanges also sponsor seminars and participate in trade shows.

THE COMMODITIES STORY

Coverage of commodities has changed. Gone are the days when journalists reported hog prices as if there were no speculators in the markets. At one time, you could assume that buyers really wanted delivery. But no more. Reporting about commodities is now more about trends or events. It's often about economic reactions rather than farming realities. Of course, you shouldn't lose sight of the real purpose of the markets, but your job only begins with the news of the day. You need to go farther and delve into the reasons for the day's activity. Every price move has a story behind it; it's your duty to find it and answer some simple questions: Who's losing or making money? How does trading in international markets, say London or Singapore, affect prices in Chicago or New York? What's the market saying about the economy or the dollar?

Be sure to get brochures published by the exchanges, brokerage houses and the FIA. You may also buy "Commodity Trading Manual" a comprehensive text on the industry published by the Chicago Board of Trade. This manual also contains the specifications for the various futures contracts.

THINGS TO KNOW

No reporter should begin the job without understanding a few basic concepts. They are:

Floor Trader or Local. A person who buys and sells futures contracts or options on the exchange floor for his/her own account and is forbidden to trade on behalf of customers. They are speculators providing liquidity to the market by their willingness to assume risk.

Broker. A member of the futures exchange who executes orders for clients for a fee, or commission. He also can trade for his own account, but the first responsibility is to fill customers' orders. Some futures exchanges require brokers to execute customers orders before their own, to prevent a broker from taking advantage of a potentially profitable situation ahead of clients.

Futures Contract. A legally binding contract, which obligates two parties to perform: the buyer to accept and the seller to deliver a specified quantity of a commodity on/or by a specific date, at the price agreed upon when the contract was made. This takes effect the moment a broker or trader indicates the acceptance of a bid or offer.

Option. A legally binding agreement that gives the holder the right but doesn't obligate her to buy or sell a specified quantity of a commodity on or by a specific date, at a price agreed upon at the time the option was purchased. The liability of the person purchasing the option is limited to the cost of the option.

Futures Exchange. The physical facilities where futures contracts are traded. The exchange doesn't buy or sell anything, but merely provides the facilities for the business to be conducted. Brokers, Account Executives or Financial Consultants who take customers' orders at the various brokerage firms aren't required to purchase seats on the exchange, but they must register with the Commodity Futures Trading Commission (CFTC) and the various exchanges where they trade.

Margin. A deposit or good faith money that clients are required to deposit with their brokers before they can trade futures.

Contract. The unit of measurement used in determining the amount of a commodity to be traded. Thus 5,000 bushels of wheat, 100 troy ounces of gold, 15,000 pounds of live hogs, 12,500,000 Japanese yen, $100,000 in Treasury bonds, 20 tons of soybean meal, 42,000 gallons of #2 Heating oil are all examples of commodity contracts traded on future exchanges.

Hedge. Selling futures contracts in amounts comparable to stocks of the physical commodity held in inventory. A person can also hedge a long or short position in the futures market by taking an opposite position in the options market.

Hedging works this way: A wheat farmer expects to reap 100,000 bushels of wheat six months hence. Currently wheat prices are high and he suspects prices will fall by the time he is ready to bring his wheat to the market. To make sure he will earn today's high prices six months from now, he orders his broker to sell 20 wheat contracts of 5,000 bushels each (for a total of 100,000 bushels), for delivery in six months, on the Kansas City Board of Trade—one of the nation's commodity futures exchanges. The farmer is protected against any price decline. However, should the price of wheat increase before he is ready to make the delivery, he is obligated to make the delivery at the lower contractual price.)

Leverage. One of the unique aspects of futures and options trading. It allows someone with a relatively small deposit to lay claim to an asset valued at several times the deposit. For example, for a margin of about $5,000 an investor can buy one gold futures contract, (100 ozs) valued at about $40,000, at New York's Commodity Exchange.

The Bond Market

by Craig Torres

Bonds. The word falls with a monosyllabic thud. But take heart! The bond beat is one of the most interesting and important components of any business page. You'll frequently write about U.S. fiscal and monetary policy. And you'll have to keep track of the major foreign economies as well.

Usually coverage breaks down into a few specific areas. There's the Treasury market: one of the largest and most liquid securities markets in the world. It's also the most important fixed income market: It's here that the Federal Reserve executes monetary policy. By buying or selling Treasury notes and bonds from banks and securities dealers, the Fed changes the level of money in the banking system. The Fed governs economic activity through the cost of money—that is, interest rates. When money is dear, interest rates are high. High interest rates slow the economy as consumers and corporations become more reluctant to expand their economic activity. Conversely, when credit is abundant, businesses and consumers are more likely to borrow and spend as interest rates fall.

Of course, the world economy, and the Fed's role in it, is vastly more complex than the simplified explanation above. The important point to remember is that you're covering an interest rate market. That's the Federal Reserve's chief monetary policy tool. Changes in interest rates in this market have a direct impact on the global economy, and other financial markets. Rates on corporate bonds, and mortgage-backed securities, for example, are affected by rate changes in the Treasury market.

When you read about the federal deficit, you might wonder where the government gets money to spend that it doesn't collect through taxes? Like any citizen, the government simply borrows. It does this by issuing debt—most commonly, Treasury securities. Since Treasury debt has the full faith and backing of the United States, it's viewed as one of the safest investments in the world.

TYPES OF SECURITIES

The Treasury issues many different types of securities, but the market is principally Treasury bills, Treasury notes and bonds. Treasury bills are discount securities. That is, they're sold at a price less than their face value at maturity. The interest earned is the appreciation of the security to its face value. Treasury bills are short-term maturities, and the common issues are 3–month, 6–month and 12–month or "year" bills.

Notes and bonds are coupon securities. Notes and bonds pay a biannual interest payment. And the owner also receives the face value at maturity. In the old days, the note and bond holders would clip paper coupons off their Treasury securities and send them to the government to receive an interest payment. The term "coupon" stuck, even though the Treasury makes most of its note and bond payments electronically. Bonds are securities with a maturity of over 10 years. Notes are securities with a maturity falling between one year and ten years. So get used to the terms; 3–month, 6–month and year bills; 10–year notes and 30–year bonds, also called long bonds.

The smallest price change on a bond or note is 1/32 of one percent of the bond's face value. Dealers refer to 32/32 as one "point." Sometimes, dealers will shave trades to 1/64th. But normally, traders will talk in terms of a "tick," or a 1/32, even though a tick may vary according to the face value of a bond. The value of a 1/32 price change on $1 million of notes or bonds is $312.50. Bond and note prices are quoted in a percentage of face value. A price of 96, for example, means 96 percent of some face amount. So a quote of 96 on $1,000 face amount of bonds means $960.00. The price may read, "96.25," meaning 96 and 25/32. Sometimes you will see a plus sign notation after a quote, like this: 96.00 + . Plus signs stand for a 1/64, so the quote is 96 1/64. Typically, quotes are listed as bid and ask—that is, the buy and sell price. For example, 96.25 to 96.28 means a dealer will buy the bond at 96 25/32, while his selling price is 96 28/32. Most traders focus on the bid side of the quote, or the buying price. The most volatile and widely watched security in the Treasury market is the long bond. Long bonds frequently thrash through a one-point range on a given day.

The smallest price change on a T-bill is a basis point, or 1/100th of one percent. A basis point's dollar value varies according to the bill's maturity, and face amount.

Bills are quoted in terms of yield to maturity. A bill quote might read, "9.10 pct, down .01 pct."

The majority of trading in the Treasury market is conducted by investment houses around the world—and around the clock. Traders in Tokyo stay up all night to trade the New York market. And vice versa. When the New York market closes at around 5 P.M. EST, Tokyo's Treasury market is about to open. The London market follows the close in Tokyo, and hands the market back to New York again at around 8:30 A.M. EST. In the institutional market, the smallest trade is $1 million. About $102 billion in Treasury securities changed hands on a given day in 1988. Compare that with the New York Stock Exchange's $1.3 billion volume in 1988. The bond market is big. And wild. As one dealer noted, "The economic forces affecting the market are so great that it's like having two massive weights to balance. Tilt one just a bit, and the whole thing starts swinging."

COVERING BONDS

Like all good craftsmen, a journalist must have some good tools. Here are some essentials for the bond beat:

Sources

Call up the Public Securities Association in New York and ask them to send you the primary dealers list they publish every year. This handy booklet lists the names of traders and their phone numbers at all of the primary dealers. Primary dealers are an elite group of firms that serve as underwriters in Treasury auctions. The Fed monitors this market for the Treasury, so each dealer has a close relationship with the central bank. In fact, the Fed buys and sells securities through these dealers when it attempts to change bank reserves in some way. Don't start calling traders right away. We'll go into source development in a minute.

Call up the large New York commercial and investment banks and get the names of their capital markets economists. Also, get the names of their bond market analysts.

Bond Calendar

Bond dealers publish a monthly calendar listing ultra-important information for your beat. These calenders list auction dates of Treasury securities and release dates and times of key economic data. Try to get a calender that lists the scheduled speeches of key officials, such as the chairman of the Federal Reserve. When testifying before Congress, for example, the Fed Chairman may shed some light on the course of monetary policy. Usually, the firm's capital markets economist puts the calendar together. Call several of them, introduce yourself, and get on their mailing lists. Ask them to send you their newsletters as well. These contain an in-depth commentary on the previous week's markets and economic events.

Quote Screen

You will need access to some kind of information system that will show you changes in the price of bonds and related markets. The major financial wire services will promptly furnish you with one.

Items at the Bottom of the Tool Box

You will need a calculator occasionally. And call up First Boston Company in New York and ask them to send you the *Handbook of Securities of the United States Government and Federal Agencies*. This is published biannually. It's a handy guide to the market, and it contains a wrap-up of market activity from the two previous years.

Get a couple of books on the bond market. A useful reference is the *Handbook of Fixed Income Securities* (Fabozzi and Pollack, eds.). William Greider's *Secrets of the Temple* provides a look inside the Federal Reserve. The importance of reading up constantly on the market cannot be overstated.

Now, you're ready to hit the Street. But first here are some maxims to memorize:

1. Bond prices move inversely to interest rates. When bond prices go up, interest rates fall. And vice versa. Memorize this. Write it on your desk if you must. It's the concept of yield to maturity.
2. The nemesis of a fixed rate bond is inflation. If inflation is rising bond prices are falling. Treasury bonds deliver a fixed rate of return which can be eaten away to nothing by rising inflation
3. The Treasury market usually reacts to or anticipates some economic event. It immediately factors in changes in the economic scenario. If the U.S. decided to trim its budget a year from now, bond prices would react as soon as the news hit the wires. Not a year from now.

GETTING THROUGH THE STORY

It's 8:00 A.M. EST. The Treasury market opens officially in an hour. First, determine if there's any important national economic news or speeches by key officials scheduled for the day. Read your calendar. Many key economic reports, such as the merchandise trade report, are released at 8:30 A.M.

Next, scour the morning press for any developments on the inflation, fiscal or monetary policy fronts. Remember, the Treasury market moves principally on supply and demand and inflation concerns. Fiscal policy news—items dealing with the government's budget—may change the supply or inflation scenarios. Monetary policy news can change expectations about the trend in interest rates and inflation.

Typically, the bond market is monomaniacal. It follows one concern —such as the price of oil—for an hour . . . or a week. The key thing to remember is that there's usually some external event that will set a trend for the market.

The previous day's bond columns in the The *Wall Street Journal* or The *New York Times* will tell you what the bond market's mania was yesterday. Never assume that it will be the same today.

After you've scoured the papers, read the overnight stories on the Tokyo and London markets if you have access to a wire service. If the market is focusing on commodity price inflation, check out the closing price of oil and precious metals in London. Are they sharply higher than New York's close the day before? Then bonds will probably open sharply lower in New York—if they're still following commodity prices. You may also want to look at the opening prices in the New York metals markets for some hint about inflation concerns.

Perhaps the bond market is following currencies. Has the dollar been rising or falling abruptly this morning? That should affect bonds. You can easily get currency quotes off a wire service screen. The dollar can register inflation expectations as strongly as bond prices. In fact, this brings up a tip: price movements in stocks, bonds and currencies are often linked to a similar economic trend or event, though they may move in different directions.

Finally, is there any news of financial distress or global distress? Has a bank failed somewhere? Is the U.S. about to enter a war? Is Brazil going belly up? Are Japanese stocks falling like rocks? Treasury prices can rise on signs of distress as dealers expect a "flight to quality." A Treasury security is viewed as one of the safest investments in the world in times of trouble.

Now you've done your homework. You're up to date on any new developments in the world economy, and you know how various markets are responding. Let's walk through some market scenarios you might face on the opening.

THE ECONOMIC EVENT

The Commerce Department has released the merchandise trade data for a given month at 8:30 this morning. If you can, print the data off a wire service and get a copy in front of you. Compare the overall figure with the expectations listed in yesterday's bond column. Is it sharply higher, lower, or right on the money? What's the bond market's reaction to the data? What's the reaction in the currency and commodity markets? Take 10 minutes and read through the report. Then look at the quote screens again. Has there been a different reaction now? Economists at the bond houses can change their interpretation of the data after they have had time to study it. Bond prices can do a complete reversal in a few minutes as economists and traders change their assumptions about what the data means.

After about 15 minutes, the market should be in a clear trend, higher or lower, depending on how its participants have interpreted the economic news. Now call an economist at one of the dealerships or dealer-banks and ask him to explain why the data is good or bad for bond prices—that is, "bullish or bearish." Often, there will be a clear consensus among economists. For example, let's say the trade data shows a deficit much higher than expectations. Economists may conclude that the dollar will have to go lower to correct the imbalance. And, usually, the foreign exchange market agrees. But test any consensus. Listen to the economist who may diverge from the crowd. Test one view against another.

Don't let economists rattle on in generalities. They assume that you, a journalist, aren't interested in the particulars. But you, a thorough journalist, are!

What particularly is bullish or bearish in the data? Is there any seasonal factor that could be exaggerating the data in one way or another? Demand an explanation for the month-to-month change in the data. Your readers will. And so will that economists' traders. What are the most important components of the data?

Don't let the economist get away with saying, "Well, I think this just shows that the trade deficit isn't improving as fast as people think." Of course, the data shows that. Of course, the bond market already knows that. Why isn't it improving as quickly? Get specific about what the numbers mean. Don't write the obvious, such as, "Today's merchandise trade deficit was sharply higher than expected and bond prices fell . . ." Write, "Bond prices fell sharply this morning as today's trade data convinced dealers that the dollar will have to drop sharply in the coming months to reverse the deficit."

After you've talked to an economist, talk to a few traders about 15 minutes after the New York opening. Traders are difficult sources to develop. They have an implicit distrust of reporters. They make split-second decisions with millions of dollars. They don't like to be bugged. They want to protect their clients and their own firms from publicity. And they want to protect their position: traders' views are often biased by their position. If a trader owns 50 million bonds and the market is falling apart, he may tell you it is only a "temporary correction."

But traders will talk to you, eventually, especially if you show them that you are a skilled reporter who knows the market almost as well as they do. (Thus, the importance of reading up on the market!) They may only speak to you on background, rendering your copy full of "traders said." Settle this matter with them right away. If you accidently quote them by name, you may lose a source for good. Usually, the head trader at the bond dealerships can be quoted by name. Use good reportorial source development sense when you're dealing with traders. Also, don't let their volatile tempers bother you. These people are like tin animals in a shooting gallery. They get shot at all day long.

Traders may not have time to consider the macroeconomic implications of a news item. They can give you a good idea of trading volume, however. Has the buying or selling been heavy or light? Have any large blocks of bonds been bought or sold, indicating a dramatic shift in strategy by an investor or dealer? What are the sources of the activity? Banks? Investment funds? Ask the trader where the market is going in the near term—higher or lower and why.

CULTIVATING SOURCES

There are two sides to every bond desk. On one side, the trader. On the other, the salesman. Traders make markets—buy and sell. Salesmen are intermediaries between the trader and client. Salesmen have more time to talk to a reporter than a trader. They can also furnish you with information about the volume and type of trading. Again, clear up the matter of attribution with them right away. Most firms have sales managers who can be quoted by name.

Another source you might want to tap is the analyst. Most Wall Street investment banks have bond market analysts. They look at a variety of data and try to project the market's trend in the coming weeks. They might issue buy or sell recommendations to the firm's clients. Analysts have plenty of glib commentary. They are good to use if you are in a hurry, or if your other sources have failed you. But they aren't as close to the market as the trader or salesman. Rarely does their commentary have the depth of an economist's. Why have an analyst? you might ask. Usually, they deal with less sophisticated investors or speculators involved in many markets who want a quick reading on a particular market's trend.

A more important source is the investor. As a reporter, you have an advantage over many bond salesmen and traders. You represent the public interest, not Salomon Brothers. Dozens of important investors are a phone call away. For example, most large corporations have a treasurer who at some point is putting money to work in bonds, stocks, or something else. Usually, most of the investment firms are in touch with these folks. But they're trying to sell them something. You can chat pleasurably with the investor. You're interested in her view of the market, not in getting her business. You give her a chance to speak to the world about how she manages money in the global marketplace.

Investors often have a different view of the market than does Wall Street. A horribly bearish market that is racking up losses for dealers may represent a good buying opportunity for the investor. Since investors usually talk to all of the bond dealers, they have access to a huge amount of information. Try to get these folks on the record. The views of large investors are very important to other investors and bond dealers.

Economic news may explain the market's move for the entire day. Often large swings in prices stimulated by economic news draw thousands of participants into the market, setting the trend for the full session. That makes your job easy, especially if you have some inciteful commentary from economists about the data. Now what happens when there is no economic news?

SLIPPIN' AND A SLIDIN'

On the rare day of no news or light news, you may find the market skates along, falling and rising again in a search for some kind of directional consensus. Typically, there will be some underlying concern in the market, such as the dollar's value against key currencies. But fluctuations in the dollar may not explain all of the bond market's moves. On days of moderate price stability, investors, dealers and speculators start to place their bets. Where will the next big move be— higher or lower? On days like this it might be good to get investors and speculators on the record. Why do they think prices are moving higher or lower? Try to elicit a view of U.S. economic trends, and world economic trends. In times of stable markets, forecasts are avidly read by bond market participants. Write your column with a forward spin.

An even rarer occurrence in the bond market is a sudden break in prices without an apparent explanation. It means that there is a large buyer or seller in the market. Now you have to use your best inside sources. Usually they will be traders. Which institution is buying or selling and why? Name names.

FED WATCHING

The professional bond market reporter must eventually become an expert "Fed watcher." With study, there's no reason why you can't become as good as some of the Wall Street Fed watchers. As of this writing, the Federal Reserve, through the New York District Bank, guides monetary policy through a borrowed reserve target. Learn more about that in your readings. More importantly, that target is affected by an instrument—an interest rate called the "federal funds rate." The Fed can change inflation expectations by moving the Fed funds rate. The Fed funds rate is determined in the Fed funds market—a market where banks buy and sell deposits. In times of rising inflation, the Fed will keep upward pressure on the rate by making money scarce. In times of deflation, or slowing economic activity, the Fed will drop the rate a notch by making the supply of money more abundant. Remember, one way the Fed changes the level of deposits in the banking system is by buying or selling Treasuries to banks and dealers.

Economists maintain a running dialogue with their traders about every jiggle in the Fed funds rate. Any aberrant move may be a tip that the Fed is pushing rates higher or lower. You should plug into that dialogue by keeping in touch with economists. They can get very technical. Ultimately, what you're looking for is some sense of where the Federal Reserve is likely to steer interest rates (see essay "The Federal Reserve," herein).

Fed watchers are frequently wrong, or biased. With the cacophony of economists in one ear, you should keep your other ear tuned to Federal Reserve Board of Governors. There are seven members of the Board, including the Chairman. The board often reflects the personality of the chairman. So, the Fed board under Chairman Alan Greenspan was quite outspoken, and often gave their views on domestic economic growth, price stability, and employment levels. Follow the speeches of Fed officials closely. Clip them. Save them. Subscribe to the "Federal Reserve Bulletin" where many of the speeches are reprinted.

Every six weeks the Board of Governors meets with five district bank presidents. This body is called the Federal Open Market Committee (FOMC). Four district bank presidents rotate through the Committee, but the New York president has a permanent seat. The reasoning is that he is closest to the financial markets, and especially the bond market, where the Fed executes monetary policy.

The FOMC may vote to raise or lower interest rates (via the Fed funds rate), or decide to leave monetary policy unchanged. You won't know what they discussed or how they voted until six weeks later when the "record" of the meeting is released. Just before an FOMC meeting, pull out your file of comments from Fed officials. Call some well regarded chief economists. Many of these people are former Fed staffers. They keep in touch with their friends at the central bank. Ask them to describe the Fed's concerns. Also, dealers have a formal meeting with the Fed at least once every two weeks. Very occasionally, Fed officials will drop a hint about the central bank's bias. Ask capital market economists about their meetings with the Fed.

The central bank has a huge influence over the market. Your understanding of Fed policy will shape everything you write about on the bond beat. It's important to get into the mind of the Fed. Subscribe to some of the "economic reviews" that are published about once a month by district banks, such as the Chicago Fed. These contain articles by key staff economists that shed light on the Governors' thinking. Get some of the Fed booklets that detail operations at the New York District Bank. Get on the mailing list for the FOMC record and scrutinize the debate between governors.

MARKET CULTURE

Every market is a human event, and therefore a human concern. If bond reporters fill their columns with interest rates and prices and economic shop talk alone, they can become so enamored or bored with the market that they forget that human beings are working the buy and sell signals behind the quote screens. They may forget that the bond business is a trade with a culture of its own. After all, bond trading is a bizarre occupation where individuals risk millions of dollars under loose supervision. When interest rates twist up or spiral down some trader's profit and loss sheet registers success or failure. It's easy to forget that the bond business is ultimately a service industry, making greed its natural enemy.

The good bond market reporter has what traders call a "feel" for the market. He or she has market instincts and knows why prices are moving before talking to sources. Additionally, this reporter speaks the market's language, while keeping jargon out of the copy. This reporter is a student of the yield curve, is interested in the techniques of trading, is keenly aware of the bond market's relation to other securities markets, and the global financial system.

Section 3

The Economy

The Economists and the Economy

by Gus Hedberg

Economics is called the Dismal Science. But why? Oh sure, because Thomas Carlyle called it that. Carlyle also called Nature "rude," the Church of England "a widow," and poets "watery personages." While these other glibnesses are long forgotten, we have kept "dismal" and "economics" bound together for over 130 years in witty editorials, after-dinner orations and informal chatter as if the adjective gave us some penetrating and clarifying insight into the nature of economics and, by extension, into the souls of professional economists.

Certainly, economists have struggled to shake off the dismal tag. They began years ago to desert the musty halls of the academy and branch out into the corridors of power. They developed comfortable roosts near heads of state and the captains of industry. They dined at the choisest tables (John Kenneth Galbraith virtually managed the French economy after World War II), squired the comeliest consorts (Alan Greenspan used to date Barbara Walters), and counseled and cajoled national leaders on wide-ranging matters of policy and ideology. From there, they have expanded into the glamorous world of television. They appear—heads and necks, mostly—on newscasts, talk shows and business forums and they come off as witty, urbane professionals. Some particularly gracious or caustic economists have even reached the outer rings of celebrity status—complete with booking agents and guest spots on Johnny Carson. (Milton Friedman, Lester Thurow and Arthur Laffer all charge more than $10,000 for an after dinner speech).

But still, "dismal" plagues them. Perhaps it's the scope and vastness of the macroeconomic purview. Gross National Product, consumer price index, world capital markets, aggregate demand—the very magnitude of these concepts instills a sense of helplessness. Is it this ingrained element of futility that causes us to mistrust economics? Who has ever seen or felt aggregate demand? Perhaps as celebrity economist George Gilder has argued there really is no such scientifically measurable thing as aggregate demand. What? So, after the reams of textbook pages and hours of lecture time devoted to explaining this basic economic concept, we find it might not exist? Dismal-making indeed.

But some economists will tell you that George Gilder is misguided. (One of the disquieting things about economics is how pathetically easy it is to find economists willing to say—or at least imply—that another economist is wrong.) Whether or not there is such a thing as aggregate demand, defined as the total amount of goods and services demanded in the economy at alternate income levels in a given period of time, it's certainly not measurable in the same sense that the temperature of liquid nitrogen, or the perihelion of Mercury, are measurable. Just try to put a dollar value on a year's worth of everything considered to be a service in the U.S.

Welcome to the world of macroeconomics—where national treasuries are squandered for the sake of pie charts and econometric models, reputations are made on luncheon napkins, and all the credentialed players are nagged by the frightening possibility that everything they're hypothesizing modeling and positing could in the end have no demonstrable relation to life as it occurs on earth.

To sense the aesthetic structure of economic analysis requires only a feeling for logic and the capacity for wonderment that such mental constructs really do have a life and death significance for billions of men and women all over the world.   —Samuelson, *Economics*

Economics has grown in the brief space of less than 200 years from a widely ignored body of musing by a migrainous Scottish professor and a gaggle of French aristocrats to a flourishing vocation, which is the choice of many of the best, brightest and most influence-crazed minds in the nation.

But we sense, and they know we sense, that something deep in their science is rotten—or at least very unscientific. The Nobel Committee, which gives no awards to the so-called soft sciences—psychology, sociology, political science—added a prize for economics to its list. The late Swedish economist Gunnar Myrdal, one of its earliest recipients, said he later regretted accepting the prize and called for its abolition on the grounds that economics was too loaded with value judgments to be classed as a true science.

Economists are well acquainted with the identity crisis that plagues their profession. But the tug-of-war between soft-science and hard-science in economics isn't a static battle. For over 100 years, up until quite recently, the forces of hard science have been steadily gaining ground. Price theory, the mechanics of supply and demand, and operations of the national economy have become increasingly described and modeled in mathematical terms. And the Holy Grail of any science—being able to use its theoretical constructions to actually accomplish things in the real world—has come very near to being realized. The austere and elegant microeconomic mechanics of the the late neoclassical economists Alfred Marshall and Wesley Mitchell, coupled with the magisterial model of a national economy devised by in the 1930s by John Maynard Keynes, yielded a scientific apparatus that economist—and politician—used to create and steer the economies of nations in much the same way that the laws of physics and chemistry are used to build and steer an oceanliner. But starting in the 1960s, when a series of economic icebergs—inflation, waning productivity, debt and deficit—were spotted off the bow, alarm and eventually panic have been breaking out on deck. The first clue came from the steering apparatus. Turn the wheel and the ship kept plowing hard ahead. Steer steady ahead and the ship zigged and zagged. In some cases the wheel seemed to work, other times it worked in reverse, and most of the time not at all.

Today economics is described as either Keynesian or non-Keynesian. Economists will object and point out that there are almost no purebred, full-bore Keynesians left; on the other hand almost every economist around uses some parts of the Keynesian vocabulary. An anecdote is instructive here. Contrary to the stubborn myth, Richard Nixon never said, "We are all Keynesians now." Milton Friedman did, in a *Time* Magazine article in 1965. But the reporter failed to quote the second phrase of his utterance, "—and nobody is any longer a Keynesian" which Friedman quickly pointed out in a letter to the editor. What he meant was that Keynes had so clearly described the working parts of the modern economy that no matter whether you agreed with his assessment or not, you had to use his terms even to disagree, which most economists were—and still are—doing. Nixon, according to Herbert Stein, his chief economic advisor, actually said, "Now, I am a Keynesian." "He meant that he was a Keynesian of the kind that by 1971 all of us were but not of the kind that by 1971 none of us were any longer," clarifies Stein.

Keynes argued that the economy is basically unstable because of the cyclical nature of investments. He further argued that the instability was correctable by the judicious intervention of government using both fiscal and monetary policies. Focus, though, on instability versus stability. The distinction is enormous, philosophically hemispheric, and essentially the distinguishing factor among all the various schools of economics. It may even go deeper and mark a division between two basically different kinds of people. At root, it divides two opposing notions of history and destiny.

In general, monetarists, neoclassicists, the proponents of rational expectations, and the libertarian "public choice" economists—all share the conviction that the economy is inherently stable. Just give it an even break and leave it pretty much to its own devices and it will plug along with minor ups and downs keeping people more or less fed and employed. Not surprisingly, these people spend more time talking to Republican politicians.

Keynes on the other hand—although politically conservative himself —argued that an economy left to itself would increasingly destablize, freezing itself alternatively to sustained stretches of high unemployment or steering itself to obliteration by inflation. His theoretical solutions to this predicament, outlined in 1936, became the classic Keynesian recipe for heavy government intervention in the working of the economy, referred to as "fine tuning." This meant generating a lot of tax revenues, borrowing into a deficit and spending all this accumulated money to stimulate the demand for goods and services and keep the economy hopping. It was a theoretical windfall beyond the wildest dreams of Democratic politicians with ambitious social programs to fund. And absolutely plausible—if economies are inherently unstable.

Marxist economists have a structural kinship with the Keynesians. They both salute the economic instability created by the business cycle. Marx saw the disequilibrium growing (those rambunctious capitalists!) with each inhale/exhale of the economy until thrombosis inevitably set in. Keynes, of course, held that the wise ministrations of a benevolent— but probably gigantic—government would keep doom in check, but right-wingers often get spooked by what they suspect is a Marxian engine chugging at the heart of Keynesian economics.

Supply-siders, who would "fine-tune" the economy on the supply side by lowering taxes and thus leaving more money around for investment, get a raspberry from both schools. Keynesians see them as doing everything exactly backwards and upside down, while the Monetarists and rational expectations people smell tinkering and panic.

All sides, however, love Joseph Schumpeter (rhymes with pumphater), first because his name is fun to pronounce and sounds right for an economist. The monetarists like him because he is basically laissez-faire and warns not to mess around with what can't be controlled anyway. The Keynesians appreciate his acceptance of the basic instability of economies due to the business cycle. Even the Marxists are respectful because he says that the whole show will eventually go to hell in a handbasket no matter what anyone does. But instead of seeing the

Golden Age of communism on the other side, Schumpeter forecasts a Hobbesian nightmare.

When covering the economy, some journalists will argue that it's better to know nothing about it and ask lots of questions, present several viewpoints and then try to sum up and present what appears to be a logical conclusion. Others will argue that so many decisions—business expansion, consumer spending, debt or credit—are made based on the economy that a story that recognizes only the conditions of the moment without understanding the relationship to yesterday and the people turning the wheels, leads to inaccurate and misleading journalism.

Regardless of your opinion, as a journalist covering the economy you can expect to face a world of visions and phantasmagoria which will make it difficult to bring back solid information for the reader whose prime economic concerns are likely to be things like buying a toaster, keeping a job or getting a mortgage. It may be up to you to find good sense, and wise counsel, in the dismal and frequently contradictory world of economics.

The Economists

by Gary Gigliotti

One may ask what value knowledge of the ideas of thinkers from the past has for a practicing journalist. In answer, I offer this famous quote from *The General Theory of Employment, Interest and Money*, by John Maynard Keynes [First Harbinger Edition, 1964, New York: Harcourt, Brace & World, 1964, p.383]

But apart from this contemporary mood, the ideas of economists and political philosophers, both when they are right and when they are wrong, are more powerful than is commonly understood. Indeed the world is ruled by little else. Practical men, who believe themselves to be quite exempt from any intellectual influences, are usually the slave of some defunct economist. Madmen in authority, who hear voices in the air, are distilling their frenzy from some academic scribbler of a few years back."

FRANÇOIS QUESNAY: Surgeon and physician to the King of France. Argued for "laissez faire" treatment of economic factors. Felt that land was the only source of value. Strongly favored the growth and development of agriculture. Devised the *Tableau Economique* (1758), in which he showed that goods circulate through the economy, from sector to sector. Marx was inspired by Quesnay's table. Modern input-output analysis, like that constructed by Leontief, is based on the principles articulated by Quesnay.

Gary Gigliotti, an associate professor of economics at Rutgers University, teaches an annual seminar on the evolution of economic thought for the fellowship.

ADAM SMITH: His enormously influential book, *An Inquiry into the Nature and Causes of the Wealth of Nations* (1776), argued that the wealth of a nation was its productive capacity, not its gold supply. His other famous book, *The Theory of the Moral Sentiment*, can be seen as a companion of the *Wealth*, though few economists have read it. He argued for competitive markets, free enterprise, and minimal government intervention in the economy. His story of the division of labor in the pin factory and the "invisible hand" are the stuff of minor legends. An old aphorism in economics states that anything worth knowing in economics can be found in Smith. It's probably true.

DAVID RICARDO: A wealthy stockbroker who liked to use abstractions to analyze economic problems. Today we would call him a builder of economic models. He wrote *The Principles of Political Economy and Taxation* (1817), a very influential book in its time. Ricardo developed the theory of comparative advantage in international trade, and using it, argued that free trade was the best policy a country could follow. He laid the foundation for the theory of capital, and tried to work out a labor theory of value. He also used the concept of diminishing returns, developed by his friend Thomas Robert Malthus, and his own theory of economic rent, to argue that the future of capitalist society was stationary. Joseph Schumpeter, a great economist of the mid-twentieth century, said Ricardo had a serious "vice"; he used highly abstracted economic models and made economic policy recommendations based on them. Some would say his vice has been passed on to the current generation of economists.

THOMAS ROBERT MALTHUS: Malthus was a friend of Ricardo, with whom he exchanged many letters dealing with their differing views of economics. In his famous work, *An Essay on the Principle of Population as It Affects the Future Improvement of Society,* Malthus argued that output per person in agriculture will grow more slowly than population, or that there are diminishing marginal returns to production. He felt that population would stabilize at the subsistence level, a "dismal" prospect, as Thomas Carlyle noted. Malthus also questioned Ricardo's view that all output would be purchased every year, so that no involuntary employment would occur. He felt that "effectual demand" would not be enough to purchase all that was produced, a precursor of Keynes' ideas, as Keynes acknowledged.

KARL MARX: A controversial figure, to say the least. Marx is best known for his dialectical materialist vision of history, his labor theory of value, and his belief in the falling rate of profit. He rediscovered the Tableau Economique of Quesnay, and based his analysis of the capitalist economy on such a multisector model. His labor theory of value, much like that of Ricardo's, is considered by most economists to be a failure. He argued that the owners of the means of production, and workers who owned nothing but their capacity for labor, would struggle over the aggregate output of the economy. This would cause capitalist economies to move in cycles over time, with unemployment rising and falling over the cycle, as the battle flowed one way, then the other. In his view, this constant battling would lead to a revolt of the workers. He also argued that capitalist economies would grow prodigiously, and not reach the stationary state predicted by Ricardo and Malthus. Chapter 10 of Volume 1 of *Capital* (1867) contains his account of the arguments for and against the limitation of the working day in Britain. It's a good example of his journalistic skills, and his attitudes toward the creation of value.

ALFRED MARSHALL: Marshall worked out a foundation for demand and supply, based on marginal utility and marginal cost, respectively. He called demand and supply the two blades of the scissors that determined price. He developed his ideas in a rigorous, mathematical fashion, using calculus in his development of marginal concepts. The distinction between statics and dynamics, and short run and long run, were introduced by him. His major work, *Principles of Economics* (1890), is a classic, and was a basic text in economics for many years. Marshall was a teacher of Keynes at Cambridge.

IRVING FISHER: Fisher was a brilliant economist, but is probably best known for his Quantity Theory of Money. (His dissertation on measuring marginal utility is considered one of the best in economics.) Fisher argued that percentage changes in the money supply would result in equal percentage changes in the price level over time, and would not cause changes in economic activity. The determinants of the level of economic activity and the rate of turnover of money in the system were assumed to be independent of changes in the money supply. Fisher also worked out a "vertical Phillips curves" model that Friedman raised to new prominence.

JOHN R. HICKS: Hicks worked in many areas of economics. His work on equilibrium determination is cited in his Nobel Prize award, but he also worked out the fundamental equation of value in economics, now usually called the Hicks-Slutsky equation. This illustrates the substitution effect and purchasing power effect on the amount of a good an individual will purchase when that good's price changes. Hicks also developed an IS-LM apparatus to model Keynes' ideas about money and expenditure. Hick's most famous work is *Value and Capital* (1939).

JOHN MAYNARD KEYNES: Samuelson has called Keynes the greatest economist of the twentieth century (though some would apply that phrase to Samuelson). In his most famous work, *The General Theory of Employment, Interest and Money* (1937), Keynes challenged the "classical view" (Keynes' term), of the role of money in the economy. He focused on the short-run effects of changes in spending, and changes in the supply of money. (One of his many famous quotes, "In the long run we are all dead.") He argued that consumption spending depended to a great extent on the level of disposable income in the economy, and used the marginal propensity to consume to illustrate this. Just as important, he argued that individuals had a preference for liquidity that was influenced by the interest rate. In a short run Keynesian model, changes in spending will cause an increase in national income. Changes in the money supply will cause changes in interest rates, which will lead to changes in spending, especially investment spending. Thus, Keynes linked spending with changes in the money market, revoking the "classical dichotomy" between them. (The dichotomy is illustrated in Fisher's model, above.) Keynesian economics was revolutionary in many senses, but in particular, it implied that government can use monetary and fiscal policy to stabilize the economy. Since Keynes felt the economy had some inherent instability, he argued for such policies.

PAUL A. SAMUELSON: Keynes was not the only revolutionary in economics in the twentieth century. Samuelson, by using mathematics as the language of economics, revolutionized the way economics is done. He used these mathematical tools to explain rigorously many propositions in economics that had been difficult to understand, and discovered many new ones. It is hard to say what he is best known for, since his work has had such pervasive influence. For an idea of his impact, review the multivolume *The Collected Scientific Papers of Paul A. Samuelson*. His dissertation, published as *Foundations of Economic Analysis* (1947), quickly became what its title claimed it was. His work in trade theory, growth theory, capital theory, have all been fundamental. His textbook, *Economics,* revolutionized the way economics was taught, and promoted the Keynesian approach to macroeconomics.

MILTON FRIEDMAN: Friedman is best known for the establishment of the Monetarist school of thought in economics. His work shifts focus away from the short-run Keynesian focus towards Fisher's long-run concerns. His permanent income hypothesis forced a reinterpretation of Keynesian consumption theory. In general, Friedman argues that changes in the money supply will affect both the price level and economic activity. But, since the economy is basically stable, discretionary fiscal or monetary policies by government will often create the instability it is supposed to cure. *A Monetary History of the United States, 1967–1960,* written with Anna Schwartz, is a compendium of information and analysis. Other important works are *Studies in the Quantity Theory of Money* (1956), and *A Theory of the Consumption Function* (1957).

The Federal Reserve

by William Glasgall

Let's say some big banks just cut the prime rate. Or mortgage rates are coming down. You want to find out what's coming next. So you call several economists. One tells you the Federal Reserve is "easing" monetary policy. Another disagrees, asserting that the Fed is still "tight," and that interest rates are falling because the economy's weakening. And just to confuse things further, a third assures you that the Fed is assuming a "neutral" stance. You hang up the telephone and wonder who's right.

So goes life on the money beat. Some say no government agency is as important as the Federal Reserve. Certainly, few agencies are as closely watched. All it takes is a wiggle in interest rates—sometimes as little as a sixteenth of a percentage point—to send squads of reporters scurrying to get out the news. And every pronouncement by the chairman of the Fed, no matter how bland, undergoes intense dissection for clues as to the central bank's future course.

There's good reason for the scrutiny. The Federal Reserve's job traditionally has been to "lean against the wind"—an apt characterization variously attributed to former chairman William McChesney Martin, Nobel-laureate economist Paul Samuelson, and others. Certainly since the first OPEC oil shock in 1973 sent consumer prices spiraling upward in the U.S. and overseas, the Fed has been doing a lot of leaning. So much, in fact, that consumers now look to the central bank as the nation's—and the industrial world's—first line of defense against inflation.

To some degree this reputation is justified: For more than a decade beginning in 1979—when Fed Chairman Paul Volcker jammed on the monetary brakes in the face of OPEC's second oil shock and double-digit increases in consumer prices—inflation was held to an annual rate of about 5 percent. Whether or not 5 percent inflation is acceptable is another matter; some say the Fed must set a zero inflation as its ideal. Whatever the outcome, monitoring inflation means keeping a constant watch on the Fed's daily doings.

WHAT'S A FED?

Before looking at how the Fed seeks to guide the economy, let's take a brief look at its history and structure. The Federal Reserve's roots date back to 1908. Congress, shocked by a severe financial panic and wave of bank failures in 1907, established a blue-ribbon commission to devise monetary reforms. Based on the panel's 38 volumes of recommendations, Congress in 1913 established the seven-member Federal Reserve Board as the nation's chief monetary authority.

In so doing, Congress cut the country into 12 districts, each with its own Federal Reserve Bank (New York, Boston, Philadelphia, Richmond, Atlanta, Chicago, Cleveland, Minneapolis, St. Louis, Kansas City, Dallas, and San Francisco) nominally owned by commercial banks in each region. The system's coordinator is the seven-member Federal Reserve Board in Washington. The Board's members are appointed by the President and confirmed by the Senate; they serve for 14 year terms and can be removed only for cause.

Both the Federal Reserve Board and the regional Federal Reserve Banks regard themselves as relatively immune from Presidential politics. The Fed's budget is not funded through budget appropriations, but from earnings on its immense portfolio of U.S. Treasury securities. And its feeling of independence was bolstered by the removal in the 1930s of the Secretary of the Treasury and the Comptroller of the Currency from Board membership. But at the same time, the Fed traditionally owes a special allegiance to Congress. Indeed, under the 1978 Full Employment and Balanced Growth Act (commonly known as Humphrey-Hawkins), the Fed's chairman is obliged to appear before Congress every February and July to detail the central bank's latest monetary growth targets—and its success in achieving its objective. Some lawmakers would make the Fed even more accountable by returning the Treasury Secretary to the Board.

HOW IT WORKS

The Fed carries out monetary policy in two basic ways, as a regulator of the financial system and as a participant in the market. In the former capacity, the Federal Reserve Board itself oversees the nation's banks, ruling on such matters as takeovers, an increasingly important and contentious area. It selects and supervises the community of primary dealers—the approximately four dozen banks and brokers that hold the exclusive right to trade U.S. government securities directly with the Fed. And it supervises the country's payments system, which transmits funds among financial institutions, and sets rules for the banking system.

In the latter role, for example, the Fed acted as the agent for the U.S. in 1988 in the international negotiations that led to adoption of common bank capital adequacy standards in the major industrial countries. In addition, through the foreign-exchange desk at the fortress-like Federal Reserve Bank of New York, the Fed buys and sells tens of billions worth of dollars, Deutsche marks, yen, and other currencies as it carries out the daily operations necessary to achieve the Treasury's goals for the value of the nation's currency overseas.

The Fed's other role, though, is even more critical: maintaining the economy on an even keel. Occasionally this requires forceful action. In the wake of the October 1987 stock market crash Fed chairman Alan Greenspan assured financial markets that the Federal Reserve would provide cash to any troubled bank or broker. But usually, the Fed's economic-guidance work is carried out by the Federal Open Market Committee (FOMC), the central bank's monetary policy-making body.

The FOMC is composed of the seven Federal Reserve Board members plus five of the 12 Federal Reserve Bank presidents. The Federal Reserve chairman also chairs the FOMC. The president of the Federal Reserve Bank of New York traditionally serves as vice chairman, and the other four slots are rotated among the 11 remaining regional bank presidents, who serve one-year terms on the FOMC.

The FOMC's main task, as a Federal Reserve Bank of St. Louis study puts it, is to pursue a "long-term objective of reasonable price stability, while promoting growth in output on a sustainable basis." That's no mean feat. To reach such lofty goals, the FOMC meets frequently, sometimes as often as eight times a year, and also holds occasional conferences by telephone to deal with pressing matters that can't wait for the next full session. Its main tactic is to set a framework for loosening or tightening monetary policy.

The FOMC does the former by ordering the Open Market Desk of the New York Fed to buy large volumes of Treasury bills or bonds from banks and brokers, thereby pumping cash into the economy. To tighten, the Fed sells securities back; the cash used to pay for the bills or bonds is removed from the financial system and less money is available for all. The technique is even more potent than it sounds because a dollar injected into the economy by the Fed is actually worth much more than that. If, say, a bank sells a Treasury bill to the Fed for $1 million, it will keep a portion in its reserves and lend the rest. The money goes back into circulation until it lands in another bank, where a portion is lent out again. One dollar pumped in at New York thus can become five or more by the time the money reaches San Francisco. The system works exactly the same in reverse, of course, when the Fed sells securities to tighten.

The FOMC never exactly says "buy" or "sell" to the Open Market Desk. But after each meeting, the committee sends sets of guidelines to New York to accomplish these goals. The FOMC's messages to New York are not disclosed until a month later, but by watching minute changes in rates, savvy traders and analysts often are able to dope out what has been decided almost as soon as the FOMC finishes meeting. A move of only 25 "basis points," or 0.25 of a percentage point, can signal a change in Fed policy.

Since 1979, the committee has focused on the level of bank reserves as its main monetary policy guide. As we have seen, a given level of reserve growth directly influences money growth. While sometimes the FOMC's directives can be quite pointed, at other times they appear extremely vague. For example, in September 1988, the FOMC, worried about inflation flaring up as a result of that summer's severe drought, advocated taking steps that "would more readily accommodate a move toward firming (of monetary policy) than an adjustment toward easing in the weeks ahead."

In so doing, the FOMC ordered the Open Market Desk to keep the widely watched Federal funds rate—the interest rate banks levy on overnight loans among themselves—to between 6 percent and 10 percent. That represented no change from the month before. But the FOMC also ordered the Open Market Desk to take steps to ensure that the annual monetary growth rate would decline about a half-percentage point from that of the month before. That's a signal that interest rates should rise. But in its order, the FOMC left it to the Open Market Desk's discretion to determine, within broad limits, just how high they should go.

The FOMC may also raise or lower the discount rate. This is the charge on loans from the regional Federal Reserve banks directly to banks that belong to the Federal Reserve System. The discount rate isn't changed very often. In fact, many banks dislike borrowing from the Fed, fearing the market will view such moves as signs of weakness or even desperation. Nonetheless, the discount rate's movements are seen as important symbols of the Fed's intentions.

In extreme cases, the FOMC also may change bank reserve requirements; forcing a bank, say, to lend out less of its deposits is one way of making less money available. Or the committee may order investors buying stocks and bonds with borrowed funds, or "margin," to put up less or more collateral. These actions also increase or decrease the amount of money in circulation.

How are the FOMC's instructions translated into inflation, growth, and jobs? Unfortunately, there's no easy answer. The monetarist school of economics, which gained wide adherence in the 1970s and early 1980s, maintains that a formal link exists between monetary growth and economic growth and inflation. That theory seems to work up to a point. The trouble is, no one yet has determined the exact timing within the relationship. If the Fed stomps down hard on monetary growth, as it did in 1979, interest rates will soar. But will that be translated first into inflation and then into a slowdown, or a recession?

Similarly, if the Fed wants to raise monetary growth by cutting interest rates, will consumers go on a spending spree that fuels inflation? Or will the outcome be noninflationary growth—a little more spending, perhaps, a little more capital investment, and better times for all. As noted above, you can get three economists to give you three equally plausible outcomes for each given change in Fed strategy. Some will even debate whether a change has, indeed, taken place.

FEDBABBLE

In trying to cut through the fog, it helps to know a bit of Fedspeak. We have already gone over how the system operates, but here are three of the key words and phrases to watch:

Money Supply

It comes in three varieties, M1, M2, and M3. The New York Fed (officially the Federal Reserve Bank of New York) releases the previous week's data each Thursday afternoon. M1 is the total of cash in circulation, travelers' checks, and checking deposits, NOW accounts, and the like. It represents the best measure of money that's "liquid," or most easily accessible. M2 comprises M1 plus bank and brokerage personal money-market accounts, repurchase agreements (contracts to buy securities with the stipulation they be sold back within a specified time), and a few other items. M3, the broadest measure of money, comprises M2 plus large savings deposits (usually called "jumbo" certificates), money-market accounts owned by institutions, and one or two additional items. Because savings and money-market accounts are nearly as accessible as cash or checking accounts these days, many analysts like to watch M2 or M3 as the most accurate measures of monetary growth.

Velocity

In simplest terms, the number of times a dollar turns over after it's created. If velocity were constant—as economists once surmised—the Fed would have much less trouble predicting the result of a change in policy. But velocity, it seems, is unpredictable, too. A given decision to boost monetary growth might not pack the wallop Fed policymakers expect if, for example, consumers decided to save instead of spending. In this case, velocity would be falling, muting the impact of higher monetary growth.

Federal Funds

Banks that need cash to meet their legal reserve requirements often borrow money overnight from other banks that have cash surpluses. This money is called federal funds. The federal funds rate is viewed as important because it's the price a bank will pay to borrow money it absolutely must have. Along with rates on Treasury bills, the federal funds rate is the chief indicator of the cost of short-term money. It's easy for the Fed to influence the federal funds rate through its Open Market Desk activities. Traders, analysts and reporters follow the rate practically trade by trade on several money-market monitor services, including Telerate, Reuters, and Bloomberg L.P.

SOURCES AND MORE SOURCES

Covering the Fed involves a lot more than keeping an eye glued to the computer screen. Although the Fed is known for a level of policymaking secrecy that rivals the Supreme Court or the CIA, it's surprisingly easy to develop central banking sources. Regional bank presidents are frequently eager to talk about monetary policy and economic conditions. Speak with enough of them, and you'll begin to get an idea of which way the FOMC may be leaning, or whether there are divisions within the Fed. For local reporters, these officials are an often-overlooked source of wisdom about the health of the regional economy.

Many Fed governors, too, are surprisingly reachable. They can be spotted on the Washington lunch-and-cocktail-party circuit, and many appear at conferences in the U.S. and abroad. Some governors become longtime sources of journalists. Don't expect them to leak. But they may point you in the right direction if the idea you try out is implausible or wrong.

The Federal Reserve Board and regional banks all house numerous researchers, many of whom go on to become Wall Street or university economists with useful contacts among those who remain at the Fed.

You can keep track of the researchers work by subscribing to the *Federal Reserve Bulletin,* a monthly magazine of comment and data published by the Federal Reserve Board in Washington. The board also publishes many "discussion papers" on current economic issues. And regional banks publish a wide range of periodicals. Standouts include the New York Fed's *Quarterly Review,* which follows international monetary affairs, among other matters; and the bimonthly Federal Reserve Bank of St. Louis *Review.* The St. Louis Fed long has been the home of dyed-in-the-wool monetarists within the Federal Reserve System and their scholarly articles often follow a unique tack. In any event, Washington and regional Fed researchers often are willing to talk about their work. And some continue to be good sources when they exit the Fed for the world of the market.

Don't forget the Fed-watchers, of course. Wall Street, and big banks, brokers, and insurance companies worldwide, are home to scores of economists who earn their livings translating monetary and economic data into buy or sell decisions for investors. It's easy to get on mailing lists of your favorites. One simple way of getting acquainted is to see who's being quoted on the wires and in national business publications. You might also leaf through the roster of analysts in *Nelson's Directory of Investment Research,* an annual available at public libraries, or study the annual list of Wall Street's "all-star" analysts that appears in *Institutional Investor* magazine.

Don't forget economic think tanks such as DRI/McGraw-Hill or the WEFA Group, both of which churn out prodigious amounts of data. And don't bypass foreign banks and brokers. The globalization of financial markets has spawned a large crop of Fed-watchers in the U.S. and abroad who work for foreign institutions. Japan's large stockbrokers— Nomura, Daiwa, Nikko, and Yamaichi—are among the world's largest purchasers of Treasury securities. In New York, London, and Tokyo, of course, each has a large staff of economists and traders who often can give you a feeling for what Japanese investors are, or aren't, buying. Similarly, Japanese, British, West German and Swiss banks maintain corps of Fed-watchers on Wall Street and at home.

Finally, when covering interest rates, try to go out into the real world. Talk, if you can, to corporate treasurers, economists and purchasing agents. Canvass consumers. Look for things that money-market folk haven't caught yet. You may find that money is tighter—or more abundant—than Wall Street thinks.

Armed with a history, operations guide, and a list of potential sources, you're ready to cover the Fed—or at least the occasional piece on interest rates. Remember that none of the three economists with the three different analyses may be right. Given the right tools, you may be able to find that a fourth answer—your own—is best by far.

Federal Budget and Economic Policy

by Debra Silimeo

The federal budget serves as the nation's financial report, but it's much more than bookkeeping. It's the government's economic game plan, a blueprint of the goals of government. In the broadest sense, since it's crafted by our elected representatives, it reflects our society.

You can find answers to important questions about our economic well-being and the priorities of the government in the budget's numbers. But, where to begin? First, establish some facts: Are the economic assumptions on which the numbers are based realistic? Where's the beef, the fat, and where are the holes? What are the budget alternatives? And what are the long-term consequences of budget actions?

Before tackling the budget, it's helpful to understand its role in economic policymaking, its special language and the uniqueness of the federal budget process.

THE POWER OF THE PURSE

The national economy responds to many factors, including changes in taste and technology. But no influence is more important than government policy. The government's role evolves from Constitutional provisions that give Congress the power to collect taxes, spend money and borrow money. Few, if any, congressional actions have such direct and enormous impact on the nation's economic well-being.

Trade policy, the regulation of business, investments in education and research all have major economic implications. However, it's generally agreed that except in rare circumstances designed to meet a specific need, the federal government's greatest direct impact is through macroeconomic tools: fiscal tools, such as taxing and spending, and monetary tools, such as changes in interest rates and the money supply (see essay "The Federal Reserve," herein).

The budget is a case study in the use of fiscal tools. It's an annual estimate of the government's revenues, new budget authority (for new spending), outlays, and the deficit or surplus, which adds to or subtracts from the federal debt. It details the types of taxes to be levied, and estimates the amount of taxes which will be collected.

Monetary tools, the other side of macroeconomic policymaking, are the prerogative of the Federal Reserve, whose Board of Governors is appointed by the President. The Fed can use its ability to influence interest rate movements and the supply of money in the economy to either stimulate a slow economy or slow an overheating one.

A dramatic example of how these monetary tools can be used is the Fed's effort to wring double-digit inflation out of the economy in the early 1980s. Inflation was "cured," but at a heavy price—the Fed's slowing actions are widely thought to have been the main cause of the deep recession of 1981–82.

A series of fiscal and monetary policy moves helped boost the economy out of that deep recession. The huge tax cut enacted in 1981 provided fiscal stimulus to a sagging economy. This was coupled with a big increase in defense spending. The Fed provided a further stimulus with its monetary vitamin—a rapid growth in the money supply.

The result was about a year and a half of rapid growth. The down side was a growing budget deficit. The federal budget deficit grew from $78.9 billion in the fiscal year 1981 to $207 billion in FY 1983. It peaked at $221 billion in FY 1986 and stood at $155 billion at the end of FY 1988.

THE BUDGET PROCESS

The current budget process, established by the 1974 Congressional Budget and Impoundment Control Act, ties numerous legislative actions to overall tax and spending totals.

The 1974 act was created by a Congress frustrated at every turn by President Richard Nixon. Nixon transformed the old Bureau of the Budget into the White House Office of Management and Budget (OMB), to put the White House in control of the budget process and to oversee, or manage, how federal agencies did their jobs. Nixon also "impounded" or refused to spend money Congress had appropriated.

The 1974 act provides Congress with a mechanism for reviewing the budget presented by the President, to write and pass its own budget, and to restrain the President from "impounding" appropriations rather than spending them.

House and Senate Budget Committees were established to keep score on congressional actions which raise and, in particular, spend money. The Budget Committees report "budget resolutions" to the full House and Senate for action. The act also gave Congress its own set of numbers crunchers, the bipartisan Congressional Budget Office (CBO), charged with providing unbiased economic information. CBO often reaches conclusions radically different than OMB's after analyzing the same economic data.

The process was amended twice in the 1980s, when the budget deficit reached record levels. The Balanced Budget and Emergency Deficit Control Acts, generally known as "Gramm-Rudman" and "Gramm-Rudman Two," set specific annual deficit reduction targets and mandated automatic across-the-board spending cuts if the targets were not met. In 1990, a weak economy, the the savings and loan bailout, and the crisis in the Persian Gulf pushed the deficit past $200 billion. The Gramm-Rudman rules would have required cuts so large that many federal programs would have been devastated, and a weak economy tipped into recession, so Congress changed the rules again. The Budget Enforcement Act of 1990 removes the focus on the sheer size of the deficit and is designed to bring down the deficit by controlling spending with a system.

HOW THE PROCESS WORKS

1. By the first Monday in February, the President gives Congress a budget request, based on economic forecasts provided by OMB and the President's Council of Economic Advisers.

2. By April 15, Congress should adopt a budget resolution, a guide for all Congressional actions relating to the budget. The Congressional Budget Office (CBO) produces its own economic forecast and provides the House and Senate Budget Committees with a list of taxing and spending options. Congressional legislative committees, such as Agriculture, Education and Labor, and Armed Services, provide the Budget Committees with estimates of the revenues needed for the programs under their jurisdictions. The Budget Committees take all of these estimates and options into account, and send comprehensive budget resolutions to the Floors of their respective houses.

3. Once a resolution is adopted, the legislative committees must reconcile the programs within their jurisdictions to the spending and revenue limits in the budget resolution. The legislative committees prepare

authorization bills, defining the goals conduct and funding levels of federal programs.

4. The House and Senate Appropriations Committees look at how much money is supposed to be spent and how much is actually available. The House and Senate vote on not one budget document but thirteen different appropriations bills. Differences between House and Senate versions of each appropriations bill are worked out in conference committees. If the normal appropriations bills have not been passed by the beginning of a new fiscal year, October 1st, Congress can keep the government running by passing a "continuing resolution," authorizing spending on a temporary basis.

5. There is an important post mortem. Fifteen days after Congress adjourns, OMB reviews Congress' work. The 1990 budget act essentially sets spending limits on the various spending categories through fiscal year 1995. New initiatives must be funded by cutting other programs within the category. New entitlement or benefit programs must be pay-as-you-go, that is, paid for by cutting other entitlements or by raising taxes. If these rules are violated, OMB can order a "sequester" or automatic cut in the category of spending that exceeds its limit by 2 percent, every program in the defense budget would be trimmed by 2 percent. The new process allows OMB to take a knife to a particular area of the budget by the same amount.

The threat of Gramm-Rudman's budget budget axe encouraged considerable game-playing. The new rules are more flexible. They allow the deficit targets and spending limits to be adjusted every year to take into account changes in economic conditions. They allow special or emergency expenses, such as Operation Desert Shield, to increase the deficit without penalizing regular programs.

ECONOMIC ASSUMPTIONS

The budget is based on assumptions about the economy's performance in the year ahead. How much will GNP grow? Will interest rates rise or fall? Will more people be working or jobless? The answers to questions like these produce estimates of tax revenues, the cost of servicing the national debt, and the price of "countercyclical" programs such as unemployment insurance and other forms of government assistance.

For example, the budget requested by President Bush in February 1989 assumed the economy would grow at a 3.5 percent clip and that interest rates would decline sharply, with yields on three-month Treasury bills falling from 8.3 percent in early 1989 to an average of 5.5 percent in 1990. It further assumed that Congress would cut the tax on capital gains from 33 percent to 15 percent. The administration claimed that this would increase, not decrease, tax revenues by $5 billion. It concluded that the federal budget deficit would be $94.8 billion, just short of the Gramm Rudman target of $100 billion for FY 90.

If you based the same budget request on CBO's economic forecast instead, you would arrive at a deficit which exceeded the Gramm Rudman target by more than $14 billion. This difference was critical when across-the-board budget cuts threatened.

Economic conditions can change drastically between the time the budget is fashioned and the end of the budget's fiscal year.

For example, if GNP growth were one percent lower than projected in the Bush FY 90 budget request, and everything else held constant, revenues would be down nearly $7 billion, outlays would increase by nearly $2 billion, resulting in a $9 billion increase in the deficit.

Assumptions about revenues are particularly fragile. The Bush budget assumed an expanding economy would produce an $80 billion increase in revenues without increasing taxes. On the other hand, a major recession would slash anticipated revenues, push the deficit way over the Gramm Rudman target. A big recession could wipe out the possibility of eliminating the federal budget deficit in this century.

WHY IS IT DIFFICULT TO BALANCE THE BUDGET?

An ever increasing portion of the federal budget is literally uncontrollable (at least, in the short run): the interest on the public debt, Social Security benefits, and entitlement programs which guarantee benefits to anyone who meets a certain standard of eligibility.

Of every dollar the federal government spent in 1989, 43 cents provided direct benefits payments to individuals, 15 cents was spent on interest payment, 25 cents supported national defense, 11 cents provided grants to states and localities. Only five cents remained for "other government operations."

A closer look at these budget commitments shows why it's so difficult to re-arrange the budget pie.

The biggest category in the budget is entitlements or benefit programs, and the biggest chunk of these is the politically white-hot Social Security/ Medicare complex. If the economy takes a downward turn, more people will rely on the "safety net" of benefit programs, so benefits payments will increase.

Fifteen cents of every federal dollar is now spent simply to cover the interest payments on the debt of past unbalanced budgets. In recent years, "debt service" has been swallowing an ever increasing percentage of the budget. If interest rates rise, the government will have to spend more to pay the interest on its debt.

As the leader of the Western alliance, the U.S. spends roughly one fourth of its budget on defense. This reflects the consensus that a strong

America is the best deterrent of war. The price tag on this commitment is increasingly high. Weapons have become more sophisticated, and more costly. Since the procurement process spans several years, it's hard to cut on a year to year basis. And much of the defense budget is for personnel; some of the cost of maintaining troops throughout the world fluctuates with the relative value of the dollar to other currencies, particularly the Japanese yen and the German mark. Finally, a politician who advocates cuts in defense spending risks being called "weak on defense."

So, what's left? The five cents of each dollar spent on "other government operations," which is everything else the federal government chooses to do, including building highways, maintaining parks, the space program, AIDS research, education and job training, the war on drugs, federal prisons, environmental programs, and toxic waste cleanup.

DEATH AND TAXES

Every American is directly affected by taxes, whether it be sales taxes, income taxes or capital gains taxes. Some Americans, however, have more to gain or lose than others; a change in the tax code which means a few dollars to the average American could have a million dollar tax effect on a business or industry group.

The tax system is a means of redistributing income, as it raises money from some citizens to spend it on others. Over the years, those with much at stake were able to obtain various tax breaks, while the middle class contributed a relatively constant portion of its income in taxes and the disadvantaged received an increasing portion of the federal budget in direct benefits.

The public became increasingly disturbed with a system which seemed to tax the rich less, give the poor more, and squeeze the middle class. The Tax Reform Act of 1986, which cut overall tax rates but eliminated many deductions and closed loopholes, was an attempt to remedy this problem (see essay "The Tax Story," herein).

Sometimes tax policy is used to achieve social goals. Tax deductions for home mortgage interest encourage home ownership. Tax deductions for charitable contributions are meant to encourage giving. Tax credits for certain energy programs are intended to encourage efficient use of energy. Tax cuts for corporations have been tried to encourage certain kinds of investment. All have budget implications. They reduce tax revenue. They also cause what economists called "distortions," in that people will do these things because they reduce tax liability and not because they are inherently desirable things to do. Because taxes affect everyone, and have such wide-ranging effects on the economy, the tax-writing committees are considered the most powerful of all congressional committees.

The Constitution specifies that all revenue measures originate in the House, so the Ways and Means Committee writes the first draft of any bill. When the full House sends the bill to the Senate, it will be referred to the Finance Committee. The Senate may then refashion and amend the bill until it's barely recognizable. The differences will be hammered out in a "Conference" committee.

READING POLITICIANS' LIPS

President Bush is remembered for his 1988 campaign promise: "Read my lips. No new taxes." His first budget did, however, propose "revenue increases" and "user fees." In 1990, his second year in office, he negotiated a budget package with Congress that did clearly raise taxes.

As a journalist, you don't necessarily need to learn to read lips, but you do need to read between the lines. Even simple statements are used to confuse budget issues:

"This program will not be cut."

If the program is an entitlement, and more people will be receiving benefits from the program in the coming year, then holding funding at the current level will in fact mean a cut in the amount of benefits available for each participant. Programs for the elderly are a good example: the elderly population is increasing and its members getting older and more frail.

"This program is fully funded."

Does that mean the program is funded at last year's level, or that this year's funding will cover inflation, or a cost-of-living increase?

Under "current services baseline" budgeting, one estimates what it will cost in the future to maintain the current level of services. If a program is not funded at that level, some will refer to this as a cut. Critics argue this reasoning gives programs immortality.

"Spending on XYZ is being increased."

Are we talking about "real" spending? That is, is the increase enough to keep up with inflation plus a "real" increase?

Is the percentage of the total budget dedicated to this program changing? Spending on "XYZ" may be increasing in absolute terms, but declining as a percentage of the total budget pie.

It's always a good idea to look for historical perspective. For example, a three-way discussion which attempts to link defense spending to budget deficits might sound like this:

"Well, in 1969 we were spending a bundle on defense and we still managed to balance the budget."

"Yes, but in 1969 there was an income tax surcharge to help finance our involvement in Vietnam. This period is more like the late 70s than the late 60s, so we should be spending a similar percentage of GNP on defense."

"In the late 70s, we couldn't even get a helicopter across a desert to complete a rescue mission."

So it goes. The first speaker has looked only at a column of numbers which shows defense spending as a percentage of GNP and the final balance on the budget for 1969. The second has also looked at the revenue situation for that year, and is trying to compare two peacetime periods. The third, in a descriptive way, is pointing out that numbers don't tell the whole story.

Those who try to make political points with budget numbers will be very selective with the numbers chosen to back up the argument.

Watch out for the "gross" versus "net" concept. For example, one might argue that a federal farm loan program isn't costing anything, since the revenue coming in from loan repayments matches exactly the amount being spent on new loans. The net effect is zero, so the cost of the new loans is hidden. What would happen if no new loans were made?

DOES THE DEFICIT REALLY MATTER?

After years of unrelenting federal budget deficits, and no Armageddon, some economists are now asking whether a mountain of debt really matters.

But the deficit the U.S. carried into the 1990s forced the government to borrow money and increase its dependence on foreign capital. The situation was compounded by unprecedented trade deficits, which meant additional borrowing from trading partners. Persistent budget and trade deficits raise serious questions about the U.S.'s ability to maintain its position as a world political leader. No nation has ever managed to be a great debtor and great leader at the same time. Further, servicing debt is an unproductive way to spend money which could be invested in education, in retraining workers, in research and development, all economic activities that strengthen the economy long-term.

The obligation to pay interest on debt for years to come means that a portion of our national wealth will be sent abroad. Debt represents a lien against the nation's future standard of living.

WHERE CAN I GET A STRAIGHT ANSWER?

Find friendly staffers on the congressional committee staffs and at OMB and CBO. Ask the press secretary to recommend someone who can offer details off the record. Then ask for the names of individuals who will talk on the record.

Compare OMB and CBO forecasts with those of private economists. Talk with citizens groups or lobbyists who are particularly interested in the numbers at hand. Lobbyists are excellent sources, if you talk with representatives of all sides. Find out who testified at earlier hearings; contact the witnesses.

Washington is home to numerous think tanks where you will find former government officials and top notch experts on almost any topic. Former CBO directors are usually available to talk about current budget issues; former Treasury officials may discuss pending tax legislation.

Your last stop should be the Senators, House members or agency heads. You may have to lurk outside committee hearing rooms for long periods of time, alongside the well-dressed lobbyists who gave these halls the nickname "Gucci Gulch." Which brings me to a final word of advice for reporters on the Hill: Wear comfortable shoes.

Economic Indicators

by Andrew Leckey

The American public must kick its way through a grueling high-hurdles course of economic data each and every month of the year—35 times a month to be exact.

As each obstacle is approached, anxious financial markets and economic pundits hold their collective breath. Their mixed response to the latest government figures may be sighs of relief, applause, shock or dejection, depending on whether the numbers seem good, too good or not nearly good enough.

The indicators do help quantify aspects of the economy and forecast its likely course, but the financial journalist is wise to approach them with skepticism. They're far from perfect, open to conflicting interpretation and don't mean much of anything unless viewed in a longer-term context.

Various indicators go in and out of style, depending on what the economy's doing and what policymakers in Washington seem to consider most important. Money supply figures were once a national fixation because the Federal Reserve supposedly based much of its policy on them. New factory orders later grabbed the spotlight as a means of determining whether economic growth was coming to an end. Inflation worries shoved the consumer price index (CPI) to the forefront.

There are many ways to interpret all these numbers. Groucho Marx once made this observation about an economic downturn: "It isn't so much that hard times are coming. The change observed is mostly soft times going."

The journalist's job is to find a simple, yet meaningful way, to make the numbers make sense. Let's say, the government reports that civilian unemployment took a significant jump in the prior month. Such a figure is immediately taken by some experts as strong evidence of an economic slowdown. The stock market, stumbling all week in anticipation of potentially damaging unemployment news, suffers a significant fall on the Friday the numbers are announced. Brokers speculate that investors are worried about what a slowing economy might mean for corporate profits. Indeed, some economists argue, this increase in the unemployment rate may signal not only the possibility of higher inflation but also the start of a truly painful recession.

But other experts seem euphoric about those same numbers. Higher unemployment should improve the prospects for a soft landing for the soaring economy, they reason. This should slow growth just enough to rein in inflation without triggering a dreaded recession. They're pleased as punch that this surprising jump could be just enough to keep the Federal Reserve Board from further credit tightening when it next gets around to evaluating monetary policy. Finally, the Administration—trying to deflect expected criticism of the numbers by the opposition party—points out, in an upbeat manner, that the percentage of working-age Americans with jobs is at an all-time high.

This maddening statistical race in which winning can be losing and losing can be winning has no end. More than a few economic experts—who, of course, have just as much of a penchant for being know-it-alls as any financial journalist—consider many of the indicators to be either frivolous, rigged or downright misleading. Some blame a lack of unified economic policy in Washington for ceding far more importance to economic reports than in the past. Because nations around the world are closely linked to the United States through trade, currency transactions and news reports, their financial markets become stricken with our paranoia.

Indicators are more widely reported in the media, becoming sort of the box scores of the economy. This also seems to have made everyone a self-proclaimed expert on the economy. Conclusions drawn about possible repercussions are usually instant and emphatic, though often quickly forgotten. When a television commentator recites the latest government indicators during a broadcast, his or her voice generally grows gradually deeper and more somber as the numbers are recited, as if to say: "This ... my friends ... is very, very serious stuff. Trust me." Newspapers, also realizing this is very serious stuff, tend in headlines placed above the typical wire story to blare out a simplistic rendering of what the numbers mean: "Unemployment up, recession may be near."

Don't take economic reports at face value. Something as simple as prolonged cold or rainy weather, for example, can have a major negative effect on housing starts or retail sales. This doesn't signal anything at all about the likely progress of the economy or consumer attitudes, but means simply that builders can't work in the mud and shoppers don't like to get wet.

It's also important to consider the local picture. If national unemployment is high, but in your state the jobless rate is low, the local effect obviously supersedes anything else in the eyes of your local audience. Yet it's surprising how many newspapers and newscasts barely acknowledge the smaller picture, simply splicing it into the national story in an identical manner each month. Whether the reporting is done for a national or local audience, it's also important to have personal contacts with leaders in areas such as construction, retailing and manufacturing so you can quickly check out whether the numbers accurately depict what's actually happening.

Relating indicators to the average citizen is no small task for a financial journalist. While anyone can grasp what it means to lose a job, buy a car or build a home, extrapolating what it means if legions of people do likewise within our world economy is quite a different matter. What's important is to tie each individual statistic to people and the quality of their life whenever possible. Never use an indicator without at least briefly explaining what it actually measures. Try to point out examples, such as an actual plant closing or opening, that can make the picture more vivid. One might as well do a recitation from the telephone book as spout statistics out of context. Indicators should be a guide and reference, but never base your hypothesis on only one month. And don't trust historical patterns. For example, many economists define a recession as three straight months of decline in the index of leading indicators, but the index dropped for five months prior to the October 1987 crash and business activity didn't slow. After the crash, the economy continued to expand.

Economists disagree on which indicators are most important. Unemployment statistics and trade balance numbers are watched closely because the first affects interest rates and the second affects the U.S. dollar. If forced to choose a preeminent indicator, many economists say they'd go with the Gross National Product, the most comprehensive measure of economic growth. Also ranking high is unemployment, the month's first release which usually sets the tone for the month.

The widely followed index of leading economic indicators is perhaps the most controversial, reviled for its flaws and the great amount of power attributed to it. Since its various components are reported before the final index comes out, its critics say it isn't saying anything new, but simply a distortion of the existing data.

All the numbers fly by so fast that it's hard to tell one set from another. Here's what financial journalists should watch for, the various quirks involved, and why the readers or viewers should care:

Consumer Price Index

The CPI, measuring change in consumer prices such as housing, food, transportation and electricity, reflects consumer buying power. As a market basket designed to gauge inflation, it's the indicator which most directly relates to the individual on the personal level. Consumers take note of these figures since all of them can remember periods of high inflation when they found numerous price stickers stuck on a can of peas at the local supermarket, which reflected rapidly escalating costs.

However, the CPI can be greatly influenced by temporary events, such as dry spells that can affect crops, making the month-to-month rates often quite questionable. The year-to-year change does a better job of ironing out aberrations and coming up with a representative inflation figure. This is a powerful indicator, with many pension and employment contracts tied directly to it. The Bureau of Labor Statistics (BLS) releases the CPI the third week of the month.

Gross National Product

The GNP, which is the value of goods and services produced in the United States, indicates whether or not the economy is growing. It's always given high visibility, sometimes without even an explanation of what the letters GNP stand for. Real GNP is in constant dollars, while nominal GNP is in current dollars. The real GNP is most widely reported because it points out to the average citizen what the economy is doing in terms of total manufactured items, services and everything else produced. In addition, the difference between growth in nominal GNP and growth in real GNP tells how much inflation has occurred. Recessions, quite simply, are periods in which the real economy slides backward.

GNP numbers are issued in preliminary and in final versions. And with each revision the numbers may widely differ. Unfortunately, even after the final numbers are released, there may be revisions, lots of them. Figures are released each month, the third week or later, and every quarter a final quarterly figure is announced. Numbers are announced by the Commerce Department.

The GNP includes several key components. The largest is consumer spending, thus the expression "consumer driven economy." Consumer spending has traditionally been about two-thirds of GNP. International transactions, loosely called trade, is becoming an increasingly large portion, now more than 25 percent. Government spending has traditionally been about 25 percent of GNP, while nongovernment investment spending, which includes outlays for plant and equipment, is usually in the 10 percent range. The percentages don't add up, but don't worry about it.

Housing Starts

Residential construction is closely followed because its turning points have accurately predicted changes in the business cycle. A solid level of housing starts usually speaks well for the coming year and is a solid barometer of economic optimism. Every recession has been signaled several months in advance by a major drop in housing starts and every recovery from recession has been anticipated by a recovery in housing starts. Generally, a rate of starts above 1.5 million is considered an indication of a strong economy in the year ahead. While housing starts receive the most publicity, another figure, the number of housing units authorized by local permits, is the one used in the index of leading indicators. One persistent problem is that weather conditions can skew these figures wildly. Housing starts are released the second or third week of the month.

Leading Economic Indicators

These 11 indicators, adjusted for inflation, include average work week of production workers; weekly claims for state unemployment insurance; new orders for consumer goods and materials; vendor performance; contracts for plant and equipment; new building permits; change in manufacturers' unfilled orders; sensitive materials prices; stock prices; money supply (M2) and index of consumer expectations. While they serve to forecast the business cycle, it may be a case of too many indicators spoiling the broth.

Since the early 1980s, the index has predicted considerably stronger economic growth than has actually taken place, in part because some of its components no longer hold as much power in the economy as they once did. For example, the movement of the stock market, while closely watched, probably doesn't have nearly as direct an effect on the economy as it once did. The leading economic indicators are reported on or near the last day of the month. The figures are compiled by the Bureau of Economic Analysis and appear in the bureau's "Business Conditions Digest," available from the Government Printing Office.

Money Supply

Represents total money in the economy, which means currency in circulation and deposits in savings and checking. Excess money in relation to output of goods may push prices and inflation up. Too little money may lower prices and spark unemployment. M1 is a narrow measure of money limited to currency and checkable deposits, while M2 is announced monthly and includes money market mutual fund assets and similar accounts at banks in addition to M1.

Money growth is a leading indicator of inflation, though its effect may not be felt immediately. Weekly figures make financial markets nervous because investors know that if the money supply grows too fast the Fed will take action to reduce it by withdrawing money from the banking system. Whether M1 is up or down depends too much on special circumstances that week and tells little about the direction of Federal Reserve policy, so monthly figures are much more worthy of consideration. Money supply figures, released weekly on Thursday, monthly figures at mid-month are available from the Federal Reserve Board.

Producer Price Index

The PPI, measuring change in prices of commodities for sale in U.S. markets, tells what's happening in industry and where prices are headed. It's worth watching as a leading indicator of inflation at the consumer level, since its price changes at the wholesale level eventually make their way to retail. PPI figures are released the second Friday of the month by the Bureau of Labor Statistics.

Retail Sales

This estimate of volume of sales to consumers, based on reports of retail establishments, outlines personal consumption and savings habits. Since consumer activity accounts for two-thirds of the U.S. economy, it's important to track. Yet these figures are based upon a small sampling and nearly always revised, with the initial figures tending to emphasize the largest vendors. The advance report, based on questions to 3,000 retail outlets and data from smaller businesses, isn't available until a month or more later. The two revisions that follow are based on 12,000 outlets. Retail sales figures are released the second week of the month.

Trade Balance

A trade deficit is an excess of imports over exports, while trade surplus is an excess of exports over imports. The balance of trade is made up of transactions in a merchandise and other movable goods and is one of the factors making up the larger current account, which includes services, tourism, transportation and interest and profits earned abroad. An important factor affecting balance of trade is strength or weakness of U.S. currency. For example, although a strong U.S. dollar is often considered a cause for rejoicing, many exporting U.S. manufacturers prosper in a period in which our currency is relatively weak. Released in mid-month.

Unemployment Rate

This is an indication of the number of civilians, 16 years old or older, who aren't employed but tried to find a job within the prior four weeks. Rises in the unemployment rate usually mean a slowing economy, so the Federal Reserve might ease credit and cause interest rates to drop. There is considerable debate among economists about the samplings used in these figures. Released the first Friday of the month by The Bureau of Labor Statistics (BLS). You might also want to take a look at Unemployment Insurance Claims, available from the Department of Labor every week.

Nonfarm Payroll Employment

Because the regular unemployment figures can be bounced around by sampling vagaries, this measure of the labor force which considers hours, wages and earnings is preferred by many economists. It's a major factor in estimates of industrial production and personal income. Released the first Friday of the month.

Manufacturer's New Orders and Inventories

New orders are the key, providing an indicator of manufacturing output. Highly volatile, these figures can foreshadow upcoming cyclical trends in the economy. The underlying problem, however, is that all those impressive orders can be canceled in the future and throw a monkey wrench into projections. Released in mid-month.

Industrial Production Index

The IPI provides hard evidence on changes in the total output at U.S. factories, mines and electric and gas utilities during the month. Remember that it emphasizes movement, rather than the value of production. Manufacturing dominates the index, mining accounting for only about 10 percent and utilities six percent. Released in mid-month.

SECONDARY INDICATORS

There are plenty of indicators. While all the above are the generally accepted measures of economic health, here are a few others that from time to time might bring added insight or some color to your story:

Purchasing power

The Bureau of Labor Statistics calls it "Spendable Average Weekly Earnings per Production Worker on Payrolls of Private Non-Agricultural Establishments." The index adjusts gross weekly paychecks to conform to price increases. It doesn't add in fringe benefits, but it's a key indicator for unions.

Standard of Living

This isn't an official index, but it's possible to see the trends by looking at the purchasing power numbers and the "Per Capita Income Series," the total of all sources of income including social security and welfare payments.

Wholesale Price Index

This is an increasingly important index since it's an indicator for the CPI and GNP. It reflects the prices of farm and industrial products.

Productivity Index

Since the Standard of Living cannot rise without a rise in productivity, the BLS indexes that express productivity are useful in determining the long-term trends in the economy.

Capital Utilization Rate

This is a measure of the efficiency of U.S. manufacturing. Rates of 85 percent or higher have been found to produce inefficiencies and bottlenecks. This number is more readily available in surveys like those done by McGraw-Hill.

Quit Rate

The BLS computes the number of people who leave their jobs as a percent of those employed. A high rate often means that workers are confident that there are plenty of jobs available.

USEFUL PUBLICATIONS

The Government Printing office will supply lots of financial documents on request, but it's better to get on the press mailing list of the Department of Commerce or the Bureau of Labor Statistics. Here is a partial list of the publications which are available from the printing office:

"Business Conditions Digest" is published monthly. It's crammed with charts and tables on dozens of indicators including income, trade and stock prices.

Economic Indicators is a monthly summary prepared by the Council of Economic Advisers with charts and tables on spending, finance, money, credit, production, etc.

Federal Reserve Bulletin is produced each month by the Federal Reserve System and is available from the Board of Governors, Federal Reserve System.

Monthly Labor Review has articles and data on labor, wages, productivity and union actions.

U.S. Industrial Outlook comes out annually and contains projections of all segments of the domestic economy.

Foreign Trade is a monthly report from the Bureau of the Census and reports trade statistics.

Population: Current Report is a monthly and annual report of population changes and changes in the characteristics of the population.

Retail Sales: Current Business Report comes out weekly and is crammed with retail data.

Joint Economic Committee of Congressional Reports these reports on economic issues are free and are available from the committee in the Dirksen Senate Office Building.

International Influences on the U.S. Economy

by Stanley Reed

The United States is part of an increasingly integrated world economic system—a system in which foreigners play a major role in the American economy. At the same time that American businesses look to foreign countries for opportunities, foreign companies are looking to the U.S. for markets, investments and profits. This flow of business and dollars across borders began to grow with the post-World War II rise of multi-national corporations and the development of international economic cooperation fostered by institutions such as the International Monetary Fund (IMF), World Bank and the General Agreement on Tariffs and Trade (GATT). International business really mushroomed in the last two decades when the communications revolution began shrinking the globe. Jet travel, fax machines and the homogenization of tastes are all working to increase and speed international economic links.

The linkage of the global economy is most apparent in financial and commodities markets, which are capable of accommodating shifts of vast amounts of assets around the globe in seconds. On any given day, as one market closes and another begins its trading day, the effects of news and investment psychology move from one market to next around the world.

In this system, the U.S. is the largest and most influential—American financial markets are favored by international investors because they are open, well-regulated and large enough to absorb huge quantities of dollars. In addition, the U.S. dollar is the currency of international reserves—the foreign currency held by governments to pay for imports and foreign debts. The dollar is also the currency used for the purchase of oil in international markets. U.S. trade imbalances with trading partners have put large numbers of dollars in the hands of foreigners who have spent them on American investments.

In recent decades the Japanese have been the dominant foreign investors in the U.S. The bull market of the late 1980s owes much of its vitality to foreign purchases of the shares of U.S. corporations. And through large purchases of U.S. government securities, the Japanese have been very important in the financing of the U.S.'s budget deficit.

This international financial network has an influence on government and policy making as well. If foreign investors lose confidence in the U.S., they may reduce their positions. For example, many experts think that in 1987, when then Treasury Secretary James Baker threatened to devalue the dollar unless Japan and West Germany stimulated their economies, he helped trigger the October stock market crash by making investors uneasy.

To be sure, his statement highlighted the economic dilemma the U.S. faces. On one hand, Baker and export-oriented American businesses wanted to lower the dollar in order to make U.S. products cheaper overseas in the hope that U.S. exports might rise and the trade deficit fall. On the other hand, foreign investors view a lower dollar as a threat to their U.S. investments.

For most journalists, the international economic story focuses primarily on the relationship between the central banks, the financial markets and economic stimulus. As the Baker statement suggested, the Federal Reserve and other major central banks can influence markets around the world. One way is by buying and selling the dollar. If the effort is coordinated, as it was in the 1980s through meetings of central bank and treasury officials, then the world economic order can be managed short-term. To weaken the dollar, the U.S. sought the assistance of other countries which sold dollars in order to increase the number of dollars in circulation so as to reduce the value of the dollar. But keep in mind that "intervention" is a short-term remedy. Eventually, economists say, a freely traded currency, like any financial asset, will find an equilibrium determined by supply and demand regardless of intervention.

The international economic story is primarily a story about the big players and the small players. Once the Arabs were major players in the economy. In recent years the Japanese have taken the spotlight. And, should the markets of the USSR and the East bloc open to trade and development, then those countries could become important to the global picture. Indeed, the Europeans may emerge as the major economic newsmakers in the 1990s if the economic unification of Europe creates the world's largest single market (see "Trade"). The presence of the European Commission in Brussels has transformed the Belgian capital into a major government and regulatory center. Whether the restructuring of Europe represents an opportunity or a threat for American businesses is grist for journalists for years to come.

Even though stories about international influences on the U.S. economy seem to have datelines like London, Brussels and Hong Kong, the influences are as apparent in Des Moines and Sacramento as they are at the negotiating tables. When the Soviet Union buys grain, Kansas wheat farmers are interested. When Malaysia begins an auto industry, it could make a difference to a plant worker in Flint, Michigan. When China cracks down on its citizens, the fallout affects Hong Kong Chinese who may become more uncertain about their economic livelihood and more likely to take their money and flee to the farmland of California.

Let's consider how a journalist might handle one assignment. Suppose, for example, a major company in your region announces that it has agreed to be acquired by a Japanese competitor. The editor asks you to look into the implications of the acquisition. Why is the acquisition happening? What will the consequences be?

THE FOREIGN ACQUISITION

In covering the foreign acquisition story, avoid falling into the trap of assuming that there's something wrong with foreign investment in the U.S. Consider each case on its own merits. Try to uncover the motivations of the company being acquired as well as the Japanese acquirer. Talk to the company, its competitors, industry analysts, and the Japanese investors. Was the company in trouble? If so, the Japanese investment may actually be saving or even creating jobs.

Find out what the Japanese intend to do with the company. If they plan to retain functions such as research and development, design and heavy manufacturing that add value, then the acquisition is likely to benefit the economy. If they plan to shut down much of the American operation down and fill the void from Japan, there would be less reason to take a positive view. If you cannot obtain satisfactory information on their plans, check into whether this firm has made other U.S. investments and, if so, how it has managed them.

Many U.S. state and local governments openly court foreign investors, offering plant sites, tax breaks and other incentives. The likely sale of a company in your region to overseas interests may give you an opening to do a more general story on foreign investment in the U.S. If so, you will probably want to provide some explanation of international economics.

In recent years, foreigners have had the wherewithal to make U.S.

acquisitions because the dollar value of goods they have sold to the U.S. has greatly exceeded what they have bought in the U.S. Foreigners have to do something with all these dollars, and have invested millions of dollars in U.S. businesses and real estate. Foreigners are also big holders of U.S. stocks and bonds, thereby helping to finance the U.S. budget deficit. The Commerce and Treasury Departments are good sources of statistical information on foreign investment.

You might also want to determine what made the company you are reporting on attractive to a foreign acquirer. Look into whether the foreign investors are paying a ridiculously high price for lackluster goods. They often do. Did the American company see its products losing market share to those produced by Japan and other overseas competitors? If so, you may have an interesting international trade story on your hands. Try to find out how the Japanese developed their competitive advantage. Do not settle for the shopworn explanation that it is lower labor costs.

Often foreign firms use sophisticated, government-orchestrated strategies in developing and marketing their products. Is this Japanese company part of a government-encouraged industry? A common tactic is to use trade barriers, government purchasing policies and other protectionist strategies to guarantee domestic producers a near monopoly of the domestic market. A protected domestic market gives a company a secure base on which to develop a product for export. The assured sales lower the risk. In cases where there is a so-called learning curve effect, meaning that manufacturing costs fall as the producer learns more efficient techniques through experience, this form of protection gives domestic firms an actual cost advantage, which may translate into higher export sales.

Government involvement in trade here and abroad is definitely on the rise, and will be an increasingly important subject for business journalism. This involvement takes many forms including trade barriers, concessional loans to buyers, tax breaks and supply of subsidized inputs to export manufacturers. The main U.S. vehicles for export subsidies are the Export-Import Bank and various Agricultural Department programs that provide developing countries with cheap U.S. grain.

GETTING THE STORY

While the sources and concepts that you'll use in reporting international stories may differ, these stories are similar to domestic ones. Do as much background work as you can on your subject. If you think you can write a great story about international banking or world energy prices without preparation, you're probably kidding yourself. You'll need to learn the terms and business procedures. You should not attempt to cover oil, for example, without understanding the structure and politics of the Organization of Petroleum Exporting Countries (OPEC) or the process of refining oil or the many grades or the pricing and delivery of oil. Your sources will respect you and may be more forthcoming if you convince them that you know what you're talking about. They'll also be less likely to feed you a party line.

If your story turns on a policy issue, figure out where the lines are drawn and who's on what side. Political interest in international economic issues is growing. If you're covering these topics on a regular basis, you'll need to cultivate sources in government—particularly congressional aides and the staff of the appropriate departments. For reasons ranging from technical complexities to geographical distances, you'll probably find yourself relying on experts more than you would like. Be aware of their interest in the outcome and use that awareness to filter what they tell you. There's nothing wrong with talking to advocates—often you'll have no choice—but know where someone stands.

PART II

WRITING STORIES

Section 4

The Basics

Sources

by Thomas C. Hayes

Developing good sources in a broad range of industries, government agencies, consulting firms, law firms and elsewhere is the cornerstone of good business reporting. You must have them and you cannot have too many.

All energetic but inexperienced reporters one day find themselves assigned to a major story when few sources are apparent for writing a clearly reasoned and well-informed piece. But plunging ahead is the only path to expand minds, resources and clip files. Alas, one success is never enough. The challenge of finding clarity amid the confusion never ends.

Old hands in business news and savvy newcomers alike realize that each story raises new questions—whether minor or staggering—that only outside experts or insiders can answer. Looked at another way, each story presents a game all its own, as the following example is meant to illustrate.

You are lingering over the last lines of a long feature one morning when a friend in investment banking calls with a hot rumor. She says a wobbly conglomerate in Los Angeles will announce within days the sale of its profitable medical-equipment subsidiary, Inventco, which happens to be the biggest employer in your city.

Quick calls to public relations contacts at Inventco and at headquarters in Los Angeles make it very plain that no one in an official role is going to address the rumor.

You are overwhelmed with possible angles: What other routes are available to confirm the rumor? Who are the likely bidders? Will Inventco's management make a bid? Could any offer be financed by its valuable assets? Is the subsidiary already overburdened by debt? Might Inventco be forced to relocate or are its local roots too strong? Could the state legislature block a sale to foreigners, if asked by Inventco? In what scenarios would Inventco's payroll likely be slashed or expanded?

By mid-day the rumor is picked up on the Dow Jones News Wire. Now you and dozens of other reporters around the nation, and perhaps abroad, are being assigned the story as editors pick up on the rumor and assess its significance. In effect, you are being handed a player's card in a new version of a reporting game that is repeated thousands of times every day.

This Inventco game, like all the other games, has three parts. One: Judge quickly where answers are needed for general and sophisticated readers and where they are not. Two: Concentrate your energy on reaching sources that will give you the fastest, most accurate and most perceptive information. Three: Repeat steps One and Two. Your raw interviews raise unforeseen issues and questions that reshape the story's initial scope and significance. The game ends at deadline. Good luck.

The way most editors see it, beat reporters have an edge on stories breaking in their field because they keep date books and card files filled with well-placed, familiar sources and their phone numbers. As beat reporters gain in experience in a field, they are expected to frame for editors new story ideas that are like compact and brightly colored puzzles with missing pieces. The beat reporters' job is to find the missing pieces and complete the picture. In the real world of tight deadlines and unreachable sources, the puzzle model is imperfect. Also, fair-minded reporters and editors can disagree about which pieces are missing and even whether they can be found.

Reporters of widely varying talents and experience always play the game. Sharp-eyed generalists who know how and where to sift for sources can and do prevail. The race to get the best stories is a sprint that is really part of a longer marathon for finding, developing and expanding a pool of good sources. For business reporters, it means devoting hours each week to carefully scanning several periodicals: *The New York Times, The Wall Street Journal, Business Week, Forbes, Fortune, The Economist,* as well as publications that cover special areas you might follow more closely, such as *Electronics Business, Institutional Investor,* or the *Oil and Gas Journal.* For regional correspondents, add several daily newspapers to the mix. Then, too, some business news programs on television are topical, informative and occasionally influence movements of stock prices. *Wall Street Week* and *The Nightly Business Report* on PBS and CNN's nightly *Moneyline* are examples.

Source prospecting requires face to face meetings—in cafes, or over breakfast, lunch or dinner—with new contacts who might be helpful down the road if they believe they can trust you. Most business sources who have dealt with reporters have been burned by sins of betrayed confidences, sloppy attribution or bungled facts. A first meeting is important for sizing up a reporter, and they wonder: How powerful and responsible is the publication? How accurate is the reporter? How much does he know about our company or agency or consulting firm? What do our contacts in public relations circles say about him? This is especially important with a group that some reporters take for granted: public relations officers. Senior executives and partners in professional firms get many requests for interviews. They rely on public relations people for advice on deciding which reporters are worth how much time, in what order, and with what likely result.

On the other hand, public relations executives vary in their usefulness to reporters. Some see their job as keeping reporters at bay and their company and its executives invisible to the public. Good ones help in suggesting financial analysts, trade associations, trade publications and industry consulting firms that are known and respected by industry executives. They also can provide tips or confirm rumors on competitors' activities.

The same is true for public relations consultants. Many account executives at public relations firms have only superficial understanding of their clients activities, but others are knowledgeable and quick to spot industry trends. In electronics technology, for instance, Regis McKenna Inc., based in Palo Alto, California, has a reputation for being associated with successful clients and for making their activities and key executives accessible to reporters.

Maintaining and developing good relationships with well-placed people is often what gives good reporters an edge. Still, there are tensions in these contacts that cannot be ignored. A source's reasons for speaking with a reporter can include promoting self-interests, retaliation against an adversary, outrage over an injustice, among others. They often work to a reporter's advantage, if the reporter uses good judgment. For instance, it's fine to report that a United States Attorney in Dallas expects that fraud is greater than believed in the savings industry. At the same time, the comment is partially self-serving because the attorney wants Congress to commit more funds so the Government can hire more and better lawyers to go after the presumed miscreants.

At times, information damaging to valued sources must be reported. Some sources will never return another phone call. Others will. Life goes on. Out of necessity, you find new sources. When reporting or editing errors occur, sources should expect and usually are satisfied with a printed correction.

WHAT NEXT?

In cases where a specific company refuses to make public statements, such as Inventco, the range of potential sources is still vast. Financial analysts at local or national investment houses and business school professors are often willing and quotable sources. Former executives, local union leaders, managers at major suppliers as well as executives at major competitors can be cultivated. So can customers or lower ranking employees who are neighbors, friends of friends, or acquaintances from social groups.

Financial analysts, usually employed by local, regional and national brokerage firms, are selling the fruits of their research on the earnings prospects for public companies to people who want to make money through shrewd investments. When the analysts are wrong, their firms' clients lose money. They often make their printed reports on companies and industries available to reporters.

How do you find financial analysts? One of the most indispensable guides for business reporters is Nelson's Directory of Investment Research. Published by Nelson Publications, in Port Chester, New York, the current volume includes more than 1,000 pages of financial analysts, listed under each of the dozens of companies they follow, as well as the firms that employ them. For instance, Bryan Jacoboski's name appears under the heading of Paine Webber, Inc., the Wall Street investment firm where he works as an oil industry analyst. It also appears under several oil companies, including Chevron, Amoco and Texaco, along with Paine Webber's general telephone number in New York City. The telephone number, address, and senior officers of most public companies are also listed in the Nelson guide. Business reporters reach for Nelson's every day. It is expensive. The 1988 volume carried a retail price of $279. Many public libraries, as well as the libraries of college and university business schools, buy it.

As in any other profession, the quality of analysts' work varies widely. Over time, business reporters develop their own lists, often noting which analysts lean toward optimism or pessimism toward a given company, regardless of the latest news. These analysts generally are avoided. The *Institutional Investor,* a monthly publication that keeps a close eye on Wall Street firms, publishes a list of research all-stars each year. It has great depth. Categories are arranged by industry, such as chemicals, pharmaceuticals or banks, and selections are based on surveys of pension funds, insurance companies and other large financial companies that buy advice on financial investments from Wall Street firms.

The Standard & Poor's *Stock Reports* is another invaluable guide. A swarm of analysts at Standard & Poor's Corporation in New York City, cover most publicly traded firms on each of the major stock exchanges, the New York Stock Exchange, the American Stock Exchange and the over-the-counter market. The complete set includes 12 volumes with each company arranged alphabetically and by the market where its stock trades. At last check, the complete set was priced at more than $2,400 a year.

The S&P guide, as it's called, is a great place to get educated quickly about a company's circumstance. A chart shows the price-and-volume movements for the company's stock over the last six or seven years. A detailed table of financial data goes back 10 years, and includes revenues, operating income, capital expenditures, net income, cash, assets, return on assets, long-term debt, common equity and return on equity.

On many occasions, when a deadline looms 30 minutes after a corporate news development is announced, an S&P sheet serves as the factual backbone for a quick story. A call to the S&P research department often produces an analyst who can assess a new development. When more time is available, the information on S&P sheets should be scoured for clues that suggest more insightful questions. For example: "I see that your operating income at the Stride Rite Corporation has rebounded beyond where it was four years ago, but you've cut long-term debt very sharply in the same period to less than 10 percent of total capital. Has your sales decline four years ago made you reluctant to use debt to finance your growth?"

There are many other ways to obtain detailed facts and analysis on public companies. In our small bureau in Dallas, we are diligent in keeping our files current for news clips, significant news releases and company publications, usually annual reports to stockholders, quarterly financial reports, executive speeches and special reports to the Securities & Exchange Commission. The annual reports and other official company documents are separated for easy access when deadlines loom and a few precise numbers are critical for illuminating financial trends.

News clips are developed the old-fashioned way, from scanning several newspapers and magazines for articles with an enduring shelf life, and marking them for clipping according to file heading and date. Many news organizations now subscribe to several electronic data services that include all articles published in dozens of publications over several years. This can markedly reduce the need to build clip files. Many libraries in major cities also have business librarians who are eager to help news organizations. The point is, it's a great waste of time for both reporter and sources when a reporter is unaware of detailed stories and reports already published about a company or industry under review.

Because they cover a narrow territory every week, trade publications often are useful guides. In many cases their editors can be quoted by reporters at general-interest newspapers and magazines as legitimate, disinterested and well-informed sources. Also, a quick scan of articles in a trade publication often produces several prospective sources among the consultants and industry experts whose opinions and analyses are regularly published by "the trades."

Trade associations, such as the American Petroleum Institute, the National Association of Manufacturers or the American Bankers Association, generally are eager to give reporters mounds of statistics and a view on issues that generally affect the industry. Most are based in Washington, the better to dispatch lobbyists to the halls of Congress. Their commentary typically is far from disinterested, but it represents an industry perspective that's important for scope and context in many stories. This is especially true in stories explaining or analyzing battles in Congress affecting an industry, such as giving banks powers to underwrite securities or curbing the independence of financial industry regulators.

Even more than consultants, accountants and other professional advisers, executives of industry trade associations adamantly resist being quoted on specific companies. One reason is because of intramural disputes within industry associations that pit company executives against one another. Trade association executives are paid from dues collected from all company members. They don't want to antagonize any of their "customers."

TRUST IS IMPORTANT

A key to creating a broad and effective range of sources is continually demonstrating in your work to chief executives, $300-an-hour lawyers and other valuable sources—including many who read and are influenced by your publication—that you go beyond getting the facts right. You know how to arrange them into a compelling analysis. Demonstrated knowledge, character and insight encourage contacts to take what they see as greater risks in giving you confidential or overlooked details on given stories. Trust, of course, works two ways. Once events suggest or prove that a source was deceptive, all future information from that source is filtered through a prism of suspicion. Your suspicion.

You develop trust in a source by consistently doing what you say you will do. That means attributing quotes and other information, for instance, that you agreed was on the record, while keeping other information on background. For instance, a spokesman or executive at a major bank often will not object to being quoted in an official capacity for a story on the bank. But they would object strenuously, and likely refuse to cooperate with you in the future, if information they leaked privately that embarrasses or criticizes a rival is attributed directly to them. Sometimes executives, lawyers and other sources will give long interviews, knowing you are a reporter, and at the conclusion say all the comments were off-the-record. It's a ridiculous request; ground rules on attribution should be established at the start of the interview. But the request might be worth honoring if you have key details confirmed on the record by others and this source can help in the future.

Management consultants at major firms like McKinsey & Company, Booz Allen & Hamilton, Arthur D. Little and Bain & Company, partners at accounting firms like Arthur Andersen, Ernst and Young, and Deloitte, Haskins & Sells, and economists at banks and economic consulting firms, such as Data Resources, in Lexington, Massachusetts., and the WEFA Group, in Bala Cynwyd, Pennsylvania, often are eager to be quoted on broad industry trends.

These firms have offices in many cities across the nation and many have public relations departments or retain outside public relations firms to lead you to their best expert. Be forewarned: these experts typically also are loath to be quoted on matters involving specific companies, especially if the view is negative. Important context and background can often be obtained, but often they simply refuse to comment on specific companies. They don't want to discourage that company from offering to pay their steep fees in a search for solutions. Venture capitalists tend to stay more in the shadows, but often are shrewd analysts of industry personalities, trends and product breakthroughs.

Outside directors of public companies are usually well-informed about the strategies, products and executive issues that occasionally erupt into important stories. Polling outside directors at a company in turmoil often is a futile exercise; many directors are unwilling to talk, especially if they don't know the reporter. But the effort is worth it. A director leading a faction against a chief executive might agree to background interviews. Union leaders, financial analysts and consultants can help identify these boardroom dissidents.

As a general rule, reporters have better luck in "smoking out" silent executives caught up in a corporate battle by making it known to them that their opponents are talking. You are going to write a story and if the reluctant executive doesn't want to respond, it doesn't mean a story will not be written. It will simply say he declined to comment. When things are going well, outside directors often are approachable and quotable. Of these, business school professors typically are more independent and outspoken. They also can be remarkably informative about industry problems.

Federal and state regulators, such as banking, insurance and public utility commissioners, are important contacts. If they trust you, many will explain complex circumstances in great detail on background. Since they are in the public arena, they frequently have designs on using news organizations to promote their programs. Public opinion in regulatory matters is very powerful. It's not unethical to play along, as long as you detect and resist attempts to trade information for favored treatment. In the end, your job is presenting a complete, clear view of reality. Former regulators also are great sources. Many return to or set up law firms, consulting firms or other advice-peddling clusters. They see news stories in which they're quoted as experts as harmonious to their private sector ambitions. They're often right.

From Wall Street to Main Street, the landscape is full of economists in financial institutions, universities and regional consulting firms who specialize in analyzing national, regional and local economies. Many cities also have market research firms—statistical boutiques, really—that analyze housing, jobs by industry, office construction and leasing, and dozens of other areas of economic activity. Be on guard for "homers," analysts who put a positive spin on even the darkest indicators.

Government agencies are most useful on industry trend stories when they are asked for statistics and general analysis. The Commerce Department, the Bureau of Labor Statistics and the Census Bureau each have officials who handle mostly requests for information from news organizations. They also can suggest articles in government publications that have dealt with the topic at hand, and the authors of those essays. Don't forget that government agencies have a responsibility to provide information to the press, even though some documents were never intended to be seen by the public. You can gain access to these documents using the Freedom of Information Act. It applies only to federal agencies, not state agencies.

Most states have commerce departments, with voluble elected or appointed senior officials, who can provide quotes and information. Many regions now have economic development agencies that are funded by both public and private sources. Their staffs often include local professors with backgrounds in urban geography, economics and social demography. In some cases, the development agencies will be offshoots of the local chamber of commerce. Chamber executives are paid to extol the wonders of their locale when they're on the record, but many provide unattributable but useful insights on personalities and companies. They can refer you to bankers, executives and consultants. Local chambers also are repositories of useful statistics on their area's economy.

Overlooked and Underused:
State and Local Sources

by David Lindorff

It was a slow news day in the Los Angeles County Hall of Administration, the county seat where I ran the bureau for the Daily News back in 1977. With nothing else going on, I had wandered down to a hearing room to listen to Equitable Life Assurance Company officials challenge their office tower assessment. The company was asking to have the assessor's market value figure of $31 million for the property reduced by $11 million.

Having not the vaguest idea of the value of such property myself, I was wondering how it might be objectively checked. Then I remembered that insurance companies are state regulated, and that like banks, they must prove they have assets to back their liabilities. Mightn't they have listed their major property holdings as assets?

The answer was yes. A call to the California State Insurance Commissioner quickly revealed that Equitable had reported the same building to the state as having a book value of $27.4 million. Looking further, I found that the company was also appealing the assessment of the UCB Tower, a downtown skyscraper it also owned, asking that it be reduced from the assessor's $62 million to just $37.2 million. Equitable had listed that building with the Insurance Commission as being worth $78 million—more than double what it was saying to the assessment appeals board. The story ran the next day under the banner head: "Tax Cuts for the Asking." A day later, the assessor's office announced it would begin defending its assessments using Insurance Commission figures.

There's a wealth of material at the state and local level that's available to reporters writing about business and economic issues—material that is all too often ignored.

"I think most reporters are unaware of how much information and documentation is floating around the archives of state and local government," says Jack Newfield, a veteran investigative reporter in New York. "I've done stories on nursing home scandals, Lilco and Shoreham (the Long Island nuclear power plant) and Teamsters Union corruption that could only be done with the help of state and local agencies like the Public Service Commission, the Department of Health and the State Department of Labor."

For certain industries, state government is almost the only source of some information. Insurance companies and public utilities are good examples. While the SEC will have the basic corporate filings of such firms, anything having to do with rate setting or actuarial experience will come from state regulators.

Similarly, states often have much more information about the health care industry than does the federal government. For the most part, the federal government's involvement in hospitals and nursing homes is limited to Medicare. States license such facilities, and investigators are often more than happy to tell you how a company is running them.

Often, state agencies can be more useful than federal regulators even where federal issues are involved. Medicare is a good example. In recent years, the federal government's data collection system has been gutted by over-zealous, and sometimes ideologically motivated budget cutters. Finding out statistics about Medicaid and Medicare at individual hospitals, for instance, is now much easier to do at the state level.

Once you know in which state a company is incorporated—or in the case of a partnership, registered—the appropriate secretary of state's or corporate commissioner's office can give you valuable information about corporate officers and owners of record—even for nonpublic companies. Often, because they get called so rarely, they'll do it over the phone —a real plus at deadline time.

State regulatory agencies, and justice departments too, have become increasingly important sources of information about business during the past decade, as the process of federal deregulation reduced the role—or at least the level of activity—of federal agencies like the Federal Trade Commission and the U.S. Justice Department's Antitrust Division. The New York Attorney General's office, for instance, located in a state where many of the nation's largest firms are headquartered, has been increasingly active in antitrust enforcement in recent years and offers a wealth of information on the subject. Other big states, notably California and Florida, have aggressive attorneys general whose offices can be very helpful. And don't forget the state court systems. When companies have legal disputes, or run afoul of public interest, they often wind up in state courts instead of federal courts, because a given state's laws work to the advantage of the plaintiff.

As the leveraged buyout binge developed in the late 1980s, a number of states, including Ohio, Indiana, Delaware and New York, passed anti-takeover statutes which have become important for business writers covering takeover stories. State attorneys general and secretaries of state have become useful sources when such laws have been invoked or challenged.

Generally speaking, every state has a secretary of state or corporate commissioner, an attorney general, a department of labor, and a tax department. Most states also have their own environmental protection laws and agencies. Some states have their own occupational health and safety agency, equal opportunity commission and consumer affairs agency and labor relations board, too. Familiarize yourself with all such offices in your own state. Just learning where your state's environmental, worker safety, labor and civil rights laws exceed federal regulations can provide you with important stories about how business is impacted. Get to know the press contacts of each agency, as each can be a terrific source of stories.

Every state also has some kind of freedom of information law (see "The Freedom of Information Act"). Find out how to use any relevant freedom of information laws in your jurisdiction, including the appeals process, and learn how not to take no for an answer. States don't have "national security" to fall back on as an excuse for not providing you with information, but some agencies can be just as information-retentive as the CIA anyway. In New York in 1988, state agencies had to be instructed to stop using the Freedom of Information Act as an excuse not to give out information. It turns out that instead of providing routine public information on request, some agencies were asking people to make requests for any information in writing under the terms of the act. Now they've been told to assume information is public.

Because reporters tend to run first to the federal government when they're doing business stories, when you do go to a state agency for information, you're likely to encounter one of two reactions: either the person you talk to will be so excited you called that he or she will bend over backwards to help, or the agency will be so calcified that it won't even know how to help you or whether it's allowed to. In the latter case, be prepared to push (that's when it helps to know your public access rights!). When you encounter trouble, the attorney general's office can often prove very useful in interpreting the state's freedom of information act. Elected officials can also help pry loose information from agency bureaucrats. (New York state has an advocate at the Secretary of State's Office, whose job it is to help citizens and members of the press make effective use of the state's freedom of information law.)

Local government too is a fount of useful information about business

—even big business. For one thing, whereas tax records concerning an individual company are unavailable at the federal and even the state level, local property tax records are always public record. Naturally, when you're doing a real estate story, this is invaluable, but such data can be important in other kinds of pieces too, providing otherwise unavailable information, for instance, on how much a company spent on a lavish headquarters building. Cultivating sources in city and county clerk's offices where property transfers are recorded can also help you get advance notice when a company buys or sells property—news that can foretell expansion or relocation plans.

A particularly interesting area of state and local government for journalists to explore is the matter of business relocation incentives. For several decades now, many states and localities have been trying to find creative ways to attract business development. Some jurisdictions will offer property tax holidays, others access to subsidized land, others job training tax credits. Still others have set up new business "incubators" in conjunction with local university research centers. Besides the fact that such programs invite corruption because of the amounts of money involved, typically, the lack of public involvement in the decision-making process raises serious questions about whether the community gets what it pays for. Companies that get tax holidays often pick up and leave when the holiday is over. And even when a business stays, the cost per job to the community can be extraordinary. For the reporter willing to look broadly at social, political and business activities, this is almost a blank page.

One last note: In addition to state and local agencies and offices, there is another very useful set of agencies at the state level that can be invaluable to business journalists. These are the state or regional offices of relevant federal agencies. Very often offices like the Regional Bureau of Labor Statistics, the regional office of the EPA, or a local U.S. Attorney's office will have much more current information about your area including in the latter cases information about corporate prosecutions— than Washington headquarters can offer. Since many of these regional agencies are not geared up to deal with the press, and don't have press officers, it again pays to develop relationships with the heads of each office in advance, so you don't have to try to get through to someone for the first time on deadline. For your efforts, you wind up talking to the big enchilada instead of the government flak you generally wind up with in Washington.

If nothing else, making better use of available state and local sources instead of ringing up Washington all the time will do wonders to keep editors and publishers off your back for running up all those phone bills.

The advent of the Reagan administration in 1980 saw a decline in the federal government's antitrust activity—always a great source of stories in years past. You can still pursue some of those juicy tales of inappropriate mergers and price conspiracies though, courtesy of a number of states' attorneys general.

Since the early 1980s, a number of states, notably Colorado, Connecticut, Florida, Maine, Maryland, Massachusetts, Minnesota, New Jersey, New York and Washington, have created or bolstered existing antitrust divisions, and have brought cases under the Sherman and Clayton Acts that once would probably have been brought by the Federal Trade Commission or the U.S. Justice Department.

In 1988, five states joined forces to bring antitrust charges against some of the nation's major insurance companies, charging them with collusion in reducing liability coverage nationwide.

A decade ago, if you wanted to write antitrust stories, you went to Washington. Now you need to know your states, especially the ten most active ones.

Even when it doesn't bring a case, you may learn a lot about big merger and acquisition stories by calling the New York Attorney General's antitrust division. That office, for instance, initiated investigations into U.S. Air's acquisition of Piedmont, and Campeau's tough battle against Macy's for the Federated retail chain. A reporter could have learned a lot by talking with attorneys there as the stories developed— attorneys who were watching closely because of the amount of business both target companies did in the state.

"We'll tell you what we're doing, but not confidential information that we are given by the companies," says Deputy Bureau Chief Alice McInerney in the New York Attorney General's office. These days, with the federal government staying aloof on many antitrust issues, you may get more from offices like hers than from the FTC. Even where the U.S. government does handle a case, state attorneys general may have another angle. McInerney's advice to reporters: "Call us, too."

The Freedom of Information Act

When the Freedom of Information Act (5 U.S.C. 552) was debated in Congress in 1965, pro-FOIA legislators argued that the peoples' right to know was a basic principle of American democracy. They quoted James Madison, a drafter of the First Amendment to the Constitution: "A popular government without popular information or the means of acquiring it, is but a prologue to a farce or a tragedy or perhaps both."

The FOIA, which allows the public to examine activities of the federal government, was adopted in 1966 and amended in 1986. The law allows anyone, including foreigners, to acquire information. It covers all "records" in the possession or control of a federal agency. (It does not apply to records of private institutions, hospitals or state governments. States have their own "open records" laws.)

Information is to be made available to any "person," which includes an individual, partnership, corporation, association, public or private organization. Under the FOIA, information must be disclosed, unless the agency can cite one of nine exemptions.

REQUESTING INFORMATION

You must file a written request. Most agencies have an FOIA officer, who, by law, must respond to requests within 10 working days. The

This section on the Freedom of Information Act was compiled by Pamela Hollie Kluge from public documents.

agency may ask for an extension, but if the agency doesn't respond within the 10 days, you may appeal to the head of the agency with an administrative appeal. The appeal must be answered within 20 working days. If you get no response after the second alternative, you can then file a lawsuit in federal court. If you win, the court will order the agency to release the documents and may award you attorney and court costs.

Your request must be specific. Identify the material you seek; include names, dates and places. You might also include newspaper clippings as background.

The documents aren't free. You should consider what you are willing to pay for information. The act requires agencies to publish the costs of search and document reproduction. Reproduction will cost about 15 cents a page. Searches may cost up to $30 an hour. Computer fees can run as much as $300 an hour.

Journalists, however, can get a break on the fees. Representatives of the media pay no search fees and get copies of 100 pages free. (Newsletters are included in this category.) Freelancers may qualify for a waiver if there is a reasonable expectation for a published story. A waiver or reduction of fees can be requested in cases where "disclosure of information is in the public interest because it is likely to contribute significantly to public understanding of the operations or activities of the government and is not primarily in the commercial interest of the requestor."

While the FOIA may appear to provide access to a world of documentation, there are nine exemptions that can cause problems. The exemptions can be challenged. The courts will decide if a request can be denied under the following exemptions:

1. *National Security.* Documents that might cause "damage" to the nation's security can be refused. The exemption applies to documents properly classified as "top secret," "secret" or "confidential"—terms defined by Presidential Executive Order. The courts can decide whether the classification is justified.

2. *Internal Agency Rules.* This exemption covers "housekeeping" records "related solely to the internal personnel rules and practices of an agency." Congress has decided some information is not of interest to the public.

3. *Catch-all Exemption.* The records covered by this exemption are "specifically exempted from disclosure" by statutes governing the operations of the various agencies. Census Bureau Records, for example, are exempt because the bureau must protect the privacy of persons who report to it. The Central Intelligence Agency is required by law to keep its procedures and methods a secret. Even the Veterans' Benefits and the Consumer Product Safety Commission can refuse to produce documents citing privacy clauses in their establishing legislation.

4. *Trade Secrets.* This is "commercial or financial information ob-

tained from a person and privileged or confidential." To withhold information under this exemption, the government must prove the information is confidential and that disclosure could cause harm to the "competitive position" of the source of the information or would impair the government's ability to get information in the future.

5. *Internal Agency Memoranda*. This exemption applies to "interagency or intra-agency memorandums or letters which would not be available by law to a party other than an agency in litigation with the agency." This exemption includes the attorney-client privilege and executive privilege as well as privileges for government-generated commercial information.

6. *Personal Privacy*. This exemption applies primarily to "personal" and "medical" records, but may apply to welfare payments, legitimacy of children and alcohol consumption records. Because the courts have often ruled in favor of disclosure, this exemption is frequently tested in court.

7. *Law Enforcement Records*. The purpose of this exemption is to prevent the premature disclosure of information that would jeopardize investigations. In 1986, this exemption was changed to allow refusal of disclosure if harm "could reasonably be expected." The previous exemption stated that the law enforcement agency had to show that harm would occur. Witnesses are protected under this exemption.

8. *Bank Reports*. This exemption protects sensitive financial reports and audits. It applies to banks, trust companies, investment banking firms and associations.

9. *Oil and Gas Well Data*. This little-used exemption protects private companies from speculators. Consequently, "geological and geophysical information and data, including maps concerning wells," cannot be obtained through the FOIA.

SOURCES OF HELP

The Office of Information and Privacy:
202-663-3642

The FOI Service Center:
202-466-6313 or 800-336-4243

Reporters Committee for Freedom of the Press
Legal Defense and Research Fund
800 18th Street, N.W.
Washington, D.C. 20006

International Business Reporting

by Sam Zuckerman

Scene: A newsroom in New York City.

It's 10 A.M. The wires report that the Federal Trade Commission has ordered a Brooklyn candy maker to stop running ads claiming bubble gum is "healthy food for real kids." Your editor assigns you the story.

You send a messenger to the Manhattan FTC office to pick up press releases and other background material. A computer data search provides background on the candy company. After an hour, the chief FTC press officer in Washington returns your call and arranges a not-for-attribution interview with a commissioner.

Meanwhile, you've already been on the telephone with the candy company flak. He told you about a company-sponsored survey that showed that gum-chewing kids got fewer colds. You get advertising text and the study in hand by 2:30 p.m. Finally, a call to an old source, a lawyer with several ad agency clients, elicits the comment that she would have advised her clients never to run such an ad. You have 700 words on your editor's screen a little before 5:00.

Scene: Your office in a Latin American capital.

During an interview on a morning news program, the finance minister announces the nationalization of Banco Riquissimo, the country's largest bank, because of "intolerable affronts to the national dignity." He accuses Riquissimo of smuggling out of the country dollars hidden in cases of Latina Cola, a locally produced soft drink.

The minister's office telephone is busy. You dial the ministry's Office of Social Communication, but that too is busy. You keep trying—it takes half an hour to get through. A woman informs you that the social communication director is not in his office. In any case, she has heard nothing about any bank nationalization and, even if she had, she isn't authorized to give out information. She assures you that Engineer Martinez, the director, will arrive in half an hour. "Don't worry," she says as you slam down the phone.

An hour later, Engineer Martinez is still out, but the woman promises he'll be there "in half an hour."

You jump in your car and speed to Banco Riquissimo headquarters. Business seems to be going on as usual. You don't even bother with the bank's public relations chief—the last time you spoke with him, he was arranging photographs for a ribbon-cutting ceremony. He knows virtually nothing about the bank's inner workings, nor will he ever comment on anything remotely sensitive.

Instead, you ask the receptionist if you may speak to a bank executive. You must have an appointment, she tells you. The board chairman's secretary is not at her desk, she says. Ten minutes more on the house phone brings word that the president's secretary is indeed at work and can arrange an interview first thing next month. You stalk off muttering about deadlines.

You call a friend at a well-connected think tank and ask what the hell is going on. Don't worry, he tells you, he's got the whole story. "The finance minister's cousin is scheming to steal the Banco Riquissimo chairman's exclusive Latina Cola dealership in the Caribbean. The whole nationalization thing is a ploy to get the franchise," he confides. Your friend has no proof, but everyone he's talked to is sure the story is true.

You don't like to use other journalists as sources, but out of desperation you check with a reporter friend from Television Panamericana. He says the Latina Cola story is a planted rumor. An "absolutely reliable source" told him what's really going on—it seems the president is trying to push the finance minister out of office. The bank move is the minister's gambit to save his job. The minister announced the Riquissimo seizure on the spur of the moment and his top aides are working feverishly to put together a plan.

"But you can't print that," your friend shouts. He says he'll be going on the air soon and won't report any of this version.

At 5:00 p.m. you call your editor in the U.S. to tell her that you have nothing to add to the minister's morning remarks. "That's OK," she says, "we weren't going to use it anyway."

Welcome to international business reporting!

There's no denying it: being a foreign correspondent has its rewards. Just as in the Navy, you'll see the world. You'll have the privilege of living overseas and earning a living at the same time. You really will meet lots of interesting people from around the world and from all walks of life (but, unfortunately, more than a few crashing bores). You'll frequent diplomatic drawing rooms and executive suites. You'll report on great matters of finance and state.

If business is your specialty, you won't spend all your time chasing quarterly profit figures for SYZ Widget, Inc. Often you'll be tackling the most critical questions of international economics—trade, debt, global capital flows. You'll get to play pundit, analyzing how your part of the world fits into the global economic picture.

You'll exercise all your reporter's skills, and more. You'll have to become a generalist capable of putting together intelligent interpretive pieces on a wide variety of subjects.

That's on your good days.

On bad days, you'll feel completely lost. The culture will seem impenetrable, people's behavior maddening, bureaucracies unmovable. Information will seem impossible to come by. You may even forget how to speak the language.

The thing about international reporting—business or otherwise—is that it really is different from working stateside. In many parts of the world, especially in developing countries, the rules of the game will seem strange and unfathomable.

Take the telephone. In the U.S. and Canada, we're used to transacting business on the phone. In these countries, a phone is a reporter's best friend. In many places, it may seem like your worst enemy.

Lines always seem either to be busy or to go unanswered. When you get through, your party isn't there or may not take your call. He or she will rarely return your call—secretaries routinely suggest you call back later. If you do manage to get your party on the line, he or she probably won't be forthcoming. Sensitive matters simply aren't discussed on the phone with strangers. You may have to speak to most of your sources in person.

More generally, in much of the world information is treated differently than in the U.S. Here, institutions are set up to promote the orderly flow of information. Statistics are more or less reliable. Public affairs offices function more or less efficiently. They will deliver press releases, give quotes for the record and arrange interviews with officials.

In the U.S., much business reporting is routine. A reporter will use his or her ingenuity to add upon a core of readily available material. Elsewhere, information may be a scarce commodity. Statistics may be untrustworthy and public relations offices may not function as such. Important developments may never be announced in an organized fashion. When official information is available, it may be even more patently a smokescreen than in the U.S. Rumors abound. What is really happening may seem to lie behind an impenetrable curtain. A reporter must be resourceful to get even the most basic information. There are days when every fact seems like a small victory.

For a business reporter, the problem is compounded. As bad as public institutions may be at providing information, the private sector usually is worse. Even large businesses may have no real public information system. Receptionists and secretaries don't know how to handle inquisitive reporters. Record keeping may be haphazard or duplicitous. Industrywide data may not exist.

Even more than in the U.S., in much of the world the way things are said to work and the way things really work are two different things. In Latin America, for example, it often seems that to say something beautifully is much more important than to say something truthfully. Government ministries prepare artful planning documents that have nothing to do with reality. Projects may be announced and forgotten the next day. A minister may assure you that the country's new debt-for-equity program will be put into effect next week, but it never will be. An organizational chart will not show how decisions are actually made. Power is often very closely held in very few hands.

Though your job is to report what is really going on, often, especially at the beginning, you won't know. You may fall into the trap of reporting what people say rather than what they do.

TRICKS OF THE TRADE

Here are some ideas—and a few tricks of the trade—for business reporting overseas. Many of these points apply specifically to Latin America, but may be relevant throughout the third world.

Be Utterly Skeptical of Statistics, Official or Otherwise

Data collection and reporting frequently can't be trusted. For example, in many countries, companies routinely keep two sets of books, one for tax purposes and another for internal use. Government officials may manipulate economic data, such as inflation or unemployment figures, for political purposes. There may be technical flaws in the data —the Bolivian central bank's 1986 balance sheet reported errors and omissions equal to 10 percent of the country's GDP (gross domestic product), the measure of goods and services produced by a country.

Don't treat all official information equally. Learn who has good data and who does not. Central Bank figures may be more trustworthy than Finance Ministry statistics or vice versa. You'll often have to use less-than-reliable data, and it may be important to note that when you write. Always cite sources and, if appropriate, indicate something about the reliability of the information.

Cultivate Sources by Building Personal Relationships

In much of the world, you'll have to work harder on developing sources than in the U.S. New sources tend to be formal and cautious, and interviews are often highly predictable. Only by investing a lot of time and energy, and developing a degree of intimacy, do you begin to get beyond a superficial level.

In many places, people do not trust purely professional relationships. You must be more personal. You may not get a businessman to show you his second set of books, but if you treat him as a friend (whether or not he is one) you may get an interesting answer when you ask, "Hey, how do you really make a profit in the widget industry here?" Even more important, a reporter can use the phone more easily with sources who are friends.

Don't neglect the secretaries of key sources. Often they are imperious gatekeepers barely accountable even to their bosses. Be friendly and courteous, and never lose your temper. Friendly gestures that might be inappropriate in the U.S. can work wonders—flowers on the secretary's birthday may get your call through when you're on a tight deadline.

Pay Attention to Your Image

Despite all of our socioeconomic and racial differences, Americans are a relatively egalitarian lot. In many countries, class and ethnic differences are sharper and prestige is more important. Sometimes secretaries are the worst snobs. As a business reporter, you'll often be dealing with members of the local elite, many of whom may be unenlightened to say the least. To get access to the important and the self-important, you must seem important.

Journalists are regarded as little more than rabble in some parts of the world. As a foreigner, you will have an advantage. But you should dress and groom yourself with some care and project an air of authority.

If you are a freelancer, don't say you are doing a story for little-known Western Widget Maker Magazine. Identify yourself as correspondent for your most prestigious outlet—even when you're writing for the widget makers. By all means, have elegant-looking business cards made up and hand them out liberally.

Master the Language, and Understand the Country's Culture and History

This obvious point must be restated. Don't be intimidated if you don't speak the language fluently, but make it a top priority to improve. Socialize with local folk. If you are single, remember that romance is said to be the world's best intensive conversation course.

If you are not entirely fluent, record all interviews. That allows you to concentrate on the conversation, not on taking notes which is stressful in a second language.

All the stuff written about how business people must be culturally sensitive goes for reporters too. Americans tend to be very abrupt and they get to the point too quickly. If time allows, stop and get to know the people you are interviewing.

Break Out of the Elite, Expatriate Ghetto

As a business reporter, you'll associate a lot with the upper crust. And you may live in a privileged upper-middle-class neighborhood. Your reporting will be slanted and one-dimensional if you don't circulate more widely. People of different social classes may have sharply divergent opinions about economic policy. For example, some foreign reporters in Chile who pronounced General Augusto Pinochet's economic program a success never journeyed to Santiago's shantytown where the policies were highly unpopular.

Use public transportation at least occasionally. Go to markets and visit poor neighborhoods. See how those in the lower-middle-class struggle to maintain their status.

Get out of the capital and into the countryside. Talk to farmers. It will enrich your writing and be good for your soul.

SOURCES OF INFORMATION

Public Officials

Unless you are very well known or very lucky, don't count on getting through to officials when you're in a hurry. Senior officials are usually inaccessible—it may take months to schedule interviews. Their aides are often reluctant to talk. The information offices of public agencies may not even be in the business of providing comments to the press.

Over time, as people get to know and trust you, and if you develop a reputation, you may succeed in cultivating official sources. But even then, when you're on deadline and desperately need a comment, your sources may not come through. Have a contingency plan for writing your story if your key interview doesn't materialize.

Broadcast Media

If you need stuff fast, nothing is more useful than radio and television. This point can't be overstressed. The print media can butcher quotes and misrepresent statements, but if you hear it on radio or TV, then you're relying on your own eyes and ears. Sometimes, with breaking news, broadcast comments may be the only quotes you have.

News broadcasts tend to consist of endless, unedited statements by politicians, officials, and other public figures. It's lousy TV, but it's great for the foreign correspondent. Public affairs interview shows on radio or TV may be key forums as well.

Local Press

Use the local press as tip sheets, but be extremely wary of its accuracy. In one story in a Peruvian newspaper, there were three different spellings of a man's name. In another, First Interstate Bank came out as Frist Interesting.

If there is an official press agency or newspaper, it may publish the text of legislation and decrees. Official outlets can themselves be cited as sources. There may be semi-official or government-linked publications which can be used similarly.

In many places, there is a highly competitive business press—often expensive newsletters published by local consulting firms. Find out which are the best and read them regularly. If you can't afford to subscribe, use the library or find a sympathetic supplier.

Your reading will provide names of commentators, economists, business leaders, etc. Call up the ones who seem sharp and develop them as sources.

Think Tanks

Sometimes it seems that the Ford Foundation, or its German or Dutch equivalent, is the only thing keeping third world intellectuals afloat. Think tanks, often foreign-funded, are big business in many parts of the world and their staffs are paid to know what is going on. At the best think tanks, you'll find thoughtful, knowledgeable people. Economic analysis is often a strength. What's more, access is usually much easier than with government officials.

Make it a point to know where the group is coming from ideologically and who is paying the bills. The political spectrum is much broader in most of the world than it is in the United States—which makes things more interesting. But left, right or center, you need to be clear where your sources stand.

Diplomats

Some diplomats seem to know more about what's happening than the chief of the secret police; others are merely serving time. Many follow economic matters closely and may know about deals involving their nationals.

U.S. embassies usually have highly professional information staffs and can arrange briefings on a variety of subjects. But beware—the U.S. is often a heavy-handed presence with a definite agenda. On third world debt, for example, the U.S. took an extreme hard line during the Reagan years. Some of the worst foreign reporting comes from journalists who rely too heavily on U.S. diplomats. Get to know, say, the Canadians or the Dutch. They may have a much humbler and wiser view of the world than Uncle Sam.

Multilateral and regional economic, trade or development agencies may be excellent for statistics and their representatives may make good news sources as well. The International Monetary Fund and the World Bank are in the business of analyzing country economic policies.

With both diplomatic and international agency sources, extreme discretion is advised. Their representatives are sensitive to their status as foreigners and rarely will talk for attribution. They will have nothing to do with you if they suspect you won't keep conversations confidential.

Trade Associations

In every country, there is a handful of major associations representing the private sector plus a galaxy of minor groups for each industry. Even street peddlers and money changers may be organized.

Officers of these groups usually are useful to get the party line and little more, but that can be helpful if you need a quote. If an association publishes a membership directory, that can be an invaluable resource. You will refer to these over and over again for names, addresses and telephone numbers of business executives.

Some associations also gather data on their industrial sector. Obviously, the accuracy and usefulness of this material may vary.

Foreign Business Community

Often you will be behind local journalists, but with foreign businesses the advantage is yours. Foreign bankers, manufacturers and sales representatives are your natural beat. They will often be able to clue you in to local business tricks and some may be quite well informed on the inner workings of government.

You're both expatriates, which is the basis for real rapport, particularly if you are the same nationality. Your source probably has war stories he or she is dying to tell. Plus, this is one source who will probably return your phone calls.

If you're going to do international business reporting, chances are you'll be a freelancer. Wire services excluded, in most places the majority of English-language resident reporters are freelancers stringing for a variety of news outlets.

Business reporting probably will be only one facet of your work. Most freelancers become jacks-of-all-trade, doing some combination of broadcast, photography, and business and general news reporting for print outlets, with perhaps some arcane specialties such as military or travel writing.

Freelancers turn to business reporting for the obvious reason. There's a market for it: Business sections of newspapers, the international financial press and trade publications.

Many freelancers get their first break reporting for trade publications. So, it is important to determine what industries in your country have international importance. It is likely that there will be trade publications outside the country that will be interested in what is going on. In Ecuador, there is interest in oil and energy. In Brazil, coffee. One friend in Chile made a nice bit of money writing for *The Packer,* a monthly magazine for North American fruit growers.

Trade publications will want details on production trends, industry outlook, major deals and important moves by the government or key firms. Writing for a trade, you will in effect become a beat reporter.

For other outlets, the whole country will be your beat. There is a market for pieces on the country's economy, as well as trend pieces on key industries. Breaking news of international interest includes major government policy moves or important deals with foreigners. A decision by a multinational company to build a factory or pull up stakes is newsworthy.

Debt stories go in and out of fashion, but in much of the world it's a critical issue. It's a cliche to lead with the "human impact"—how debt has worsened the living standards of a poor family—but, let's face it: That is the story. The task becomes to write about the human effects of debt in a fresh way.

In fact, the debt crisis has given an enormous shot in the arm to international business reporting. Banking and finance publications that never noticed the world beyond North America, Western Europe and East Asia now compete hotly for debt-related news from Latin America, Africa and Eastern Europe. Especially sought after are stories on innovations like debt-for-equity swaps.

One final tip: if you are choosing where to go, pick a country with international direct dial and international collect call service. And if you are able to file by computer or fax, you won't spend half the day waiting for your calls to get through to editors. If you do go elsewhere, don't despair—valium is sold over-the-counter in most of the third world.

Not Just Business as Usual

by John Gallagher

Every business reporter has had the experience. At a dinner party or wedding reception, an attractive stranger asks what you do for a living. "I'm a newspaper reporter," you say with pride. "Oooh! That must be interesting," comes the reply. "And what do you write about?" "Business," you say.

Your new acquaintance's eyes glaze over.

Why, 10 or 15 years after most newspapers "discovered" business writing, is most of it still so dull? To be sure, business journalism has come a long, long way. No longer can we say that the business pages contain a mere recitation of numbers, statistics, earnings reports and the like, unrelieved by a single quote, insight or human emotion. Some of the best prize-winning writing in journalism has been business writing, and business sections routinely carry profiles, analyses of product quality, and light features.

But, mostly, it's still an insider's game, inaccessible to the majority of readers. I venture to say it's our own fault. Business reporters seldom conceive of their beats as dealing with anything beyond business itself. Banking reporters still talk mostly to bankers, regulators and analysts. Manufacturing reporters stick pretty much to stock pickers and trade groupies, industry and union chiefs. There's a wall of our own making that cuts us off from the wider readership we deserve.

It cannot be for lack of material. The business world is filled with egotistical, talented, brash, adventuresome souls, people whose lives ought to translate into vivid copy. Moreover, in a far more direct way than politicians, business people touch our daily lives in ways our readers need and want to know.

So, how do we breach the wall for good? Or, put another way, how do we make the most of our beats?

I venture that the best way is to be something of a hybrid reporter, part numbers-crunching specialist and part socially conscious city-side scribe. The best stories always seem to be the ones that straddle the line between business and city desks. A piece on interstate banking laws packs less impact than asking whether local banks make mortgage loans in poorer neighborhoods. A profile of a developer can advance to the front page if you write about his political contributions and critique what his buildings do to the local skyline, and include some vivid personal description, too. And the real story of merger mania is the impact that takeovers have on local communities across America.

It's hardly unfair to hold business leaders—and business journalists—socially accountable. After all, sports writers demand answers from athletes about race relations, drug use and the pernicious effects of runaway salaries in sports. We ought to be at least as tough on business executives.

But even when writing about strictly "business" issues, it's essential to make the most of a beat. First, it helps to expand the usual circle of sources. Think unconventionally. Don't let the trade insiders set the agenda. Our typical banking reporter, for example, could ask a developer about getting a commercial loan from a local bank for a significant local project. Are local banks supporting the community? Or ask a travel agent what it's like to open a small business account with a bank that caters to corporations. Or ask a local pastor in a poor neighborhood how his parishioners get treated when they visit the local branch of the bank. From such unconventional sources, a bank begins to emerge with a personality, and banking itself seems less abstract.

It works with other beats, too. In general, whether covering manufacturing, health care or real estate, always try to talk to some customers. Highly promoted images of personal service tend to melt away beneath routine stories of customer frustration. A company, any company, seems less remote when placed in a vivid social context. Revealed as confused, opportunistic and often arbitrary, a company acquires a human, if not always humane, face.

And let's not assume that all creative stories are negative. Some of the best positive stories come from similar unconventional thinking. Oftentimes, stories emerge from places that you might think are completely off a beat.

Computer experts, for example, run our financial and communications worlds today. Reporters who care little for computers may drop by a computer conference and turn up a story about their local bank or utility. These days, any hospital conference almost certainly will buzz with talk about insurance rates. And remember that politicians keep a line on local businesses, if only to know whom to tap for contributions. Politicians love to talk.

Energetic reporters are not afraid to waste a little time. They read trade journals, looking for trends, gossip, and the occasional mention of a local company. They also meet sources informally, over lunch or coffee, just to plug into the gossip network. Try it, and you'll find yourself coming away with stories; and they'll have a freshness that can't be found in canned press releases.

Like a roving foreign correspondent, a business reporter ought to look upon his or her beat as just a home base from which to venture forth. There are all sorts of political and social concerns that we, as business writers, are uniquely qualified to write about. Journalists who understand the workings of business and the economy have a powerful advantage over reporters who tremble at the sight of a budget story. Let's not waste our advantage by treating our beats as business as usual.

HANDLING THE BEAT

A beat assignment at many news organizations is a vaguely defined area of coverage. Some beats are so broadly defined, that it is impossible to know what to do. A popular beat on some business desks may be called simply "consumers." Does that mean all the consumer companies? Does that mean only the products that consumers might be interested in? Does that mean new products? Does the beat include consumer protection and safety? Chances are, if you ask these questions the answer will be "yes."

Covering any beat requires organization and clear thinking. If your editor isn't sure what the beat is, then you should be. Defining the beat is the reporter's responsibility and that is why reporters like beats. It gives the reporter the authority to decide about coverage for a specific area of business.

For this same reason, the beat system has been abandoned at some news organizations. Many editors are not comfortable with the autonomy that the beat system gives reporters. If story ideas at your organization come from the top, then the beat system may not provide the freedom it was designed to give reporters.

Still, there is value in taking a beat. The obvious advantage is specialization and a chance to find and nurture stories of your own. Here are some tips on how to organize and use your beat to your advantage:

Choosing a Beat

If you have an opportunity to select your beat, look for one that the news organization is interested in. On large papers, those beats are advertising and the media, energy, computers, real estate, labor and the financial markets. Magazines always need people who understand corporate and personal finance. The networks need people who can translate the economy.

Organizing the Beat

Sources are always the important component in good coverage. The better the sources, the better the story. Those sources should represent every aspect of your beat's activities and include industry lobbyists, lawyers, accountants, labor leaders and executives. You should have office and home telephone numbers.

Becoming an Expert

Because you are supposed to be the specialist on a certain subject, you should read everything about your beat you can and attend briefings. Read trade publications and scholarly works as well. Find out if there is any research going on that might eventually lead to a story.

Selling Your Ideas.

When you are a beat reporter, you have to sell your stories harder, especially if the editor is unfamiliar with the subject. It may be necessary to write proposals to your editor, explaining the focus of the story and its importance. The advantage to this approach is that when the story your editor turned down shows up in a competitor's publication, you have evidence that you had the idea first.

Expanding the Beat

To get the most out of your beat, you should think in macro terms. In other words, if you focus too much on the details of your beat, the small twists and turns of a company's activities, your stories will become limited. Try to see the big picture.

Using the Beat to get Ahead

Since you have staked out a territory, investigate and develop it in a way that will result in a series of carefully reported articles. Use your on-going coverage to develop several stories at once. Turn beat stories into magazine articles.

Broadcasting Business

by Jan Hopkins

October 19, 1987. There's chaos on the floor of the New York Stock Exchange.

Above the floor, in the balcony, a dozen cameras record the action for millions of viewers. The three major networks interrupt programming for stock market updates. Some cable networks provide continuous coverage. For the first time in the history of broadcast journalism, television and radio become the primary media for national business and economic news.

Black Monday marked a coming of age for broadcasting. Rather than the usual, and sometimes incomprehensible, recitation of numbers at the end of a newscast, broadcasters focused for nearly a day on a single financial event, covering it as they would a Presidential assassination or an armed conflict involving American troops.

While financial crisis coverage is not commonplace, many broadcasters on October 19, 1987 realized that financial news broadcasting lacked the sophistication of political, military or public crisis reporting. Some fumbled for the right words and the right tone, realizing that words like "crash" and "panic" could affect the stability of the already weak securities markets. Broadcasters had to be careful about the emotional level of the broadcast. While broadcasters are trained to grab audience attention with catchy words this was an event that required caution and restraint. This was an event that required play-by-play coverage with a healthy dose of historical context balanced with even-handed analysis.

It was not long ago that the idea of business news on television struck people as a poor idea. But that was before events like Black Monday proved broadcasters were the natural heirs of wire services in the mass communication of financial news. Weekly programs like ABC's *Business World*, Adam Smith's *Money World*, *The Wall Street Journal Report on Television*, and CNN's *Moneyweek* draw sizable viewing audiences. Daily television programs include CNN's *Business Day, Business Morning*, and *Moneyline*. PBS broadcasts *The Nightly Business Report*.

This new era for economics and business broadcasting created a need for intelligent and thoughtful reporting of the type usually associated with print journalism. The best business stories on television or radio are like the best stories in the *Wall Street Journal*. They are compelling. They include the human element; the victims and the beneficiaries. They make clear the significance of the story, how important it is and how it reflects lifestyles or business practices.

PRODUCING A SEGMENT

The typical broadcast reporter begins work at 9:30 A.M. and may work until 8 P.M. Usually the day begins with reading of morning papers and reviewing the business wires. The reporter may be assigned a story or may suggest one. Reporters working on daily broadcast generally have one day to complete a story, although some may have days, even weeks, to prepare a story. In either case, the reporter is responsible for researching the story and writing a proposal for the producer or assignment desk. A proposal will include the locations where the story will be shot, the requirements for crew and the amount of time needed to complete the project.

Before anyone is interviewed on camera, the reporter should conduct a pre-interview conversation over the telephone to determine what the person will say. The actual interview may take an hour. Only about 15 seconds will be used.

Before departure for interviews, the reporter must consider the best visuals for the story. Are the pictures available in the video library or will they need to be taken that day? The reporter also needs to think about charts or graphs. Keep this simple. Use only one or two illustrations to make a point. Remember that the graphics department may need several hours to prepare the illustrations.

After the interviews have been shot, it's the reporter's job to transcribe the tape and make notes on the segments to be used. This process takes anywhere from 30 minutes to an hour. The reporter is looking for the best 10 or 15 second section of sound to go with the available pictures.

Most business stories have a simple format. The first section of about 15 seconds is narration. Then the interview is introduced. The narrator will give the title of the interviewee and comment on what that person will say without summarizing the interview. The next 10– or 15–second section is the interview, which is called a sound bite. Following the sound bite there's more narration, again about 15 seconds, with perhaps a comment from another expert with a slightly different opinion or a kicker for the story. The story ends with a summation or a look forward. The conclusion should be short, 10 or 15 seconds. If the reporter is on camera, it's called a "standup." Generally standups are filmed in the field during the day's shooting. But some reporters prefer to shoot the standup late in the day after the script has been approved by the editor.

Broadcast stories are usually ready for editing about two hours before they go on the air. The first step in editing is to record the reporter's reading of the narration. The narration is then transferred to the master tape. The interview sound bites are inserted on the master tape as they appear in the story and the reporter's standup is added. When all the sound is laid down the editor rewinds the master tape to the beginning and starts laying down the pictures, leaving room for the graphics which are inserted last.

THE BROADCAST STAFF

Associate Producers and Field Producers

In some news departments associate producers and field producers do everything a reporter does except provide the face and voice. He or she may interview, log tapes, go with the camera crew to get video, write the story and sit through the video editing.

In other news organizations the producer or associate is called in by a reporter or is assigned to work with a reporter to research a story. He or she may set up interviews, do interviews with a camera crew, think up and get video to cover the story, as well as sit through the edit, but not do any writing.

In some departments the producer is given a completed script and must come up with video from the library and find graphics to cover the story.

Show Producers

Some producers are responsible for an entire program. They keep on top of all the day's events, usually by reading the wires. Show producers find out what stories reporters are doing and calculate how to fit everything or stretch everything to fit a half hour. It's the producer's job to decide which stories appear in the broadcast and in what order. The producer also assigns writers to put together the transitions between stories and to write the stories that aren't handled by reporters. The producer is responsible for the flow of the program and usually decides what headlines to use and what stories to "tease" at the end of the segment. The producer may decide that a live interview is needed. If so, he or she will assign someone to book the guest and put together research for the anchor.

It helps to be very organized in this job, since it's the producer's responsibility to make sure the show is ready on time. If not, the producer better have an alternative plan.

Producers must be organized and yet flexible. Often events happen late in the day. An entire show may have to be changed at the last minute. In addition to all of these responsibilities, the producer must time the program to the second. And while the show is on the air, he or she must make adjustments to ensure that what is scheduled fits into the allotted time.

Writers

It's the writer's job to make the news come alive and make sense. Broadcast writers must write quickly, clearly and crisply. Material will come from the wires, from phone interviews and from reporters. Direction comes from the producer before the writers begin their task. A writer must keep in mind what stories come before and after the one he or she is working on so there is a smooth transition. Perhaps most important, the writer must keep in mind the style preferred by the anchor.

In some organizations writers get involved in putting together a segment of the program or a complete story. In this case, they take on the role of an associate producer.

Anchor

The anchor is the most visible television job and usually the highest paid.

The anchor is ultimately responsible for how everything comes together on the air. He or she is usually involved throughout the day on developing events. The anchor must also prepare for live interviews.

Once on the air the anchor becomes the focus of the communication of the news. The best anchors understand and care about what they're saying and reporting. They aren't just reading news.

For an anchor, presence is crucial. Anchors are supposed to be natural, confident, in control yet compassionate and trustworthy. An anchor should be believable. Many anchors have these qualities naturally. Others acquire them with the help of voice lessons and wardrobe consultants.

In some ways the anchor's job seems the easiest on television, especially in terms of hours. But it's a stressful occupation. Anchors are expected to be calm in times of panic and confusion. In times of crisis, the anchor earns her salary.

BROADCASTING JOBS

Television broadcasting is a group effort with many jobs for journalists and managers of news. There are various management jobs such as supervising producer and assignment editor. These are the people who run the department. They oversee the operation to make sure everything runs smoothly. They are responsible for seeing that news is being gathered and that the rest of the staff has the proper resources to do the job. Generally these positions are filled from the ranks of producers and writers.

Radio cannot be overlooked. Radio is an especially good place for business journalists. Most networks and large stations have a business anchor. Usually this person gives stock market updates on an hourly basis, using the wire services. But the job of radio business reporters is expanding, primarily because many radio reporters are able to do more for specific business stories than television can. Many more stories can be covered in a day, since the equipment requirements are less inhibiting. And, radio reporters are less obvious among the press. Their advantage is that they can get their stories out much faster than print journalists and cover a story more thoroughly than television journalists. Radio reporters have the advantage of sending tape to the station by phone and reporting live from events.

Usually a radio reporter will go back to the station to edit sound pieces to be inserted in a voiced report. At this point, the work is similar to that done by television reporters.

Radio reporting is a good place to start in broadcasting. Many television journalists were radio reporters first.

THE STORIES

Television and radio stories should be compelling. They should include the human element. They should make clear the significance of the story, how large it is and how it fits into the scheme of things. Obviously, broadcast works best when the audience can see or hear people with whom they can identify. This usually means using a cross section of man on the street interviews or an individual who represents others who have been affected by the news.

All broadcasters use experts. They're important because they provide perspective. If they are good, they can put an event into context and explain its significance. Part of the reason why some experts tend to be used over and over again is that they consistently perform well and return phone calls. That's important for reporters who are working on a tight deadline. But try to expand your pool of experts. Too often experts represent a single viewpoint, for example, an urban perspective. Since most national business reporting is done from New York, most experts who appear on the national news also come from New York. This creates a New York bias that often misrepresents the events in smaller cities. Balance is very important and a variety of views may help a story.

Generally, reporters should make an effort to include new views and faces. Radio reporters have the advantage here. They can do an interview over the phone. They don't have to travel to an office with a camera crew and tons of equipment.

Most important, broadcast reporters shouldn't forget the power of the media. Business reporters, especially, need to remember that they can be used by people who will benefit financially from getting a particular view on the air. Be leery of people who call the station and volunteer their views. Figure out what they might gain from the publicity.

TIPS FOR THE BROADCASTER

There is no substitute for being prepared. Think carefully about your audience. Consider how you will explain a complicated business concept. Would it be better to use an illustration to make the point?

Rehearse the script. Read it aloud to see how it sounds. Sentences should be short. The key points should be spelled out simply. Make sure you can pronounce all the names and titles.

Try to get the best interviews you can. In companies, generally the higher you go the better the interview. Underlings tend to worry about what the boss will think.

Stay clear of jargon. No one will be impressed if they can't understand you.

Try to think of ways to turn numbers into pictures. There are some routine ways broadcasters are expected to cover economic stories. For example, home sales are used as a news peg for stories on housing; unemployment numbers for stories on work issues, and trade numbers for a story on a local business that is exporting. Think of other ways to illustrate economic data.

Never forget that most of your audience won't care much about what is happening outside their homes. So personalize your reporting when you can. Compare what is happening on a national level with what may be happening locally. Use people that your audience can identify with. Do not depend solely on experts. Instead of looking to the labor department for help on a story about unemployment, look at the want ads. Find out who in your area is hiring or firing.

Using Video in Business Broadcasts

by Sarah Kidwell

The basic tenet of television journalism is to tell a story with pictures. If the story is a fire or a plane crash, the choice is easy. But if the assignment is to cover a corporate takeover or report an unexpected increase in the producer price index (PPI), the choice of video is less clear. As a result, many broadcast business stories are "wallpapered," that is, covered with generic pictures. With careful planning and creativity, this can be avoided.

Business stories for television can often require reporting two stories: one through interviews, the other with pictures. It's important to decide on the video early in the reporting process, even before the interviews. This enables the library staff to track down footage and the assignment desk to assign pictures to be shot early in the day. If for example, the story involves a company in a remote location, the assignment desk may get video from other bureaus or affiliates when you are out on interviews. Your crew can be an important resource. Be sure to discuss the story with them, as they may have good ideas about what to shoot.

If your video library is a good one, there should be file footage of business leaders, various financial exchanges and economic sectors like housing, retail and automobiles that you can use for generic pictures. However, choose this footage carefully. Seasons should be considered; one can hardly use video of residential homes covered with snow for a story on the June housing numbers.

Video easily becomes outdated. For example, the most common footage of former Federal Reserve Board chairman Paul Volcker shows him puffing on a cigar during testimony on Capitol Hill. He has since said he'll no longer smoke while testifying. Care should also be taken when using corporation logos, too. So many companies have merged and reorganized in recent years that it's easy to make a mistake when showing company-specific products, corporate headquarters and company symbols.

Since graphics are an important visual aid, they can also be useful in explaining a business story. But beware. Overuse of graphics can confuse or even bore the viewer. Full screen graphics work best when interspersed with video.

Business Journalism Ethics

by Philip Moeller

Ethical discussions among business journalists are seldom about the grave issue of honesty. The discussions are more likely to be about "free lunch" issues: Are you dining to cultivate a source or is the meal a subtle payoff for past or future favorable coverage?

Some reporters have abused the "free lunch." A journalist at a newspaper where I once worked always drove a new car. I later learned that the journalist, who occasionally dabbled in automotive coverage, had simply accepted all of the local auto dealers' offers to "test drive" the latest models for story "background." I never checked to see if the Car of the Week became the Story of the Week, but the writer's acceptance of these vehicles seemed wrong to me—even if he never wrote a word about any car.

A couple of years later, I was standing in line at a hotel waiting to register for a seminar sponsored by a nonprofit journalism group that was paying my expenses. Before I got to the front of the line, I heard the loud voice of another reporter. He was letting everyone know his paper would be paying for all his expenses because his paper never accepted favors from any organization, even a publicly-funded journalism group. I felt a little less smug about my high ethical standards. But I also knew that my newspaper simply would not have sent me if it had to pay my expenses. So I went ahead and registered.

So, who was the hack this time?

As older hands know, ethical standards change. To be sure, there are times when you know what's acceptable and what's not. It is clearly wrong for journalists to accept gifts before or after a story, although there are probably some journalists who accept invitations to concerts or box seats at the ballgame without thinking of these courtesies as gifts. It is clearly wrong to tell sources or others outside the office about the timing of an important story, although we all know that word gets around that you're "working" on something. (In fact, you tell sources what you're working on to get their cooperation.)

The point is that the clear wrongs aren't so clear after all. And the gray areas—the "maybe" and the "it depends" situations—are so numerous that most journalists have to trust their instincts when making their way through the ethical jungle.

There are many reasons this happens, of course. Journalism, for example, has no generally accepted professional code of conduct. There are lots of rules we are supposed to honor: deadlines, accuracy, fairness, attribution, protection of sources and the like. But most, if not all, of these basic rules get broken from time to time, often with the approval of editors.

If (always the big if) the story is worth it, we simply break the rules. We break deadlines all the time. And many of us sacrifice accuracy to time pressures, while knowing that the risk of errors is high when competitive pressure forces us to go into print before we're ready.

Relationships with sources are incredibly messy. Do we protect them at all costs? Is it worth misinforming our readers and listeners? Should we use a misleading source attribution to disguise the identity of our source?

If we know the rules are vague, why should it matter if business journalists have ethical standards at all? It matters a great deal, because business journalists have a special responsibility. Unlike many other journalists, the news we handle has value, financial value, for those able to use it. Content is as important as timing. Those with access to financial information first have a market advantage over those who don't have the information. Financial information is so valuable that business journalists are subject to insider trading laws.

As part of the chain of information dissemination, business journalists are responsible for maintaining the doctrine of the level playing field: the generally accepted concept of fair play that holds that no investor should have an advantage over another because of access to privileged information. To help maintain that playing field, most news organizations have established guidelines for the investment behavior of financial journalists. Reporters, editors and others who might profit from early access to financial information must list their financial holdings and report to their employers the purchases and sales they make. Many business journalists find that to avoid any question of impropriety it is easier to own no stock at all.

BUSINESS AND THE PRESS

Since the 1970s, journalists have become much more aware of how things look to the public. This is, in part, the result of the focus on business behavior beginning with coverage of the oil crisis in the 1970s and public suspicions about the motives of the nation's energy companies. An active period of consumerism followed in the 1980s. Now, it no longer seems advisable for journalists to maintain their once cozy relationship with corporate America.

Companies view the press differently now than when business could safely assume that continuing profitability would result in favorable coverage. Reporters are no longer happy to rewrite and embellish corporate press releases as they did in the early days of business journalism. Most companies have adjusted to this changed environment by creating favorable news when they can, focusing on corporate image and corporate personalities. Companies anticipate unfavorable developments and plan for them. But reporters are outsiders, not insiders. The exclusive— the result of a company and a reporter working together—has almost entirely disappeared from the business pages.

In recent years, the relationships between journalists and some corporations have become downright hostile. Business journalists often bypass public relations departments when they can. The once cordial relationships that business journalists had with the heads of communications are rare. Some journalists still dine with sources and journalists still make personal friends among the staff of the companies they cover, but everyone is more careful these days about the appearance of a conflict of interest, insider trading and leaks.

While this evolution of press-business relationships may not seem important to a discussion of ethics, it helps explain why the ethical dilemmas are personal rather than professional. How do you handle stories you have a personal opinion about? Is it fair to do a profile of a person you dislike? How do you cover the real estate development in your neighborhood? How do you report on employment cutbacks at companies where your friends work? How do you deal with government contracts decided by, and even awarded to, people you see socially?

The answer to most ethical questions is "take the high road." But we all know the problem is more subtle than that. By choosing one word over another, we can slant a piece or make a personal statement.

There are no clear answers to most ethical dilemmas. That is why journalists are lucky to have a network of reporters, supervising editors, copy editors and top editors, through whom stories pass before the public sees them. Running this gauntlet can be a humbling experience, but also a cleansing one, that identifies conflicts of interest. At times, you may decide the best course is to be taken off an assignment you can't handle objectively.

WHAT WE WANT FROM COMPANIES

One unresolved ethical dilemma for the business press is what we expect companies to do for us. We depend a great deal on companies to help us do our reporting. Consider what most journalists and their employers tacitly expect of those they cover. We expect companies to provide substantial staff time, access to highly paid executives and lots of printed background material to supplement our direct reporting. We often ask for stock photographs and, in this age of color, transparencies as well. We attend thousands of press conferences, seminars and conventions that feature well-stocked press rooms, extra telephones and computers. This stuff all costs money, and if we accept it, aren't we creating the wrong impression? My guess is that lots of business executives think so. And while their disdain for the press may have several origins, I suspect one of them is the annoyance which comes from spending so much money so that we can do our jobs—producing coverage that often galls the companies that help us the most.

The prevailing view of this process is that it's all right to accept such support items in the normal course of doing your job, so long as you are not receiving any favored treatment that might be viewed, as an exchange of "goods": your favorable coverage for your source's largess. Reporters should not forget that exchanges involving influence and access to sources are sometimes favors that put you in debt to those who have provided the help.

CODE OF CONDUCT

When journalists think of ethics, they think about situations involving money. Ethical lapses involving money are the stuff of the headlines. In the most celebrated case of the 1980s, R. Foster Winans gave advance notice of the contents of his "Heard on the Street" columns in the *Wall Street Journal* to individuals who profited from it. Because WSJ stories are widely read and because the column had demonstrated its ability to move stock prices, Winans' indiscretion undercut the *Journal's* reputation and cast a shadow over business journalism in general. (Winans was convicted of wire fraud in August 1985 and given a reduced sentence of 1 year, a $5,000 fine and 400 hours of community service.)

It certainly wasn't the *WSJ's* ethics policy that led Winans astray. The *WSJ,* well aware of its position and the sensitivity of the information in its news columns, has long had one of the profession's most comprehensive ethics policies.

Explicit codes of conduct are helpful to journalists, especially newcomers who need to know the rules of the game—what types of investments are forbidden, what kind of disclosure of holdings, if any, is required, what kinds of outside work are frowned upon and what are considered competing news organizations and thus off limits as far as freelance work is concerned (see "Code of Conduct").

The codes should—but usually don't—deal with the methods of obtaining information. Reporters and editors trade information all the time with sources, it's one of the time-honored cornerstones of how the press operates. While few journalists trade information for money, most of us pass on tidbits as part of the price of keeping information channels open. If we're good, we receive a lot more than we pass on.

Our ability to translate information into money is awesome, thanks to the technological marvels that now characterize our investment markets. Today, nearly any credible source with access to a telephone can move a market quickly. How fast should we pass on the information we know? How long should we hold it if confirmations are slow in coming? We know that business news gathering is a very competitive business and that getting it first increases its value. How do we know who to trust on the telephone?

Let's take a hypothetical example. What if you're interviewing an investment analyst for a story about XYZ Company, and the analyst, who also happens to make a living gathering information, asks you what you think of its latest new product offering. Should you answer? Consider the following questions: If you're really sharp, maybe you know so much about the product that your intelligence is of real value to the analyst. Should you trade your information in hopes of getting something you don't know or should you keep it for your own story? Further, can you tell if the analyst is playing fair and not directing you toward a story to support his viewpoint? It's also possible you will tip your hand letting the analyst know the tone of your upcoming story, which may give him some valuable information.

Although this example suggests the various situations a journalist must consider, it shouldn't suggest that every word a reporter utters must be weighed for its ethical implications. Still, business reporters must always exercise caution with unpublished information.

HANDLING SOURCES

To a journalist, of course, nothing is more important than access— access to executives, documents, reports, shareholders, employees. You simply can't get the kinds of information you need for great stories without having access. And don't kid yourself. Everybody has access problems and conflicts. Everybody.

Providing unfavorable coverage is usually not a prescription for continued, cooperative access. Unlike government, no one in business plays the role of "loyal opposition"—people who will give you the other side of the story, complete with negative quotes and documentation, so getting a balanced story may mean upsetting your sources inside the company. And, if you lose access to the company, where else are you going to go to get information? Often, time can overcome this limitation. If you have enough time to work on a story, you can find other sources.

Developing and maintaining access can be difficult especially if the executive sitting across from you in an interview has his own access—to the publisher of your paper or the general manager of your station. Subtle and not-so-subtle threats from powerful people are part of your landscape, I'm afraid, and they make it much tougher to take the ethical high road. News organizations tend not to bite the advertising hands that feed them, and there's not been nearly enough change in that attitude over the past two decades, despite the lip service to professional standards.

Given the bottom-line preoccupations of most, if not all, media corporations these days, it's easy for reporters and editors to feel that their managements are not particularly interested in standing up for principles when there's a lot of money at stake or the newspaper's corporate image is on the line. Still, if it's any comfort, I've found that the guys who say they'll call "my good friend, the publisher" are usually lying on two counts—they don't call, because the publisher isn't their friend. Even when the threat is not a bluff, most corporate news executives find such efforts distasteful and, when taking sides becomes the issue, will often take your side.

Accepting the inevitability of trade-offs doesn't mean that you have to accept unethical situations as well. The best journalists manage to strike a fair balance. They are guided by not only their consciences but also their peers and the forces of competition—among news organizations as well as among sources—that over time will give unmistakable warning signals if you stray too far off a balanced course.

If you still harbor doubts about the basic rules for business journalism the following may be of help:

Never accept gifts from sources. It would be better never to attend a ballgame than to become indebted to the friendship and kindness of a company or individuals you must cover closely.

If your news organization doesn't have an ethics policy regarding staff investments, it's safest to own no stock at all. (This is an extreme, but practical suggestion.) Also be careful about stock activity in your retirement plan even if you cannot get the immediate benefits.

It's wise to refrain from giving investment advice, particularly about the companies you cover.

Do not talk about the story you are working on with anyone except your editor. Never tell an outsider when a story will appear.

When you have valuable information, the safest thing to do is publish it as quickly as possible.

Code of Conduct

On May 7, 1980, Stephen D. Isaacs, editor of the *Minneapolis Star*, implemented the following code of conduct to help the newspaper's staff "avoid impropriety or conflicts of interest." It has been reprinted here with Mr. Isaacs' permission as an illustration of guidelines for journalistic conduct.

The philosophy underlying these guidelines is that each staff member should hold paramount the integrity of the newspaper. Consequently, each staff member should conduct both the private and public aspects of his or her life in a manner that leaves him or her free of obligation to sources or makers of news.

1. *Investments.* Staff members should not buy or sell or hold beneficial interest in stock of a company within three months of handling news regarding that company. Those staff members who frequently cover business news should avoid investing in local companies. At least, such staff members should disclose their local investments to the managing editor or the opinion editor, with the knowledge that those investments might affect their job assignments. Top executives of the newspaper who have news responsibility will disclose any outside in-

NOTE: The *Minneapolis Star* was merged with the Minneapolis Tribune in 1982. In 1987, the paper became the *Star Tribune.*

vestments to the senior editors of *The Star* and, if appropriate, to the readers.

2. *Outside employment.* Staff members should not accept compensation for services from any person or organization whose news they cover or handle. Those receiving compensation for services from any party other than the newspaper must report the identities of those persons or organizations to the managing editor or opinion editor.

3. *Gifts.* Star staff members do not accept gifts when their employment at the newspaper may have been a factor in the decision to offer the gift. Gifts worth more than $25 should be returned to the donor, with a letter citing the newspaper's policy (if desired, along with a standard letter from the editor stating that policy and explaining it) and requesting that such gifts not be proffered in the future. Gifts valued at less than $25 will be donated to charity. The editor's office will handle the logistics. A standard letter from the editor notifying the giver of the donation, and the reason for donating it, will be available when needed.

4. *Samples.* Samples of any products, including but not limited to books, records and tapes, generally should be regarded as gifts, in that those not used for news purposes should be donated to charity, with a letter to the giver explaining the action. Those samples, books, records, tapes, etc. that are desired for news purposes will be purchased from the sender by *The Star* at the standard retail price and will remain the property of *The Star*. Logistics will be handled by the editor's office. This policy includes all samples, including those sent to individual staff members at home or at work. (Samples should never be sold for personal profit.)

5. *Admissions. The Star*'s preference for paying its own way applies to all admissions, including cultural and sporting events. No free tickets will be accepted for any event, whether for reporting, educational or recreational purposes. In instances where the promoter of an event has obviously priced tickets to include contributions to a cause (as in $500–a-plate fundraising dinners), *The Star* will pay the cost of an equivalent normal meal or event. In the cases involving news coverage of conventions or similar events in which no extraordinary expense has been incurred in providing access to reporters, *The Star* will not be expected to pay the full admission charged to normal attendees. In the case of advance showings of entertainment for review purposes, *The Star* should disclose publicly the circumstances of each showing.

6. *Trips, meals, lodging and entertainment. The Star* will pay for any trips and/or lodging for staff members on news assignments. Staff members will avoid accepting offers of free entertainment when employment at *The Star* may have been a factor in the offer. *The Star* prefers to pay for meals that staff members have with news sources. (In instances where insistence on paying would be awkward or otherwise inappropriate,

staff members should make it clear that the newspaper will reciprocate in the future.) While acting as public citizens, staff members should avoid using their employment at *The Star* to solicit special consideration.

7. *Advocacy.* All involvements of staff members in outside organizations should be disclosed to the managing editor and, when appropriate, to the public in the newspaper. News staff members should avoid memberships, affiliations or partisan activities in organizations that concern themselves with public policies and that may be covered by the newspaper (professional, religious and military organizations are exempt from this provision). *The Star* prefers that news staff members avoid public roles of any kind in political activities (including contributions of time or money), in this way recognizing that, even with regard to issues that individual staff members do not cover or handle, such roles can be perceived publicly as an indication of the newspaper's lack of fairness.

Any staff member who opts to take the role of advocate can assume it will affect his or her job assignment.

Although spouses and intimate friends have independent existences, every news employee must recognize that a spouse's or friend's activities could create an appearance of conflict of interest that could influence a staff member's job assignment.

8. *Misrepresentations. The Star* prefers that its staff members not misrepresent themselves. Reporters should gather information by identifying themselves as reporters. Exceptions are permissible. When information cannot be obtained because of an identification, or when the newspaper clearly can anticipate that information or treatment of materials will be altered because of the identification, the managing editor should be consulted.

To secure admission to public places, meetings and the like, staff members do not need to volunteer their identities. If asked, however, they should acknowledge their capacity. (Staff members should not cover up or lie when specifically challenged as to their true identity.)

9. *Interview disclosure.* Under ordinary circumstances, when reporters for *The Star* seek out a person for information or comment, they should identify themselves as working for *The Star*. They should not assume that ordinary citizens are familiar with journalistic ground rules. If a person is likely to be quoted, a reporter should make that clear at the beginning of the interview. If a reporter feels some special rules are in effect, the reporter should ensure that the person understands the situation. This approach puts reporters on firm ground if, at the interview's end, the person attempts to change the rules, contending after the fact to be speaking off the record.

10. *Surreptitious coverage.* Staff members should not violate laws or the spirit of this code to gain access to documents or conversations.

If reporters happen to overhear a conversation or see a document, they may use that information to lead them to further investigation. Reporters should not publish quotes obtained by such measures if they are from an ordinary citizen—not a public official or other person dealing with public business. In the case of public officials and/or public businesses, the quotes or facts may be used so long as the article also fully describes the measures by which they were obtained.

11. *Accurate quotations.* Persons should be quoted as accurately as possible, including idiosyncrasies in speech patterns if they are pertinent to the article. If a person's slip of the tongue is not typical of his or her normal speech, and if the slip is not important to the essential point of the story the quote may be restated in context. (Profanity is excluded from this guideline subject to the specific policy on use of profanity.)

Reporters may use tape recorders to assure the accuracy of quotations or to acquire corroboration of conversations for use in libel defense. Reporters should request permission in advance from sources if they wish to record any conversations for purposes other than notetaking or libel defense.

12. *Attempts to influence coverage.* Staff members should resist any untoward attempt by persons outside the newspaper to influence news coverage. Such attempts could include, but not be limited to, bribery or extortion. All such attempts should be reported immediately to the managing editor or deputy managing editors.

13. *Confidentiality.* Given that a newspaper's business is information, the staff of *The Star* expects that information it gathers and has not yet published will not be leaked or otherwise disclosed to persons outside *The Star,* except for purposes of gathering further information for a story.

14. *Plagiarism.* Material taken from other sources and other media must be attributed at all times.

15. *Waivers.* If the managing editor or the opinion editor permits a relaxation of these guidelines, he or she should consider disclosing the occasion in the newspaper.

Section 5

Types of Stories

The Troubled Company

by Leah Beth Ward

XYZ Inc. has just released its quarterly report and you notice a downward blip in earnings. The company says in a financial footnote that there was a one-time write-off in connection with the sale of a screw division in an obscure Ohio town.

While the company may only have been tossing off an unproductive Rustbelt relic, something else might be going on. XYZ may be troubled.

Trouble either starts small and builds fast, or it festers while management ignores it until the problems bring about a crisis. Either way, your job is to scratch around beneath the footnote and find the more interesting story: What is going on inside this company?

Companies in trouble go through phases. In many ways you are writing about an organism that is metamorphosing. A press release, a balance sheet, any piece of paper the company puts out at a particular point in time will only give you a snapshot of the company—and through a rose colored lens at that. It is the journalist's job to take these pieces of information and analyze them. Often the result is a not-so-touched-up picture.

Here are some specific things to look for that will indicate whether there's more red ink than just in the screw division.

Match XYZ's targeted growth rate—the one the CEO boasted about in a recent speech or press release—against the expected industry growth rate. How is XYZ doing? If the industry is doing poorly, then your company may be reflecting its environment. But you still don't know enough.

Try to analyze the origin of the company's earnings. Is a large percentage from revenues? That's a good sign because it means the company's assets are productive. But the company is unhealthy if a large percentage of income is coming from asset sales.

XYZ could be well along in its decline if you spot the following: A drop in the bond rating; the loss of several big customers; the loss of a single large supplier; a product recall; successive write-offs; resignations from the board of directors (unless it's a rubber-stamp board); the fire sale of any division or bundle of assets; the loss of a big lawsuit; cancellation of a new marketing program, product or factory or a change in accounting practice.

GETTING INFORMATION

When a company is ill, it's usually spending money faster than it can balance its checkbook. You should identify the source of the drain. Get an annual report, if the company is public, and copy the funds statement, also called the statement of cash receipts and disbursements. Take an accountant source to lunch. (You should have already developed such a source simply by virtue of being a business reporter.) Ask for help interpreting the sources and uses of funds, which means how much cash is going out the door versus how much is coming in.

Call competitors. They may be guessing at why XYZ is leaking cash, and they obviously have an interest in seeing that the trend continues. But competitors are often the first to know what's going on, because business people gossip as much as news people.

Locate former employees. Go through old press releases that announced the appointment of a new mid-level manager, a vice president of sales or an assistant to the executive vice president. Pull out every management name you can find. Are they still with the company? Ask the public relations manager, a competitor or a head-hunter.

If the company's problems have been long in the making, its middle-management ranks probably are, or were, bloated with managers. It is common for companies to overexpand in good years. Many of these people may now be cast-offs, refugees or revolutionaries who quit. Find them. When used with journalistic caution, they make excellent sources.

Seek out possible creditors and current suppliers. If the company is already in a Chapter 11 bankruptcy, these people may be the same. Trade magazines are good sources of suppliers because they are the main advertisers. Randomly call suppliers to XYZ's industry. Once you establish that they are suppliers to the company, start asking questions: Is

XYZ paying its bills? How late are they in paying? What is their explanation? How many times have they changed controllers?

Try members of the boards of directors of XYZ's biggest customers and its biggest suppliers. They may know something.

Bankers are tougher. They won't talk about specific troubled loans, not only because they consider the relationship with the borrower confidential but also because the lender looks stupid when the loan goes bad.

But loan officers only get to be president of the bank by saving their loans, and you may find one who will tell the story of the "turnaround" he's leading at XYZ. Usually large banks have a specialist who evaluates strategy. He or she can tell quickly whether the company has enough liquidity to make a comeback or whether bankruptcy is inevitable.

Bankruptcy is one strategy the troubled company may choose. Bankruptcy as defined by the Federal Bankruptcy Act of 1898 means total insolvency. That law allowed for only one solution, the orderly liquidation of the debtor's assets. Later chapters were added to allow for reorganization of the company and other arrangements to provide fair and friendly settlements of debts. Once the company has filed for bankruptcy in the courts, your job is easier because the records are public information (see "Corporate Strategies," herein).

Troubled public companies are difficult enough to cover. Troubled private ones are even harder (see "Private Companies," herein). But here's an investigative tip for constructing at least part of the private company's balance sheet: Drive by XYZ's parking lot and get a count of the cars. Get an industry schedule that lists typical ratios of employees to sales. (A business school librarian can look this up for you.) Multiply that number by the number of employees per car. For example, assume 1.5 employees per car and multiply it by $100,000, the industry average of annual sales per employee for a manufacturing operation. This approximates the company's sales. (The technique comes from an investment banker who has used it and says it is used by creditors and their lawyers to prepare bankruptcy strategies.)

THE COMPANY'S STRATEGY

As soon as you have a picture of the company's internal condition, you'll want the interview with the chief executive officer. Tell your already battered public relations contact that you are interested in how the chief is tackling the evident problems. Cash is king in a troubled company. As a result, the management team that's trying to keep the company afloat will be preoccupied with converting assets to greenbacks. Ask the CEO how he's doing this. What's on the block? Is any division a leveraged buyout candidate? Is the company developing a new product to help its sales? Is it returning to its core business? Is it seeking a merger partner? A joint venture with a larger, stronger firm? Does it have any products or services that it could license or franchise as a source of royalties? How is the company paying off its debt? Is it borrowing to pay dividends? Has it restructured debt? What is the CEO's turnaround strategy? He or she may not have one, not to mention a job for much longer. That's a story.

Also look for what turnaround artists say are signs of corporate largess, including continued use of limousines and corporate jetcraft even after losses have mounted. (Talk to private jet pilots. They know who is flying what, when and where.) If top management has insulated itself, it will continue using these perks. Subordinates may be shielding them from the real problems, however. That's also a story.

Layoffs, possibly massive, will probably be part of your continuing coverage. Try to get the lay-off plan drawn up by the company or its consultants. Are women the main employees laid off? If so, does this comply with Equal Employment Opportunity Commission regulations? Is the company cutting fat or muscle?

It's common sense—but be kind to the public relations person with whom you talk at least five times a day.—He or she may be about to be laid off. The public relations department is usually the first to be cut.

If the faltering company is in a small town, you may face some unexpected problems, especially if the company is the largest employer. Some may feel that your coverage is hurting rather than helping the situation. Your report of layoffs and problems may make the whole town feel ashamed or depressed. People might accuse you of trying to sink the company by writing about its problems. While the criticism won't deter you, empathy and objectivity aren't mutually exclusive.

A NOTE ON ACCOUNTING CHANGES

Look at your troubled company's past annual reports for any changes in accounting practices, particularly two methods that are often the bane of first-year accounting students: LIFO and FIFO.

LIFO (last in, first out) and FIFO (first in, first out) are methods for valuing inventory. If the company has changed from one to the other recently, it's either trying to increase its net income or lower it for tax purposes. The LIFO method ties the cost of the goods sold to the cost of the most recent purchases. FIFO assumes the inventory is to be sold in the order in which it was purchased.

Generally, in times of inflation, a company will use LIFO to lower its taxes. It may switch in times of deflation. Often, the change in methods will come at a time when LIFO will reduce taxable income since LIFO produces a lower ending inventory figure, a higher cost of goods sold number and a lower reported profit.

While there are valid management reasons for changing accounting practices—the company wants to look good or bad for some reason—the change may signal internal problems that the company wants to cover up. Therefore, any change should be a red flag to carry off your trusted accountant source for interpretation.

Be forewarned about financial statements. They are unreal documents. Here's what a Touche Ross accountant told a first-year accounting class at Columbia Business School about his corporate clients: "Clients can be stupid, venal and weak. They have their own agendas. There's got to be a large amount of skepticism and a low amount of trust when dealing with clients." That's good advice for reporters, too.

TERMS YOU NEED TO KNOW

Financial Ratios. A variety of ratios—comparisons—can give you a handle on the company's financial fitness. Comparisons are more meaningful than just raw figures. For example, comparing current assets with current liabilities, which gives you the current ratio, is better than just looking at the dollar value of assets given on the balance sheet. This is because current assets are generally considered the pool of resources from which current obligations can be met. And that is important to a company in jeopardy. There are numerous ratios measuring efficiency and profitability. Start out with the current ratio, current assets divided by current liabilities, to get a measure of a company's liquidity and indebtedness. Compare the result to a competitor or the industry.

Restructuring. Also called downsizing or turnaround, the term describes a corporate plan for reducing debt, increasing value for shareholders and making the most out of corporate assets. Essential to a restructuring is a strategic plan to enable the company to become more adaptive, market driven and innovative.

Chapter 11 Bankruptcy. Increasingly a method used to bring about a "turnaround. This type of filing usually buys time, but often not a new lease on life. There is no such thing as an involuntary Chapter 11 case. Debtors like Chapter 11, however, because once it's filed, the debtor's property and future income are under the court's protection. There is automatically a stay against litigation, collection and liquidation. (Other forms of bankruptcy are described in the essay on strategies.)

Pro Forma Operating and Balance Sheet Statements. These are a company's forecasts of future business activity. They are hypothetical statements useful for comparing against a company's actual performance. The operating statement is built around expected sales. The balance sheet is based, in part, on expectations about how funds will flow through the company.

The Concept of Funds Flow. Managers are essentially concerned with how they can put the company's present funds to best use and where they will get future funds to take advantage of business opportunities that will benefit the owners. This is why cash is king—or tyrant—in the troubled company. Cash projections sum up everything that's going on in a company. Identifying the flow of funds, receipts and disbursements, is the first task of the turnaround artist, who wants to wring cash out of every possible source in order to reduce debt, which is the monster that can swallow whole companies.

The Successful Company

by David Kinney

The best businesses often make the worst stories. When writing about a successful company, you're at a disadvantage, something many business writers, even those who've been at it awhile, don't realize.

Blame it on the nature of news, but even more so on human nature. Failure, especially if it's draped in the dark tones of tragedy or, better yet, tarted up with a touch of knavery, will always score higher on the reader-meter than a place on "Bilbo Bulbs' Bright Future."

The problem is, a business writer can't survive on a steady diet of opening one can of worms after another. Over the course of a career, assignments to cover a "good" company far outnumber chances to watch a rogue one unravel. But that's no excuse for much of what you read on newspaper business pages and between the covers of business magazines.

A lot of it can be laid to laziness, an affliction that not just journalism's business subspecies suffers, or to treating these stories as penance, the price you pay for running the kind of stories the business community doesn't like—but loves to read. Reporters often act as if writing a success story will ruin their reputations, an admission that they're going soft or, worse yet, are on the take.

Regardless of reasons, the result has been a double standard of how we cover business. Too often, reporters approach a successful company in a way they never would a troubled one. They leave behind the skepticism and intellectual curiosity so essential to their craft, satisfied simply to regurgitate whatever is spoon-fed to them. On occasion, they wind up with profile of rock-solid companies that two months later turn out to be papier-mâché. More often, they commit the gravest sin a writer can against their readers: They bore them.

It need not be this way. A reporter can produce something of substance—and genuine reader interest—even when the assignment doesn't culminate in flushing out a fake. And it's done the same way you cover a company going down the tubes: Find out what went wrong and who's to blame.

That's not as strange as it sounds. On the surface, the free-enterprise system seems simple: You make/buy something, then sell/distribute it at a profit. Heed that rule and you come out a winner. But, often as not, business success is born of aberration: A company does something different, something that sets it apart, something liable to be labeled wrong if what the rest do is considered right. Behind that course, whether it initially was set by choice or chance, can be found one or more few key individuals.

THE INTERVIEW

Discovering who these people are and what they've done can prove more difficult with a successful business than with one where the wagons are circled. Sure, a company that's doing well is more likely to cooperate. But be forewarned: Even top officials might not know or fully understand what it is they do that is so right.

Often, they lack the self-awareness you find at a foundering company, where executives have spent a lot of their time trying to figure out what went wrong, if for no other reason than to keep the blame off their heads. Like most people, executives learn by their mistakes, not their successes, and the people who run successful companies are usually more interested in taking care of business than in soul-searching.

They also tend to spread the praise around. Claiming that everyone, from the janitor to the CEO, shares the credit makes for good company morale but bad journalism. If, as the saying goes, "victory has a hundred fathers but defeat is an orphan," then business success and failure are their close kin.

A reporter covering a successful company often winds up in the awkward position of having to squeeze things out of people. In your quest for a brilliant story, don't be afraid to ask dumb questions: Is there a visionary at the helm? Did a team effort pay off? Is success due to careful strategy or blind luck? Did the company buy out its competitors or crush them? What incentives are there to keep the company growing? Do executives get big bonuses? Does the boss really know what he's doing?

Remember: Success doesn't come easily, and a company—or, for that matter, a reporter—slavishly following a formula will likely find failure. Not every company produces goods and services efficiently. Most don't manage their people very well. Some can control their costs; many can't. Some have an uncanny instinct for what people want to buy and what they'll pay for it; for others, the market moves in mysterious ways.

It's no mean feat for a company to do all the things necessary to make a profit, plus satisfy regulators, unions, consumers and shareholders. If, on top of that, it can sustain reasonable growth and be a good corporate citizen, you can hardly blame the CEO for blowing his stack when a reporter informs him that the company doesn't add up to enough for a "real" story.

THE APPROACH

There's no secret to covering a successful company. You go at it the same way, with the same commitment and intensity with which you cover a troubled company. But here are a few things to keep in mind:

It takes time. Often as not, an impatient editor deserves as much blame for a shallow story as the lazy reporter who wrote it. What these stories lack in sexiness, they must make up for with insight. They must speak with authority, which comes from understanding, which comes from mastering details. A good reporter will stand her ground and insist the story get the time it deserves.

Talk behind their backs. The subjects of your story may have important things to say, but so do others. A good reporter works sources, talking to analysts, consultants, rivals, friends, family—the same people you talk to about a company on the ropes. Use sources to lead to other sources.

One thing leads to another. Do your background interviews before meeting the key players, then keep working those sources until you've finished writing the story. And call them back after the story appears. Remember: The more you know, the more you're likely to find out.

Numbers don't always add up to anything. A business story isn't an income statement, and a business reporter who puts too much faith in figures is a fool. In many cases, such as with a private company, they might not be available. The story lies not in the numbers but in how they got that way.

Now isn't forever. To determine where a company is, a reporter must know where it's been and where it's going. What kind of challenges has it faced in the past? How is that history likely to affect its future? A reporter who fails to hedge his bets often winds up a loser.

Tell them something they don't know. "They," in this case, are subjects as well as the readers. Compiling facts doesn't make a story: It's the depth and insight the reporter brings that adds value.

Basic Stories

In the course of a career, business and economics journalists will write hundreds of look-alike stories: the corporations' names will differ, the numbers will change, but the format of the story will remain pretty much the same. While innovation and style are encouraged on the business page, no journalist will survive long without learning the generally accepted forms for basic business and economics stories. Here are examples of the stories journalists encounter every day and how they might be written.

EARNINGS

Publicly traded companies must report their earnings quarterly. Each quarter is important and should lead the story. The results for the "half year," or the "six month report," the nine-month results and the annual earnings are secondary.

When reporting the quarter's results, compare "like quarters." In other words, compare the third quarter this year to the third quarter last year. It doesn't matter very much how a company performs from one quarter to the next, since seasonal adjustments or the business cycle (retailers have quarters that vary widely because of annual sales and holidays) may result in misleading comparisons. However, when writing about a company that has seasonal swings in earnings, it's important to say so, particularly if this year's traditionally strong second quarter is stronger, or weaker, than usual.

The earnings story should lead with the quarter's results, stating which quarter it is and the dates it ended, if the company has an unusual year. Many companies operate on "fiscal years" which don't end on December. 31. If the company reports on a calendar year basis, then you needn't state the date of the quarter. It's assumed that the first quarter ends on March 31, the second at the end of June, and the third at the end of September.

When looking for the correct numbers to use in your story, look for the "net income," also called profit or earnings. This is the money the company earned after paying taxes. It's the money the company will share with its stockholders. Be aware that net income may include "extraordinary items" which add to, or subtract from, the company's results. A large "extraordinary gain" can add millions to the bottom line and push the earnings figure higher than it would ordinarily have been. Since extraordinary items are one-time gains or charges (also called an extraordinary loss), don't compare the results of a reporting period with an extraordinary item to one without one. In other words, compare the results that measure the same activity year to year. Use "continuing operations," also called "income before extraordinary items."

The next important number is the "per-share earnings." Per share is found by dividing the company's earnings by the number of shares outstanding. Shares outstanding are the shares in public hands. The per share number provides an easy gauge for measuring a company's performance over time.

The third most important number is the percentage increase or decrease in earnings. If the percentage is small, less than 10 percent, it may not be necessary to include a percentage in your story. But if the rise or fall in earnings is large, using percentages helps readers to understand the magnitude of the change.

And don't forget about sales, also known as revenues. This measures all the money a company takes in. Sales are used as a measure of the size of a company. TTT Inc., for example, might be a $1 billion company, which means its revenues are $1 billion or more. Sales are less important than profits.

An earnings lead might look like this:

New York—DDD Corp. reported a 50 percent increase in third quarter earnings, before accounting for a $50,000 extraordinary gain from the sale of a factory in July. Earnings for the mining company, excluding the extraordinary item, were $150,000, or $2.00 a share, up from $75,000, or $1.00 a share in the year earlier quarter. Sales rose 25 percent to $1 million from $750,000 a year ago. The company said that earnings benefited from . . .

ACQUISITIONS

The number of companies in the United States changes every day. Many of those that disappear from the public market are absorbed into other companies through acquisitions. Acquisitions happen in stages. And depending on the size of the company, you may write just one story: the one that reports the acquisition agreement. Or you may write several stories leading up to a completed deal. Those stories might be one of the following:

The Intention Story

This story lets the public know that a company is looking for acquisitions. Such a story might also be written about a company that wants the public to know it's for sale. Whether a company is looking to buy or to be sold, the story should explain why the decision was made and how this strategy will benefit the company, or shareholders, long-term. Be sure to include the company's cash position or any other information that would help the reader understand the reason for the announcement. Remember that the numbers an analyst or the company quotes as its value don't mean much. The only value you can write about—unless there is a bidder with an offer—is the value computed by taking the most recent closing price of the publicly traded stock and multiplying by the number of shares outstanding. This won't be the price the company is actually bought or sold for (see "Analyzing Acquisition," to learn how companies are valued). Try to find out who is the deal-maker for the company; usually it's the company's investment banker.

The "Maybe I'll Buy" Story

Once it's known a company is for sale, there may be many interested parties. Some may come forward and announce their interest, but others may not. If you are an alert reporter, you may be able to get ahead of an official announcement by watching the company's stock activity. When a buyer acquires 5 percent of a publicly listed stock, the Securities and Exchange Commission requires the buyer to file a 13–D. This is a clue to a possible buyer, even though the buyer may be a speculator or an investor with no intention of taking over the company. When a company decides to make a purchase, negotiations will begin. Check the finances of the interested party. Does it look as though the potential buyer can afford—or find financing for—the target company? Talk to analysts.

The Agreement in Principle

This is not the final stage of an acquisition. It just means that two parties have agreed to the basic details of a possible deal. It means that the two parties are friendly—it doesn't mean they will stay friendly. At this stage of the negotiations, some of the terms of the acquisition might be available. And, it's likely that the market has reacted in a positive or negative way to a possible acquisition announcement. Remember, it's common for the stock price of the acquiring company to drop because acquisitions are expensive and result in higher debt for the acquirer and extra costs associated with consolidation. The stock price of the target company usually rises because speculators want to buy in anticipation of a higher-than-market offer for the company.

The Acquisition

This is the announcement that the two parties have agreed to terms for a deal. The terms are usually made public. This story should include an analysis of the transaction, supplied by analysts. It should also look carefully at financing. The annual earnings of each company should appear in the story. Don't forget to say when the "closing" is expected. You might want to talk to unions or other interested parties. Don't forget the major shareholders and company executives, who may have gotten a different deal than the common shareholders. Is anyone upset about the deal?

A typical acquisition story looks like this:

New York—PPP Corp. agreed to buy Paperback Exchange, a Chicago-based chain of bookstores, for $12.25 a share, or about $12 million in cash and stock. The acquisition will expand PPP's presence in retail book distribution in the Midwest. PPP, a publisher of quality softcover educational texts, owns and operates about 150 book outlets. The acquisition will double its distribution capabilities. The transaction calls for . . .

FINANCING

Companies raise money by either selling common or preferred stock (equity financing) or by selling bonds, debentures or other debt (debt financing). If companies sell to just a few investors it's a "private placement." If the financing involves the public, the company will use an underwriter in a "public issue." Sometimes the arrangements involve combinations of debt instruments.

Creative financing flowered in the 1980s with the proliferation of leveraged buyouts and takeovers using high yield, high risk "junk bonds." But most financing stories are straight-forward announcements. They take two basic forms: equity and debt.

Equity

When companies need money they often sell stock. An equity story should state the number of shares offered and the class of shares (see

"Publicly Held Companies," herein). The story should include the anticipated offering price, if it's the first offering. If this is an offering of shares already publicly traded, then report the most recent closing price. It's important to explain the use of the funds and who is doing the underwriting.

An equity story might look like this:

New York—FFF Corp. said it plans to raise $10 million through a public offering of 500,000 common shares. The proceeds will be used to finance the expansion of its New Jersey manufacturing division.

The maker of widgets said the company's Employee Stock Ownership Plan had committed to purchase 100,000 of the shares. The remaining 400,000 will be offered to the public. FFF's stock closed yesterday on the Big Time Exchange at $11.50 a share unchanged.

A syndicate led by XXX Banking will underwrite . . .

Debt

As in any business story, the first question is "how much" debt? Then it is important to explain the types of debt and the terms, including the interest rate. Sometimes the terms of a debt story are complicated and of little interest to the reader. But often complex debt arrangement includes restrictions on dividends or the sale of property. This is important information, since it can inhibit a company's long-term growth and tie the hands of management.

A debt story might read like this:

New York . . . EEE Inc. said it has arranged partial financing through KKK Bank for its tender offer of $25 a share for all of LLL Corp.'s shares outstanding. The bank is committed to provide a facility of as much as $150 million to finance the offer and to pay related fees and expenses.

The electronics firm said that the remaining $100 million of the $250 million purchase price will be financed through a unit offering of debt and equity. The company registered 100,000 units with the Securities and Exchange Commission on Tuesday.

The offering will consist of $100 million of debentures, due 2000. Each unit will consist of $1,000 face value debentures and an as-yet- undetermined amount of common stock. An investment group headed by YYY Banking . . .

BANKRUPTCY

Sometimes companies fail. And in some cases, they file for bankruptcy. But bankruptcy doesn't always mean the company will dissolve. Often businesses encounter temporary financial difficulties but aren't insolvent. Some companies are capable of making a profit but file bankruptcy because high debt has crippled the company and its officers want relief from the company's creditors. That's why it's important to analyze the reasons for bankruptcy.

The classic reasons for corporate failure are: poor financial planning, inefficient management of income, errors of judgment, overexpansion, poor pricing practices and poor merchandise. Sometimes these problems can be remedied; sometimes they can't. When a company gives up, it files a Chapter 7 of the Bankruptcy Code, which calls for liquidation.

When there is hope for the company, it files a Chapter 11, which allows companies to reorganize with the help of the courts. In the case of Chapter 11 stories, the first article will be a straight-forward explanation of the company's problems: how much money is owed and what may happen to the operations of the company. The more important story is the follow-up, which explains the company's reorganization plans.

It should read something like this:

New York—QQQ Company, which filed for protection from creditors under Chapter 11 of the federal Bankruptcy Code last month, filed a plan for reorganization yesterday.

The reorganization will result in the sale of 80 percent of the company's assets and the reorganization of its remaining businesses under its two largest subsidiaries, RRR, a Chicago commodity firm and SSS, a New York brewer.

Under the plan, the firm will distribute to creditors and shareholders a total of $7 million in cash, 5 million preferred shares, 6 million common shares, $12 million face value secured convertible notes, and warrants to buy four million QQQ common shares at 25 cents each.

ECONOMIC NEWS

Periodically, the government issues data about the health of the national economy. Reporters can't avoid doing these stories, despite the sometimes abstract nature of the numbers. Generally, there are two important facts to remember. First, compare "real numbers" to real numbers and "nominal numbers" to nominal numbers. Real numbers are the results before inflation. Nominal numbers include inflation. So, economic growth, Gross National Product (GNP), may appear in documents in both forms. Use the "real" GNP, unless your publication has another policy.

Second, it's important to remember that government numbers are revised repeatedly. So, use caution when drawing conclusions about what the numbers mean; they might be revised up or down in coming months or years. It's best to focus on the short-term impact of economic data. And, unlike an earnings story, an economic story will compare the most recent figures to the previous month's numbers and then refer to the year ago figures. For economic data, it's important to show how the year is progressing month by month and at what annual percentage rate.

The typical economic story might read like this:

Washington—Consumer credit surged in November at a 9.8 percent rate, helped by a upswing in auto loans, the Federal Reserve Board reported yesterday.

Borrowing for cars grew $4 billion in the month, or at a 13 percent annual rate, far above the previous month's increase of $2.5 billion, or a 6 percent annual rate. The numbers are adjusted for seasonal fluctuations.

The recent two month increase in consumer credit follows three months of slow growth in consumer due to rising interest rates. Interest rates during the last 10 weeks have fallen five-tenths of one percent. Lower interest rates and dealer incentives are expected to contribute to a continuation of high demand for consumer credit . . .

STOCK MARKET

At the close of each market day, it's a reporter's job to tell the world what happened in the financial markets that day and why. This is a difficult assignment because the market is unpredictable and increasingly driven by emotion. Often the anticipation of economic news will move the stock and commodities markets, even when buyers and sellers of stocks know that economic data isn't always accurate. Still, the market reporter must say, with some authority, what moved the market.

Every stock market story has similar elements. It must state the closing level, usually the Dow Jones Industrial Average, followed by the volume, usually on the New York Stock Exchange, and then the trend in the market. Technical analysts at brokerage firms are helpful here. Usually the story will include a mention of the most active stocks and the losers for the day. If there was a rumor of takeovers or announcements of acquisitions, information about the stocks affected should be included.

A stock market story might say this:

New York—Stocks slumped after three days of gains. The Dow Jones Industrial Average lost 8 points to close at 2110.10. Volume on the New York Stock Exchange contracted to 140,350,000 shares from 162,123,000 on Tuesday.

The Dow was hurt particularly by TTT Corp.'s 3–1/8 decline to $45 a share on a disappointing earnings projection. The company said it expects to report a 60 percent drop in second quarter earnings.

Analyzing the Acquisition

by Elyse T. Tanouye

When an offer to buy a company is announced, the press release might read something like this:

Company B said that it is commencing a $65–a-share tender offer for up to 49 percent of Company A shares. Following the tender offer, and subject to the approval of Company A shareholders, Company A will be merged into a subsidiary of Company B and each share of Company A common stock will be converted into Company B common stock with a value of $65 a share, or $65 in cash. No more than 49 percent of Company A shares will be bought for cash. The tender offer will expire at midnight EST, February 24th, 1999.

What should the public and, more specifically, the shareholders make of this offer? Is $65 a share a fair price? Should a shareholder tender (sell) shares now or wait? Why is the deal structured with just 49 percent cash? What effect will the merger have on Company B shareholders?

Many of the answers to these questions are contained in the formal document called, appropriately, the Offer to Purchase. You can obtain a copy from the acquiring company's investment relations office, or the agent listed in the paid offer announcement in the *Wall Street Journal*.

In the offer document, the buyer must disclose all material details of its proposal so that the shareholder can make a reasonably informed decision. It will detail the events that led up to the offer, terms, financial information about both the target and buying companies, how the deal will be financed, the tax implications of the deal, conditions of the offer and other valuable information.

VALUE: WHAT IS A FAIR PRICE?

Often the target company's board of directors will urge its shareholders not to tender their shares because it believes the price is not fair. The board usually will present a letter from its highly respected, credible investment bank testifying that the price is inadequate and doesn't reflect the full value of the company's assets or operations. Then the bank will give its own estimate of the company's value, which invariably will far exceed the buyer's offer. For example, Company A's investment bank may claim the company is worth $95 a share, not $65 a share.

But wait. The offer document contains a statement by the buying company that its highly respected, credible investment bank considers the offer price fair. How can both prices be fair?

And, if $95 or even $65 is fair, why was the stock trading on the Big Time Exchange at only $41 a share yesterday? Were those transactions unfair?

First, let's look at how the prices are calculated. Investment bankers use several techniques to assess the "fair" value of companies. Depending on the method, and the assumptions used in making the calculations, "fair" values can vary widely. That's because nearly all of the methods are flawed, and most contain subjective components.

One of the most common techniques is the price-to-earnings multiple (P/E). Values are determined by comparing the selling price of comparable companies against their earnings. For example, if Company X earned $2.50 a share and was recently sold to Company Y for $25 a share, the P/E multiple was 10. Company A, then, could expect to receive 10 times its earnings per share, according to this method.

The problem with the P/E multiple is the E, the earnings figure, which is an accounting artifice subject to any number of manipulations by management. Earnings, then, may not be an accurate reflection of a company's true performance or value. And differences in accounting methods between firms make comparison difficult, at best.

The same type of calculation can be done for multiples of book value and cash flow. The book value multiple is rarely used alone, since it measures the depreciated historical cost of assets and doesn't reflect subsequent changes in market value. Land is the classic example of an asset that is typically listed at a fraction of its current market value.

Cash flow, on the other hand, is the rising star in financial analysis. Many members of the financial community believe that cash flow is the true measure of a company's health since its ability to pay its bills, pay dividends, grow or restructure depends on cash flow, not earnings. In takeovers and leveraged buyouts, cash flow receives especially close scrutiny since it determines the amount of debt a company can service.

In calculating the multiples of cash flow, however, historical figures are generally used, which may not be representative of current or future cash flows. Because of that, many financial analysts advocate the discounted cash flow methods (discussed later) as a better approach since it uses cash flow projections.

In most takeovers, the acquiring company pays a substantially higher price over the previous day's stock exchange quote. This premium over market price is paid for control of the company—the power to make or direct its decisions. Again, the appropriate premium in any given deal is derived by looking at premiums paid in comparable recent acquisitions.

Liquidation value estimates the cash that would be generated after the company sold its assets and paid off its liabilities. This method, of course, requires estimates of the prices the assets would fetch in a sale, a highly subjective judgment. It also assumes, perhaps wrongly, that the assets are sellable. Conversely, replacement value shows simply what it would cost to startup a similar company today.

These days the technique of choice is discounted cash flow. In a nutshell, the discounted cash flow method measures value according to the company's free cash flow, or the cash from operations left after making capital investments necessary to maintain existing production. Consider free cash flow as the cash available to shareholders to take out as dividends or to reinvest in the company. It represents the true return on their investment, according to current financial theory.

But problems arise immediately in putting the theory into practice. The discounted cash flow method requires a projection of the target company's cash flow at least five to ten years into the future. The banker then calculates the present value of the cash flow (a complicated formula which requires predicting interest rate trends and the company's relative risk profile).

Prescience, as you can see, is the key talent required of investment bankers who use the discounted cash flow method. But most veteran company managers, who know their companies far better than bankers, would attest that projecting financial performance more than one or two years ahead becomes pure guesswork, since economic, political and competitive factors are unpredictable. And little needs to be said about the vagaries of interest rate forecasting.

Since so much of what goes into the discounted cash flow formulas are predictions, the results depend on who is making the forecast. You may want to ask the banker or company what interest rate (part of the "discount factor") and cash flow assumptions are inherent in their valuations.

Often a bidder will factor in the benefits of "synergies" arising from merging the two companies. For example, synergies are created if combining Company One and Company Three would produce higher profits than would result from adding up the profits of each. In that case,

Company Three can justify offering a higher price for Company One than for Company Two, which would not benefit from synergies.

Now that we know what's behind the numbers, how do we interpret them for "fairness?" Most investment bankers combine several of the above techniques to come up with a range of defensible prices. Here again, determining one price as "fair" within that range is a subjective call.

Of course, we would suspect that Company B, in the initial example, is low-balling its bid, since it wants to get the best price possible. And it's a safe bet that Company A's price reflects the most optimistic of assumptions about the company's asset and operational value.

Ultimately, you should view both prices simply as negotiating positions. The final price, of course, will be determined by each side's negotiating strengths, whether other bidders emerge and factors such as executives' hidden agenda to keep their jobs.

What is a fair price? It is the final price, the price that both sides voluntarily agree is "fair."

DEAL STRUCTURE AND TAX CONSIDERATIONS

In our scenario, Company B proposes to buy Company A shares for 49 percent cash and the balance in common stock. In other deals, you will see different percentages of each, or other structures involving preferred stock, convertible preferred, convertible debt, installment notes, and other securities. Given all the possible combinations, what determines how a deal is structured? In general, you need to focus on a few key points.

Shareholders are solely concerned with getting the highest return on their investment. But that doesn't mean they'll jump at the highest price offered. What needs to be calculated into the price is the tax effect of the transaction. All-cash deals, for example, are immediately taxable, and shareholders lose a big chunk of the sale's proceeds to capital gains taxes.

Deals that offer at least 50 percent of the purchase price in the acquiring company's equity (common, preferred, or convertible preferred stock) are called "tax-free." To be accurate, they should be called tax-deferred, since the shareholder pays no capital gains tax until the securities are sold. Cash and other assets that make up the other 50 percent are taxable.

The offer document will describe in detail the tax effects relevant to the shareholder, usually under a section titled, "Certain Federal Income Tax Consequences."

The buying company, on the other hand, may want to limit the amount of stock it issues to avoid dilution of earnings per share. For example, if Company B had four million shares outstanding and earnings of $12 million, its earnings per share would be $3.00. If it issued 500,000 more shares to pay for Company A, which added only $1 million more to earnings, the EPS is reduced to $2.89. Earnings, then, are "diluted," since they are spread among more stockholders. And, needless to say, Company B shareholders are sure to be up in arms over what they will perceive as a loss of value in their investment.

On the other hand, if the buying company offers to pay cash, it often must borrow the money, which raises its debt-to-equity ratio. That may lower its credit rating, which in turn may increase its borrowing interest rate. Investors also tend to shy away from companies with a high debt-to-equity ratio.

Finally, the handling of asset valuation for tax purposes varies under different deal structures, and will affect the combined companies' taxes and cash flow. For example, acquiring companies can "step-up" the acquired company's assets (put them on their tax books at full market value). That gives them a larger depreciation deduction in years ahead and lowers their taxes. Paying less tax means more cash available to the company and its shareholders. The tax effect depends on the individual circumstance of each deal, and you should probably have your friendly tax lawyer help you analyze any complicated deal.

LOOK FOR LOCK-UPS

Especially in friendly deals, where the target company's board agrees to the buyer's offer, you'll want to scour the offer document for conditional agreements, called "lock-ups" or "crown jewels" in M&A (mergers and acquisitions) lingo. These agreements kick in if, in the end, the tender offer isn't successful. Most frequently this happens when another bidder emerges with a better offer. You'll usually have to comb through the fine print since such agreements are not usually pointed out in public statements.

A lock-up is an agreement between the target and acquiring companies that, if a third party ends up buying the target company, the original bidder will still get something. In many cases, that something is an option to buy or exchange securities of the target company. Or, it may be the right to purchase a "crown jewel," a highly prized asset of the target company, such as a profitable subsidiary or other operation.

One interesting arrangement is the joint venture lock-up, where two companies contribute their crown jewels to a joint venture, each with a 50 percent interest. In the event one of the companies is acquired, the lock-up agreement allows the other to purchase a majority interest in the joint venture.

Finally, even if there are no lock-ups, friendly merger agreements usually include a provision to compensate the buying company if the target company withdraws its support for the deal and/or agrees to be acquired by another company. In many cases, this sum is a significant penalty.

Most of these agreements are insurance for the target company. But they also play the dual role of warding off competing bids. And that interferes with the bidding process, which shareholders may contend prevents them from obtaining the best deal possible. By agreeing to allow lock-ups, the board might be sued for violating its responsibility to work in the best interest of the shareholders (see "Publicly Held Companies"). If you find a lock-up agreement, you should question the target company on who benefits from it.

TACTICAL MANEUVERS

The target company has essentially three options to choose from in responding to an offer. It can accept the offer and encourage shareholders to tender their shares to the acquiring company. Or, the board may want to fight and retain control. Finally, the board may want to force the target company to the bargaining table so that it can negotiate a higher price or better terms. In the latter two cases, here are some defensive tactics you can expect the target company board to employ:

Declare the Offer Inadequate and Recommend Shareholders Not Tender Their Shares

This is the weakest alternative and unlikely to spur the buying company into negotiations or to increase its offer. Nor is it likely to dissuade shareholders from tendering if there is a substantial premium, as there usually is, or if there are no competing bids. Institutional investors, in fact, are likely to consider it their fiduciary responsibility to tender and collect the premium.

Consider Litigation

Reviewing the tender offer for regulatory and/or antitrust violations or errors is, of course, routine. But it is often used as a delaying tactic to substantially raise the cost of the acquisition to the buyer. To avoid such an escalation in cost, the buyer may instead agree to negotiate.

Seek Government Protection

The target company can raise fears among public officials about the intentions of the buyer. Typically, it points to past acquisitions where the buying company laid off employees, closed down factories, or did a "bust-up," selling off the company in pieces. As has been shown many times in recent years, government support—by introducing anti-take-over laws or threatening to withdraw business—gives management tremendous bargaining clout. It may then be able to force the buyer to raise the price, or go away altogether. This effort usually takes time—at least a few weeks—and depends on the local government's attitude toward the takeover. But it can be powerfully effective.

Deploy Its "Poison Pill," aka Share Purchase Rights Plans or Shareholder Protection Plan

The Poison Pill comes in a number of forms but usually works by dramatically increasing the number of shares outstanding—or by issuing a new series of preferred stock that would give shareholders the right to redeem them at a premium price in the event of a takeover—thereby making the company prohibitively expensive. But these tactics are usually effective and, in some cases, legal, only if prepared in advance of an attack. Even so, there is still a risk of invalidation by courts when put to the test. If upheld, they do give the target company a strong bargaining position to force the buyer into negotiations.

Offer Greenmail

The legality of getting rid of a suitor by buying back his shares at a premium, which is not available to other shareholders, is hotly debated. If accepted, this strategy stops the buying company's offer and can be implemented fairly quickly if the company has or can arrange for the cash. The risk, however, is that the company may attract other buyers seeking greenmail.

Seek a White Knight

Again, advance preparation would help here since finding a willing and suitable buyer may take more time than the company has. It may not make the raider go away but this tactic forces an auction—and a better price for the shareholder.

Actively Auction the Company

Once it is clear that remaining independent is unlikely, boards often throw the doors open and announce the company will consider all offers and will accept the best. This tactic gives the board a measure of control over the sale of the company. Since a sale appears inevitable and a higher price likely, shareholders would have an incentive to wait until the auction is completed before tendering. The original bidder may ultimately win the company, but probably will pay a higher price.

Recapitalize the Firm

This would include a leveraged buyout, spinning off operations, or trading debt for equity by borrowing money to pay a large dividend or buy back shares.

Finally, beware of hidden agendas in defensive maneuverings by the company. Although board members must uphold their responsibility to act in the best interest of the shareholders, most boards are controlled or strongly influenced by management, who want to keep their jobs. And board members themselves are all too human and may want to keep their directorships, or their friendships with management, intact. In your analysis of a takeover bid, consider whether the target company's resistance benefits the shareholders or is simply an effort by management to maintain the status quo.

A takeover can be one of the toughest topics to cover in business journalism. But, as with all power struggles, it can also be one of the most intriguing and exciting.

The Annual Meeting

by Barbara French

A company's annual meeting, on first thought, may seem to the business reporter to be what the city council meeting is to the metro reporter. It's a public occasion when all the principals gather to talk about business before an audience, their voting constituents.

The annual meeting is a once-a-year event. It's a highly orchestrated, invitation-only event. The chairman presides from a podium. A dozen vice presidents and divisional heads may be seated on the dais. There might be a corporate promotional film or a screening of upcoming television commercials. If the company is a cosmetics firm, there may be free samples. If it makes toys, the lobby outside the meeting hall may become a toy store. If it has had a good year, the shareholders will smile and talk calmly. If the company is not doing well, they may not look so happy. And if the company has activities that certain shareholders oppose, say selling goods to South Africa, they may be demonstrating.

Annual meetings tend to be either very businesslike or circuses. The majority of them are over almost before they start—the requirements of an annual meeting can be concluded in less than 30 minutes. Rarely do such meetings give way to raucous banter. Unlike government bodies, corporations seldom encourage discussion. And it is quite unlikely that the rhythm of the meeting will be upset by surprises. Even before the first shareholder takes a seat, the management knows well how the votes will be cast. The chairman can smile with confidence, even though the official election of the board of directors has not been announced (see "Publicly Held Companies"). Quite unlike a city council meeting, an annual meeting is not a democratic assembly.

Yet despite its shortcomings, which include the prospect of no news, the annual meeting can be useful to a business reporter. It is one of the few times when a company's top officers and directors are accessible. It offers an opportunity to meet and talk with many of the company's key employees, as well as its shareholders. And it often attracts analysts who track the company for brokerage firms or institutional investors.

Publicly traded companies are required by the stock exchanges (New York Stock Exchange, American Stock Exchange, National Association of Securities Dealers) and by states' corporation laws to hold annual meetings. The purpose of the meetings is for shareholders to elect a board of directors and to vote on proposed changes in corporate policy that, under the company's charter or bylaws, require shareholder consideration. The company's top executives—chairman, chief executive or president—typically discuss the outlook for the upcoming year, and answer shareholders' questions.

PREPARING FOR THE MEETING

To get the most out of an annual meeting, reporters should prepare by:

• Finding out when and where the annual meeting will be held (they are not always held in the city where the company is headquartered, which may require travel plans).
• Obtaining and reading the proxy statement, which can usually be obtained from the company, the Securities and Exchange Commission or any of the data retrieval services that provide prompt access to SEC records.
• Obtaining and reading the company's 10–K and annual report—including the footnotes and chairman's discussion of operations, financial status and prospects. (The 10–K and annual report can be obtained through the same sources as the proxy statement.)
• Checking other sources—for example, your newspaper's or magazine's library, the current news edition of Standard & Poor's corporation records, and stock analysts—for recent news about the company. Also find out if the resolutions to be voted on by shareholders are noteworthy, either because they follow a trend or break from a trend.
• Selecting two or three top executives to interview, and ask the company in advance for time to interview them at the meeting's conclusion. (Sometimes directors do not have a lot of time for interviews because the company has scheduled a board meeting immediately following the annual meeting. Get whatever time you can.)

Annual meetings, unlike council meetings, are not public events. They are open to shareholders. Companies routinely permit reporters to attend the meetings, but generally require advance notice.

The agenda for an annual meeting is contained in a proxy statement, which the SEC requires be sent to all shareholders prior to the meeting. The proxy statement will say when and where the meeting will be held and what resolutions on corporate policy will be put to a vote of shareholders. Shareholders unable to attend the annual meeting can vote for directors and resolutions by proxy—a sort of corporate absentee ballot.

Resolutions are submitted by the board of directors and by shareholders. The directors nominate candidates for the board of directors and recommend an accounting firm to serve as the company's independent auditor. Scan these recommendations. (It's helpful to check the current proxy against the previous year's to find out what has changed.) Are all nominees to the board incumbents? If not, why not? If incumbents are not up for reelection, find out why. Maybe they are displeased with something. If the accounting firm is different from last years', what's behind the parting of ways? The answers are often straightforward, but change occasionally indicates a good story.

The board's resolutions can also propose significant changes in corporate policy: for example, strengthening the company's defense against a hostile takeover can be achieved through staggered terms for the board of directors or through the establishment of a new class of stock. These proposals may indicate that the company has reason to believe that it is or will be the target of an unfriendly takeover bid. Or maybe it is adopting a policy that other companies adopted long ago.

Shareholder proposals are often more controversial—recommending that the company stop doing business in South Africa or stop making loans to the Chilean government. These proposals, which management routinely recommends shareholders oppose, can reveal aspects of a company's business dealings that have not received much public attention. These shareholder groups can also be good sources of information on your company's business operations.

The proxy statement also contains short biographies on nominees to the board (including their age, occupation, membership on other boards and stockholdings in the company), salaries and stockholdings of most senior executives, retainers paid to outside directors, details on severance deals made with top executives (also called golden parachutes), the names of investors holding more than 5 percent of the company's outstanding stock, and information on the company's bonus and option plans.

The proxy statement also contains information about business dealings the company has had with its directors or top executives. This information is often found under nondescript headings such as "certain transactions." These business dealings can include low interest or non-interest loans extended by the company, and fees paid for services from companies owned in part or full by executives or directors.

FINDING THE STORY

Once armed with information, the reporter has a sense of what will be happening at the meeting. But what's news?

Shareholders rarely reject the company's board nominees, or the recommended accounting firm. They also approve management's resolutions and oppose shareholder resolutions. If shareholders reject any of the company's recommendations, it's news. It is also news if the resolutions win by narrow margins. (Note: Shareholder proposals have been getting more votes in recent years, due to the lobbying efforts of large shareholder groups. Track those votes and compare them year-to-year.)

Listen to shareholder questions, even the questions posed by the professional gadflies—those people who own a few shares of stock in many companies and attend all the meetings. Listen to the company's responses. Are you satisfied with the answers? If not, follow up.

If a company is having financial troubles, the annual meeting might be the first face-to-face exchange between company officials and shareholders since those troubles were revealed, which could mean some heated exchanges.

Listen to speeches of the chairman, chief executive and president. Be sure to ask for copies of the speeches at the beginning of the meeting and read along as the executive speaks. Sometimes paragraphs will be dropped or items added. You may want to ask the executive why. And since you have read the background material and talked to industry analysts, is management addressing the issues? If not, why not? Catch them in an interview at the meeting's conclusion for further explanation.

A final tip: It is a good idea to go to an annual meeting with your own story ideas. Never let an opportunity to talk with the company's key officials slip by without being prepared to ask questions.

Consumer Reporting

by Trudy Lieberman

Modern consumer reporting traces its roots back to the days of the early-twentieth-century muckrakers. Ida M. Tarbell's expose of the Standard Oil Co. and Upton Sinclair's revelations of unsanitary practices in the meat-packing industry stand out as journalistic classics that led to passage of the antitrust laws and the Pure Food and Drug Act, the cornerstone of federal consumer protection.

In the activist 1960s, journalists again returned to muckraking. Following the example set by Ralph Nader, whose book *Unsafe at Any Speed* prompted passage of federally mandated safety standards for cars and a federal agency to oversee auto safety, reporters delved into the unsavory business practices of automobile dealers, supermarkets, drug manufacturers, building contractors, physicians, and even that pillar among American institutions—the local bank. They exposed shoddy and unsafe products as well as the deceptive, misleading, and fraudulent sales practices that enticed people to buy them. Sometimes their stories prompted new laws to protect consumers. Laws banning deceptive sales practices, eliminating outmoded and unfair clauses in credit contracts, and requiring safer products often grew out of journalistic efforts.

But good consumer reporting had its enemies—the publications' advertisers. When a reporter revealed that a supermarket sold an inferior cut of meat, called it by a fanciful name, and charged an exorbitant price, or when a reporter discovered that a car dealer had set back an odometer to make a used car appear newer, advertisers and the business community complained bitterly.

One advertising director for a major newspaper warned editors to "play down" consumer coverage. The reason for the tough reporting, as he saw it, was the low starting salaries paid to reporters. "A young reporter fresh out of college with a baby and wife to support, lands a job on a paper at $145 a week, which is much too little," he noted in 1972. "After seeing most of his salary going for groceries and rent, this individual begins to take a negative view against business for charging what he thinks are high prices. Eventually all this reporter wants to write about are stories that make businessmen look bad."

A supermarket executive charged that newspapers "largely, if not totally, carry news of price increases and make little reference to the true value of food." A California advertising executive even called consumerism a "form of economic McCarthyism" and blamed the media for giving it too much coverage.

For a few years, editors withstood the onslaught. But eventually advertising and circulation wars, plus the practice of linking the compensation of senior editors to profit objectives, made even the most tolerant editor reluctant to "bite the hand that feeds." Exposing the misdeeds of local businesses conflicted with the goal of increasing advertising revenue.

"Aggressive consumer reporting was not encouraged and subtly discouraged," said J. Edward Murray, a former Knight-Ridder executive and past president of the American Society of Newspaper Editors. "Journalists abandoned the old leadership they gave to hard-hitting stories in order to give readers what they wanted." (Or thought they wanted.) At some publications, the discouragement was not so subtle. Editors simply killed stories that were too hard on advertisers or local businessmen. By 1973 tough consumer reporting was history at many papers.

Instead of tough reporting, editors wanted stories that encouraged readers to shop and, if possible, patronize their advertisers. Hence a genre of writing grew up that told consumers where to find the best of everything—from ice cream and pizza to bonbons and pastrami sandwiches. Unfortunately these "shopping mood" stories came to pass for consumer reporting in the 1980s.

About the same time, deregulation, a recent version of laissez-faire, became fashionable. The media, as well as the consumer movement, embraced deregulation as a new way to help consumers by promoting competition, which would in turn lower prices for everything from phone calls to airline tickets.

Luckily for the media, deregulation of financial institutions came along just as editors were trying to make their publications a friendly source for shopping information. Financial products proliferated, and readers needed help. Instead of having only fixed-rate mortgages which had put two-thirds of American families in houses, consumers could now choose adjustable-rate mortgages that made it more likely they could lose those homes. No longer were there simple checking and savings accounts, but checking accounts that paid interest and savings accounts that allowed customers to write checks.

Personal finance stories were perfect for the shopping-mood school of writing. They were the ultimate service piece. Such stories were seemingly simple and cheap to do, and above all, created the right mood for shoppers. All a reporter had to do was call a few experts on personal finance topics, get a few quotes, string five or six tips together on choosing a savings account or a mutual fund, and voilà, the story was complete. These advice stories appeared to impart needed information and kept advertisers happy.

ASSESSING PERSONAL FINANCE COVERAGE

Perhaps one could live with the loss of tough consumer reporting in the pages of America's publications if the personal finance reporting that replaced it was helpful and of high quality. But it's not. Many personal finance stories are superficial. They may be cleverly written, sprinkled with anecdotes, and geared for a fast read, but they're often misleading and fail to discuss the nub of an issue. And sometimes the advice is simply wrong.

For example, a major financial publication advised its readers who were thinking about buying annuities to look for products with a "bail-out" clause, a contract provision that allows the owner to cash in the annuity without paying the normal penalty if the annuity is surrendered (cashed in) during the early years. But the clause is usually triggered only if the rate the annuity is earning at the time of surrender is lower than the initial interest rate by some percentage point or points. In reality, such clauses may be so restrictive they're unlikely ever to be used. Generally they aren't worth the extra premium insurance companies charge for them.

On the surface, telling readers to look for a bail-out clause seems like good advice, but readers who followed that advice, are likely to be disappointed when they find their bail-out clause doesn't save them a nickel.

Personal finance journalism has also tended to focus on the micro aspects of the subject; for example, which savings and loan offers the cheapest mortgage or where to get the cheapest airline ticket to Bermuda. The macro aspects have largely been ignored, at least by the journalists assigned to the personal finance beat. Much of the reporting has failed to put some of the equally important, larger issues into perspective. Take deregulation, for example.

Reporters and their sources were eager to tell people how they would benefit from deregulation, at least in the short term. Prices would come down, and choices would expand—the perfect solution in a market economy. But few journalists recognized that deregulation had long-term consequences, not all of them favorable to consumers. Few questioned the flip side of bank deregulation. Customers could indeed earn a market rate on their savings accounts and money wouldn't flow out of savings and loans during periods of "disintermediation" when interest rates rose. But who predicted the high fees banks eventually charged for services that were once free? (Bounced check charges are now a profit center at some banks.) Who foresaw that allowing savings and loans to stray from their central purpose of making mortgage loans would invite fraud and corruption on the part of bank officers trying their hands at new forms of lending? Deregulation left a broken deposit insurance system and a high price tag to fix it.

In reporting the virtues of airline deregulation, journalists failed to remember what happened in the railroad industry when fierce competition eventually led to consolidation by the Interstate Commerce Commission and ultimately less competition. Disturbing parallels are emerging with airlines. Deregulation brought new carriers into the business, and for a while lively competition followed. But many of the new carriers were gone as quickly as they'd come, leaving consumers few transportation choices in some markets. From this pattern, a journalist could conclude that the possibility of an airline monopoly, with its implications for consumer prices, is all too real. Furthermore, such a consolidation would occur without the watchful eye of a regulatory agency, unlike the railroads' consolidation.

Good consumer and personal finance reporting must discuss these larger issues as well as the ones that directly and immediately affect readers' pocketbooks. It must sift through the blandishments of economists and politicians who are touting some economic reform as the greatest thing since Adam Smith (see "The Economists," herein). Consumer reporting now focuses on the small, narrow issues much the same way some political reporting now tends to spotlight the personal venality of politicians rather than the larger questions of the day.

THE CHALLENGE TO REPORTERS

To revive consumer reporting as it existed in those golden years in the late 1960s and early 1970s is a worthy goal. But realistically the chance to do that kind of reporting may be limited. Publications must nurture and support such reporting, and many do not. Nevertheless, reporters can do a better job on the stories they are allowed to cover by following a few rules:

Take on consumers as your clients and represent them by reporting all the important facts that help them in the marketplace. Whether you're writing about a new financial product or a local scam, put yourself in the consumer's shoes. If you were going to purchase the product or service you're writing about, what do you need to know? Find out and tell the reader. Learn not only how a product works, but why the sales people are pushing it. Evaluating the sales pitch is as important as understanding the product itself (see "Marketing Strategies," herein). Identifying what you as a shopper really need to know will help pinpoint all angles of a story. It will help you think of a problem or issue in its totality and allow you to see both its micro and macro aspects. Realize there are trade-offs in any economic reform. Who benefits? Who pays? Discuss these in your stories.

Financial journalists, as well as all journalists, rely on quotes from experts to make their points. And in financial as in other types of journalism, the same experts are quoted over and over again. Obviously the "experts" have learned to tailor their answers for maximum media effect, and journalists have learned who gives the juicy quote. The good consumer reporter must go beyond the quotable experts, and not be afraid to make judgments for readers. To the extent your publication allows you to be the expert, be one.

Learn to sift through the inane and misleading quotes and identify the experts' biases; certainly they are present. Be wary of experts on both sides: the so-called consumer expert who has a private cause to pursue and the industry spokesperson who must protect the interests of his or her company or industry. The positions advocated by consumer organizations may not always be the correct ones. Nor are the positions advocated by business. As is so often the case in journalism, the answers may be gray, not an easy black or white. You may conclude that neither side's position is as clear-cut as it seems. Don't be afraid to report that.

Consumer reporting demands the highest standards of fairness, accuracy, and honesty. When you are writing about other people's livelihoods, you can't afford to make mistakes. Above all, a good consumer reporter must be courageous. Good stories may sting. They may attack conventional wisdom or the businessman's balance sheet, and they seldom will make everyone happy.

In 1971 the *Columbia Journalism Review* carried a story headlined "Consumer Reporting: Underdeveloped Region." It still is.

Investment Options

by Pauline Tai

Deregulation of financial institutions, technology and market innovation during the 1970s and 1980s have generated intense competition in the banking and securities business. Today, financial services are the largest and fastest growing sector within the U.S. services industry. Financial institutions that succeed in this largely unregulated environment tend to be the ones that are either very innovative in terms of technology and marketing, or very adept at copying new inventions before the competition. Most have proved very savvy at copying others.

Besides competing for new products, institutions are also vying to offer the largest number of services. For example, when convertible adjustable rate mortgages were the rage during the spring of 1988, Greater Metro Financial of Wayne, New Jersey had some 30 versions. Too many choices can be as big a problem for the consumer as for bankers and brokers. In the trial and error environment of investing, mistakes are made.

The journalist who specializes in personal finance must remember that the job is not one of adviser, but of a well-informed researcher of financial information. If you're faced with the job, here are some guidelines. When analyzing and evaluating investments, keep in mind three major points:

1. *The product itself:*
What is it? Is it regulated and if so, by whom?

How does it work?

What are its advantages and disadvantages?

Where does it fit in the larger investment universe?

Who is the issuer and what is its credit rating?

Who is the sponsor?

Where do the managers come from? What kind of track record do they have? How do they compare with others in the industry? How do they compare with others managing the same type of investments?

What is the price?

What are the fees? Be sure to include both front-end and back-end charges, that is, those fees paid when an investment is purchased and those paid when it is sold or surrendered.

Find out as much as you can about the product and list all comparable alternatives currently available. State and federal regulatory agencies, trade groups and often the issuers themselves can tell you much about a particular investment offering.

Caution: an offering registered with a governmental agency such as the Securities and Exchange Commission doesn't come with a seal of safety. Registration means only that the company has complied with current rules for disclosing required information.

2. The current economic climate:

Is the economy in a recession, recovery or expansion? Where is the economy heading?

Are interest rates trending upward or downward?

Is the trend for a higher or a lower inflation rate? Is the U.S. dollar on the way up or down?

Are there important elections coming up?

Since market timing is crucial to successful investing, knowing the current economic climate will help pinpoint whether a product is compatible with the existing environment. For example, if interest rates are rising, a person might want to purchase an investment that locks in a high yield.

3. The individual investor:

Who benefits from this product?

What goals will it satisfy?

How should one use it as part of an overall strategy?

When and where to buy it?

When and how to sell it?

Any transaction tends to have some effect on an investor's total financial well-being. Good advice means giving the reader sufficient relevant information to make a sound decision.

Give as many examples as you can to illustrate specific situations.

This is especially important, when writing about complicated abstract ideas which include mathematical calculations. If you're writing about the tax implications of a particular investment, examples are almost a necessity.

All investments entail one kind of risk or another, and they can be evaluated in terms of the risks they present. These are the potential risks all investors face with any investment:

Interest Rate Risk is the risk that the income a particular investment generates may rise or fall depending on interest rates. Some investments guarantee a rate of return for a certain period; others do not. If money is locked up in a particular investment and interest rates suddenly rise, the investor may have the unpleasant choice of keeping his or her money where it is and forgoing the higher income or pulling the money out to invest elsewhere. The latter option often involves a cost.

Credit Risk is the risk that the entity to whom an investor has lent money, through a bond or stock, for instance, will go bankrupt, leaving investors to stand in line for their money along with other creditors.

Principal Risk is the risk that your principal will fluctuate in value over the short term so that if you want to withdraw your money, you may have to take a loss in order to do so.

Liquidity Risk is the risk that you may not be able to withdraw money when you want without incurring severe penalties. Investors also experience liquidity risk when there's no one to purchase an instrument they want to sell.

TYPES OF INVESTMENT VEHICLES

The following is a brief summary, including a risk assessment, of some of the most popular investment vehicles:

Financial Assets

These are cash or cash equivalents, bonds and stocks. Mutual funds, and some insurance products, such as annuities, which may invest in mutual funds are included under this umbrella. Most retirement savings are also invested in financial assets. Cash assures liquidity and preserves capital, but bears interest-rate risk. That is, your money might be locked up at a relatively low rate. The rates suddenly rise; the investor must forgo the higher interest or pull money out and pay a penalty on the amounts withdrawn. During periods of great uncertainty, investors like to keep a large percentage of their assets in cash or cash-equivalent investments. Conservative or income-oriented investors who abhor risk and like the security of knowing exactly how much their money is earning, are attracted to cash and cash equivalents.

Banks, savings and loan associations, and credit unions offer products that are essentially cash and cash equivalents. These include traditional passbook or statement savings accounts; the more modern money market deposit account (MMD) which is a savings account with check-writing privileges, and Certificates of Deposit (CDs) with maturities ranging from one month to five years or more. Deposit insurance from the Federal Deposit Insurance Corp. (FDIC), the Federal Savings and Loan Insurance Corp. (FSLIC), or the National Credit Union Share Insurance Fund covers all accounts up to $100,000. A few institutions, however, are covered by state deposit insurance funds.

The U.S. government sells Treasury bills (T-bills) with maturities of three, six, or twelve months. A direct obligation of the U.S. government, these securities carry the highest credit rating and interest is exempt from state and local income taxes. After a person makes an initial investment of $10,000, he or she can buy additional bills in multiples of $5,000.

Auctions for three-month and six-month bills are usually held every Monday and for 12–month bills every fourth Thursday. Federal Reserve Banks and branches do not charge buyers fees for purchasing T-bills. But banks and brokers who can also sell Treasury issues usually charge $20 to $30 for this service.

Mutual funds offer both taxable and tax-exempt money market funds (MMFs). Like the MMDs offered by banks, MMFs are actually savings accounts with check-writing privileges. But unlike the MMDs, these funds are usually not insured. The mutual funds, however, tend to be more flexible than their bank counterparts. The funds may require a minimum initial deposit of $1,000, but shareholders are not required to maintain a minimum balance. Bank money market deposit accounts usually require both. Money funds allow customers to write an unlimited number of checks, but money market deposit accounts limit check writing to three checks a month. They also impose a hefty fee ($10 or more) for each check over the maximum.

Bonds

These are obligations of municipalities or corporations. When interest rates are low, governments and corporations like to borrow in the credit markets by floating bond issues. In return for the use of an investor's money, the issuer promises to pay an annual fixed interest rate plus the principal at a predetermined maturity date. Some bonds have "call" provisions; that means the creditor can ask for the bond back and return the principal to the investor. The investor then loses the interest. Bonds are senior securities. In case of default, bondholders are paid off before a company's shareholders.

Bonds are usually considered safe investments that yield steady income for investors. But that image was shattered in the 1970s when high interest and inflation threw the credit markets into chaos. Bond prices vary inversely with interest rates. Investors suffered huge losses as interest rates shot up, forcing bond prices to new lows. Those lucky enough to lock up high returns also lost when high inflation canceled out their gains.

All bonds carry varying degrees of interest-rate risk, and depending on the issuer, there may also be some liquidity or credit risk.

The U.S. Treasury offers notes with maturities from two to ten years, and long-term bonds with maturities ranging from 10 to 30 years. As with T-bills, these securities carry the highest credit rating and are considered the direct obligation of the U.S. government. You can buy Treasury notes with maturities of two and three years for an initial investment of $5,000. For notes with longer maturities and for bonds, the initial investment is only $1,000.

U.S. Savings Bonds, often available through payroll deduction for as little as $25, give workers a convenient and inexpensive way to invest. Rates are set every six months and are generally comparable with other money market investments. Although interest paid on savings bonds is often lower than on other Treasury issues, the bonds' accrued interest can be deferred until they mature or are redeemed.

Corporations may issue bonds or debentures with face amounts of $1,000 or $5,000. To protect bond investors most such bonds carry a call protection clause that limits a corporation's ability to call in the bond. Typically such clauses say a bond can't be called for five years after it's issued. Corporate bonds are rated by investment services such as Standard & Poor's and Moody's, which evaluate a bond issuer's credit worthiness.

Junk bonds are a new twist in the bond markets. These are low-grade unsecured debt issued by companies involved in large corporate takeovers to finance part of the deal. They carry high rates, but also high risk.

State and local governments issue mostly tax-exempt or municipal bonds to finance various projects. The interest income from "munis," as they are called, is exempt from federal taxes. The interest may also be exempt from state and local taxes if investors own bonds issued by an entity in the same state where they live. Municipal bonds are usually issued in $5,000 denominations.

Investors who are in high tax brackets receive maximum benefit from tax-exempt bonds. For example, the taxable equivalent yield of a 9 percent tax-exempt bond is 12.50 percent for a taxpayer in the 28 percent tax bracket, but the yield is only 10.59 percent for someone in the 15 percent bracket.

Because some munis are traded infrequently, tax-exempts may not be as liquid as other investment options. An inactive market also makes buying and selling odd lots of munis a costly affair. Small investors who want some munis in their investment portfolio should consider mutual funds or unit trusts that invest in municipal bonds.

Zero coupon bonds are typically Treasury securities, corporate or tax-exempt bonds, in which the coupons have been stripped from the principal payments. The two parts are repacked and sold with feline names like CATS offered by Salomon Brothers and TIGRS by Merrill Lynch. Zeros pay no regular interest, have a set value at maturity and a fixed rate of interest, but they are sold at a big discount. These features make zeros ideal for investors saving for some specific goal such as a Caribbean cruise, college or retirement. Since the interest rate is fixed, the investor takes an interest-rate risk if rates should rise sharply.

Stocks

Stocks are issued by corporations needing money for expansion or other purposes. A person who purchases a bond becomes the lender to the corporation, a person buying stock becomes an owner of the company and thus will enjoy its good or bad fortunes. Stock investing involves varying degrees of capital risk. For investors who are comfortable with this risk, stocks are a good way to invest for growth. Over the long term, stocks tend to outperform both bonds and cash equivalents. Here are the major types of stocks:

Blue chips are the stocks of America's premier corporations and are included in the Dow Jones Industrial Average, a commonly used indicator of the market's performance. Blue chip stocks are issued by such familiar corporations as AT&T, American Express, Eastman Kodak, General Motors, IBM, McDonald's, Merck, Philip Morris and Texaco. Blue Chips tend to command high prices, but also pay high dividends.

Growth stocks are usually issued by smaller firms and have good potential for capital gains. They pay little or no current income.

New issues are shares from new public offerings. They tend to be volatile, especially if their initial price is far above their true value.

Penny stocks are usually priced under $1 and are offered by developing firms. They are very volatile.

American depository receipts (ADRs) are issued by foreign firms to facilitate the sale of shares in the U.S. markets. ADR prices are published in the financial pages of major newspapers such as The *Wall Street Journal* and the *New York Times*.

Mutual Funds

These investments are designed for investors who don't want to pick their own stocks, bonds, options, or commodities. They may give their money to investment companies that operate mutual funds. Mutual funds offer investors diversification as well as professional management. For these services the funds typically charge an annual management fee of 1 percent (or less) of the fund's assets.

Mutual funds may be closed-end or open-end. In a closed-end fund, the number of shares available is fixed. There is no continuous offering of new shares and no redemption of outstanding shares. These shares, usually traded on a stock exchange, are available through brokers. Most funds on the market are open-end funds and accept new purchases and redeem shares from existing holders on a continuous basis. "No-load" funds charge no commission and are available directly from the investment companies. Those sold through brokers charge a fee, or "load," that often starts at 8.5 percent of the investment and declines as the size of the initial investment increases.

Like ice cream, mutual funds come in many flavors. The types of stock funds include: aggressive, balanced, growth, income, growth and income, sector, international or global, and precious metals. Bond funds may invest in a variety of bonds including Treasury securities; corporates; tax-exempts, including single-state issues; and mortgage-backed securities.

Cash Value Life Insurance

Insurance can be thought of as a financial asset if it combines death protection with a savings element. Historically the rates of return on cash value policies have been lower than from those on competing investments, but new types of policies have made the returns more respectable. Cash value insurance is expensive and most breadwinners cannot afford enough of it to adequately protect their families. The income earned on the savings portion is tax-deferred until the policy is cashed in.

Annuities are an insurance product that provide a way to accumulate money at a fixed or guaranteed rate. At the end of the accumulation phase, the owner may convert her savings to payments made at regular intervals, such as monthly, quarterly, or yearly. During the accumulation phase, interest earned is tax deferred; it receives tax treatment similar to that of a life insurance policy.

Retirement Options

To encourage savings for retirement, the federal government gives investors special tax incentives allowing the interest and sometimes the contributions themselves to accumulate tax deferred.

401(k) plans are company-operated tax-deferred savings plans for employees. An employee may contribute a certain percentage of income each year. (The amount increases annually.) With some plans employees also contribute to their plans.

Individual Retirement Accounts (IRAs) are generally for workers not covered by company pensions plans. Depending on the amount of income and whether a person is covered by a company-sponsored pension plan, individuals may deduct up to $2,000 a year (those with non-working spouses may deduct $2,250). Early withdrawals before age 59 1/2 are subject to a 10 percent tax penalty. In addition, amounts withdrawn must be included as regular income and are thus taxed at the individual's tax rate.

Simplified Employee Pension Plans (SEPs) allow both employers and employees to contribute to an IRA. Individuals can contribute $2,000 or 100 percent of their salary, whichever is less, while employers can contribute $15,000 or 15 percent of their employee's salary, whichever is less.

Keogh Plans are designed for full-time or part-time self-employed workers or for employees of unincorporated businesses. Those eligible can contribute up to 25 percent of earned income, up to a maximum of $30,000.

Tangible Assets

Also called hard assets, tangibles include gold, silver, diamonds and collectibles such as art, stamps and coins. During periods of high inflation, they are ideal hedges. Tangible assets also includes commodities hedges which don't fare as well during periods of high inflation.

Three points to keep in mind about tangible assets: most carry some liquidity risk; most produce no income; they often need to be stored.

The following are common tangible assets.

Commodities tend to carry a very high risk and are extremely volatile. The most commonly traded commodities are: agricultural products such as corn, wheat and soybeans; cattle and pork bellies and precious metals such as gold, platinum and silver. You can buy precious metals in the form of bullion, coins and certificates or in the form of stocks, mutual fund shares invested in metals. Metals are also traded as futures and options. Although low inflation in recent years has discouraged these investments, many investment advisers still suggest that any well-designed portfolio should have 5 percent to 10 percent in precious metals as a hedge against inflation.

Foreign currencies tend to be volatile. That means you can achieve great profits as well as sustain great losses in short periods of time. For several years beginning in 1985 the U.S. dollar declined steadily against the Japanese yen, German mark, British pound and other major currencies.

Real estate presents some interest rate and liquidity risk, but offers substantial advantages. The many ways to invest in real estate include single-family houses, apartment houses or condominiums, commercial property such as offices and shopping malls, mortgage-backed securities, or real estate investment trusts (REITs). REITs invest in a diversified portfolio of real estate ranging from hotels to warehouses.

Limited partnerships involve a general partner who manages investments in real estate, oil and gas, equipment leasing, movies and research and development. Investors are called limited partners because their liability is limited to the amount of their investment which is usually purchased through brokers or financial planners. The minimum investment in a public limited partnership is $5,000; a private one, $25,000. Such partnerships offer income, capital gains and tax advantages. Recent tax law changes have tried to eliminate abuses in these partnerships. Investors should carefully check the economic soundness of these programs before plunking down money. It's also important to check out the general partners—how reliable are they and how much do they charge for their services?

Collectibles have become increasingly popular as investments. Americans are fervent collectors of a great variety of things including stamps, coins, comic books, photographs, prints, classic cars, plates, and of course, paintings.

Hybrids or Derivatives

These are the new risk-transferring innovations: hedging instruments such as financial options, financial futures and interest rates that permit various risks to be unbundled, priced separately and sold to new investors willing to assume the risk.

Such hybrids include:

Options which give investors the right to buy (known as a call) or to sell (a put) a fixed number of shares of a specified common stock or a set amount of a commodity at a fixed (or striking) price at any time until a fixed (expiration) date. Options may be purchased through individual stocks or in baskets of shares.

Futures contracts are agreements to buy or sell a specific amount of a commodity or financial instrument at a particular price on a stipulated future date. The price between the buyer and the seller is established in a commodity exchange, such as the Chicago Board of Trade or the Mercantile Exchange.

Mortgage-backed securities invest in insured and guaranteed mortgages such as those offered by the Federal Housing Administration, Veterans Administration, or Farmers Home Administration. Those guaranteed by the Government National Mortgage Association are called Ginnie Maes while those from the Federal Home Loan Mortgage Corporation are called Freddy Macs.

Financial Planning

by Ellen James

Many stories involving financial planning are about rip-offs: how Mrs. Grey, the 94–year-old widow, lost her fortune on bean futures touted by the planner she met over the phone. Another category is the how-to-survive story, help for investors about the dos and don'ts of financial planning and quoting planners on a host of investment or personal finance topics. And there is the success story: how Mr. Smart made some wise choices and ended up a millionaire.

Since the early 1980s, financial planning stories have become increasingly popular, the result of new individual investment opportunities resulting from deregulation, tax changes and new retirement options. Until recent years, financial planning was only for the rich, individuals with more than $100,000 to be invested and managed. Now an individual with a few thousand dollars can make a variety of investments, some which require as little as $1,000. (See essay on investment options.) Unfortunately, for some individuals this open door to investment opportunities creates all kinds of problems and lots of confusion.

Enter the financial planning reporter. Consumer and financial reporting meet in the financial planning story. How to finance a home is not only about helping a consumer through the maze of mortgage offerings, it's also about interest rates and the health of the residential housing market. How to plan for retirement is as much a story about tax policy as it is about the long-term vitality of the U.S. economy.

In short, financial planning is life planning. That means financial planning stories can be either very specific or very general. Since reporters should not give advice, your role is to provide examples of possible strategies and present the calculations necessary to show the advantages or disadvantages of one financial plan over another.

THE FINANCIAL PLANNERS

One of the difficulties of financial planning stories is the sources of information. Whatever sort of financial planning story you're doing, it's important to realize that the financial planning business is a thorny thicket. With virtually no licensing or regulation and more than 50,000 self-proclaimed practitioners, it's extremely important for reporters to know with whom they are dealing. Some who identify themselves as financial planners are frankly charlatans or flimflam artists whose aim is to swindle the naive on unregistered securities or nonexistent goldmines. Such fraud has always gone on. It's only been within recent years that many such crooks have found a respectable sounding name for their work: financial planning.

Apart from the crooks, many financial planners are honest but incompetent. Some are competent in one area of finance but not in others, though they may claim to be general practitioners. And many in the field are laden with undisclosed or only partially disclosed conflicts of interest that make their advice highly suspect. They're really insurance salesmen, stockbrokers or realty agents in disguise.

To make matters worse, the financial planning field has become crowded with those drawn by the lure of self-employment and the prospect of collecting high fees. At this point, there are so many wild cards in the deck that it's tough to find the aces. Granted, there are more truly qualified people entering the field—including those with impressive backgrounds in such areas as accountancy and tax law, plus specialized financial planning training. But intensified competition has meant that even the aces must spend more time on marketing and promotion and less on keeping abreast of ever-changing financial markets.

Fortunately, many lesser players in the financial planning field, basically tax shelter salesmen who hung out a financial planning shingle to sell real estate partnerships, dropped out of the field after the Tax Reform Act of 1986 killed most such shelters. The stock market crash of 1987, however, had mixed results for the industry. It discouraged some financial planners heavily involved in equity sales, but with a cutback in Wall Street employment, many of the financial district's unemployed went into financial planning.

The biggest danger is misinformation. Make sure your source has the requisite background and experience in the area of your reporting. A mutual fund specialist, for instance, may know nothing about tax shelters. And someone capable of helping high-income couples grapple with college costs, may be ill equipped to address the subject of estate planning with the same couples. Despite billing to the contrary, it's a rare financial planner who's truly a jack-of-all-trades.

It's advisable to seek out material from financial planners who work on a fee-only basis rather than from planners who are compensated only through commissions. Usually material coming from commission-only planners tends to be biased toward products the planner wishes to sell.

Often the financial planner is not the first place to start. Begin with economists to establish the economic environment. What are the expectations for interest rates? Is the economy expected to grow? Then establish the trends in various markets. Never write a housing story without knowing whether residential housing is strong or weak or whether interest rates are rising or falling. Consult an accountant or tax attorney often. Almost every investment has tax consequences. Likewise, lawyers may be of use in some stories. For example, a lawyer who structures estates might be able to shed light on the legal aspects of one estate planning strategy over another, in the event of early death.

In other words, explore the aspects of each story with the individuals who would know the most about the subject before trying to put the entire picture together. And when you do use a financial planner, you might ask what training he or she has. Here are some of the more common credentials:

Chartered Financial Analyst (CFA): This requires three years as a financial analyst and three six-hour exams over three years.

Chartered Financial Consultant (ChFC): A minimum of three years' experience and the successful completion of ten courses and ten two-hour exams.

Certified Financial Planner (CFP): At least three years' experience and six three-hour exams, usually following courses in investment and tax planning courses.

Member of Registry of Financial Planning Practitioners: At least three years' experience and the completion of a four-hour exam. Members must also be certified public accountants or a CFP or hold a law or business degree.

Registered Financial Planner: At least three years' experience, a financial planning, business or law degree, 40 hours of continuing education and two exams.

THE AUDIENCE

The overall proliferation of financial planning services comes at a time when Americans hanker more than ever for solid advice on personal finance. There are several demographic explanations. The most important is that the population is aging, which naturally means that there are more people thinking about retirement and what must be done to ensure that old age is comfortable. Not surprisingly, a survey by the International Association for Financial Planning (IAFP), a dominant Atlanta-based trade association with 19,000 members, found that the average financial planning client is a middle-aged individual in a high income bracket.

With the front line of the postwar baby boom generation advancing into middle-age, there are added concerns about the ability of social systems to provide for the millions of retirees in the 21st century. These concerns—health care, social security, retirement benefits—are all important stories. For many of the postwar generation there are dual concerns about college costs for their offspring and retirement planning for themselves.

A second demographic element is the rise of the career woman. There are more two-career families, with the accompanying higher expectations for a comfortable life. In some cases, two income families create considerable discretionary cash and lots of investment opportunities. The intelligent two-career family wants the best combination of investments to ensure long-term prosperity. But regardless of the education or careers of prosperous two-career families, even the most financially conscious couple cannot be expected to track investments, follow the ups and downs of the market, mutual funds, bonds and real estate. That's where the journalist comes in. You're supposed to help them know what's news, what's risky and what's high yield.

DOING THE JOB

Affluent individuals, with incomes above $50,000, are the most frequent clients of financial planners. But your stories should reach a wider audience. For every wealthy socialite trying to rearrange her finances following divorce, there are many suddenly-single secretaries who, in the wake of separation, are struggling against eviction.

To avoid the tendency to write for the rich, it's often a good idea to approach stories by categories—the tax story, the retirement story and the planning for the kid's education story. Subject stories are generally more useful to readers. And keep in mind that readers are generally interested in maintaining the value of their investments and seeing their money go farther. So a key element in many of your stories will be "getting your money's worth."

TIPS AND TRAPS

Avoid single-sourcing of stories. Financial planning stories should include many voices and many views, so the reader can come to a conclusion based on the viable alternatives presented.

Go out of the office and look your sources in the eye. It's too easy for personal finance reporters to fall victim to inertia and do their interviewing by telephone. But in a field as riddled with problems as financial planning, it's important to remain skeptical. And it's often easier to know who you're dealing with if you see planners in operation on their own turf.

Don't be lulled into thinking that a financial planner is worthy or honorable simply because he's been certified by a financial planning organization or has his name on a national registry. The motives of these organizations may be noble—establishing ethical standards, and so forth. But most are relatively loose knit associations that can offer few guarantees about the quality or integrity of their members.

The Tax Story

by Deborah Rankin

Tax stories come with a built-in advantage. Most readers want to know how tax law changes will affect them. As long as you maintain a "what's in it for me" approach, you'll probably keep your readers until the end of the story.

With any major tax cut or tax increase, the idea is to present the broad outlines of the change first, and then show how it will affect different segments of the taxpaying public. For example, if there is a significant tax boost, first tell how large the increase is in absolute dollar terms and then enumerate the different items that will provide revenue for the increase. Is the increase coming from higher tax rates on all personal income, from higher rates on just certain items such as capital gains, or from taxing income that had previously been tax-free such as Social Security benefits in the early 1980s?

If you're writing about federal taxes, the basic broad-brush information comes from the U.S. government. Start with the public affairs division of the Internal Revenue Service (IRS) in Washington, D.C. Staffers are remarkably pleasant, and can quickly come up with statistics and information on the current law. But their replies, while technically correct, are often not colloquial. So you may need help (usually from an obliging public accounting firm) in translating the response into laymen's language. You should also be aware that the information provided by the IRS reflects the government's view, and may omit, ignore, or dismiss conflicting views handed down by the courts or held by tax experts in the private sector.

Another source of information, particularly about the reasoning behind a certain piece of legislation, is Congressional staff members who are responsible for most of the behind-the-scenes work on tax legislation. Key staffers change with each new administration and/or election. Start with the Joint Committee on Taxation, and then contact the two tax-writing committees, the House Ways and Means Committee and the Senate Finance Committee. Your own congressman may be of help.

Staffers on these committees can tell you, for example, the "legislative intent" of a provision—that is, exactly what Congress was trying to accomplish by enacting a particular change in the law; sometimes the IRS goes overboard in interpreting a change, and legislative intent is often invoked by lawyers and accountants who then challenge the IRS interpretation. Congressional staffers can also provide revenue figures on different provisions—that is, how much revenue (taxes) the government expects to gain or lose from the changes.

This information can help you in organizing your story. By leading with provisions that have the biggest revenue impact and working down to those which have the smallest impact, you will automatically be highlighting provisions that affect the largest number of taxpayers.

Sometimes, however, certain tax provisions will have a relatively modest revenue impact but nonetheless be highly controversial. In such cases, you should be sure to discuss them high up in the story, but put their role into perspective by noting that the revenue impact of the particular provision is relatively small.

Congressional aides can also be helpful in discussing what segments of the population will be helped (or hurt) by a piece of tax legislation. For example, while the tax reform bill in the second term of the Reagan administration was ballyhooed as a major tax cut for the lower and middle classes, Congressional staffers had information that clearly showed the biggest beneficiaries were wealthy individuals making over $200,000.

Your biggest allies in interpreting the impact of tax legislation on individuals will probably be large nationwide CPA firms, such as Arthur Andersen, Price Waterhouse or Peat Marwick Main, and tax publishing firms, such as Prentice Hall, Commerce Clearing House, or Research Institute of America. When writing about change in state laws, contact the revenue or tax department in your state capital, and call smaller local CPA firms for an analysis of the changes.

These organizations closely follow the development of tax bills, and after enactment will usually publish books, booklets and pamphlets analyzing the provisions of the new laws. They are usually delighted to help reporters (in return for some sort of credit for the information they have provided).

Examples are a crucial element in developing the impact of tax legislation, and CPA and tax publishing firms are usually glad to provide them. The trick is to choose examples which apply to broad categories of taxpayers. For example, when writing about a tax cut, you might want to use examples that show how it would affect a lower-income family with children; a single person with a moderate income; an affluent couple with children; and a retired couple.

Since many tax changes are phased in gradually (to give taxpayers a chance to adjust their behavior), it's important to tell readers what the impact will be when the changes are fully effective. If you limit yourself to the first-year impact only, you will almost certainly understate the total impact.

In discussing the impact of a federal tax cut (or increase), don't forget to include the impact of Social Security taxes. After all, what the reader is concerned about is his or her total tax bill, not just the income tax segment of it. And while personal income tax rates were cut sharply during the 1980s, Social Security taxes—especially those earmarked for Medicare—moved in the opposite direction, and for many individuals, they wiped out any net benefits.

You should also be aware of a continuing attempt to broaden the items that are subject to federal income tax. With the deficit a continuing problem, Congress has been trying to stretch the notion of what constitutes taxable income. Employee benefits, which includes such things as group life insurance, health insurance, and pensions, are an increasingly popular target of proposed new tax legislation. Employee benefit consulting firms, such as Hewitt Associates, Towers Perrin Forster & Crosby, and Buck Consultants, can be helpful resources in analyzing the impact of any proposed or actual changes.

TIPS AND TRAPS

Don't accept the official government view as gospel (whether it's coming from Washington or your state capitol). Discuss the conventional wisdom with tax experts in the private sector. Talk with certified public accountants and tax publishing firms to get their views.

By the same token, take with a grain of salt moaning from the private sector about the dire impact of tax changes. Most tax firms don't have an egalitarian attitude toward the tax system, but rather a bias toward safeguarding the interests of wealthy executives and business owners. That's understandable since this is their client base. Much of their hand-wringing is a calculated step to change the mind of Congress, and it often succeeds.

Don't forget to include the impact of Social Security taxes (including changes in Medicare) and state taxes when analyzing a federal tax cut or increase. Changes in these taxes can often outweigh changes in the individual income tax.

Use lots of examples. Even if the examples don't precisely parallel the situation of your readers, they help personalize a story. In a sense, they're an acceptable form of financial voyeurism.

TAX TALK

Adjusted Gross Income

This is an individual's gross income, reduced by certain adjustments allowed by law, such as alimony payments and contributions to a Keogh or Individual Retirement Account.

Capital Gain and Loss

The gain or loss arising from the sale or exchange of capital assets, such as securities or real estate. The gain or loss is determined by comparing the amount you receive from the sale to the amount you originally paid. If you receive more than the original cost, plus certain adjustments, you have a gain; if you receive less, you have a loss.

The tax treatment of capital gains, which is traditionally considered something only the wealthy have the luxury of worrying about, has varied over the last few decades. In 1990, capital gains were treated as ordinary income; but in the past, as much as 60 percent of long-term gains could be excluded from income.

Deduction

Expenses allowed by the law that reduce your taxable income. Some of the most common deductions include mortgage interest, state and local taxes, real estate taxes, charitable contributions and medical expenses. The value of a deduction varies, depending on one's tax bracket. A $1,000 deduction, for example, will save someone in the 33 percent bracket $330 in taxes; but it will save someone in the 15 percent bracket only $150 in taxes.

Depreciation

A deductible business expense that reflects a reasonable allowance for wear and tear of property. Only property that has a useful life of more than one year and is used for business or income-producing purposes may be depreciated. Depreciation may be calculated under various methods, depending upon the laws in effect at the time the property is put into service.

Earned Income

This is compensation, such as wages, salary, bonus and tips, that one receives for performing personal services. One must have earned income in order to make deductible IRA contributions.

Individual Retirement Account

An IRA is a personal retirement account to which up to $2,000 ($2,250 if it covers a nonworking spouse) may be contributed annually. Your ability to claim a deduction for your contributions depends upon your income and whether you are covered by a pension plan at work.

Kiddie Tax

A tax on the investment income of a child under the age of 14, if that income exceeds $1,000. The tax is based on the parents' marginal tax rate.

Marginal Tax Rate

The rate of tax you pay on each additional dollar of income you earn above a certain level. If, for example, your marginal tax rate is 33 percent, that means that the IRS will get 33 percent of your income on any investment and you will get to keep 67 percent. So, if you earn $1,000 on a certificate of deposit, the government takes $330 and you keep $670.

Ordinary Income

Income that is not derived from capital gains and is not subject to any preferential tax treatment.

Passive Activity Loss Rules

Rules that limit the deduction of losses from passive activities, such as certain tax shelters, to income from other passive activities. Passive activities include rental operations or businesses in which investors do not actively participate.

Personal Exemption

An amount determined by Congress that you are entitled to deduct from your income before computing your tax. It is equivalent to a deduction that each taxpayer is permitted to claim for himself or herself as well as for each dependent.

Standard Deduction

A deduction that can be claimed by taxpayers, instead of itemizing deductions. The amount of deduction depends upon one's filing status, whether one is 65 or older or blind, and whether one can be claimed as a dependent on somebody else's return.

Taxable Income

The amount of income on which your federal income tax is figured. This is your adjusted gross income, minus your itemized deductions and personal exemptions.

Tax Credit

A credit reduces your taxes dollar-for-dollar, which makes it more valuable than a deduction, which reduces only your taxable income. The most common credits include the child care credit available to working parents, the earned income credit available to certain low-income tax-payers, and the foreign tax credit, which offsets income taxes paid to a foreign government.

Tax-Preference Item

These are certain deductions, such as accelerated depreciation on real property that may subject you to a special tax. Tax-preference items are generally a consideration only for the very rich who invest in tax shelters.

Tax Shelter

An investment designed to generate maximum writeoffs in the early years of the investment so that wealthy investors can offset their taxable income from other sources. Traditionally, shelters produced large deductions through depreciation and interest expense. But, Congress has virtually eliminated the tax benefits that once were associated with shelters such as apartment buildings, shopping centers, oil and gas drilling programs, research and development projects and business equipment leasing programs.

Housing

by Mike Sheridan

For decades, the demand for homes, the building of those homes, the financing and selling of them as well as the renovation, redecoration and redevelopment of residential housing have been important signs of the nation's prosperity. Economists are fond of saying that housing numbers are the first clues to the start of a recession and the signs of the end of one. Since consumers fuel the housing machine, how they feel about the economy will affect housing. If they feel the economy is going well, they buy a house. If they are apprehensive about the future or worried about the direction of the economy, they hold back and housing starts sputter and housing sales slacken. So, housing becomes an indirect measure of consumer attitudes and a direct measure of their spending and borrowing capabilities.

Looking at the Gross National Product, residential investment represents a mere 5 percent piece of the pie—some $200 billion a year of gross private domestic investment. But that's only part of the story, since home construction provides jobs, wages and tax revenues. And other industries, such as utilities and transportation, depend on housing for their economic health.

According to the National Association of Home Builders, the construction of 1,000 single-family homes typically generates 1,800 worker-years of employment in construction and construction-related industries, $39.3 million in wages, $16.1 million in combined federal state and local tax revenues, $1.6 million in local property taxes during the first year and $19 million in local property taxes over 20 years (assuming a 5 percent annual increase in property values), all of which is distributed throughout the system.

THE HOUSING STORY

Real estate journalism has come of age. Like reporting on science and medicine, reporting on housing requires not only certain skills but also a basic knowledge of the economics of the field. It involves scrutinizing a number of bellwether economic indicators such as single-family housing starts (if builders aren't beginning construction on houses, does that mean people can't afford to buy them?), sales of previously occupied dwellings (home resales, and their activity, can quickly pinpoint the vitality of a community) construction of multifamily units (a shortage of apartments will force people to seek shelter elsewhere, usually single-family homes), and so forth. Today, real estate is discussed as casually as a Little League baseball game. Rare is the conversation that doesn't contain some reference to housing: buying a home, selling one, or contemplating doing one or the other. From time to time, housing becomes a hot topic. When housing booms, the print and electronic media devote extra resources; some even form housing task forces to report consumer and industry issues.

In the most basic sense, housing can be reported by watching a handful of key indicators. One—probably the most important—is interest rates. Rates skyrocket. They inch downward. They spurt up again. They decline dramatically. Like a frenzied robot short circuited after being hit by lightning, interest rates jump all around. Such activity concerns the consumer, who seeks the answers to a number of questions. Should I buy a house now? Wait for a better time? Will rates move up or down now? Within three months? Six months? The answers can be contradictory, because mortgage rates are indirectly tied to three measures of money: to the discount rate, to the federal funds rate and the legendary prime rate, and to long bond rates, like the 30–year Treasury Bond. Yet these rates determine whether more, or fewer, Americans will be able to fulfill the American Dream.

It wasn't always so. Years ago, the local financial institution—oftentimes a savings and loan, which back then was called a building and loan—provided mortgage money. Members of the association pooled assets and then took turns using the funds to buy a home. Loans were small and usually paid back within five years or so, enabling the next individual in line to take his or her turn. Rates charged for home loans used to be set, for the most part, by the community lenders. If the local financial institution paid its small depositors 2 percent interest, it would often charge 3 1/2 or 4 percent to a customer taking out a mortgage. The bank would earn a profit, the saver would accumulate interest, and the homeowner would obtain a house. Savings continue to be the cornerstone of mortgage lending, whether from passbook accounts or profits from major corporations. But what has changed over the years is the provincialism. Most areas of the country aren't self-sufficient any more in the mortgage lending department; they now seek funds from noncommunity sources such as out-of-state lenders, large financial institutions on both coasts and the international marketplace. Competition for mortgage money thus has increased, and oftentimes that hasn't boded well for the American Dream. Supply and demand takes over, and the sector willing to pay the highest rate usually obtains the needed funds.

WHO OR WHAT DETERMINES MORTGAGE RATES?

Actually, no single element controls the marketplace. It is controlled instead by a combination of factors—the Discount Rate, the Federal Funds Rate, and the Prime Rate. The Discount Rate is the amount of interest charged by the Federal Reserve to member banks who borrow funds on a short term basis. The Federal Funds Rate is the cost of overnight borrowing between member banks—a sort of check overdraft protection. The Prime Rate is the rate which many financial institutions charge their best customers. Mortgage rates are affected by the terrible trio because, in simple terms, if the interest rates charged banks or companies increases, mortgage rates will usually follow suit. Thus an increase in these three rates can affect Americans seeking to buy a home as well as those who already own their own.

One of the most consistent indicators of mortgage rates is the yield of long term bonds, like Treasuries, or Ginnie Maes (issued through the Government National Mortgage Association, Ginnie Maes are actually secured by home mortgages). If rates rise, chances are that home sales will slow, because fewer people can qualify for a loan or make those monthly payments. Rising rates can choke off home buying—unless would-be buyers become creative, thereby adding another component to the mortgage market.

For decades, fulfilling the American Dream was virtually identical for everyone. A couple bought a house by agreeing to a 30–year mortgage. They paid the same monthly payment for the loan the first month as on the 360th. Simple. Easy. Unexciting. But then came the 1980s when the Federal Reserve, seeking to stem inflation, tightened the money supply (see "The Federal Reserve"). The Fed move made borrowing money more expensive, thereby pricing more Americans out of the housing market. But the dream of home ownership doesn't fade easily. Americans still wanted to own their own home, but either they couldn't afford the higher mortgage payment (each half percentage point increase in the mortgage rates on a $100,000 loan typically translates into an extra $45 payment per month) or they didn't earn enough money to qualify for the loan (as rates rise, so does the income needed to apply for that mortgage). Shut out of the shelter market, people—and lenders—began to ponder the situation. Why was the mortgage pegged at 30 years? Why couldn't it be 15 years in length—or even 20? Why should monthly mortgage payments be the same? Why couldn't they fluctuate, particularly since a home buyer would undoubtedly be earning more in the future and thus could afford higher payments then? And what about making a mortgage available to the millions who weren't currently earning as much as they needed to qualify for a loan—but would soon?

The answer was innovative mortgage financing. Before long, the home loan market had new mortgage products and these instruments spurred housing demand. The most popular form of this financing was the Adjustable Rate Mortgage (ARM), where payments fluctuated as interest rates increased or declined. ARMs were among the first in an alphabet soup of home loans that enabled millions to buy a house. Alternative mortgage, continually evolving, enabled Americans to buy that house. The means to buying a home had changed, but not the result.

THE SECONDARY MORTGAGE MARKET

Consumers like the lower interest rates of adjustable mortgages, of course, and as ARMs succeeded, they also appealed to private and government investors. Over the past half-century, these investors have created a market for mortgages, whether made in Portland, Maine or Portland, Oregon, enabling financial institutions to replenish their supply of mortgage money and make more loans. Real estate loans typically have been traded, but the problem has been that oftentimes what was popular in Philadelphia wasn't flying in Phoenix. Enter a pair of mortgage market players with the unlikely names of Fannie Mae and Freddie Mac. Together, these two financial giants now control what's called the secondary mortgage market, which handles several hundred billion dollars of mortgage loans each year.

Formally known as the Federal National Mortgage Association, Fannie Mae is a federally chartered, New York Stock Exchange-listed corporation that is owned by some 30,000 stockholders. The third largest corporation in America—it has more than $100 billion in assets—Fannie Mae purchases mortgages for its own portfolio as well as issues and guarantees mortgage-backed securities. The Federal Home Loan Mortgage Corporation, affectionately known as Freddie Mac, is a Congressionally chartered corporation that purchases loans from lenders and then sells securities backed by those mortgages to investors. Freddie

Mac and Fannie Mae free up not only mortgage money, enabling more Americans to obtain a home loan, but also billions of dollars for use in the economy.

More importantly, Fannie Mae and Freddie Mac have standardized the mortgage writing business; each mortgage issued that wants to enter the secondary marketplace must conform to Fannie's and Freddie's underwriting criteria, thereby enabling an investor in Oregon to purchase a mortgage issued in Oklahoma. Freddie Mac and Fannie Mae purchase adjustable rate mortgages and package them to investors, but they're not miracle workers. The yields on mortgages must be sufficient to entice investors. If the rates are too low, mortgages won't be sold and the supply of mortgage money won't be replaced. And if the bond market is producing better yields, investors will flock there. If that happens, mortgage rates will shoot up to attract investors back—and that isn't beneficial for house-hungry Americans (see "The bond market," herein).

Housing issues in the future will no doubt hinge heavily on interest rates. As the global markets become more sophisticated, and investors seek higher and better yields, housing will be affected. No longer is mortgage lending confined to the community. It's international in scope and mortgage rates are being influenced by yet another indicator since some new mortgages are being tied to LIBOR (London Interbank Offered Rate), which is the interest rate most credit-worthy international banks charge each other for large, short-term loans made using U.S. dollars.

What will remain the same, however, is the American Dream. Despite mortgage rate uncertainty, despite the high cost of homes in some areas of the country, despite the lack of available land to build in other sectors, Americans still want to fulfill the American Dream. It's a legacy that has been passed down from generation to generation. The end has not changed, only the means.

Writing about Insurance

by Trudy Lieberman

You're asked to write a story about a rate increase for the local Blue Cross and Blue Shield plan, and you don't know beans about insurance. "How boring," you grumble to yourself. Insurance is one's idea of reportorial glamour, but this seemingly "boring" subject can yield gems for the reporter willing to learn the ins and outs of the subject. After food and shelter, insurance is the next largest expenditure in the family budget. Helping families use their insurance dollars more effectively can be as important as explaining the effects of a leveraged buyout.

Because of the subject's reputation for complexity, your second reaction may be to grab the phone and get a few quotes from the so-called experts in the insurance business. Try a renegade from the industry who thinks he or she has something important to say or one of the self-styled consumer experts who may have an axe to grind that's not apparent to the beginning reporter. Many of these "experts" are only too willing to "educate" reporters in exchange for a quote or two in a newspaper or magazine article. It's never a good idea to rely on these people, even if you're on a tight deadline. What do you do?

When writing about insurance, there's no substitute for homework. What follows is an insurance primer.

THE SUBJECT

Insurance is divided into life and health policies and property/casualty policies. In the first category, you'll most likely be called upon to write about life insurance policies that have some sort of investment component, or you may be asked to discuss the reasons behind rate increases for Blue Cross and Blue Shield, usually a complicated and politically-charged issue. In the second category, you'll probably write about auto insurance policies and the reasons for their ever-increasing premiums. When State Farm announces a 20 percent increase in liability rates, a well-informed reporter will know what that means.

Life Insurance Policies

For starters, you'll need to know how a life insurance policy is structured, how it's priced, how the different types work, and what bells and whistles companies string on to differentiate their offerings. Basically there are term policies and cash-value policies. Term policies provide only protection—a death benefit when the insured dies. Cash-value policies offer a death benefit as well as a kind of savings account, which a policyholder can tap during the life of the policy (at a cost, of course). The newfangled policies on the market today—variable life and universal life—are simply variations on the cash-value theme. Life insurance companies, like all financial intermediaries, take your money, invest it at a profit, and pay you for the use of it. Companies collect your premiums, deduct their expenses and the cost of providing the death benefit (the mortality charge), and invest the rest. Keep in mind that any new policy will work basically this way.

Health-Insurance Policies

Blue Cross and Blue Shield organizations as well as regular commercial companies sell hospital coverage and major medical policies. The latter usually cover 80 percent of the cost of doctor visits, lab work, X-rays, and so on. Policyholders almost always pay deductibles to help keep premiums lower; that is, they must pay the first $100, $200, or $300 of a bill before the insurance company picks up the remainder. Employers pay the premiums for health-insurance coverage for most workers in this country. But some 37 million Americans have no health insurance: their employers don't provide it, and they can't afford to pay for coverage themselves.

For those over 65, the federal Medicare program is the primary insurer. But most of those over 65 also buy other insurance to supplement Medicare. Some of the policies are useful; others are a waste of money. The most useful ones are Medicare-supplement policies that cover some of the gaps Medicare leaves and long-term-care policies that pay for nursing home stays. Neither Medicare nor Medicare-supplement policies pay for most long-term care in nursing homes. Nursing-home policies are a new breed of insurance. Many of the early policies were riddled with restrictions and limitations that rendered them virtually useless if someone tried to collect. The market for this product is still evolving, and future policies should improve somewhat. Dread-disease insurance and accident policies that pay a small amount per day if some serious illness or accident should befall a policyholder land in the category of wasteful insurance. Despite the blandishments of television celebrities, these policies are seldom good buys.

Property/Casualty Policies

Auto and homeowners insurance are the main types of property/casualty policies a reporter will confront.

An automobile policy is actually a package of different coverages. Liability coverage pays for damage a driver causes to other people or their property; collision coverage pays for damage drivers cause to their own cars; comprehensive coverage pays for damage caused by hail storms, and for theft losses; uninsured motorist and underinsured motorist coverage pay if someone is injured by a driver who has no insurance or very little; and medical payments coverage acts as a mini-health-insurance policy that pays medical expenses up to certain limits.

Some states have "no fault" laws which require drivers to buy personal-injury protection coverage that pays for medical bills and lost wages due to an auto accident. In these states, drivers can't sue the other party to recover damages unless certain conditions are met. No fault laws were supposed to help keep premiums from rising so fast and to make the automobile reparations system more equitable. (In a no fault state, more money should theoretically go into compensating injured victims than into the pockets of trial attorneys who have benefited handsomely from the tort liability system.) But with the exception of a few states, no fault has not accomplished its goals. The trial lawyers, who vigorously opposed no fault laws, persuaded state legislatures to water down no fault bills by keeping parts of the tort system in place. In some states, the result has been two very expensive systems.

Auto insurance coverages are generally the same from state to state, but rates aren't. Rates vary widely among states, and even within cities and towns in the same state.

A homeowner's policy also consists of several coverages. There's basic coverage for losses caused by such calamities as fire, windstorms, hail, explosions, and for losses due to vandalism and theft. And there's liability coverage that protects policyholders against lawsuits filed by those who are injured on their property. Policies also pick up some part of a homeowner's expenses if the family must live somewhere else while their property is repaired.

Companies offer seven types of homeowner's policies. Four policies are actually sold to people who own houses, and they vary in their comprehensiveness; one policy is for renters who live in apartments; another is for condominium owners; and one specialized policy is for those who own very old homes. When a catastrophe strikes, a policy pays the actual cash value—the replacement value minus a depreciation allowance—unless the policyholder has purchased replacement-cost coverage (for a higher premium). This coverage pays the actual cost of replacing a particular item.

WHERE TO LEARN ABOUT POLICIES

Insurance company actuaries who design the policies are excellent sources. At this point, don't worry about industry bias; you're simply trying to find out how a policy works. Actuaries who work for independent consulting firms are also good sources. Some of the major national consulting firms are Thillinghast/Towers Perrin, Milliman and Robertson, and The Wyatt Company. Sometimes the industry trade association. The American Council of Life Insurance, the Health Insurance Association of America, the American Insurance Association, the Alliance of American Insurers, and agent groups such as the National Association of Life Underwriters and the Independent Insurance Agents of America may be helpful. But a morning spent with an actuary at a company is likely to bear more fruit than a phone call to public relations officials at a trade association.

A word about academics. Many universities have insurance departments within their business schools, and sometimes you'll find a professor who talks to reporters. Such a person can be helpful in understanding the mechanics of a policy, but may not always be in touch with the real world aspects of this business. Use such sources carefully!

Some periodicals are useful. *The National Underwriter,* both life and health and property/casualty editions, provide a good view of the policies available as well as the marketing and political issues affecting the industry. *Best's Insurance Reports,* published by A.M. Best in Oldwick, New Jersey, is a thick volume found in most libraries. It details the corporate ownership of insurance companies, their financial condition, and assigns ratings to each company based on Best's perception of a company's financial strength. An A+ is the highest rating; a C is the lowest. Some companies are "not assigned," either because they are too small, have too little experience, are in receivership, or have provided incomplete financial information. While Best's rating is a useful guide to a company's financial condition, it's not perfect. Insurance companies have plunged into insolvency while carrying an A or A+ rating from A.M. Best.

Standard & Poor's also rates insurance companies if companies pay for the rating. S&P evaluates a company's ability to meet its contractual obligations and also tries to evaluate its future performance. S&P ratings range from AAA to D.

THE SALES PITCH

There's a saying in the life insurance business that policies are sold, not bought. The same is true for other lines of insurance. But the way insurance is sold leaves much to be desired. For some types of insurance, sales tactics are shoddy, deceptive, misleading, and even border on outright fraud.

Most policies are sold by "independent" agents who sell for many companies or by "captive" agents who sell for only one. Agents receive commissions—a fixed percentage of the first-year premium and a fixed percentage of renewal premiums. For a life policy, that commission can run as high as 100 percent of the first-year premium.

Other policies are sold through the mail; prospective buyers respond to an advertisement on television or in a newspaper or magazine, and the insurance company sends materials to examine. As a general rule, policies sold through the mail cost less because companies don't need to pay commissions. Some companies, particularly those selling life policies, have experimented with new ways to sell their products, thus bypassing the agency system. These experiments have not been entirely successful.

The mix of high commissions and a complicated product often result in sales presentations waiting to be exposed. The best way to see how policies are sold is to sit through the pitches yourself. Find a person who is a suitable prospect for the kind of insurance you're writing about—you wouldn't want a 25–year-old to listen to a pitch for Medicare-supplement insurance, for example. Pose as a family friend or relative, and ask some agents to give a presentation. You can do this for almost any kind of insurance, but the most outrageous sales pitches are made by those selling life and health policies.

Before you hear any pitches, however, you must be thoroughly conversant with the subject. If you're not, it will be hard to spot the misstatements and deceptions agents undertake.

THE REGULATION

Insurance is regulated by 50 state insurance commissioners who head departments of insurance that are part of the executive branch of state government. The commissioners are usually appointed by the governor, but some are elected. Many departments are very small and lack adequate staff to monitor policies, let alone the sales practices and advertising. For example, many have no actuary on staff to examine policies that companies submit for review. Some states don't even approve the policies that companies offer for sale.

With few exceptions, most departments are not forceful regulators, and the industry pretty much gets its way. Only recently have some departments paid attention to the concerns of policyholders. Some departments publish buying guides for various types of policies. The guides are a legacy of the consumer activism of the late 1960s and early 1970s. While helpful to some extent, these guides usually don't give advice about specific policies. Some of the guides for auto insurance are more useful, detailing premiums for specific policies and companies. Usually though, state insurance departments aren't in the business of telling consumers which policies to buy.

Each insurance commissioner belongs to an association called the National Association of Insurance Commissioners (NAIC) which proposes model laws and regulations for states to adopt. Before the NAIC adopts a model, it listens to its advisory committees which are largely composed of insurance company representatives. (Occasionally, though, a consumer representative or two turns up on one of the committees.) The model laws and regulations the NAIC finally proposes and the states subsequently adopt have the industry's imprimatur.

The federal government stays out of the insurance business. The McCarran-Ferguson Act passed in 1945 exempts insurance companies from federal antitrust laws if the companies are regulated by the states. Courts have broadly interpreted this exemption, giving insurance companies a great deal of freedom. Certain practices in the insurance industry wouldn't be tolerated in other industries.

HOW TO USE THE REGULATORS

Cultivate sources at your state's department of insurance. Staffers can tell you about policies and problems with companies. Departments usually maintain a policyholders' service section which handles complaints from the public. Even though some departments keep poor records, (for example, all complaints about health and accident policies may be lumped together), the policyholders' service section may be a good source of story ideas. It can also provide backup for a problem you've already uncovered.

Many states require insurance companies to file their policies with insurance regulators. This doesn't mean that the regulators approve the policies before they're offered to the public. They may or may not do that. Some departments also require companies to file their rates as well as their policy forms. Once a rate is approved it becomes public information. Auto insurance rates filed with the states can be useful if you're doing a story on the premiums companies are charging.

YOUR EVALUATION

Once you have mastered the subject of insurance, don't be afraid to make judgments for the consumer. Buyers of insurance policies need all the help they can get. The product is arcane, complex, and the salespeople can't be trusted to impart information free of bias and propaganda. If your research leads to the conclusion that term insurance is best for most families or that the premiums charged by a particular auto insurance carrier are way out of line, don't hesitate to say so. If your publication won't allow you to make your own judgments about insurance products, and you must rely on the judgments (and quotations) of others, be careful. Even a seemingly unbiased financial planner may be pushing a particular product. (Some planners also earn commissions from selling insurance policies.) If you're quoting someone about an insurance product, try to identify his or her biases, or at least try to put the quote into perspective. For instance, if someone from a life insurance company says people should buy cash-value policies, note that such policies are the life blood of the company.

The more judgments you can make, the better the public will be served.

Trade

by Linda Corman

Trade, one of the nation's many economic indicators, is a political and business story no financial journalist can ignore. Trade, once just six percent of the nation's Gross National Product, now accounts for more than a quarter of GNP. And its influence on the vitality of the American economy and American lifestyles continues to grow.

As a result, trade isn't simply a story about what countries bought and sold to other countries. It's a story about domestic and international issues involving Congressional debate, labor demands, social concerns, international negotiations and intellectual and philosophical debate.

The trade story was not always a major business beat. For decades little attention was paid to the monthly numbers. Then in 1985 the United States acknowledged that it had become a net debtor nation. Attention quickly focused on the U.S. relationship with other nations. For many Americans, it came as a surprise that somehow the U.S. had changed from a country which in 1980 was owed $106 billion by the rest of the world to a country which owed other nations $263.6 billion. What happened?

Let's look at how the recent U.S. trade imbalance developed. As far back as the 1960s and for two decades thereafter, the nation was reporting a deficit in merchandise trade. The merchandise trade is the value of domestically produced goods exported compared to foreign-produced goods imported. Usually a country prefers a "favorable trade balance," a situation in which exports exceed imports. But the continuing merchandise trade deficit caused no alarm because the "current account" was in the black until 1982. The reason the current account (the value of all goods and services imported or exported) remained positive was that profits from U.S. investments overseas were offsetting the merchandise trade imbalance. The current account includes payment and receipt of dividends and interest.

The U.S. might have been able to avoid the trade problem had other factors not come into play. But oil prices rose in the 1970s, raising the country's energy expenses. An increase in the value of the dollar beginning in 1979 made U.S. exports more expensive. And an increasing budget deficit during the Reagan administration encouraged more borrowing, which further boosted the nation's debts to foreign investors. The economic result for the early 1980s was higher interest rates, which further pushed up the value of the dollar, making U.S. goods even more expensive, and less competitive.

All of these factors turned what were underlying weaknesses in the U.S. economy—including what appeared to be complacency in many industries—and growing manufacturing and technological competition from overseas, into a crisis by the late 1980s. As Americans bought more of their goods from overseas, foreigners accumulated more dollars which they used to buy American assets.

So, the first important fact about trade data is that it's not independent of other economic factors. A second important fact is that trade figures are more than a measure of goods and services. They also reflect the value of the dollar, the nation's ability to compete.

At the center of any trade debate is the question of economic control. This tends to be a political question. How should a country take steps to correct its trade imbalances? Can a country control its destiny if it depends heavily on the finances and production of other countries?

There are experts who can argue every nuance of trade. But be careful. Many experts are connected with the government and therefore have a biased view. Others oppose the government's approach. Still others have their own theories about trade and the economy. Unfortunately, most journalists find that quoting experts results in a story that says little and provides conflicting information. For example, some trade experts will argue that if foreigners invest in U.S. manufacturing for export, Americans will lose control over jobs and homegrown profits. Others will argue that as long as foreigners are willing to invest, it shows their confidence in the U.S., and that they often create jobs and provide wealth Americans can't produce for themselves.

MAKE THE STORY MANAGEABLE

It's easy for journalists to get caught up in the trade argument. So to make the issues understandable, it helps to break the story down into digestible parts. Here are some aspects of the trade story that may help you explain why trade is important to the economy.

Productivity

Let's say the trade deficit is widening this month. If that's the case, it may mean that the U.S. isn't using its resources—human, capital, financial, etc. as effectively as possible. Productivity is the output of an average worker over a period of time, usually a year. So, productivity is a key to improving the trade picture. Try to find out how productive local industries are. What is being done to improve productivity?

Labor

Again, if there is a trade deficit, the U.S. is probably losing jobs, because production from overseas is meeting the demand here. Labor leaders refer to this as "jobs are being lost overseas." Why is this happening? Are there jobs that could be and should be brought back on shore? How could this be done? Then again, are there some advantages to letting others make at least some of what the U.S. wants?

Foreign Policy

If the U.S. is dependent on foreign countries to invest here, does that constrain its foreign policy? If the local jet radar manufacturer, which employs 10 percent of the local population, has a lucrative business with a South American country's air force, would the local congressional delegation vote to impose sanctions when political tensions develop between that country and the U.S.?

Dollar Relationship

As the dollar rises and falls against other currencies, local companies involved in trade must weigh the costs of foreign sales and manufacturing operations. If the dollar plummets, even though the cost of labor in the Philippines remains at rock bottom, perhaps the cost of shipping electronic parts there and back becomes prohibitive and it makes sense to bring operations back on shore.

Foreign Investment

How is increasing foreign investment changing the local landscape—in real estate, in labor relationships, in job opportunities? What happens when foreign companies set up plants in the U.S.? Do they adapt to American ways or do they introduce their own? How does it work? Are Americans closed out of top management? What happens with unions?

Trade Deficit

As local manufacturers find themselves becoming less competitive, they may tend to push for protection. Who are they pressuring? How much clout do they have? How many jobs are at stake? Could workers be retrained? What do local congressional representatives have at stake? What are they willing to trade off? Are these the wisest trade offs?

Competition

As the U.S. attempts to keep up with other countries, are some of its principles, values, the national character jeopardized? What about anti-trust law? Labor protections? Is the U.S. in danger of becoming a nation of single-minded workaholics, bent only on out-producing the rest of the world?

GETTING THE STORY

The trade story is based on numbers obtained from the U.S. Department of Commerce, which releases statistics once a month on the deficit and on total U.S. imports and exports. These figures reveal what has occurred a month and a half earlier. But, it's important to note that they're widely viewed with skepticism, since the data isn't adjusted for inflation. They also have not been adjusted for seasonal influences or the number of working days in a given month.

In writing a story on the merchandise trade figures for a given month, one logical approach is to lead with the key trend which has influenced the figures for that month. For example, a surge in oil imports might explain a widening of the gap.

Besides the gross figures, also report how they compare with previous months and years and to previous highs and lows. If the trend in the current year continues, what would it mean for the year? Give the figures for exports and imports and note whether an increase or decrease in the deficit is due to unusual activity, up or down, in either category.

To back up your lead graph, note whether the reason given for the change in the month to month figures is part of a pattern, an anomaly, or whether it signals a trend. If the reason is higher oil imports, is the U.S. becoming increasingly dependent on foreign oil? Is this trend likely to sabotage efforts to correct the trade deficit? Besides government officials (the U.S. Trade Representative, the Commerce Department, the White House), talk with economists and industry representatives. Don't make the mistake of focusing only on one factor in the figures. Note the two or three other factors that brought about a change in the figures and say whether there seems to be a trend developing.

Also note bilateral trade deficits with particular countries. Did the deficit with Japan grow while that with Western Europe shrank? Again, what were the products involved? Is this a trend that is likely to continue? Does it bode ill or well for the overall deficit?

Besides reporting the trade figures, mention what happened with the value of the dollar in relation to other currencies in the aftermath of the trade announcement and how the stock market reacted. The dollar is prone to increase in value with a shrinking of the deficit, decrease with a widening. But this result is often shortlived.

The stock market too reacts to the trade figures. Primarily, the reaction is based on expectations. Before the trade figures are announced, the stock market will take into account what is expected. If the announced numbers come in higher or lower than expected, the market will react and adjust to the news.

It's important to note what the numbers may mean for the economy overall. Does a narrowing reveal a slowdown in consumer activity corresponding with a slowdown suggested by other economic numbers? Does a widening of the gap indicate high levels of spending, a squeeze on output and additional inflationary pressures?

After getting government reaction and assessment of the figures, get some economists to comment. Don't forget the think tanks (e.g., Brookings and the Institute for International Economics, DRI/McGraw-Hill) and the international economists at major banks.

AVOIDING CONFUSION

Beware of revised figures. When a set of new monthly figures comes out, the Commerce Department issues revised figures for the previous month as well. These figures are based on the accumulation of additional data. When you make comparisons, say what numbers you're using, such as "revised October" figures and say which way they were revised. If it's a large revision, you must say why.

A few days before the merchandise trade balance is released, the balance of payments or current account figures for two and a half months previous is released. This number, the most comprehensive measure of trade, is often at odds with the merchandise trade figures, but it's the most telling number on the status of U.S. trade. Since the merchandise trade component of this figure will have been reported a month earlier, concentrate on trends in service and investment. But re-report the highlights of the merchandise trade figures in the context of the additional current accounts information. For example, the euphoria expressed by the President over a $20 billion narrowing of the trade gap might be qualified by a $50 billion widening of the current account for the same period.

PROTECTIONISM

A major topic in the trade discussion is protectionism. The debate usually arises over whether the U.S. should become more protectionist to reduce its trade deficit. Generally protectionism means quotas, which limit the amount of goods that one country can import into another, or tariffs, which add to the price of goods imported so that they aren't cheaper than domestically produced goods. These are more subtle forms of protectionism usually referred to as nontariff barriers.

Generally speaking, protectionism isn't good for an economy because it pits countries against each other and causes higher prices, inefficient use of world resources, contraction of trade and sometimes recession. But economists also argue that protectionism may be absolutely necessary to help a struggling industry. The problem is, who has a genuine need and when do the interests of the world trade community take precedence over those of individual industries?

In the U.S., Republicans in recent years have opposed protectionism. They claim they believe in the free market system. Democrats are more inclined to say that theoretically protectionism is bad, but some is needed. Unions are among the chief advocates of protectionism. Some classic cases of industries that have sought, and gained, protection are steel, textiles, computer chips and agriculture.

The next big story may be trading blocs. Countries in trading blocs allow relatively free trade among countries within the bloc while maintaining long-recognized barriers against goods from countries outside the bloc. There are three potentially strong trading blocs; North America, Europe and the Pacific Rim. The notion of a North American trading bloc was fed by the 1989 U.S./Canada Free Trade Agreement. Predictions of a European bloc are based on the Common Market's plans for a so-called Single Market. The Pacific Rim bloc arises from the ascendancy of Japan and the economic relations it's building with other Pacific Rim countries.

THE EEC'S SINGLE MARKET

The European Economic Community has 286 directives to eliminate remaining trade barriers between its 12 member countries. Most of those barriers are so-called nontariff barriers, since tariff barriers were theoretically eliminated with the forming of the EEC in 1957. But obstacles such as differing product standards, different licensing requirements for professionals and rules against multinational banks, insurance companies and other services, have continued to restrict trade between the Common Market countries. After numerous false starts, in 1985 the European Commission drafted a plan to revitalize the European economy, to combat the infamous "Eurosclerosis," and take advantage of economies of scale. That plan—a White Paper—laid out how to make the community a large, unified Single Market.

For Americans, the most important issue is, naturally, what does it mean for the U.S.? This question has boiled down to, will the Single Market become Fortress Europe—i.e., will the EEC, while removing internal barriers, erect barriers to keep out non-EEC goods and services? And, what will be the role of a unified Germany in this partnership? Will Eastern Europe be welcomed or rejected?

Many argue that Europe is too dependent on the rest of the world for trade to isolate itself from the rest of the world. Those who predict a fortress, however, say it's a long EEC tradition to protect its members— exemplified by its Common Agricultural Policy which provides enormous farm subsidies to protect European farmers.

There are stories for journalists in how American companies are preparing. Companies seem to have taken one of three options: sit tight and continue to export from the U.S. and hope for the best; set up factories in the EEC so that goods produced there would be accepted as EEC products; or, set up a joint venture or licensing arrangement so goods could gain the status of EEC products, through marriage with EEC companies.

Logical stories include what's happening with the directives concerning specific industries? Are the standards or the local content requirements being set, effectively exclusionary?

Another approach to attempting to predict the likely tenor of directives is to report on the state of specific industries on the continent. Are these industries well developed, fledgling, ignored? Are they a priority of governments to nurture? That could give clues as to how welcome U.S. companies in those industries will be.

Good sources of information are the European Commission in Washington, D.C. and Brussels, the U.S. Trade Representative, the U.S. Department of Commerce and the U.S. Chamber of Commerce.

U.S./CANADA FREE TRADE AGREEMENT

Just as the EEC strenuously denies that it's forming a trading bloc, the U.S. and Canada don't consider their Free Trade Agreement (FTA) the pact for a bloc. The agreement eliminates tariffs between the U.S. and Canada by 1999. It met considerable opposition in Canada among the Liberal Party especially, and the conservative government of Brian Mulroney was nearly voted out of office over the issue in the 1980s. Canadians opposing the agreement were concerned that the country would be ceding autonomy to the U.S. and would lose its more comprehensive social service system, including national health care, because it couldn't compete with the sparer U.S. economy. Canadians also feared their industries would flee to the U.S. to take advantage of lower costs.

Although debate about the FTA quickly subsided, retrospectives in the next few years on whether Canada's fears were realized, or just what have been the consequences, would make good stories.

It may also be interesting to see whether the "bloc" expands to include Mexico, other Central American countries or the Caribbean.

THE GENERAL AGREEMENT ON TARIFFS AND TRADE

The major international organization which concerns itself with trade —particularly protectionism—is the General Agreement on Tariffs and Trade (GATT). Chastened by the rampant protectionism of the 1920s and 1930s, which helped send the world into a major recession, 23 nations created the organization in 1948.

The organization, now with 96 signatories, is based in Geneva. When a round of negotiations is not being held to negotiate new rules for trade, it operates as a deliberative body on various trade issues and tries to resolve trade disputes between signatories.

Since the GATT was organized, negotiations over trade regulations have been conducted in a series of rounds, many of them lasting for several years. The rounds have sometimes been named for the site of the meetings. In 1986, the eighth round, was dubbed the Uruguay Round after Punta del Este, Uruguay. In recent years, the agenda has shifted to the discussion of nontariff barriers. A major issue at the Uruguay round was whether intellectual property rights would be protected through the GATT. Such rights are administered by the World Intellectual Property Organization (WIPO), a United Nations body based in Geneva. The U.S. and other developed countries are on the side of greater protection and GATT jurisdiction over intellectual rights. Third World countries were inclined to argue that WIPO is all that's needed. Another major issue in the Uruguay Round is whether trade in services would be regulated by the GATT. Only merchandise trade had been regulated by the agreement.

Like many trade issues, the sides are often drawn along economic power lines. And the intellectual property rights and trade debate pitted less developed countries (LDCs) against industrialized countries. The most developed countries, hoping to maximize profits from their technological developments, wanted to insure the best protections possible to guarantee that their technology was not stolen. Less developed countries were eager to get new technology as cheaply as possible. Some, too, like India, argued that there shouldn't be protections for certain types of intellectual property, like pharmaceuticals, because products on which people's lives depend should not be limited for profit.

In services, the trade argument was reversed. Developed countries generally sought unrestricted access to offer services in any country. Less developed countries were inclined to want to keep them out or circumscribe their operations in order to give their own service industries an opportunity to capture some market share. Also they wanted free movement of labor to be part of a liberalization in service trade agreement.

Farm subsidies is a trade issue that may be debated for decades. The U.S., which once supported the elimination of subsidies by the year 2000, has gradually moderated its position in favor of seeking reductions. The U.S. and the EEC were the major opponents in this farm battle. The EEC has refused to eliminate subsidies, contending that doing so would undermine the Common Market, which devotes enormous proportions of its budget to farm subsidies.

While GATT has provided an international forum for trade discussions, its usefulness is in question. Some argue that the organization is steadily losing its stature. Some countries, impatient with the glacial pace of GATT remedies, prefer to make bilateral arrangements. Others argue that modern-day trade problems tend to be specific and lend themselves more to bilateralism than multilateralism. Wary observers of the evolution of the EEC's Single Market predict that in order to erect barriers to non-EEC players, the EEC will have to defy some GATT rules, further undermining an already shaky organization.

Conversely, there are those who say GATT will increase in importance and influence. They cite increased use of GATT's dispute resolution mechanism and signatories' interest in putting more muscle in the mechanism as causes for optimism.

Remarkably, there are very few people who know much about what is going on in the GATT. The best place to start is the U.S. Trade Representative's office in Washington and the GATT Secretariat in Geneva.

THIRD WORLD DEBT

The Third World Debt crisis, although far from strictly a trade issue, has important implications for trade.

The debt crisis erupted in 1981 when Mexico declared it could not meet its debt payments. Its debt, and those of numerous other Third

World countries, began to assume unmanageable proportions with the rise in interest rates and the world recession that meant a decline in their export earnings at the end of the 1970s and early 1980s. These countries had taken on sizeable debts in the 1970s, when interest rates were low. They were eager to sustain growth despite the constraints high oil prices had placed on them, and Western banks were eager to lend oil dollars.

Mexico's default was followed by that of many other countries. Under a plan proposed during the Reagan administration, some countries received new loans on the condition that they undertook severe austerity measures and restructured their economies. In most instances, the plan was a failure, in part because banks weren't willing to lend more money. The Bush administration followed with the Brady Plan, which called for banks to forgive part of their loans in exchange for guarantees on the balance from the World Bank and the International Monetary Fund.

One of the major implications of the Third World Debt crisis for trade is that Latin America—the hardest hit by the crisis—has traditionally been an extremely important market for the U.S., accounting for some $30 billion annually before the debt crisis. With the continent floundering in debt, the U.S. lost an enormous market, which contributed significantly to its trade deficit. So, in addition to the need to assist U.S. banks and boost Latin American economies, the U.S. had a compelling interest in finding a solution to the problem.

Because South America is a neighbor and remains a source of inexpensive labor and raw materials, this region provides interesting trade and development stories. It's a region where the U.S. has repeatedly sought schemes to encourage economic growth. The Caribbean Basin Initiative (CBI) was one such U.S. effort to foster economic development. That initiative, which took effect in 1984, provided preferential treatment for exports from 22 Caribbean Basin countries and territories and incentives for U.S. business to invest there.

TECHNOLOGY TRANSFER

Another major issue in international trade is technology transfer. It's a rich subject. The issue, which emerged with the Cold War, boils down to types of technology the West should make available to the Soviet Union and other communist countries.

There are many schools of thought. Traditionally the hawks say the U.S. shouldn't sell anything more complicated than a clothespin to the Soviet Union because anything the U.S. sells will help the Soviet's economic development. They argue that any easing of the Soviet's economic development difficulties releases resources for a military buildup. Since Mikhail S. Gorbachev's perestroika initiatives, the hawks have represented a minority point of view. An anticipated Peace Dividend, resulting from a reduction of weapons by the U.S. and the Soviet Union, is expected to shift opinion toward a more liberal trade policy for the Soviets. Still, it is likely that high technology, which could be applied to military use, will be restricted.

There are numerous definitions of what should be classified as high technology. Some would say personal computers are high technology. Others say it's ridiculous to restrict sales of technology that communist countries could get from any number of other sources, if not from the U.S.

The issue is more complicated, and fascinating, because it's not simply one between the U.S. and communist countries. It has often been described as more of a West/West issue than an East/West issue. That is, disputes between Western countries over what should be restricted and what should not be, has become more of a problem than disputes between East and West over what to restrict.

The West/West dispute has arisen because the U.S. realized that unless it persuaded the other producers of technology not to sell to communist countries, its efforts to contain those countries or simply keep weapons out of their hands, were futile. The U.S. also realized that unless the Western countries agreed on what not to sell to communist countries, anything it sold to its allies could easily find its way to those countries.

To try to forge agreements, the NATO members (minus Iceland) and Japan, formed the Coordinating Committee for Multilateral Export Controls (commonly referred to as CoCom), based in Paris, in 1949.

CoCom draws up lists of controlled goods under various degrees of restrictions. But, the parties to it are constantly squabbling over what should and should not be on the list and accusing each other of violating the agreements. The U.S. is usually most adamant about controlling technology and has expended a lot of political capital with its allies, chastising them over selling technology to communist countries. There are numerous classic battles. One was the gas pipeline fiasco of the late 1970s and early 1980s. When the Soviet Union was planning to construct massive gas pipelines to supply Western Europe, many Western European countries offered not only to buy the gas but also to supply the equipment needed to build the lines. The U.S. tried to discourage Western Europe from signing up for the gas. Then, with the imposition of martial law in Poland, the U.S. government imposed sanctions on the Soviet Union which barred the export of much of the equipment that would be needed for the pipeline. Not only did the U.S. lose business to European competitors, but it alienated Europeans when it imposed sanctions on European companies to which U.S. technology was licensed, that was then sold to the Soviet Union.

Western Europeans were not only angry over the interference, but also charged that the U.S. was being hypocritical, since it continued to sell huge amounts of subsidized wheat to the Soviets. Perestroika added a new element to the equation in the late 1980s.

In technology transfer stories, issues of economics, security and politics coincide. And, in the U.S., numerous government agencies will play a role. Permission for export of specific technology may require approval from the Department of Commerce and sometimes State, Defense, Treasury. The issue also can create some surprising allies.

TRADE TERMS

National Accounts: The Balance of Payments is a record of a country's international transactions that generate flows of funds. The BOP is divided into the current account, comprised of exports, imports, service receipts, investment income, and other current items, and the Capital Account, which records direct investment in companies and real estate, and portfolio investment in securities. The trade balance, a subcategory of the current account, shows the difference between merchandise exports and imports. Because the BOP must balance, the imbalance in the current account will be accompanied by an offsetting imbalance in the capital account. Thus, the much-publicized flows of Japanese investment funds into the U.S. are a predictable accompaniment to a huge trade deficit with Japan.

Trade Law: American companies can appeal to the Commerce Department or the International Trade Commission for protection, if they think they are the victims of unfair trade practices. Such practices include dumping, which is the sale of products at below cost; subsidies of exports by foreign governments; and discriminatory import rules against U.S. exports. Even if no unfair practices are involved, companies may be granted protection if they can demonstrate that their business is threatened by a sudden surge of imports.

Trade Barriers: Tariffs, which are direct levies on imports, are declining in significance. The use of nontariff barriers is increasing. Nontariff barriers include import quotas, regulations and bureaucratic procedures that inhibit imports, and Voluntary Export Restraints, such as the agreement that sets limits on Japanese car sales to the U.S. Studies have shown that in purely economic terms the costs of such measures outweigh the benefits. Consumers wind up paying higher prices that are in aggregate greater than the value of the jobs preserved.

—Stanley Reed

Founding the Fellowship

by Stephen B. Shepard

The Walter Bagehot Fellowship, renamed the Knight-Bagehot Fellowship in Economics and Business Journalism in 1987, has endured for 15 years, training more than 100 journalists in economics and business—and vastly enriching our profession's coverage of those often-difficult subjects. I had the great privilege of starting the program in 1975 and serving as its director in that rewarding first year. Before its origins recede from memory, let me tell you how it all came about.

The person who thought up the program was Elie Abel, then dean of the Graduate School of Journalism at Columbia University. At the time, I was an editor at *Business Week* and an adjunct professor at the J-School. Together with my good friend Soma Golden of the *New York Times*, I was teaching a spring semester seminar on economics and business writing. In the early 1970s, the class was small, perhaps seven or eight students. Business reporting in those days just didn't have the glamour of politics, the trench-coat intrigue of foreign news, or the social relevance of urban affairs. But then in the mid-1970s, business and economics became front page news. There was the oil crisis, the near-bankruptcy of New York City, and the mysterious simultaneous appearances of both inflation and recession—a phenomenon so new

Stephen B. Shepherd is editor of *Business Week*

that we had to coin a word for it: Stagflation. Suddenly business news was hot. Our seminar grew—to 15 students one year, 22 the next.

When we realized what was happening, Elie Abel got a bright idea: Establish a program, similar to the Nieman program at Harvard, for working journalists who wanted to spend an academic year at Columbia. They would study economics and business, drawing on the resources of the entire university—from the business school and the economics department to the law school and the school of international affairs. The program would be rigorous: five courses per semester, at least two of them for credit. Yes, that meant final exams, a novel idea for a Nieman-type program. In addition, the program would be rooted in the Journalism School, with special seminars and dinners tailored to the needs of journalists. We were acutely aware that we were training journalists, not academics.

Because Soma was in a new job at the *Times,* we all agreed that I should run the program. *Business Week* offered me a year's leave if we could get the program up and running by September 1975. That was a tall order, largely because we weren't sure where the money would come from. There was another pesky question: What name should we give the program?

Surprisingly, the funding was easier than the naming. Elie decided we wouldn't proceed unless we had our finances guaranteed for five years. Rather than doing it in dribs and drabs, he asked only a handful of corporations and foundations for relatively large donations. Among those that responded: Alcoa Foundation, AT&T Foundation, Exxon Education Foundation, IBM Corporation and Prudential Insurance.

The name? Again, it was Elie's idea: name it after that eminent Victorian, Walter Bagehot, who was editor of the *Economist* a century ago. But Elie and I were worried about the choice. Why an Englishman? And why someone whose name was sure to be mispronounced? Well, we couldn't think of an eminent American, a Walter Lippman of economics. As for the pronunciation, we simply decided the heck with it. Those who didn't know his name would just have to learn.

And so the program was born. We advertised, mailed flyers, did some recruiting—and about 40 applications came in for ten places. I was the admissions committee, with Elie looking over my shoulder. Somehow, on very short notice, we attracted a good group of fellows. I remember Doreen Chu Jagoda, still with the *Today* Show, struggling with a statistics course until she mastered it. And Phil Moeller, now business editor of the *Baltimore Sun,* outshining MBA candidates in the Business School. I remember, too, the cooperation we had from Bob Yavitz, dean of the B-school, Professors Cagan, Thomas, and Seneca from the economics department, and numerous guests who came to our dinners—from Paul Volcker, later to be chairman of the Federal Reserve Board, to Frank

Cary of IBM. Not least, I remember how much I too learned—from the seminars and from the fellows themselves.

By May of 1976 it was time for all of us to leave: the fellows to their original jobs, and I to a new job as a senior editor at *Newsweek,* where I stayed for five years before returning to *Business Week.* It was Soma's turn to run the program for a year. I'm grateful to her and the other directors who followed: Chris Welles, now my esteemed colleague at *Business Week;* Mary Bralove, formerly of the *Wall Street Journal;* and Pamela Hollie Kluge also from the *New York Times.* All of them, in different ways, greatly enriched the program, thus contributing to the vast improvement in our profession's coverage of business and economics and in the public's understanding.

Glossary

ABANDONMENT The voluntary surrender of a capital asset which is no longer useful or valuable. Damaged or obsolete assets may be abandoned. The sale of abandoned assets may result in a capital gain or loss. Abandonment value is the amount that can be realized as a result of liquidation.

ABILITY TO PAY A doctrine which states that those who can pay taxes should. It assumes that the benefits of government spending will be received by people other than those who pay the taxes.

ACCELERATED DEPRECIATION A method to permit greater amounts of deductions from the loss of an asset's value than the straight-line depreciation method, which assumes equal depreciation during each year of the asset's life. Acceleration is expressed as a percentage.

ACCELERATION CLAUSE A provision in an indenture (bond contract) that authorizes a trustee to collect all the outstanding principal and interest on the issue, even if there's just one default on payment of principal or interest by the debtor.

ACCOUNTS PAYABLE A list of the amounts a company owes its suppliers of goods and services. "Open accounts" are payable in 30, 60 or 90 days. Accounts payable debts appear under the "current" section of the balance sheet. Payroll, notes and taxes aren't included.

ACCUMULATED EARNINGS TAX   A penalty charged companies that earn net profits far in excess of their reasonable needs. It's a tax designed to encourage companies to pay their excess income to shareholders in the form of dividends.

ACID TEST RATIO   A ratio used to measure the extent of cash available to meet current debt obligations. It's found by dividing cash and receivables by current liabilities. An acid test ratio of one-to-one is considered acceptable in most industries.

ACCRUED INTEREST   Interest paid to bond holders at stated times, usually twice a year. If a bond is sold, the usual practice is for the new owner to pay the old owner the amount of earnings—the accrued interest—when purchasing the bond, because payment for the full amount of earnings will be made to the new owner at the end of the period.

ACQUISITION   The acquiring of control of one company by another. In a friendly takeover, the potential buying company may offer a price above the market price established by trading on an exchange and may offer inducements to attract shareholders of the company to sell their shares to the acquirer. An acquisition may result in a merger or consolidation.

ACQUISITION COST   The price and all fees required to obtain a property. Fees will include attorneys' fees, loan fees and appraisal costs.

ACTUAL CASH VALUE   Sometimes used as a substitute for market value. Also a contract's value at maturation or redemption.

ADJUSTABLE RATE MORTGAGE (ARM)   A real estate loan that allows the interest rate to change at specific intervals over the life of the loan.

ADMINISTRATIVE LAW   Decisions from government agencies, with no specific legislative approval or judicial precedent, that become binding on businesses or individuals unless challenged and overturned by the courts.

AFFILIATED COMPANY   Two companies that are allied because one owns less than a majority of the voting stock of the other or because both companies are owned by a third company. In banking, such a company is owned or controlled by a bank or its shareholders and its officers are also directors of the bank.

AFTERMARKET   A term used to describe the trading in a security following its initial public offering.

AFTERTAX BASIS   Used for comparing returns on corporate bonds and municipal tax-free bonds. For example, a corporate bond paying 12 percent would have an after-tax return of 8.64 percent for someone in a 28 percent tax bracket. A nontaxable investment paying 8.64 percent would yield a higher return.

AGGLOMERATION   The accumulation of several diverse unrelated activities under one corporate entity, such as a holding company. Conglomerates are agglomerations.

AGGREGATE DEMAND The total quantity of all goods and services purchased in an entire economy, expressed in terms of dollars expended.

AGING SCHEDULE A report showing how long accounts receivable have been outstanding. It gives the percentage of receivables not past due and the percentage of those past due in categories of one month, two months, etc.

AGREEMENT OF SALE A written agreement between seller and purchaser which is also called a contract of sale.

AMERICAN DEPOSITORY RECEIPT (ADR) A receipt issued by U.S. banks to domestic buyers as a substitute for direct ownership of stock in foreign companies. ADRs are negotiable and are used by foreign corporations to sell shares in the U.S.

AMERICAN STOCK EXCHANGE (AMEX) The second largest exchange in the United States, located in the financial district of New York City. Formerly known as the Curb Exchange.

AMORTIZATION An accounting term referring to the reduction of debt by periodic changes to assets or liabilities, such as the payments on mortgages. A systematic write-off of costs incurred to acquire an intangible asset such as patents and copyrights.

ANNUAL REPORT A formal annual financial statement issued by a company. Designed to be read by shareholders, it shows assets, liabilities and earnings. A longer more detailed account of the company's financial results can be found in the 10–K, a document required by the Securities and Exchange Commission.

ANNUITY A series of payments of a fixed amount for a specified number of years, usually a contract sold by insurance companies that carries an income benefit for life. The basic purpose is life insurance, but it's most commonly used for retirement planning.

ANTIDUMPING DUTY An import tariff which is imposed for the purpose of raising the domestic price of a product being exported by another country at an unjustifiably low price.

ANTITRUST LAWS Legislation principally designed to protect competitive competition by outlawing monopolistic and anticompetitive practices. In the U.S., the major federal antitrust law is the Sherman Act of 1890.

APPRECIATION An increase in the value of an asset. Investors, such as homeowners, invest for appreciation, which may result from prices keeping up with inflation, increased demand for housing or shortages.

ARBITRAGE Simultaneous purchases and sales of an asset in different markets with a profitable price or yield differential. Arbitrage positions are completely hedged—the performance of both sides of the transaction is guaranteed at the time the position is assumed—and are thus without risk of loss.

ARBITRAGEUR A person or entity practicing arbitrage, usually the individual is a broker-dealer.

ARBITRATION A remedy to disputes when the alternative is litigation. The process results in a decision which is binding for both parties.

ARREARAGE Overdue payment, sometimes an omitted dividend on a preferred stock.

ARTICLES OF INCORPORATION Also called certificate of incorporation, it's a document that formally indicates the approval of authorities for the creation of a corporation.

ASKED PRICE A stock market term indicating the lowest price that will be taken by a holder of a security. Also called a quotation, it's compared to the bid, which is the highest price offered by a potential buyer.

ASSESSMENT A claim that a certain payment is required, usually a tax levied by the government or a regulatory agency. Often a penalty payment.

ASSETS The properties or items with value that are owned by an individual, business or institution. Liquid, or current, assets include cash and other items that can be converted to cash within 12 months. Long term assets are equipment and machinery and other capital assets after accounting for depreciation. Prepaid and deferred assets are items such as insurance, rent or interest. Intangible assets include such items as patents and copyrights.

ASSUMABLE MORTGAGE A loan on a property its owner can assign to a buyer upon sale of the property. In other words, if a home with a mortgage with an interest rate of 9.5 percent is purchased, the new owner can assume the mortgage at the same rate.

AT THE CLOSE An order to buy or sell a security within the final 30 seconds of trading. Brokers will not guarantee such orders.

AT THE OPENING An order to a broker to buy or sell a security at the price that applies when an exchange opens. If the order isn't executed at that time, it's canceled automatically.

AUCTION MARKET A system of trading securities through brokers or agents on a exchange. Buyers compete among themselves for the most advantageous price.

AUTHORIZED STOCK The total amount of capital stock which a company has approved for sale. The amount it actually sells is issued stock; the amount it holds for possible future sale is authorized but unissued stock.

AVERAGES Ways of measuring the trend of securities prices. One of the most popular is the Dow Jones average of 30 industrial stocks listed on the New York Stock Exchange. The prices of the 30 stocks are totaled and then divided by a divisor that's intended to compensate for past stock splits and stock dividends. Changes in this index have little relationship to the price changes.

BABY BOOMERS   Individuals born in the years immediately following World War II. Because of its size, this group has influenced the marketing habits of businesses.

BACKWARD VERTICAL INTEGRATION   A company increases its control over its supply systems by taking ownership of its suppliers or by becoming its own supplier. This strategy streamlines the company, provides better cost controls and eliminates middlemen. It allows companies to lower costs and become more competitive.

BALANCE OF PAYMENTS   A record of a nation's international economic transactions including such items as exports, imports, foreign aid and international investments.

BALANCE OF TRADE   The difference between the goods and services exported by a country and the goods and services imported into that same country during a given period. The measurement may represent trade between two countries or one country and the rest of the world. If exports are less than imports there is a trade deficit. If imports are more than exports, there is a trade surplus.

BALANCE SHEET   An itemized financial statement showing assets, liabilities and net worth of a company on a given date. The left side of the sheet is the "debit" side and shows the value of assets. The right side is the "credit" side and shows liabilities and owners' equity. The two sides must exactly balance.

BANK HOLDING COMPANY   A company owning 25 percent or more of the voting stock in a bank or in several banks. Holding companies are regulated by the board of governors of the Federal Reserve.

BANKRUPTCY   Insolvency of an individual or corporation because of an inability to repay debts. In the U.S. there are two kinds of legal bankruptcy under the 1978 Bankruptcy Reform Act; Chapter 7, or involuntary bankruptcy which calls for liquidation and for a court appointed trustee, and Chapter 11, or voluntary bankruptcy which calls for reorganization. In this latter case, the debtor remains in possession of the property and in control of the assets and operations. The goal of bankruptcy is the orderly settlement of debts.

BARTER   To trade goods without using money. It is one of the earliest trading practices, but is still used by economies in which the population has little or no confidence in the banking system or in the value of the money. In the international arena, barter is common among countries with unattractive currencies. For example, many of the trade deals between the U.S.S.R. and other countries involves barter since the Ruble is not convertible into other currencies.

BASIS POINT   One gradation on a 100-point scale, which represents one percent. It's used to express variations in yields. For example, the difference between 10.73 percent and 10.77 percent is four basis points.

BEAR MARKET   A prolonged period of falling stock prices, usually the result of declining economic activity or the anticipation of an economic downturn.

BEAR RAID   An illegal act in which investors manipulate the price of a stock downward by selling large numbers of shares.

BEARER BOND   A bond which doesn't have the owner's name registered on the books of the issuer and therefore payable to the holder.

BEARER SECURITY   A security which doesn't state the name of the owner and is therefore considered to be owned by the person who holds it.

BELLWETHER   A security which is considered an indicator of the movement of other stocks in the same market. International Business Machines, because of its size, has long been considered a bellwether stock. In bonds, the 20–year treasury bond is considered a market bellwether.

BEST'S RATING   A rating of the financial soundness of insurance companies. The top rating is A +.

BID AND ASKED   A stock market term. The bid is the highest price anyone is willing to pay. The asked is the lowest price anyone will take.

BIG BOARD   The New York Stock Exchange.

BIG THREE   Refers to automakers General Motors Corporation, Ford Motor Company and Chrysler Corporation.

BLACK FRIDAY   A term referring to a sharp drop in the financial markets on Sept. 24, 1869 when a group of financiers attempted to corner the gold market. A depression followed. Another Black Friday occurred in 1873.

BLACK MONDAY   The name given to a major stock market correction on Oct. 19, 1987. The shock of a more than 500 point drop on that day was felt around the world. Investors were warned of the drop the previous Friday. A similar pattern of trading occurred in 1989, but the drop of nearly 200 points did not create a second Black Monday.

BLOCK   In the stock market, it's a large holding of stock, usually 10,000 shares or more.

BLOWOUT   A quick sale of all shares in a new offering of securities, which results in a high stock price. Investors have difficulty getting the number of shares they want in a blowout.

BLUE CHIP STOCK   Common stock of a nationally known company that has a long track record of profitability, growth and dividend payout. The company usually has a reputation for good products and services.

BLUE SKY LAWS   A name for state laws that protect the public against security fraud. The term is said to have its origins in a ruling by a unknown judge who commented that a particular stock had about the same value as a patch of blue sky.

BOARDROOM Historically, a room for registered representatives and customers in a broker's office where the opening, high, low and last prices of stocks were once posted on a board throughout the day. Such postings are now done electronically.

BOND A certificate of indebtedness, an IOU, which obligates the issuer to pay interest coupons at regular intervals to the purchaser and to repay the principal on a specified date. Bonds are usually issued to obtain financing for a fixed asset such as a hospital.

BOND FUNDS Registered investment companies with assets invested in a portfolio of bonds.

BOND RATING An evaluation of the likelihood that a bond issuer will default. Standard & Poor's, Moody's Investors Service and Fitch Investors Service provide analysis of the bond issuers. The highest rating is AAA. D means default.

BOOK A notebook used by stock specialists to keep a record of buy and sell orders. It provides a record of the sequence of orders left with the specialist by brokers.

BOOK VALUE The value of an asset on the balance sheet or the asset value of a company's securities. On tangible assets, the value is calculated as actual cost less allowances for depreciation. When using the term for stocks, remember that book value isn't the same as market value.

BOTTOM LINE The net profit or loss for a transaction or for a company's business activity. It usually refers to the earnings statement issued by corporations and means net income or profits after taxes, expenses and extraordinary items.

BOX A term referring to the safekeeping of securities. Brokerage firms are required to keep a separate box for their clients' securities.

BREAKEVEN POINT The point at which revenues equal costs. Young companies talk in terms of reaching the breakeven point in about three to five years after the beginning of operations. For investors it means no profit, since the transaction, net of commission costs, is a wash.

BREAKOUT The movement of a stock above or below a range bounded at the upper end by the security's previous high and at the lower end by the lowest price at which the security has traded.

BRETTON WOODS In June 1944, 44 nations met in Bretton Woods, New Hampshire to prepare for European reconstruction after World War II. The World Bank, officially called the International Bank for Reconstruction and Development, and the International Monetary Fund (IMF) were the resulting world agencies. This was the beginning of efforts to establish a world economic order. A fixed exchange rate system, later abandoned, was established based on the U.S. dollar.

BROKER   An agent who handles public orders to buy and sell securities, commodities, real estate or other financial or to buy and sell securities, commodities, real estate or other financial or tangible property. Brokers usually work on a commission basis.

BROKER LOAN RATE   The interest rate bankers offer stockbrokers who ask for loans to cover the securities positions of their clients. The loan rate is usually close to the prime rate.

BUFFER STOCK PLAN   A method to smooth out the peaks and valleys in economic fluctuations. For a company it means building inventories during recessions in order to create additional employment and reducing inventories during inflationary periods.

BULL MARKET   A prolonged period of rising stock prices.

BUNCHING   A ticker tape pattern in which a series of trades in the same security appear consecutively.

BURNOUT   When tax shelter benefits are exhausted and investors begin to receive income from the investment.

BUSINESS CYCLE   A recurring pattern of expansion and contraction in the level of business activity. The cycle averages 2.5 years and moves through a period of recovery, prosperity, decline, recession and then recovery again as the next cycle begins.

BUY-BACK AGREEMENT   A contract with a provision that allows a seller of a property to repurchase it at a stated price within a certain period.

BUY ON BAD NEWS   An investment strategy that assumes that just after a company announces bad news the stock price will fall to a point below what it's worth and that it will rise again when news improves.

BUY ON MARGIN   Buying securities with credit provided by a broker through a margin account. Such activities are regulated by the Federal Reserve Board.

BUYOUT   The purchase of control of a company through negotiation or a tender offer. The purpose of a buyout is to acquire the assets and operations of the company. In a leveraged buyout, a small group, using borrowed funds, buys the company with the idea of repaying the loan from cash generated by the company or from the sale of its assets.

BUY THE BOOK   The book is the notebook that specialists—the individuals or firms assigned to individual stocks and who are responsible for orderly markets in those stocks at the New York Stock Exchange—to keep track of buy and sell orders. An order to buy the book would mean buying all the shares of a single stock that are available from all dealers or brokers of the stock at the current offer price.

BYLAWS Guidelines addressing the internal management of an organization. For companies the bylaws are initially drawn up at incorporation, but may be amended by a vote of shareholders at a later date.

CALL In banking, a demand to repay a loan usually after a debtor has failed to meet some condition of the loan. In bonds, it means that the issuer of the bond has redeemed it. In options, it means the right to buy a specific number of shares at a specified price by a fixed date.

CALLABLE A bond issue, all or part of which may be redeemed by the issuing corporation under specified conditions before maturity. It also applies to preferred shares.

CALL OPTION The right to buy 100 shares of a stock or stock index at a predetermined price before a preset deadline in exchange for a premium. For buyers who expect a stock to rise, call options allow a profit from a smaller investment than it would take to buy the stock.

CALL PREMIUM The amount in excess of par value that a company must pay when it redeems a security.

CALL PRIVILEGE A provision in a bond or preferred stock agreement that gives the issuer the right to redeem the security at a specified price.

CAPITAL ASSET An asset with a life of more than a year.

CAPITAL EXPENDITURE Outlay of money to acquire or improve capital assets such as buildings and machinery.

CAPITAL FLIGHT The movement of large sums of money from one country to another to escape political or economic turmoil or to benefit from investments with higher returns.

CAPITAL GAIN OR CAPITAL LOSS The profit or loss from the sale of a capital asset usually described as short-term (12 months or less) or long-term (more than 12 months).

CAPITALISM An economic system based on the assumption that the marketplace will determine the amount of goods produced and the prices of those goods. At the core is private ownership or production and property. And a minimum of government of involvement is assumed. A pure capitalist economy doesn't exist; most are mixed.

CAPITAL MARKETS Transactions involving financial instruments with maturities of greater than one year.

CAPITAL STOCK Shares representing ownership in a business—includes preferred and common stock.

CAPITAL STRUCTURE The financing of a firm represented by its long-term debt, preferred stock and net worth (capital, capital surplus and retained earnings).

CAPITALIZATION The total of the securities issued by a corporation and may include bonds, debentures, preferred and common stock. The securities are often accounted for by different methods: bonds and debentures are listed at par or face value; preferred and common stock at par or stated value.

CARRY-FORWARD This is a method used by companies to reduce federal income taxes. Losses can be carried forward or backward.

CARTEL A group of businesses or nations that agree to influence prices by influencing production and marketing of a product. The Organization of Petroleum Exporting Countries (OPEC) is the most famous of the contemporary cartels. The United States prohibits such organizations.

CASH COW Business that generates a steady and predictable flow of cash. Such a business usually has a well established brand name with high consumer recognition. Stocks that are cash cows have dependable dividends.

CASH CYCLE The time between the purchase of raw materials and the collection of accounts receivable from the sale of the finished product.

CASH FLOW The money that an enterprise can depend on to pay for operations and debt. A company has a positive cash flow when more cash comes in than goes out. A negative cash flow is the opposite situation. Investors focus on cash flow because it's an indicator of the company's ability to pay dividends.

CASH SALE A stock exchange term referring to delivery of the securities the same day as the transaction. Normally, delivery may come several days after a trade.

CENTRAL BANK A bank which coordinates the money and banking functions of a nation. In the United States, the central bank's functions are the responsibility of the Federal Reserve System which acts through monetary policy.

CENTRALLY PLANNED ECONOMY Considered the opposite of capitalism, since central authorities, rather than the market, are responsible for the national economy, including what's produced at what quantities and at what price to consumers.

CHURNING Excessive trading of a client's account. This illegal practice increases a broker's commissions, but usually leaves the client worse off or no better than before.

CLASSIFIED STOCK More than one class of common stock, usually created with the intention of giving a minority of shareholders control of the company. In cases of Class A and Class B stock, one class usually retains voting rights while the other has only equity participation. Because the voting rights remain in the hands of a minority, often a family, classified stock is a anti-takeover tactic.

CLOSED CORPORATION A firm owned by a few people, usually management or family members. There's no public market in the shares. Also called a private corporation.

CLOSED END MANAGEMENT COMPANY An investment company that operates a mutual fund with a limited number of shares outstanding.

COLLATERAL An asset pledged to a lender until a loan is repaid. If the borrower defaults, the lender has the legal right to seize the collateral and sell it to pay off the loan.

COLLUSION When two or more enterprises work together to provide benefits that would not exist for them if the market were free to function and economic forces determined supply and demand.

COMMERCIAL PAPER Short-term obligations with maturities ranging from 2 to 270 days, issued by banks, corporations, and other borrowers to investors with temporarily idle cash. Such instruments are unsecured and usually discounted, although some are interest bearing. Investors like such forms of debt because, if the paper is issued by top-rated companies and backed by bank lines of credit, the investment is relatively safe. Maturities are flexible and the rates are usually a bit lower than bank rates.

COMMITMENT FEE A fee paid to a lender for a formal line of credit.

COMMON STOCK Units of ownership in a public corporation. Holders of such stock are entitled to vote on the selection of directors and other important corporate matters. Shareholders are also entitled to a share in the earnings of the company through dividends.

COMMON STOCK RATIO The percentage of total capitalization represented by common stock. For purposes of analysis, the ratio depends on the stability of the company's earnings. A high ratio can mean lack of leverage. Generally, if the ratio is below 30 percent, analysts take a careful look at the company.

COMMUNISM In its pure form, this economic system has only one class, the proletariat, which contributes the labor of individuals to society according to their abilities. There is no need for government in such a plan. Since no pure example exists, the closest to the principals of communism are the centrally planned economies.

COMMUNIST MANIFESTO A pamphlet written by Karl Marx in 1848 describing the abuses of capitalists during the Industrial Revolution. It was written to encourage workers to overthrow capitalism and establish socialism.

COMPOSITION An informal reorganization that voluntarily reduces a creditor's claims on the debtor firm.

COMPOUND INTEREST An interest rate that's applicable when interest in succeeding periods is earned not only on the initial principal but also on the accumulated interest of prior periods. With simple interest, returns aren't earned on interest received.

COMPOUNDING The arithmetic process of determining the final value of a payment or series of payments when compound interest is applied.

CONGLOMERATE A corporation that has diversified its operation usually by acquiring enterprises in widely varied industries.

CONSOLIDATED TAPE The NYSE and AMEX ticker systems that report transactions on the NYSE and regional exchanges as well as all transactions of AMEX listed companies.

CONSORTIUM A group of companies formed to promote a common objective or engage in a project of benefit to all its members. It usually means sharing resources or technology.

CONSUMER PRICE INDEX (CPI) This index is based on the price of about 400 items which are selected to represent the movement of prices of all goods. The index has been altered and redefined many times since it was initiated after World War I. Available from the U.S. Department of Labor's Bureau of Labor Statistics, the monthly number is an indicator of inflation in the economy.

CONTRARIAN An investor who does the opposite of what most investors do at any given time. Such investors buy when others are selling.

CONTROLLING INTEREST Ownership of more than 50 percent of a corporation's voting shares. A smaller interest, owned individually or by a group in combination, can create a situation of controlling interest, if the other shares are widely dispersed and not actively voted.

CONVERSION PRICE The dollar value at which convertible bonds, debentures or preferred stock can be converted into common stock, as announced when the convertible is issued.

CONVERSION RATIO The relationship that determines how many shares of common stock will be received in exchange for each convertible bond or preferred share when conversion takes place. It's determined at the time of issue.

CONVERTIBLE SECURITIES Usually bonds or preferred stocks that are exchangeable at the option of the holder for common stock of the same company.

COOLING-OFF PERIOD An interval of about three weeks between the filing of a preliminary prospectus with the SEC and the offer of the securities to the public.

CORNERING THE MARKET Illegal activity, resulting from the purchase of a security or commodity in such volume that control over the price is achieved.

CORRECTION A reverse movement, usually downward, in the price of a stock, bond, commodity or index. Whenever a market moves in one direction over a long period of time, a correction is expected.

CORRESPONDENT A financial organization, usually a securities firm or a bank, that performs services for another in a market that's inaccessible to the other.

COST OF CAPITAL   Rate of return that a business could earn if it chose another investment with equivalent risk. Cost of capital is also calculated using a weighted average of the firm's cost of debt and classes of equity.

COST-PUSH INFLATION   Inflation caused by rising prices which follow on the heels of rising costs. Also called sellers' inflation, the term recognizes that the economy may depart from stability.

COUNCIL OF ECONOMIC ADVISERS   A group of economists appointed by the U.S. President to provide counsel on economic policy. The advisers help prepare the Presidential budget message to Congress.

COUPON   A once-common method for paying interest on bonds. Holders clipped coupons and presented them for payment. The coupon rate is stated on the bond.

COVENANT   Clauses in loan agreements designed to protect the lender. Covenants may include terms that limit total indebtedness or restrict dividends or acquisitions.

CRASH   A precipitate drop in stock prices and economic activity, as in the crash of 1929, which brought on the Great Depression. Crashes usually follow a loss of investor confidence which occurs during times of anticipated high inflation. The October 19, 1987 stock market drop doesn't meet this criteria, so many argue that it wasn't a crash but a correction.

CREDIT RATING   Formal evaluation of an individual or company's credit history. For corporations, Dun & Bradstreet is the primary source of credit ratings. For individuals, TRW provides ratings. Standard & Poor's and Moody's provide credit ratings for bonds.

CROWDING OUT   When there is heavy federal borrowing at a time that businesses and consumers also want to borrow money, the latter may be crowded out of the market for funds. Because the government can pay any interest rate it must to get funds and individuals and businesses can't, high interest rates discourage nongovernment borrowers. This circumstance can cause economic activity to slow.

CROWN JEWELS   The most desirable pieces of a diversified company measured by asset value, earning power and business opportunities. The crown jewels are usually the targets of takeover attempts, since they can be sold off easily and usually at a profit.

CUMULATIVE DIVIDENDS   A protective feature on preferred stock that requires all past preferred dividends to be paid before common dividends can be paid.

CUMULATIVE PREFERRED   A stock provision that requires that common stock dividends not be paid until the omitted dividends of the preferred stock are paid.

CUMULATIVE VOTING   A voting method that improves minority shareholders' chances to get representatives on the board of directors. It allows shareholders to cast all of their votes for one candidate; an exception rather than the rule.

CURB EXCHANGE   Nickname for the American Stock Exchange. Before 1921 the exchange operated out of doors and was known as the New York Curb Exchange.

CURRENCY CONTROLS   When currency controls are used, the currency is inconvertible since all buying and selling of foreign money is through a designated government agency in order to establish rates favorable to products and businesses the government wants to protect.

CURRENCY FUTURES   Contracts in futures markets for delivery in a major currency such as U.S. dollars, British pounds, French francs, Japanese yen, etc. Currency risks can be hedged with these futures.

CURRENT RATIO   A method to determine financial soundness. Current assets divided by current liabilities. It shows a company's ability to pay current obligations from current assets.

CURRENT YIELD   The earnings on an investment based on market value or the amount paid for the investment. It's the actual rate of return, so a bond with a maturity value of $1000 that pays 10 percent interest would pay $100 a year. But if the investor buys the bond for $900 the current yield would be 11.1 percent.

CUT OFF POINT   The minimum rate of return on acceptable investment opportunities.

CYCLICALLY SENSITIVE   Industries or economic conditions that grow faster than the Gross National Product during expansions and decline faster during a slowdown.

CYCLICAL STOCK   A stock that tends to rise quickly when the economy turns up and to fall quickly when it turns down. Cyclical stocks are housing, automobiles, and paper.

DAISY CHAIN   Trading between market manipulators to create the appearance of active volume. This is done to lure legitimate investors. Once the price is driven up, the manipulators unload their holdings, leaving unwary investors without buyers to trade with.

DAS KAPITAL   The famous presentation of Karl Marx's theories, which are based on his premise that the value of a good is based on the labor in it. Final editing on the 1867 book was done by Fredrich Engels.

DATE OF RECORD   Date on which shareholders must officially own shares to be entitled to a dividend. Also called the record date.

DAY ORDER   An order to buy or sell which, if not executed, expires at the end of the trading on the day it was entered.

DEALER An individual or firm in the securities business which acts as a principal rather than an agent. Usually a dealer buys for his own account and sells to customers from his inventory.

DEBENTURE A general debt obligation backed only by the integrity of the borrower rather than by specific property. An unsecured bond is a debenture.

DEBT INSTRUMENT A written promise to repay a debt; a bill, note bond, banker's acceptance, certificate of deposit or commercial paper.

DEBT RETIREMENT Repayment of debt. Usually a company will retire debt by setting a little money aside each year in a sinking fund.

DEBT TO EQUITY RATIO Total liabilities divided by total shareholders' equity. It shows whether owners' equity can cushion creditors' claims in the event of liquidation.

DECISION TREE Using a series of branches, various courses of action are drawn so that the alternatives are clear and the most efficient course of action is apparent.

DECLARE To authorize payment of a dividend on a specified date. An act of the board of directors.

DEEP DISCOUNT BOND A bond selling for a discount of more than 20 percent from its face value.

DEFICIT Excess liabilities and debts over income and assets.

DEFICIT FINANCING Borrowing by a government agency to make up for revenue shortfall. It stimulates the economy for a while, but eventually can become an economic drag by pushing up interest rates.

DEFLATION Decline in the prices of goods and services. The reverse of inflation, it's not the same as disinflation, which is a slowing in the rate of price increases.

DEFAULT Failure to fulfill a contract. Usually, default refers to the failure to pay interest or principal on debt obligations.

DELISTING Removal of a company's security from an exchange because the firm doesn't meet the requirements for listing. Requirements might be minimum financial ratios or sales performance.

DEMAND-PULL INFLATION Price increases occurring when supply doesn't adequately meet demand.

DENOMINATION The face amount or par value of a security which the issuer promises to pay on the maturity date. For example, municipal bonds are usually sold in denominations of $5,000.

DEPRECIATION A loss in the value of an asset, which in accounting terms can create tax-free income equal to the loss in the value of the asset.

DEPRESSION An economic situation when prices fall, purchasing power is reduced, there's an excess of supply over demand, unemployment rises and there's a decrease in business activity.

DEVALUATION Lowering the value of a country's currency relative to gold or other currencies. Devaluation can also result from a rise in the value of other currencies.

DIP A slight drop in securities prices after a sustained uptrend. Analysts advise investors to buy on dips, since the assumption is the drop in prices is momentary.

DISCLOSURE Release by companies of all information, positive or negative, that might affect investment decisions. It's required by the Securities and Exchange Commission and the stock exchanges of all member companies. Businesses may also have internal disclosure requirements for directors, executives and officers.

DISCOUNT For bonds and preferred stock, it's the amount these securities may sell below par value.

DISCOUNT RATE The interest rate used in the discounting process.

DISCRETIONARY ACCOUNT An account in which the customer gives a broker, or other individual, the right to buy or sell securities on behalf of the owner.

DIVERSIFICATION Spreading investments among different companies in different fields. Investors also seek diversification of their securities portfolios.

DIVIDEND Payment designated by the board of directors of a corporation to be distributed pro rata among the shares outstanding. Preferred shares get a fixed amount. Common share dividends may vary.

DIVIDEND YIELD The ratio of the current dividend to the current price of a share of stock.

DOLLAR COST AVERAGING A system for buying securities at regular intervals with a fixed dollar amount. Because investors buy only the amount of shares the fixed dollar amount can afford, they buy more shares when prices are low and fewer when prices are high.

DOUBLE EXEMPTION Refers to securities that are exempt from state and federal income taxes.

DOUBLE TAXATION Short for double taxation of dividends. The federal government taxes corporations profits as corporate income and the portion distributed to shareholders in dividends is taxed again as personal income.

DOW THEORY Market analysis based on the performance of the Dow Jones industrial and transportation stock price averages. The theory says the market is in a basic upward trend if one of these averages advances above a previous important high, accompanied or followed by a similar advance in the other. When the averages both dip before previous important lows this is considered confirmation of a basic downward trend. It's not a method for forecasting.

EARNINGS REPORT A statement, also called an income statement, issued by a company to show its profits or losses during a designated period, usually a three-month period, or quarter. Quarterly statements, six-month, nine-month and annual reports are issued.

EQUITY The net worth of a business, consisting of capital stock, capital surplus, earned surplus and sometimes net worth reserves. The common equity is the part of total net worth that belongs to the common shareholders.

EXCHANGE RATE The rate at which one currency can be exchanged for another.

EXCISE TAX A tax on the manufacture, sale or consumption of specified commodities.

EX DIVIDEND Also called "without dividend." The buyer of a stock selling an ex dividend doesn't receive the recently declared dividend. Every dividend is payable on a fixed date to all shareholders holding stock at another earlier specified date, called the date of record. When stocks go ex dividend they are designated in the stock tables with an "x."

EXERCISE PRICE The price that must be paid for a share of common stock when it's bought by exercising a warrant.

EX-RIGHTS The date on which stock purchase rights are no longer transferred to the purchaser of the stock.

EXTRA Shorthand for an extra dividend, which may be in stock or cash. This payment is in addition to the usual payment to shareholders.

FACE VALUE Value of a bond that appears on the face of the security. Usually it's the amount the issuing company agrees to pay at maturity. It's not the same as market value.

FACTORING A method of financing accounts receivable. A firm sells its accounts to a financial institution, which serves as the factor. The receivables are then sold. If accounts prove uncollectible, the factor can't turn to the original seller.

FINANCIAL ACCOUNTING STANDARDS BOARD A private agency which operates as an accounting standards-setting body.

FINANCIAL MARKET Markets for the exchange of capital and credit such as stock markets, bond markets, foreign exchange markets and commodities markets.

FINANCIAL STATEMENT   A record of the financial condition of a business, association or individual. It includes a balance sheet and income statement and may also include net worth.

FIRST IN, FIRST OUT (FIFO)   An inventory valuation in which raw materials and finished goods purchased first in the inventory are charged against the goods most recently sold. During times of rapid inflation, FIFO inflates profits since the least expensive inventory is charged against current sales.

FISCAL YEAR   An accounting year which ends on a date other than December 31.

FIXED EXCHANGE RATE   In 1944, the Bretton Woods International Monetary Conference set up a system of fixed exchange rates based on a set relationship between the dollar and other currencies. The arrangement was abandoned by the United States when President Richard Nixon took the U.S. off the gold standard.

FLAT INCOME BOND   The price that a bond is traded at which includes consideration for all unpaid accruals of interest. Bonds in default of interest or principal are traded flat.

FLAT TAX   A tax applied equally to all income levels. Supporters of flat tax say that if people are able to keep larger portions of a higher income they'd have an incentive to earn more and therefore stimulate the economy.

FLOAT   The amount of funds tied up in checks that have been written but are still not collected because they are in the process of collection.

FLOATING EXCHANGE RATES   Currency values that move up or down with world supply and demand. The rates are based on a number of factors, including national reserves of hard currency such as gold. Rates are closely linked to the rate of inflation or interest rates.

FLOOR BROKER   A member of the stock exchange who executes orders to buy and sell listed securities on the floor of the exchange.

FLOWCHART   A method of tracking the steps in a procedure such as the manufacture of a product. It may also show how to solve a problem.

FOREIGN TRADE ZONE   A designated area, sometimes a port, where goods may be stored or inspected without duties being assessed. Also called a free trade zone.

FORMULA INVESTING   A technique where an investor might shift funds from common shares to preferred shares or bonds when a selected market indicator rises above a certain predetermined level. The investor then might return to common stock when the indicator drops.

401(K) PLAN   A salary reduction plan allowing employees to contribute pretax earnings to a company pool of investments. The earnings are taxed when they are withdrawn, usually at retirement.

FRANCHISE A license to operate an enterprise, such as the stores of an ice cream chain. The franchisee has the right to use the logo and other products and services of the franchiser. In broadcasting, a local or state government may grant a broadcaster a franchise to serve a designed area.

FRAUD Intentional deception, such as nondisclosure of information or misrepresentation, which results in injury to another party.

FULL DISCLOSURE Under the Securities Act of 1933 and the Securities Exchange Act of 1934 and requirements of the stock exchanges, public companies must make certain, but not all, information about their operations public.

FULLY DILUTED EARNINGS This figure, usually expressed per share, assumes the exercise of all outstanding stock options and warrants as well as the conversion of convertible bonds and preferred stock. It reflects all the potentially dilutive elements.

FUNDED DEBT Usually interest-bearing bonds or debentures, but may include long-term bank loans.

FUTURES CONTRACT An agreement to buy or sell a commodity or financial index which specifies a future date of delivery or receipt of goods or financial instruments. Futures are used as a hedge. They include commodities traded in future markets such as corn, soybeans and pork bellies as well as oil and metals, financial instruments and stock index futures.

GENERAL ACCOUNTING OFFICE (GAO) A congressional agency organized in 1921 to review federal financial transactions.

GENERAL PARTNER A partner whose liability in a partnership isn't limited.

GENERAL MORTGAGE BOND A bond that's secured by a blanket mortgage on the company's property, but may be outranked by one or more other mortgages.

GENERIC BRAND An unadvertised, plain-label product which usually sells at prices well below advertised brand name products.

GIFT TAX When assets are transferred from one person to another, the state or federal government may levy a tax.

GINNIE MAE The nickname for the Government National Mortgage Association, which issues mortgage-based securities.

GLASS-STEAGALL ACT OF 1933 Banks were prohibited from owning brokerage firms and engaging in investment banking activities. However, bank holding companies may hold a subsidiary broker-dealer organization.

GLUT Overproduction which economists define as a situation when the available supply won't be bought at the current price.

GOING PUBLIC   A term used to describe a private company's selling its shares to the public for the first time.

GOLDEN HANDSHAKE   Early retirement incentives.

GOLDEN PARACHUTE   A contract which provides lavish benefits to executives who leave their jobs. Parachutes are associated with anti-takeover measures, since many provide such expensive benefits to executives forced to leave a company after an acquisition that the contracts make acquisitions too costly to undertake. Shareholders have challenged golden parachutes because they discourage takeovers, which can bring investors high returns.

GOLD FIX   Setting the price of gold by dealers. There's a twice daily fixing in London. The fix is the fundamental worldwide price and reflects market conditions.

GOODWILL   An intangible business asset that reflects a company's relationship and reputation with unions, suppliers, customers or the communities it serves. Charitable gifts is one way of building goodwill. An acquiring company may calculate a part of its purchase price on goodwill.

GRANDFATHER CLAUSE   An exemption for people already engaged in a business that's coming under new regulations.

GREENMAIL   In potential acquisitions, a hostile suitor might acquire a large number of a company's shares, then negotiate with the company for the repurchase of the shares by the company at a premium to its market value in exchange for abandoning a takeover. It's considered an unethical act.

GREEN REVOLUTION   Rapid changes in the methods and technology of agriculture.

GRESHAM'S LAW   An economic theory relating to the value of money. The law says that people will save or hoard what they believe to be good money and spend the bad. In other words, people may spend dollars and save gold, if there is a perception that dollars have less value.

GROSS INCOME   Earnings before deductions.

GROWTH FUND   A mutual fund invested in growth stocks. These funds tend to be more volatile than conservative investments such as money market funds.

GROWTH STOCK   Company stock with a record of rapid earnings growth.

HEDGE   A method to reduce risk which may involve the purchase of a derivative security such as options or futures, in order to reduce or neutralize all or some portion of the risk of holding another security.

HEMLINE THEORY   The theory that stocks move in the same direction as women's hemlines. Short skirts are considered bullish. Long skirts are said to be a bearish indicator.

HIDDEN ASSET   Value that's understated on a company balance sheet because of deliberate action of the company's management or because of an accounting procedure.

HOLDING COMPANY   A corporation that owns the securities of another, in most cases having voting control.

HOT STOCK   Stolen securities or newly issued stock that rises quickly in price.

HYBRID ANNUITY   An insurance company product that lets the investor mix the benefits of a fixed annuity, which offers a fixed rate of return, and a variable annuity, which offers a higher rate of return but a greater risk.

HYPOTHECATION   Pledging securities as collateral without losing possession of them. The creditor has a right to have the securities sold to settle the debt.

INDEPENDENT BROKER   Members on the NYSE floor who execute orders for other brokers. They were formerly known as two-dollar brokers from the time when they received $2 per hundred shares executed. Their fees today are paid by the commission broker.

INDEX   A statistical measurement expressed in percentages of a base year. A frequently used base year is 1967 (identified as 100), since that year predates the oil crisis and other unusual economic events of the 1970s and 1980s.

INFLATION   Rising prices for goods and services. Generally, the economic assumption is that buying power declines because there is an abundance of cash in circulation, often the result of government spending.

INFLATIONARY SPIRAL   A condition of inflation in which price increases occur at an increasing rate, resulting in a rapid loss in the value of currency.

INITIAL PUBLIC OFFERING (IPO)   A company's first stock offering to the public. Also called going public.

INSOLVENCY   A condition when a company can't meet its financial obligations when they come due. Generally, it means more liabilities than assets at a given time.

INSTITUTIONAL INVESTOR   An organization which invests its own assets or those held in trust for others. Such investors include pension funds, insurance companies, banks and universities.

INTEREST   Payments borrowers pay lenders for the use of money. A corporation pays interest on bonds to its bondholders.

INTRINSIC VALUE   The difference between the exercise price of an option and the current cash value of the underlying security, expressed in dollars.

INVESTMENT BANKER   Also known as an underwriter, this is the middleman between the corporation issuing new securities and the public. The usual practice is for investment bankers to buy a new issue of stocks or bonds directly from a corporation for resale. A group may form a syndicate to sell the securities to individuals and institutions.

IRA (INDIVIDUAL RETIREMENT ACCOUNT)   A pension plan with some tax advantages. Investments can be made in mutual funds, stocks and other instruments. Many are self-directed, which mean the investor may chose his investments. Investors begin drawing from the fund at retirement, or no sooner than age 59 1/2.

J-CURVE   An economic description of a turnaround. In theory the present situation continues for a while, then bottoms out and improves quickly, forming the look of a J, if graphed.

JOB SECURITY   A way of talking about the chance of dismissal. A job with the government is said to have high job security, whereas a job in the private sector has less job security.

JOINT VENTURE   An agreement between at least two parties to work together for a limited amount of time or for a single project.

JUNK BOND   A term referring to bonds rated BB or lower by rating agencies, such as Standard & Poor's. The lower the rating the more risky the investment. However, the returns for junk bonds rise with the risk. Junk is often associated with leveraged buyouts and takeovers by companies with little, or no, credit history or a poor borrowing track record.

KEOGH PLAN   Named for New York Congressman Eugene J. Keogh, the plan was created in 1962 to allow self-employed people to save for retirement. It's a tax advantaged personal retirement program which allows the individual to invest in stocks, bonds, mutual funds, annuities, partnerships and other assets.

KEYNESIAN ECONOMICS   The theories of John Maynard Keynes, a British economist who is best known for his theory that to avoid depression, government should spend more to encourage investment and higher employment. He said that insufficient demand created unemployment. Excessive demand creates inflation. He endorse government manipulation of the economy.

LABOR EFFICIENCY VARIANCE   The difference between actual hours worked and the standard hours of actual production, multiplied by the standard labor rate. This gives the difference in costs attributed to changes in labor efficiency.

LABOR-MANAGEMENT RELATIONS ACT   The Taft-Hartley Act of 1947, which outlawed unfair labor practices by unions and allowed suits for breach of contract against unions among other provisions.

LAFFER CURVE   A suppy-side economics approach named for economist Arthur Laffer, who postulated that noninflationary growth is spurred by tax policies that encourage investment and productivity. In short, an increase in the marginal tax rate will raise total revenue, but only for a short time. At a point, rising tax rates result in decreasing tax revenues.

LAGGING INDICATOR   A statistic which doesn't change until after the economy has changed. Construction is a lagging indicator since the economy may adjust to the expectations for construction when plans are announced even though the actual construction may take many months to complete.

LAISSEZ-FAIRE   It means minimal government involvement in business affairs. In 1776, Adam Smith in *The Wealth of Nations* called this theory the "invisible hand," since it allowed businesses to seek their maximum opportunities without interference. Deregulation is seen as a movement toward a laissez-faire philosophy and a retrenchment from Keynesian economics, which advocated government intervention.

LAST IN, FIRST OUT (LIFO)   Inventory accounting that records the cost of items brought out of inventory in reverse order from those that enter the inventory. It may result in an artificially low inventory balance sheet. This method is useful during times of inflation.

LAW OF DIMINISHING RETURNS   As more and more cost is expended on a given task, the benefits per unit of cost become less and less. It often applies to the addition of labor. At a certain point, adding more labor will not add significantly to production, while the labor costs will continue to rise at a constant rate.

LAW OF SUPPLY   An economic principle that assumes that if market forces are operating, producers will produce goods when the profit is highest.

LEADING INDICATORS   The U.S. Commerce Department's Bureau of Economic Analysis issues measures of the health of the national economy. They measure a number of sectors including employment, business formation and consumer demand.

LETTER OF INTENT   Written indication that an action may be taken. When two companies come to a preliminary agreement—possibly about a mergers—they may issue a letter of intent.

LEVERAGE   The effect on a company's per-share earnings when the company has interest to pay on bonds or preferred stock, or both. Leverage may be good when earnings are good. But leverage may be bad for a company when earnings drop, since the effect of leverage is to direct funds away from the payment of dividends to common shareholders and toward the payment of others.

LIABILITIES   All claims against a corporation, which may include wages, dividends, accured taxess, mortgage bonds, etc. There are short-term liabilities and long-term liabilities. Liabilities must equal assets on a balance sheet.

LIQUID ASSETS RATIO   The ratio of liquid assets to current liabilities, used to assess the adequacy of liquid funds of an organization.

LIQUIDATION   The processs of coverting securities or other property to cash. However, in business it usually means the dissolution of a company. The cash remaining after the sale is used to pay off the company's indebtedness.

LIQUIDITY   The ease with which an asset can be converted to cash.

LISTING   Stocks are listed on exchanges and must meet exchange requirements. The New York Stock Exchange requires a minimum of 1.1 million shares publicly held and not less than 2,000 round-lot stockholders. The value of the common shares must be at least $18 million and the company should have net income or over $2.5 million.

LONG   It means ownership of securities, options or futures. Someone who is "short" has sold the securities. A broker is long when he has more securities than he's sold.

MAINTENANCE CALL   When a brokerage customer's margin account equity falls below the requirement of the National Association of Securities Dealers (NASD), a call is made for additional money or securities. If the account isn't brought up to compliance, the client's holdings may be sold to make up the shortfall.

MANAGED MONEY SUPPLY   Also called a controlled money supply, it's a decision to make short term adjustments in the supply of money rather than relying on factors out of the control of the government. It's a method of monetary policy.

MANIPULATION   An illegal act of buying or selling a security for the purpose of creating a false or misleading appearance of active trading for the purpose of raising or depressing the price to induce purchases or sales by others.

MARGIN   The amount paid by the customer when using a broker's credit to buy or sell a security. The Federal Reserve regulations since 1945 have required a minumum, which has ranged from 50 percent recently to 100 percent.

MARGIN CALL   A demand for a customer to put up money or securities with the broker. A call is made when a purchase is made; also, if a customer's equity in a margin account declines below a minimum standard set by the exchange or the customer's borkers firm, then a call is made.

MARKET PRICE   The last reported price at which a stock or bond sold. It may also be the current quote.

MARKET SHARE   The percentage of total sales of a product which one seller has. Achieving a larger market share is the goal of marketing, advertising and promotion.

MATCHED ORDERS   Normally, an illegal buying and selling of orders to create the impression of activity in a security, which causes an upward price movement. However, it's the job of specialists to create an opening price on the NYSE by counterbalancing orders or trades to narrow the spread between prices. This is a legal activity to produce orderly markets.

MERCANTILIST   A popular belief in the early 1700s and 1800s that nations would greatly benefit from holding precious metals. Policies achieving this goal were encouraged.

MERGER Any combination of enterprises. Mergers are of many types, such as the horizontal merger, which combines direct competitors with similar markets and products. A vertical merger combines customer and company or supplier and company. A merger may also result in extending product lines.

MINORITY INTEREST Shareholders who own less than half the shares of a company.

MONETARIST An economist who believes that changes in the growth of the rate of money supplied to the system has important effects on spending, price, production and employment. An effective way to control a nation's economy is through monetary policy.

MONETARY POLICY Government influence over the economy by controlling money and interest rates. The Federal Reserve System does this by using open market operations, changing reserve ratios and influencing the discount rate.

MONEY MARKET FUND A mutual fund whose investments are in high-yield money market instruments such as federal securities, CDs and commercial paper. Its intent is to make such instruments, normally purchased in large denominations by institutions, available indirectly to individuals.

MORTGAGE A transaction in which purchased property is used as collateral for the loan which is then used to buy the property. Mortgages for homes are normally written for 15 or 30 year periods.

MUTUAL FUND Investment companies operate funds that raise money from shareholders to invest in bonds, stocks, options, commodities or other securities. These funds normally offer investors a choice of an aggressive or conservative strategy to earn returns.

NAKED POSITION When an option isn't offset by an equal and opposite position. In other words, the position isn't hedged so the risk is greater than for a covered position.

NASD The National Association of Securities Dealers, an association of brokers and dealers in the over-the-counter securities business.

NASDAQ The automatic quotation system of the National Association of Securities Dealers. It provides brokers and dealers with price quotes for over-the-counter stocks.

NATIONAL DEBT Money owed by the federal government. It includes Treasury notes, bills and bonds. The interest on the national debt is an annual expense which results from balancing the deficit against the surplus for any given year.

NATIONALIZATION The takeover of a private company by a government. Sometimes the company is compensated, sometimes not.

NEGATIVE YIELD CURVE When yields on short-term securities are higher than those on long-term securities of the same quality. This is the reverse of normal yield curve where long-term securities have a higher yield because interest rates tend to be higher for long-term investments to encourage investment. High interest rates in the short term can produce a negative yield curve.

NEOCLASSICAL ECONOMICS Economic theory which flourished from the turn of the nineteenth century until the adoption of Keynesian economics. The assumption was that market forces would always lead to efficient allocation of resources and full employment. Keynes maintained that, at times, the market failed and that it was the responsibility of government to intervene.

NET After everything has been deducted, the net is the result. It's both a noun and a verb, since one can net a million dollars. Net is also the difference between business additions and subtractions. Net assets, for example, are the difference between total assets and liabilities.

NET ASSET VALUE Net asset per share is calculated by taking the market value of all securities owned and deducting the liabilities. The balance is divided by the outstanding shares.

NET INCOME/NET PROFIT Also called the bottom line, it is the amount remaining after all expenses and taxes are paid or deducted from the proceeds of a venture. For businesses, the net income is expressed in dollars and in per share earnings.

NET OPERATING INCOME The earnings of an enterprise after deducting the expenses of its operation, but before deducting taxes and financing expenses.

NET WORTH The capital and surplus of a firm, including the paid-in capital and retained earnings. Usually it refers to the worth of common shareholders rather than preferred shareholders.

NEW DEAL Political and economic policies under the first two administrations of President Franklin D. Roosevelt aimed at overcoming the miseries of the Great Depression.

NEW ISSUE The first time a company sells stocks or bonds. Proceeds may be used to retire outstanding securities, to improve plants or buy new equipment, to raise additional working capital or to acquire public ownership in the company for private owners.

NEW YORK FUTURES EXCHANGE A subsidiary of the New York Stock Exchange devoted to the trading of futures products.

NEW YORK STOCK EXCHANGE The largest organized securities market in the United States. Founded in 1792, it's a nonprofit corporation governed by a board of directors. The Exchange doesn't buy, sell, own or set the prices of securities traded on the exchange.

NYSE COMPOSITE INDEX The index covering price movements of all common stocks listed on the New York Stock Exchange. It's based on the close of the market December 31, 1965 as 50.00 and is weighted according to the number of shares listed for each issue. The index is computed continuously and printed on the ticker tape. Point changes in the index are converted to dollars to measure the changes in the average price of listed stocks.

NO-GROWTH   No change in the Gross National Product from year to year.

NO-LOAD   Refers to mutual funds which have no sales charge. Shares are bought directly from the fund companies, rather than through a broker, which is the practice with load funds.

NONCUMULATIVE PREFERRED STOCK   Preferred stock in which unpaid dividends don't accrue. Omitted dividends are lost.

NOT FOR PROFIT   An incorporated organization in which the activity of the enterprise is directed toward some charitable, humanitarian or educational purpose. Such groups are exempt from corporate income taxes and some donations are tax deductible to the supporters of the enterprise.

OBLIGATION BOND   A mortgage bond with a face value greater than the value of the underlying property. The difference compensates the lender for costs exceeding the mortgage value.

OBSOLESCENCE   As a result of scientific or technological changes, property may become useless. This process doesn't refer to physical deterioration.

OCCUPATIONAL HAZARD   Conditions in a work environment that increase the probability of death, disability or illness to workers.

ODD LOT   Less than a "round lot," which is a stock trading unit of 100 shares.

OKUN'S LAW   Named for economist Arthur Okun, the rule says that at levels higher than full employment, a change of one percent in the unemployment will cause a change of three percent in the nation's total output.

OLIGOPOLY   Market domination by a few large suppliers. In a true competitive situation, there'll be a large number of small suppliers.

OPEN ACCOUNT   Until final payment is made to a creditor and the account is closed, it's said to be an open account.

OPEN BID   A method to set the price of work or goods which allows bidders to quote a price at which they can provide the needed services. They have the right to reduce the price to meet the quotes made by others for the same work. The winner of the bid is the lowest acceptable bid.

OPEN DOOR POLICY   A national trading policy which allows equal treatment for foreign citizens and products and domestic citizens and products. In the workplace, it's a policy encouraging an informal environment. The manager's door, for example, might be left open to encourage interaction with employees.

OPEN-END CONTRACT A contract providing an unspecified amount of goods or services over a period of time.

OPEN MARKET It usually means a lack of restrictions on the price or type of goods traded. In the Federal Reserve System, it refers to the activities of the Securities Department and the operations used to regulate money supply.

OPEN OUTCRY A method of trading used on commodity exchanges. Traders come together in a trading ring or pit where they shout their buy or sell orders. The two sides make a contract in the open.

OPERATING RATIO There are a number of ratios that reflect the strength of a company's operations. The ratios usually show the relationship between various income and expense figures using the profit and loss statement or the balance sheet figures. Common ratios relate sales to cost of goods sold; operating expenses to operating income or net income to net worth.

OPPORTUNITY COST This is the cost of taking one course of action rather than another. There's cost associated with foregoing a particular opportunity.

ORDINARY INTEREST Also called "simple interest," it's based on a 360–day year rather than a 365–day year, which is called "exact interest."

ORIGINATION FEE A borrower's fee, usually associated with a mortgage. It may cover the cost of issuing the loan, of making credit checks, of appraisal or of completing a title search.

OUTSOURCING When a firm goes to other firms for goods or services rather than producing them itself. Many clothing manufacturers will outsource to foreign manufacturers in Hong Kong or Taiwan because labor is cheaper there or manufacturing technology is more advanced. A company outsources when another company can do the job more cheaply.

OVERAGE The opposite of shortage.

OVERHANG A large block of securities or commodities contracts that, if released on the market, would result in a drop in prices.

OVERHEAD This is cost not directly related to the production of a product, but costs associated with the activity of the firm, such as the cost of a corporate attorney.

OVER-THE-COUNTER A market for securities of companies that are usually small and often young. Generally, these companies are without sufficient shares, shareholders or earnings to enable them to be listed on the AMEX or the NYSE. The market is conducted over the phone. OTC dealers may act either as principals or as brokers for customers. The NASDAQ provides quotes.

PAC MAN DEFENSE Named for a once-popular video game, it refers to a defense used to fight off corporate mergers and acquisitions. Instead of stubbornly opposing a takeover, the target company turns the tables and makes a counter-offer to buy the unwelcome suitor.

PAPER PROFIT Unrealized gain in an investment or portfolio. The profit is calculated by comparing the current market price to the investor's cost.

PAR Equal to the face amount or stated value of a negotiable instrument, stock or bond. It's not the actual value in the open market. "At par" means that the securities sell at their stated value.

PAR VALUE It's the face value or the value of a stock for accounting and tax purposes. The market value of the stock is the price at which it actually trades. For bonds, the par value usually refers to the maturity value.

PARKINSON'S LAW A rule describing the paralysis of organizations. Named for C. Northcote Parkinson, it describes an organizational infection called "injelitis," which causes firms to become moribund, resulting in little constructive activity or accomplishment.

PATENT PENDING This statement is issued from the U.S. patent office when a patent search is being conduct in the U.S. and other countries to determine if the invention is really new and therefore patentable under law.

PATERNALISM A management style that assumes the ultimate responsibility for employee welfare rests with the employer. The company decides what's best for the employees and makes benefit decisions, job assignments and promotions for the employee.

PENNY STOCK A stock that sells for less than $1 a share. Such stocks are generally issued by companies with a short history of sales and earnings performance. Penny stocks are more volatile than those of large, well-established enterprises on large equity exchanges.

PER CAPITA Anything calculated to reflect the cost or value per individual.

PER DIEM The daily rate an employer pays employees who are traveling on company business. Per diem is provided to cover expenses. It isn't considered earned income.

PERFECT COMPETITION Also called pure competition, this is the ideal condition for competition—large numbers of sellers and buyers.

PERQUISITE Also called a perk, these are benefits other than wages, such as the use of a corporate health club or the assignment of a secretary.

PERSONAL INCOME A component of the national account, it's the total of all income including wages and salaries, rental income and dividends.

PETER PRINCIPLE Based on a book, *The Peter Principle and Why Things Always Go Wrong,* by Lawrence J. Peter, this theory maintains that people rise in their careers to the level of their own incompetence.

PHILLIPS CURVE The relationship between price changes and unemployment. The curve shows an inverse relationship, low rates of unemployment go with high rates of price change, or inflation.

PLANNED ECONOMY An economy in which government planning dominates the economic activity. Market forces, the basis of capitalism, aren't allowed to function freely. Socialist, and especially communist, economies are planned economies.

POISON PILL A defense against takeovers, this is a strategy to make a company's stock less attractive to acquirers. Poison pills have been challenged by shareholders, since they may prevent shareholders from realizing a handsome return on their stock investment in the event of a takeover.

PORTFOLIO All the securities, including stocks, bonds, real estate and certificates of deposit, owned by an individual or organization.

PORTFOLIO THEORY An investment strategy designed to allow an investor to classify and control the kind and amount of risk and return. The point is to select the portfolio which will provide the highest return.

POSITIVE LEVERAGE Use of borrowed funds that increases the return on the investment.

POSITIVE YIELD CURVE When interest rates are higher on long-term debt than on short-term debt securities. A positive yield curve is the expected situation for investments of the same quality. A negative yield curve exists when interest is higher on short-term debt securities.

POVERTY An inexact measure of income and wealth based as much on perception as on actual calculations. Generally it means income and wealth at or below subsistence.

PREFERRED STOCK A class of stock without ordinary voting rights, but which allows the owners certain privileges including preference over common stockholders in the payment of dividends or in the liquidation of assets.

PREMIUM Usually an incentive payment. But in insurance it refers to the fee paid for the policy. In stocks it's the amount paid over the market price for shares. For example, an acquirer may pay a premium in order to entice shareholders to sell the acquirer their holdings. Premium may also refer to the trading price of a new issue above its offering price.

PRESIDENTIAL ELECTION CYCLE THEORY Some investment advisers maintain that major stock market moves can be predicted on a four-year presidential election cycle. Historical patterns show that incumbent presidents seek to encourage an economic program that flowers by election day.

PRICE EARNINGS RATIO (P/E) A standard measure of risk, the market value of a share of stock is divided by earnings per share for a twelve month period. A low P/E ratio is considered relatively safe, but less likely to increase in a rising market.

PRIMARY MARKET The first market for new issues of securities. When a stock issuing company sells new securities directly to the public, it gets the proceeds. Once investors hold the shares they may buy or sell them among themselves in the "secondary market" and keep the proceeds. A stock exchange is a secondary equity market.

PRIME RATE   This is the lowest interest rate commercial banks charge their best customers, usually large strong corporations. The rate is determined by market forces affecting a bank's cost of funds and the rates that borrowers will accept. Banks may offer some customers discounts on the prime rate.

PRINCIPAL   The person for whom a broker executes an order, or a dealer who buy or sells for his or her own account. The term is used to refer to an individual's capital or the face amount of a bond.

PRIVATE PLACEMENT   This is the direct sale of securities by a company to institutional investors, like insurance companies. Because the securities don't involve the public, private placements don't come under the jurisdiction of the SEC.

PRIVATIZATION   In general, a firm shifts ownership from public to private investors. For a publicly held company, this may mean "going private" by repurchasing its outstanding stock from public shareholders. In an international context, privatization is associated with economic restructuring in which state-owned enterprises are sold to the private sector.

PRODUCER PRICE INDEX.   This measure of inflationary trends is based on changes in wholesale prices. The index is broken down into components that reflect the price of products as they move through manufacturing and distribution before reaching the consumer.

PROFIT AND LOSS STATEMENT (P&L)   A summary of a company's sales and expenses during an accounting period. It's the same financial statement referred to as the operating statement or income and expense statement.

PROFIT CENTER   A unit of a company which operates in a decentralized environment. Profit centers have a calculable rate of return and may report sales and earnings independent of the parent company.

PROFIT MARGIN   Generally, the ratio of net profits, after taxes, to sales. But profit margins may also involve a calculation of the return on sales based on gross profit or operating profits.

PROFIT SHARING   An employee benefit which allows workers to share in the profits of the firm. The company makes contributions to an account for the employee. The profit-sharing may be in cash or invested for the employee.

PROFIT TAKING   When stock appreciates, investors realize their profits by selling. This is a term often used to explain a downturn in equity markets.

PROGRAM TRADING   This strategy used by institutions calls for buying and selling stocks in a program or index on which options and futures are traded. Computers assist in the buying and selling with the objective of capturing the arbitrage profits available when stock indexes and their futures or options are being traded.

PROSPECTUS   An official selling document registered with the Securities and Exchange Commission that must be given to purchasers of new securities so that they can evaluate the securities before a purchase. It describes the history, lists officers and outlines the financial background of a company, real estate, mutual fund or other investment.

PROXY   A person with the authority or power to act for another. Shareholders may vote by proxy. In some cases, a proxy is a power of attorney.

PROXY FIGHT   This is one way to gain control of a company. The point is to get enough shareholders, through the vote of their proxies, to vote out a company's board of directors, unseat the management and replace the company's officers and board with candidates sympathetic to those seeking control. Proxy fights usually erupt between factions within the company, but they may also involve shareholders outside the company who seek support for a takeover.

PROXY STATEMENT   Information the SEC requires companies to give shareholders prior to solicitation of proxies. The statement lists the board of directors and the directors to be elected by a vote of shareholders in person or by proxy. Other information about the company, including resolutions and changes in corporate procedure are outlined in the statement.

PUNITIVE DAMAGES   A form of punishment that increases the damages for wrongdoing by providing compensation above the actual damages.

PURCHASING POWER   This is the value of money measured in terms of the goods and services it buys. The index of consumer prices, with calculations for inflation, is used to determine purchasing power.

PUT   An option to sell a specific security at a specific price within a designated period.

QUOTA   A quota sets a maximum, minimum, or both for the quantity of goods in circulation. In international trade, it's used to regulate the amount of imports of certain goods into a country. It's a form of protectionism.

RAID   This is an attempt to acquire enough shares of a company to gain control. Companies are usually not aware a raid is coming and are therefore too surprised to mount an immediate defense. Sometimes a raid may involve selling stock, rather than buying it. But selling isn't a raid unless the intention is to buy the stock back at a lower price.

RAIDER   An individual or company seeking control of an enterprise by buying stock. It implies that the target company hasn't been asked to negotiate. However, a raider cannot act in secret for long, since the SEC requires that any purchase of 5 percent of a public company's stock must be announced in a 13–D, which states the purpose of the stock purchase. It's after this filing that many companies realize that there's interest by a raider.

RALLY   A rapid rise in the overall market or in an individual stock following a period of decline in the general price level.

RANDOM WALK   A stock theory based on the belief that stock price movements are completely random and unpredictable.

RATE OF RETURN   Generally, this means earnings as a percent of investment. So for stocks, the dividend yield is calculated by dividing the annual dividend by the stock purchase price.

RATINGS   A measure of the likelihood that a bond issuer will repay the principal amount at maturity and meet the scheduled interest payments. Bonds are rated by agencies such as Standard & Poor's Corporation (highest rating is AAA) and Moody's Investor Service Inc. (highest rating AAA).

REAL ESTATE INVESTMENT TRUST (REIT)   Usually a publicly traded company set up to manage a portfolio of real estate for shareholders. There are several types of REITS, including ones that lend money to building developers.

RECESSION   A downward turn in economic activity. Defined in different ways, most economists accept the definition that it's at least two consecutive quarters of decline in the Gross National Product.

RECORD DATE   The date a shareholder must be registered on the stock book of a company in order to receive a declared dividend or to vote on company affairs.

RED HERRING   A preliminary prospectus that's not complete or final. It's identified by its red cover.

RED INK   Slang for a loss.

REFINANCING   A technique for increasing debt or exchanging one debt agreement for another. In personal finance, one usually refinances to lower the interest rate on a loan or change the method of payment. In bonds, the issuing party may retire existing bonds and issue new debt. In almost all cases, the result is a longer payment period. Also called refunding.

REGISTRATION   The Securities and Exchange Acts of 1933 and 1934 state that securities must be reviewed by the SEC before they can be sold to the public. Registration outlines the plans and financial health of the company issuing the securities.

REINSURANCE   An insurance company practice for sharing risk. One company will accept a policy and then sell all or part of it to other insurers. The companies that assume part of this risk are paid part of the premium fee collected from the insured.

REORGANIZATION   Not to be confused with bankruptcy, when a company is liquidated. Under reorganization a troubled company continues to operate, but its assets are restated to reflect their current market value. There is, however, a provision of bankruptcy law that allows a company to reorganize to meet its obligations to creditors. But reorganization doesn't necessarily mean a company is considering bankruptcy.

RESERVE In order to pay upcoming expenses such as dividends, improvements or retirement costs, a company may put aside some of its earnings. Often a company has hidden reserves, the result of understatements on the balance sheet. Governments maintain reserves in foreign currencies and gold to pay for imports and foreign debts.

RESERVE REQUIREMENT The Federal Reserve System requires member banks to maintain a certain level of cash or other liquid assets as a percentage of demand deposits. The higher the reserve, the tighter the money supply and the slower the economy grows.

RESISTANCE LEVEL This is the expected price range for a stock or commodity. The ceiling is referred to as the resistance level. The lower end of the range is called the support level. When a stock breaks through the resistance level, it usually causes investors to re-evaluate a company.

RETAINED EARNINGS Also called undistributed profits, a company may keep some of its earnings after paying dividends to put back into its operations. The earned surplus is an important part of a company's shareholders' equity.

RETURN ON EQUITY A percentage that reflects how well a company is doing against itself and competitors. It's calculated by dividing common stock equity at the beginning of an accounting period into net income (before paying the common stock dividends but after paying preferred dividends). The resulting percentage can be used to compare a company's performance against other companies.

REVENUE This figure measures all the money that comes into a business or government during a certain period of time. The figure is more comprehensive than sales, since it also includes capital gains and dividends and other sources of funds that aren't from the daily activities of the enterprise.

REVERSE SPLIT Occasionally, companies reduce the number of shares in public hands. A reverse split accomplishes this while raising the value of each share. For example, if there are 100 million shares in public hands valued by the equity market at $1 each and the company announces a 1 for 10 split, the number of shares outstanding is reduced to 10 million and each share rises in value to $10.

RIGHTS OFFERING Sometimes companies may give common shareholders the right to buy newly issued shares at a discount from what the public might pay at a later date. The stock is by the company to shareholders through investment bankers.

RISK ARBITRAGE This strategy involves the simultaneous purchase of stock in a company being acquired and the sale of stock in the company that's acquiring it. The profit, if any, is made when the price of the target company's shares rise and the acquiring company's shares fall, as they often do in takeover situations.

ROUND LOT This standard unit of trading is 100 shares for stocks and $1,000 par value for bonds. Sometimes for thinly traded stocks, a round lot may be as small as 10 shares.

RUN ON THE BANK When depositors lose confidence in the banking system, they withdraw their money. If the run is serious enough, banks fail, as hundreds did during the Great Depression of the 1930s.

S CORPORATION Short for Subchapter S Corporation, this is a common form for small businesses. It requires that all earned profits and other income be passed to the shareholders each year. The shareholders are taxed as a partnership.

SALES This is the total dollar amount of goods and services sold by an enterprise. Sometimes called revenues, sales are actually a part of revenues, which include other company income such as dividends and capital gains.

SATURDAY NIGHT SPECIAL A once popular surprise takeover tactic, this method was curtailed by the Williams Act of 1968 which put severe restrictions on how tender offers (a public offer to buy stock from shareholders) should proceed. The technique gets its name from takeover maneuvers in the 1960s that were planned on weekends for Monday morning announcement.

SAVING In economics, saving is income minus expenses. However, this assumes all income is spent or saved, which isn't always the case. The savings rate is the rate at which savings occur out of income. Since savings is an indicator of the economy's potential for growth and investment, the proportion of additional income that will be saved, rather than consumed, is important and is called the marginal propensity to save.

SAY'S LAW Named for nineteenth-century French economist J.B. Say, the law maintains that supply creates its own demand. Therefore, whatever quantity is supplied, it's assumed that the amount will also be demanded.

SEAT An expression for the right to trade directly on the floor of major securities exchanges. The number of seats is fixed, so there's an informal market among those who buy and sell seats.

SECONDARY MARKET When a company initially sells shares to the public, the company does it directly to the public and takes the proceeds. But once the shares are in circulation, investors sell among themselves. They buy and sell in the secondary market where the equity exchanges have a major role.

SECURITIES This is a general term for stocks, bonds and other instruments of ownership or debt used to finance business and government.

SECURITIES AND EXCHANGE COMMISSION (SEC) Established by Congress to help protect investors, the SEC administers the Securities Act of 1933, the Securities Exchange Act of 1934, the Securities Act Amendments of 1975, the Trust Indenture Act, the Investment Company Act, the Investment Advisers Act and the Public Utility Holding Company Act.

SEIZURE While seizures are common in drug related cases and in some instances of real estate fraud, in a larger economic context—the government takeover of management and control of a private enterprise—seizure is rare.

SENIOR PREFERRED When there are classes of preferred stock, the senior preferred has priority over the junior preferred and both have priority over common stock.

SHARES OUTSTANDING These are the authorized shares of a corporation in the hands of shareholders. Authorized shares are the maximum number of shares a company can issue under its charter.

SHARE OF THE MARKET A company will seek to expand its market share, which is the percentage of total sales of a product, by advertising, pricing and other competitive tactics. The larger the market share, the easier it is for a producer to control prices and profit.

SHARK REPELLENT A term that refers to a number of measures a company may take to prevent a takeover. Tactics may include poison pills or golden parachutes. The point of shark repellent is to increase the cost or the difficulty of taking over a company.

SHELL CORPORATION Usually an incorporated company with no significant assets or operations. Such companies are often formed in order to obtain financing to begin business. They're highly risky investments. The term often describes fraudulent tax evasion schemes.

SHERMAN ANTITRUST ACT Passed July 2, 1890, the law was enacted to curb the growing concentrations of economic power during the industrialization of the United States.

SHORT It means owing money or securities. A short position occurs when an investor has sold securities with the obligation to close the position by buying the same security at a later date.

SILENT PARTNER The term usually refers to a general partner with no role in management but who receives a share of the investment and shares in the liability. A silent partner may also be a limited partner with no direct role in management and no liability beyond the individual investment.

SINKING FUND When a firm has an obligation to redeem its bonds, debentures or preferred stock, it may decide to regularly set aside a certain amount of money in a sinking fund to pay these obligations. This isn't the same as a reserve fund, since sinking funds are generally required by bond or preferred stock charters.

SOCIALISM It's an economic system associated with central planning. The government owns the major means of production.

SOCIAL SECURITY A plan designed to provide a "safety net" for individuals and families. It provides continuing income when family earnings are reduced because of retirement, liability or death. The fourth, and newest component of the U.S. system, is Medicare.

SOFT MONEY   A term used in many ways, it often refers to money that is tax deductible. In currency markets, however, it refers to money that is risky to hold because it fluctuates in value or has no value outside of specific trading circles. In the case of the Soviet Union's ruble, the currency is set at unrealistic exchange rates, and is therefore not easily converted to other currencies. **Hard money** refers to gold and convertible currencies.

SOLVENCY   This is the ability to repay debts.

SOVEREIGN RISK   Involving governments, this risk reflects the likelihood that a government will default on its loan or fail to honor other business commitments because of a national policy change. The U.S. is able to attract foreign investment because it has a low sovereign risk.

SPECIAL DRAWING RIGHTS (SDR)   A measure of a nation's reserve assets in the International Monetary Fund (IMF). These rights are designed to supplement the reserves of gold and convertible currencies (or hard currencies) used to maintain stability in the foreign exchange markets.

SPECIALIST   A member of the New York Stock Exchange whose job is to match buy and sell orders and to maintain an orderly market in securities registered to the specialist. Maintaining an orderly market may mean that the specialist must buy or sell for his own account when there's a temporary disparity between supply and demand. The specialist acts as a broker's broker.

SPECIE   Money which has an intrinsic value, such as gold or silver coins.

SPINOFF   A way of creating a new corporation from a subsidiary or division of an existing corporation. Often, new shares are issued in the newly created company. Shareholders of the parent company receive shares in the new company in proportion to their original holding. The total value of the shares in the spinoff and the existing parent company would retain about the same value at the time of the spinoff.

SPLIT   A way of distributing shares to the public by giving existing shareholders additional shares based on their holdings. In a two for one split, shareholders would receive an additional share for each one they hold. Sometimes new stock is exchanged for all old shares, so a shareholder would get two new shares for each old share. In a two for one split, the number of shares would double and the price of the stock (at the time of the split) would be reduced by half.

SPREAD   Generally, it's the profit from selling at a higher price than the purchase price. In securities, it's the bid minus the offering price. For an underwriter of securities, it's the profit in a public offering.

SPREADSHEET   A company ledger showing in columns and rows its financial situation. It may include a balance sheet, income statement and sales report. Spreadsheets are used by securities analysts in researching companies and industries.

STAGFLATION A combination of the words "stagnation" and "inflation." The word described a condition in the 1970s when slow economic growth and high unemployment occurred at the same time as rising prices.

STANDARD & POOR'S INDEX This gauge of market performance includes the price movements of 500 publicly traded industrial, transportation, financial and public utility stocks.

STOCK These units of a company represent partial ownership. The purchasers of these units have rights as owners and may receive income through dividends. Stock may be bought or sold without an effect on a company's operations. In a stock market, the price of the stock, also called shares, is set by the buyers and sellers of the stock.

STOCK OPTION These options, or rights, allow an employee to purchase a stated number of shares of capital stock—almost always stock of the corporation for which he or she works—at a stated price per share. The purpose of options is to provide incentives for employees and to reward executives.

STRAIGHT-LINE DEPRECIATION For tax and accounting purposes, assets lose value over time. This method of depreciation writes off the falling value in equal amounts each year. In the case of real property, the time may be 18 years.

STRIKE A labor-organized work stoppage with the purpose of exerting pressure on management to agree to better work conditions. Usually associated with the negotiation of a new labor contract, union members may take a strike vote to authorize action. Sometimes strikes are used to force management to accept a union as a bargaining agent.

SUBORDINATED The word suggests that others have priority. In the case of loans, subordinated debt has a secondary claim to assets after those with higher claims.

SUBSCRIPTION PRIVILEGE The right of common shareholders to purchase new issues of a company's stock. The privilege must be exercised within a stated period of time, usually a month or two.

SUBSIDIARY Usually a company owned by another and considered part of its parent's operations. Technically, it's a company more than 50 percent owned by another.

SUBSISTENCE When it refers to standard of living, it means at a maintenance level without a prospect for growth. As a theory of wages, it says that if wages fall below the subsistence level a labor force cannot be maintained.

SUBSTITUTE GOODS When goods perform about the same function or satisfy wants equally they can be substituted. The importance of watching substitute goods is that small price changes in certain goods may result in large changes in the quantity of goods demanded, if there's a close substitute whose price doesn't change.

SUNSHINE LAWS A response to the Watergate years when the public was concerned with government secrecy, these laws refer to state or federal laws that require meetings of regulatory bodies to be held in public or for their decisions and records to be disclosed. The most important of the laws is the Freedom of Information Act, which makes most documents of federal agencies available to the public.

SUPPLY-SIDE ECONOMICS A theory championed by Arthur Laffer in the late 1970s, the theory says that drastic reductions in tax rates should stimulate productive investment by corporations and wealthy individuals with the result benefiting the entire society.

SWAPPING Selling one security and buying a similar one almost at the same time to take a loss, usually for tax purposes.

SWEAT EQUITY A reference to the unpaid personal time and effort put into a project, usually real estate.

SWEATSHOP A place of employment with unacceptable work conditions, usually low pay and inhumane treatment of the employees.

SYNDICATE Investment bankers who agree to raise capital to purchase the securities of an issuer. Also called an underwriter, the syndicate works with the selling group to market shares or units of the issue at a fixed price.

TAKEOVER A change in the controlling interest of a corporation. Takeovers may be friendly or unfriendly and involve a takeover company and a target company. Target companies may resist a takeover by using a number of tactics to make the purchase unattractive.

TARIFF Usually, a federal tax on imports or exports in order to raise money, although the effect may be to discourage trade of certain goods. The term also refers to fees or charges for freight.

TAXABLE INCOME The amount of income after deductions that's subject to tax. For an individual, it's called the adjusted gross income. For a corporation, it's the net income before taxes.

TAX CREDIT A direct dollar for dollar reduction in the tax liability, different from a tax deduction, which reduces taxes only by the percentage of a taxpayer's tax bracket.

TAX DEFERRED An investment whose accumulated earnings are free from taxation until the investor takes possession of them, such as an individual retirement account.

TAX EXEMPT Some investments, such as municipal bonds, allow investors to collect interest without paying taxes on the income. While the return on such investments are less than taxable ones, the tax-free status is supposed to compensate for the lower return. This tax status is given investments in order to encourage investments in such activities as state hospital construction. Some investments are double or triple tax free, which means that the investor pays no federal, state or local tax on the income.

TAX SHELTER A method used by investors to legally avoid or reduce taxes. Depreciation and depletion are two common methods of reducing taxes. Tax reform in the 1980s greatly reduced the benefits of tax shelters.

TENANCY IN COMMON In real estate, the ownership of property by two or more people each of whom has an undivided interest without the right of survivorship.

TENDER OFFER A public offer to buy shares from existing stockholders of a public corporation. The tender offer states the terms and price of the offer. Shareholders usually receive a premium above current market price for their shares, subject to the tendering of a minimum and maximum number of shares.

TERM LOAN A loan of typically two to ten years given by financial institutions such as a finance company for equipment or working capital.

THRIFT INSTITUTION Generic for savings and loans, savings banks and credit unions, these institutions collect consumer deposits and make loans mostly to individuals. Traditionally, thrifts provided loans for residential housing, but now make commercial and consumer loans. Credit unions are still limited primarily to car and other consumer loans.

TICK A movement in a security. Analysts watch ticks to get a feel for the trend in price for a stock or security. An up-tick describes a transaction made at a price higher than the preceding transaction price.

TIGHT MARKET In an active market, the bid and offer prices tend to occur within a narrow range. When the difference in bid and offer shrink and the "spread narrows," the market is tight. The opposite is a "slack market."

TIGHT MONEY Usually the result of a Federal Reserve Board action to restrict the money supply, the result is that credit becomes more difficult.

TIP In investments, it's information passed on to an investor which may encourage the purchase or sale of an investment. Since tips are information not readily available to the public, certain information, if acted upon, may leave the investor open to charges of "insider trading."

TRADE DEFICIT The opposite of surplus, the volume of goods and services sold is less than the amount purchased. The result is a negative balance of trade.

TRADEMARK Any designation, such as a name, design or color, that distinguishes goods or companies from others. Trademarks are protected from infringement by law.

TRADING RANGE In securities, it refers to the highest and lowest prices at which the securities trade. In commodities it refers to the limit set by a commodities exchange for a single commodity.

TREASURIES U.S. government debt secured by the full faith and credit of the federal government. Issued in various schedules and maturities, income is exempt from state and local, but not federal taxes.

TRICKLE-DOWN The idea that if individuals and businesses are allowed, and encouraged, to flourish then their prosperity will eventually benefit everyone through improved economic activity.

TRIPLE WITCHING HOUR On the last Friday of March, June, September and December, options and futures on stock indexes expire at the same time. Unusual activity results from large trades by arbitrageurs and other hedgers.

TRUST A legal relationship which allows an owner of property to hand over title of the property to another, called a trustee, for the benefit of a third party, called a beneficiary.

TRUSTEE IN BANKRUPTCY In a bankruptcy proceeding, a court may charge someone to act as a trustee with the title to property or money to be distributed to creditors of the company in bankruptcy.

TURNAROUND Assuming that a company is doing poorly, a turnaround is the reversal of this condition. Turnarounds are possible for markets and economies too.

UNDERCAPITALIZATION Generally, it means a shortage of funds. This condition exists when a business doesn't have enough money to carry out normal business functions.

UNDEREMPLOYED Individuals are underemployed when their jobs don't require their full capabilities or fail to take advantage of education, talent or experience.

UNDERGROUND ECONOMY An unrecorded part of the economy made up of legal and illegal activities. Most of the transactions are in barter or in cash to avoid taxation or detection by government or law enforcement agencies.

UNDERVALUED When a company's stock doesn't reflect the full value of the firm's assets, it's said to be undervalued. Undervalued companies are frequently targets of takeover attempts, since acquirers can buy assets cheaply this way. Value is determined by estimating the profit that might result from liquidating the company.

UNDERWRITER An underwriter of stock investments will buy stock from a issuing company and then sell it to the public. The profit is the difference between the price paid to the issuer of the investment and the public offering price. In insurance, the underwriter assumes the risk of the policy and collects a premium.

UNEARNED INCOME For tax purposes, it's income from sources other than salaries, wages or tips such as dividends, interest or rent.

UNION RATE Through collective bargaining, a union will set an hourly rate for wages for its members. The rate is usually the minimum that will be paid for a particular job classification.

UNION SHOP A company where all the employees must be members of the union.

UNISSUED STOCK A company's balance sheet will show the number of shares authorized by the company and how many are issued and unissued. The unissued stock doesn't pay dividends and can't be voted.

USURY A level of interest rates above what's permitted by state law. Usury limits vary according to the type of lender and the type of loan.

VALUE ADDED TAX (VAT) A method of taxation common in European countries, it's a tax charged against the steps of production that add value to a product. Taxpayers, therefore, pay the difference between the cost of a good at the beginning of its processing and the amount of value added at each step of production.

VENTURE CAPITAL This is financing needed to begin a business, usually a risky or unproven venture. In exchange for the capital, the investor gets partial ownership in the business. High risk venture capital also offers the potential for substantial profits.

VERTICAL SPREAD An investment strategy that calls for simultaneous buying and selling of options on the same security, with the options having identical expiration dates but a different strike price—the predetermined exercise price of the stock option.

VESTING At most companies, employees are able to receive employer-contributed benefits, such as a pension fund, after working a minimum number of years. By federal law, employees at most firms are fully vested within seven years.

VOLUME The number of shares traded during a period of time. Daily volume of the entire market indicates investor interest, and periodic comparisons points to trends that technical analysts use to forecast movements. The NYSE, alone, can handle in excess of 600 million shares a day.

WAGE FREEZE To contain costs, a government or company may place a limit on pay increases for workers. On a national scale, wage freezes are usually accompanied by price freezes. When such freezes are eliminated, the result is usually a rapid escalation of wages and prices.

WAGE-PUSH INFLATION An economic condition when wages increase faster than productivity, so that costs rise and therefore the price of goods increase.

WARRANT A certificate issued directly to shareholders giving them the right to purchase securities at a predetermined price, usually for a predetermined time.

WASTING ASSETS   Resources, such as oil or gas, that are depleted over time by extraction.

WATCH LIST   Securities singled out for special surveillance by brokerage firms or regulatory organizations. Firms on the list may be takeover targets or companies with high stock activity.

WELFARE ECONOMICS   An economic specialty that concentrates on the effect of different actions that affect the well-being of the nation and its population.

WHITE COLLAR   A reference to people who do non-manual work, such as administrators and professionals. Blue collar workers are people who wear uniforms, which are sometimes blue.

WHITE KNIGHT   A suitor who comes to the rescue of a company that's fighting off a takeover attempt by another company.

WHOLESALER   This word has several meanings. In business, it's a middleman who takes delivery from producers of goods for resale and distribution to consumer outlets, such as supermarkets or retailers. It also refers to a broker/dealer who trades securities with other broker/dealers for prices below market value or for a selling concession.

WILDCAT STRIKE   An illegal, unannounced work stoppage while a labor contract is still in effect. Like other strikes, wildcat strikes arise over wages and working conditions.

WORKING CAPITAL   Also referred to as net working capital, this is the difference between current assets and the current liabilities of a company. The calculation is used to judge the strength of cash flow and management of financial resources.

WORLD BANK   This is the common name for the International Bank of Reconstruction and Development.

WRITE-OFF   Write-offs occur when assets are worthless or when debts cannot be collected or other negative events affect operations. The effect is to reduce profits.

YANKEE BOND   This is a bond issued outside the United States but registered for sale in the U.S and traded in dollars.

YEN BOND   While still a small factor in international credit markets, these are bonds denominated in Japanese yen and valued by investors who want to diversify their holdings in currencies other than dollars or German marks.

YIELD   Also referred to as the return (it doesn't involve capital gains or losses), yield is expressed as a percentage of dividends or interest paid by a company to the current price.

ZAIBATSU This is a large Japanese complex of industrial enterprises controlled by a small group—usually one or two families. The term is widely, but usually incorrectly, used to refer to Japanese trading companies.

ZERO-BASE BUDGETING This type of budgeting requires justification for all expenditures. Therefore, all lines on the budget begin at zero. Funding is provided according to merit.

ZERO COUPON BOND A security sold at a deep discount from its face value. Since the rate of return is achieved by gradual appreciation of the security, there are no interest payments. The face value is redeemable at maturity.

Contributors

Ovid Abrams, a 1976 fellow, is a former product manager, precious metals, for Merrill Lynch & Co. He is currently president of his own publishing firm.

Charles G. Blaine, Jr., a 1982 fellow, is the business/financial editor of the *Times-Picayune* in New Orleans.

Linda Corman, a 1990 fellow, is a reporter at *American Banker* newspaper in Washington, D.C.

Stephen Dunphy, a 1976 fellow, is a business editor at the *Seattle Times.*

Barbara French, a 1981 fellow, is a business editor at the *San Francisco Examiner.*

John Gallagher, a 1987 fellow, is a business reporter at the *Detroit Free Press.*

Gary Gigliotti, is an associate professor of economics at Rutgers University.

Victoria Rea Gits, a 1984 fellow, is a business writer for the *Daily Camera* in Boulder, Colorado.

William Glasgall, a 1978 fellow, is an international economics editor at *Business Week* in New York.

Stephen J. Govoni, a 1984 fellow, is a contributing editor at *Corporate Finance* magazine.

Udayan Gupta, a 1982 fellow, is a senior special reporter at the *Wall Street Journal* in New York.

Thomas Hayes, a 1979 fellow, is an economic correspondent for the *New York Times* in Dallas, Texas.

Gus Hedberg, a 1986 fellow, is a senior editor at *Money* Magazine in New York.

Ellen James, a 1982 fellow, is a business reporter at the *Baltimore Sun.*

Cynthia Kasabian, a 1982 fellow, is a vice president & director of public relations at Bank of America, San Francisco.

Sarah Kidwell, a 1989 fellow, is field producer at Cable News Network in New York.

David Kinney, a 1980 fellow, is editor and publisher at *Business North Carolina* Magazine.

Pamela Hollie Kluge, a former national and foreign correspondent for the *New York Times,* was director of the Knight-Bagehot Fellowship in Economics and Business Journalism from 1987–90.

Kevin Lahart, a 1982 fellow, is a free-lance writer and author.

Andrew Leckey, a 1979 fellow, is an investment columnist at the *Chicago Tribune.*

Joshua Levine, a 1982 fellow, is an associate editor, in charge of marketing coverage at *Forbes* in New York.

Trudy Lieberman, a 1977 fellow, is a senior editor at *Consumer Reports* in Mount Vernon, New York.

Dave Lindorff, a 1979 fellow, is a former television producer who is an assistant professor at Alfred University.

Pamela Luecke, a 1987 fellow, is an assistant managing editor at the *Hartford Courant.*

Philip Moeller, a 1976 fellow, is a business editor at the *Baltimore Sun.*

Floyd Norris, a 1982 fellow, is a market place columnist at the *New York Times.*

Deborah Rankin, a 1977 fellow, is a former business reporter at the *New York Times.*

Stanley Reed, a 1988 fellow, is an international editor at *Business Week* in New York.

Jaye Scholl, a 1982 fellow, is west coast editor at *Barron's* in Los Angeles, California.

Stephen Shepard, a former director of the fellowship, is editor-in-chief of *Business Week* in New York.

Mike Sheridan, a 1980 fellow, is a business writer at the *Orange County Register* in Santa Ana, California.

Debra Silimeo, a 1987 fellow, is director of public affairs at Joint Economic Committee in Washington, D.C.

Pauline Tai, a 1989 fellow, is a former editor at *Money* Magazine. She became the Fellowship's director in 1990.

Elyse Tanouye, a 1987 fellow, is a reporter for the *Dow Jones Professional Investor Report* in New York.

Craig Torres, a 1989 fellow, is a staff reporter at the *Wall Street Journal* in New York.

Leslie Wayne, a 1980 fellow, is a Business Day reporter at the *New York Times*.

Leah Beth Ward, a 1988 fellow, is the statehouse reporter for the *Albuquerque Journal.*

Chris Welles, a former director of the fellowship, is a senior writer at *Business Week.*

Jack Willoughby, a 1984 fellow, is a senior writer at *Money* Magazine in New York.

Sam Zuckerman, a 1989 fellow, is San Francisco bureau chief for *American Banker* Newspaper.